"Harris has written the best guide yet to Japan's subtle but important political shift towards 'the new conservatives'—its origins, meaning, limitations and failures—of which the country's longest-serving prime minister, Abe, is the prime exponent."

Bill Emmott, editor of *The Economist*, 1993–2006,
chairman of the Japan Society of the UK,
and author of *Japan's Far More Female Future*

"Throughout a period of tumult, both international and domestic, Abe has remained a grimly determined steady hand, a conservative force in a world of radical uncertainty. In translucent prose, Tobias Harris is a subtle commentator on Japan and a remarkably sure-footed guide to the inner workings of its longest-serving prime minister in history."

David Pilling, *Financial Times*, and author of
Bending Adversity: Japan and the Art of Survival

"Harris has very skilfully told one of the great political comeback stories of our era—the fall and rise of not just Abe, but Japan itself. With colourful anecdotes and insightful analysis, the author shows us how Abe, a political blue-blood, pulled off the most remarkable second act in modern Japanese history by being an iconoclast. Harris tells how Abe challenged taboos and broke the mould to help Japan reclaim its confidence, and its rightful place in the world."

Martin Fackler, former Tokyo bureau chief, *The New York Times*

"A superb biography of Abe, as well as a remarkably detailed political history of Japan, from Abe's grandfather Prime Minister Kishi Nobusuke (1957–60) to Prime Minister Abe. Thoroughly researched, lucidly written. A great achievement."

Ezra Vogel, Henry Ford II Professor of the Social Sciences Emeritus,
Harvard University

"No political figure looms larger in Japan's bid for national renaissance than the country's longest-serving prime minister, Abe Shinzō. In *The Iconoclast* Tobias Harris offers a nuanced depiction of the many shades of Abe—from conservative cultural warrior to champion of globalization—and his uneven domestic and international legacy. In telling the story of one man, Harris captures the little appreciated pulses of change redefining Japan."

Mireya Solis, Director, Center for East Asia Policy Studies,
The Brookings Institution

"*The Iconoclast* is a well-written and comprehensive chronicle of the politics and policies of Japan's longest-serving prime minister."

Gerald L. Curtis, Burgess Professor Emeritus of Political Science,
Columbia University

"Tobias Harris's timely biography expertly uncovers the complex interplay between Abe's pragmatism and nationalism at a pivotal moment for Japan in the changing international relations of East Asia. Judiciously blending a wealth of Japanese and English-language sources, Harris paints a portrait of Abe that combines historical drama, indispensable analysis of Japan's postwar politics and a brilliant dissection of the strategic ambitions and policy achievements of this most influential of prime ministers."

John Nilsson-Wright, Senior Lecturer, Japanese Politics & IR,
University of Cambridge, and Senior Research Fellow
for Northeast Asia, Chatham House

"Harris delivers a gripping chronicle of the rise, fall, and rise again of Abe Shinzō, a 'young politician uniquely burdened by history'. Crafting Abenomics, rebuilding the military, adroitly managing China and the US, Abe rightfully boasted that 'I am back, and so is Japan'. *The Iconoclast* is an instant classic of Japanese politics and a must-read to understand how America's most important ally has been transformed by its most skilful prime minister."

James Shinn, Senior Advisor, US Department of State

"In this crisp, readable and studiously fair biography of one of the world's most underestimated leaders, Abe, Tobias Harris manages to bring to life Japan's complex postwar politics, and the struggle to keep the country's economic edge and nurture a new nationalism in an increasingly combustible region."

Richard McGregor, Senior Fellow at the Lowy Institute, Sydney,
and author of *The Party* and *Asia's Reckoning*

"A compelling portrait of Japan's longest-serving prime minister, tracing both the world that shaped him and his place in history. *The Iconoclast* faces head-on the controversies that have marked Abe's career and his determination to strengthen Japan's geostrategic role and settle the country's culture war. Tobias Harris is one of the most knowledgeable observers of Japanese politics, and his mastery of the subject is visible on every page."

Yoichi Funabashi, Chairman, Asia Pacific Initiative,
and former editor-in-chief, *Asahi Shimbun*

"Much anticipated political biography of a consequential politician, by an astute Japan watcher. A vivid portrayal of the rise, fall and resurrection of an unexpected global statesman. Harris has done a superb job in helping us understand who Abe Shinzō is and where he came from. His depiction of Abe is nuanced, reliable and engaging."

Toshihiro Nakayama, Professor, Keio University

"At a time when Japan's security environment deteriorates amidst China's aggressive military behaviour and North Korea's nuclear devel-opment, Prime Minister Abe Shinzō has sought to secure Japan by upholding the international order alongside the US and other liberal democracies. Tobias Harris successfully examines Abe's strategic vision with compelling insight into how his thinking evolved through-out his life."

Yoso Furumoto, Washington Bureau Chief, *Mainichi Shimbun*

THE ICONOCLAST

TOBIAS S. HARRIS

The Iconoclast

Shinzō Abe and the New Japan

HURST & COMPANY, LONDON

First published in the United Kingdom in 2020 by
C. Hurst & Co. (Publishers) Ltd.,
41 Great Russell Street, London, WC1B 3PL

Printed in the United Kingdom

Distributed in the United States, Canada and Latin America by
Oxford University Press, 198 Madison Avenue, New York, NY 10016,
United States of America.

A Cataloguing-in-Publication data record for this book
is available from the British Library.

ISBN: 9781787383104

This book is printed using paper from registered sustainable
and managed sources.

www.hurstpublishers.com

Printed in Great Britain by Bell and Bain Ltd, Glasgow

To Nathan and Caleb
May books bring you as much pleasure as they have brought me

&

To Jennifer
For everything

“Politics is a strong and slow boring of hard boards.”

Max Weber

“Japan’s regulatory regime is like solid bedrock. I myself intend to serve as the drill bit that will break through that bedrock.”

Abe Shinzō

CONTENTS

NOTE ON SUBJECT'S NAME

Throughout this book its subject is referred to as Abe Shinzō, using the correct word order in Japanese. However on the cover of *The Iconoclast* the publisher chose to refer to him as Shinzō Abe, to avoid bibliographic, cataloguing and search engine confusion.

ACKNOWLEDGEMENTS

Despite a lifetime of reading books, when I embarked on this project, I honestly did not appreciate the extent to which producing a book is truly a collective enterprise. I received so much help in so many ways from so many people that it would be impossible to acknowledge everyone—but I will try.

First, I have to thank Kevin Kajiwara and Wolfgango Piccoli, co-presidents of Teneo Intelligence, where I have been the Japan analyst since 2013. When I told Kevin and Wolf that I was working on this book, they did not hesitate to give their support. In a larger sense, this book would not have been possible without Teneo, which gave me an excellent perch from which to analyze Abe's return to power and the intellectual freedom to explore all facets of Japan's politics during the second Abe administration. Declan Kelly, Paul Keary, and Doug Band have created a special company that genuinely appreciates and rewards intellectual achievement, and I am fortunate to have been part of it. Other Teneo colleagues—Orson Porter, Thomas Schoenfelder, Antonio Barroso, Alexandra Rogan, Bob Herrera-Lim, Gabriel Wildau, Otilia Dhand, Anne Fruhauf, Carsten Nickel, Nicholas Watson, Meghan McDonough—have been sources of encouragement and insight before and during the process of writing this book. By generously sharing his insight into the Korean Peninsula, Victor Cha has expanded my understanding of Japan's regional environment and it has been a privilege to work with him. I am also grateful to Jim Shinn, who, though no longer with Teneo, helped bring me to the company and has been a constant supporter, especially during the writing of this book.

Second, I am indebted to the Sasakawa Peace Foundation USA and the Sasakawa Peace Foundation in Tokyo. As a research fellow from 2014–2020, I was able to dig deeply into the Abe government's economic policies and to develop Japan Political Pulse, a Japanese public opinion poll aggregator, work that contributed immeasurably to this book. I am immensely grateful to current and former SPFUSA staffers, Jim Zumwalt, Chris Rodeman, Kazuyo Kato, Joy Champaloux, Adam Morrow, Darah Phillip, Susan Dalzell, Misa Imanaka-Miller, Keiji Iwatake, Sayuri Romei, Phyllis Yoshida, Satohiro Akimoto and many others for their support. I am indebted to former research director Dan Bob for encouraging me to undertake this project in the earliest stages, as well as to Admiral Dennis Blair for bringing me on board as a fellow. I am also grateful for support from SPF headquarters in Tokyo, particularly from Aya Murata and Junko Chano, who took an early interest in my work and provided steady support along the way.

SPFUSA not only provided financial support for research trips to Japan but also hosted workshops that enabled me to receive feedback on early drafts from some of Washington's best analysts of Japan. That group—including Ben Self, Ben Goldberg, Andrew Oros, Giulio Pugliese, Emma Chanlett-Avery, Mark Manyin, Jacob Schlesinger, Ben Rimland, Ali Wyne, and Sherry Martin—generously volunteered their time to read and comment on this book as it took shape and I believe helped make it significantly better.

Getting this book into your hands also required a certain degree of serendipity. Ankit Panda told me that he was writing a book for Hurst Publishers and that it might be a good fit for the Abe book I had in mind. It turned out that a professor from graduate school, Brendan Simms, had edited a series for Hurst, and he promptly introduced me to Hurst's Michael Dwyer, who was enthusiastic about the idea of publishing the first English-language biography of Abe. I am grateful to Michael for his enthusiasm about this project and grateful for the work he put into making it a reality. I am also deeply appreciative to Hurst's production head Daisy Leitch, publicist Alison Alexanian, and marketing head Kathleen May for their work making this book a reality, and to copy editor Cate Bickmore and proofreader Susan Boxall for hammering the text into shape. Finally, I am indebted to Linda Kulman for her help refining my proposal and Micah Salb for his help finalizing a contract. I am also grateful to W. David Marx and Geoffrey Cain for taking the time to answer my questions about their experiences in the publishing industry.

Over the course of my career, I have benefited greatly from the wisdom of other Japan watchers, who shared their knowledge with me and made me a better analyst. Asao Keiichirō gave me the opportunity to observe Japanese politics up close as a member of his staff, and has been generous with his time ever since. The Maureen and Mike Mansfield Foundation's U.S.-Japan Network for the Future —the third cohort of which I am a member—helped me stay connected to old friends from academia, introduced me to new scholars, and helped me stay up to date on the debates that political scientists who study Japan were having about Abe. In the six years that I have lived in greater Washington, DC, I have also benefited immensely from DC's community of Japan specialists. Jim Schoff, Sheila Smith, Mireya Solis, Mike Green, Mike Mochizuki, and Glen Fukushima have all generously included me in discussions and given me opportunities to refine my thinking. Others, including Gerald Curtis, Chris Nelson, Brad Glosserman, Dan Sneider, Richard Katz, and Alicia Ogawa have been valued friends and supporters, and have a knack for doling out praise just when it is most needed. David Nakamura generously shared his insights into Abe's relationship with Donald Trump. I am especially grateful for the friendship of my fellow Midwesterner Jeffrey Hornung, who has read and commented on multiple drafts, been a source of encouragement, and a friend. Ben Self has generously answered panicked texts at unusual hours and provided advice at every step of the way. Some of the earliest ideas in this book began with a guest lecture for his course at George Washington University.

I am also indebted to the broader world of Japan specialists, who have helped bring this book into being in various ways. Stephen Nagy of International Christian University in Tokyo hosted me for talks in 2018 that ultimately became parts of several chapters. Harvard University's Susan Pharr and Ezra Vogel, who also serve as advisers to the Mansfield Foundation's U.S.-Japan network, kindly hosted me at Harvard in 2017 for a discussion of Abe's legacy with Andrew Oros. Greg Merkley at Northwestern University invited me to guest lecture twice while I was working on this book, giving me a chance to present some of these ideas to a non-specialist audience. Yoichi Funabashi has been generous with his time and his wisdom for years, and served as a sounding board when I was figuring out how to structure this book. Corey Wallace generously read drafts at a late stage. Peter Drysdale, Shiro Armstrong, and the rest of the team at Australian National University's East Asia Forum have given me multiple opportunities to develop and present arguments that eventually made their way into this book. Robert Dujarric, Greg Noble, and David Leheny have been excellent dining companions whenever I am back in Tokyo, and the source of ideas that have made their way into this book.

Michael Cucek and Jun Okumura found me when I was an anonymous blogger writing about Japanese politics. Their encouragement made me think I was writing something worthwhile and the back-and-forth conversation across blogs provided me with a fast-paced tutorial in Japanese politics. Our conversations have largely migrated to Twitter, but my admiration for their insight and wit has never waned.

I am also grateful to two members of this community no longer with us. Early in my career, I was fortunate to meet the late Sam Jameson, with whom I would regularly dine at his table at Komahachi Honten and who would regale me with stories from his long career as a foreign correspondent in Tokyo. The world of Japanese political analysis is poorer without him. It is similarly worse off without the late Peter Ennis, from whose knowledge of the US–Japan relationship I benefited immensely.

Many others have helped arrange interviews that strengthened the arguments in this book. Sato Setsuya, Kinoshita Hidetomi, Murai Hideki, Nagashima Akihisa, Miyake Kunihiko, Wendy Cutler, Tom Taniguchi, Paul Haenle, and others facilitated meetings that informed my writing in addition to sharing their own insights.

I left the Ph.D. program in MIT's political science department sooner than I had hoped, but a glance at the references in this book will quickly reveal that I never stopped being a student of Richard Samuels. I was attracted to MIT because I believed that he worked on what I thought were the most fundamental questions about how Japan is governed—and I still believe that to be true. I have never forgotten the intellectual debt I owe to him. Other scholars at MIT with whom I had the privilege to work—Suzanne Berger, Kathy Thelen, Ken Oye, Taylor

Fravel, David Singer, and Melissa Noble—have influenced this book in ways large and small. I have also benefited immensely from friendships forged in Cambridge, and am grateful to Sameer Lalwani, Dan Altman, Kentaro Maeda, Josh Shifrinson, Llewelyn Hughes, and Joseph Torigian for their support at different stages of this project.

Teachers at other stages of my education—Mark Hulliung, George Ross, Robert Art, and the late Eugene Black at Brandeis University, Charles Jones, Philip Towle, and Shogo Suzuki at the University of Cambridge, and Chris Schwarz, David Klingenberger, Michael Conroy, Joseph Meyer, and Dana DesJardins at Niles West High School in Skokie, Illinois—all played instrumental roles in preparing me for life spent thinking and writing. Special thanks also go to Hiroko Sekino, to whom I am especially indebted for making room in her overbooked introductory Japanese class in my first semester at Brandeis.

I thank my parents, Yra and Janice Harris, who raised me in a house full of books, encouraged me to write, and gave me the education and the opportunities to travel that made my career possible. I especially treasure the time that I have spent with them exploring Japan, and I appreciate the effort that they have made to understand my passion for Japanese history and culture.

When I first thought of writing a biography of Prime Minister Abe, my eldest son Nathan was a newborn. As I write the final words, Nathan is six and learning how to read, and his younger brother Caleb is three. Writing a book with two small children was not the easiest undertaking—for them or for me—but I hope that they will find as much comfort in the printed word as I have. Our household is complete with the addition of two cats—I found Penelope outside of my apartment in Tokyo during my Fulbright year, and Elsa is a rescue who joined our family halfway through this project; they have both been my constant writing companions.

Finally, this book could simply not have happened without the love and support of my wife, Jennifer T. Gordon. She carved out time for me to work on weekends, read chapters late at night, and has shared in my enthusiasm for the life story of Abe Shinzō. Jennifer has been a sounding board, an editor, and my best friend, and I am so fortunate to have her as my partner in all things.

It is to her—and to the two boys we have made—that this book is dedicated.

ABBREVIATIONS

ADIZ	Air Defense Identification Zone
AIIB	Asian Infrastructure Investment Bank
APEC	Asia-Pacific Economic Cooperation
ASDF	Air Self-Defense Forces
ASEAN	Association of Southeast Asian Nations
BOJ	Bank of Japan
BRI	Belt and Road Initiative
CCP	Chinese Communist Party
CEFP	Council on Economic and Fiscal Policy
CLB	Cabinet Legislation Bureau
CPB	Cabinet Personnel Bureau
CPTPP	Comprehensive and Progressive Agreement for the Trans-Pacific Partnership
DPJ	Democratic Party of Japan
DPRK	Democratic People's Republic of Korea
DSP	Democratic Socialist Party
ETF	Exchange-traded fund
FDI	Foreign Direct Investment
FSA	Financial Services Agency
FTA	Free Trade Agreement
GPIF	Government Pension Investment Fund
GSOMIA	General Security of Military Information Agreement
IMF	International Monetary Fund
IOC	International Olympic Committee
IRAA	Imperial Rule Assistance Association
JA	Japan Agriculture

JCG	Japan Coast Guard
JCP	Japan Communist Party
JDA	Japan Defense Agency
JGB	Japanese government bond
JNP	Japan New Party
JRP	Japan Renewal Party (1993–1994) or, later, the Japan Restoration Party (2012–)
JSP	Japan Socialist Party
LDP	Liberal Democratic Party
MAFF	Ministry of Agriculture, Forestry, and Fisheries
MCI	Ministry of Commerce and Industry (see: MITI, METI)
METI	Ministry of Economy, Trade, and Industry
MHLW	Ministry of Health, Labor, and Welfare
MITI	Ministry of International Trade and Industry
MMT	Modern Monetary Theory
MOD	Ministry of Defense
MOF	Ministry of Finance
MOFA	Ministry of Foreign Affairs
MSDF	Maritime Self-Defense Forces
NAFTA	North American Free Trade Agreement
NDPG	National Defense Program Guidelines
NEET	Not in Employment, Education, or Training
NFP	New Frontier Party
NIRP	Negative Interest Rate Policy
NPA	National Police Agency
NPS	New Party Sakigake
NRA	Nuclear Regulation Authority
NSC	National Security Council
OECD	Organization for Economic Cooperation and Development
PKO	Peacekeeping operations
PLA	People's Liberation Army
PR	Proportional representation
PRC	People's Republic of China
QQE	Quantitative and Qualitative Easing
RCEP	Regional Comprehensive Economic Partnership
REIT	Real Estate Investment Trust
SDF	Self-Defense Forces

SEALDs	Students Emergency Action for Liberal Democracy
SIA	Social Insurance Agency
SMD	Single-member district
TEPCO	Tokyo Electric Power Company
TPA	Trade Promotion Authority
TPP	Trans-Pacific Partnership
TSE	Tokyo Stock Exchange
USMCA	US-Mexico-Canada Agreement
WHO	World Health Organization
WMD	Weapons of Mass Destruction
WTO	World Trade Organization
YCC	Yield Curve Control
YP	Your Party
ZIRP	Zero Interest Rate Policy

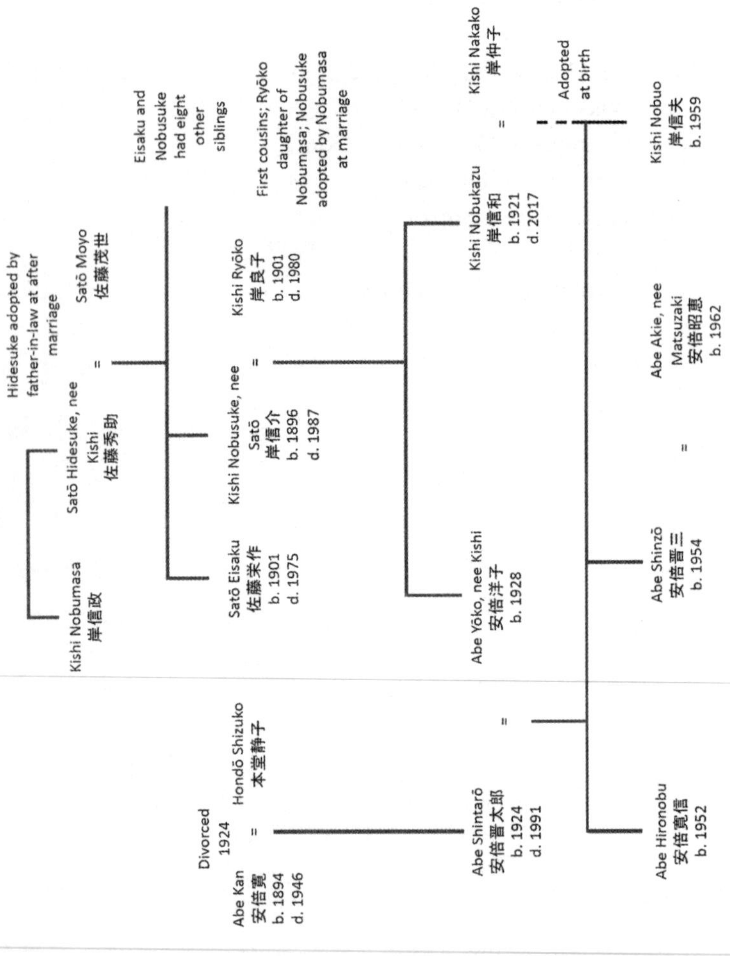

Abe family tree

1

THE LAST HEISEI PRIME MINISTER

Nine leaders—including a university president, a novelist, a newspaper chairman, and the head of the national broadcaster, NHK—gathered at the Kantei, the residence of Japan's prime minister, on the first day of April 2019. At the end of the month, Emperor Akihito would abdicate and on 1 May, his son Naruhito would become emperor. It would be the first abdication in 200 years. The panel gathered that spring morning were responsible for choosing a *gengō*, the new emperor's reign name.

It was a decision invested with tremendous symbolic importance. A reign name becomes a cultural touchstone, a single word that evokes moments of collective trauma and jubilation that are the building blocks of the nation's identity. The Heisei era, Akihito's reign, began with the bursting of Japan's financial bubble in the early 1990s and would be profoundly shaped by economic malaise, natural disasters, political turbulence, and the awareness that Japan's population had begun its seemingly inexorable decline. The panel's decision would shape how millions of Japanese would remember much of the twenty-first century.

At the highest levels of the Japanese government, seventy submissions from experts for possible names had been whittled down to ten, and then to six, which were then presented to the panel.[1] At 11:41am, after the panel had finalized its decision and communicated it to political and imperial authorities, Chief Cabinet Secretary Suga Yoshihide stood in the Kantei's briefing room, holding up a white placard bearing two Japanese characters drawn in thick, black brushstrokes: *Reiwa*(令和). Unlike previous reign names, which had customarily been drawn from ancient Chinese classics, *Reiwa* came from the *Manyōshū*, a collection of Japanese poems compiled during the eighth century. The characters came from a line referring to the anticipation preceding the first plum blossoms in spring.

A short while later, Prime Minister Abe Shinzō mounted the stage to explain the decision.

"Just as the plum blossoms announce the arrival of spring after the harsh cold of winter and bloom splendidly in all their glory," Abe said. "All Japanese will be able to make their own blossoms come into full bloom, together with their hopes for tomorrow. We decided on '*Reiwa*' with the hope that Japan will be just such a nation."[2]

The foreign ministry recommended an appropriate translation: "beautiful harmony." But the prime minister's critics quickly suggested a darker meaning, noting that in contemporary Japanese a more appropriate translation would be "commanded peace," implying Abe intended to put an authoritarian stamp on the new era.[3] The notion that Abe would use the reign name as a declaration of authoritarian designs was far-fetched—and ultimately, it would be up to the Japanese people to imbue *Reiwa* with social and cultural significance. But there are more subtle ways in which the selection of a reign name was a revealing moment in the life and career of Abe Shinzō.

* * *

By April 2019, Abe had been the prime minister for more than six years, more than seven counting a stint from 2006 to 2007. He would soon become Japan's longest-serving prime minister since the birth of constitutional government in 1889. But for Abe too, the end was approaching. His third term as leader of the Liberal Democratic Party would end in September 2021. His party had changed the rules once to enable him to run a third time; it was unlikely to do so again. He too was contemplating his place in Japanese history.

Abe had always been burdened by Japan's past and Japan's future. He entered the Diet, Japan's legislature, in 1993 as the heir to a storied political dynasty. As a lawmaker from Yamaguchi prefecture, which until 1871 had been known as Chōshū, he was acutely aware of its pivotal role in the Meiji Restoration, the "revolution from above" that built the modern Japanese state that eventually set Japan down the path of empire, war, and ruin.[4] A third-generation Diet member, he was the grandson of a postwar prime minister who had served in the wartime government and been imprisoned as a war criminal by the US occupation, and he bristled at how left-wing Japanese and Japan's neighbors characterized imperial Japan and chafed at the US-imposed encumbrances that had constrained Japan's independence.

He regularly spoke of having a mission in political life. By his own reckoning, he would achieve great and necessary things for the nation—including important tasks left unfinished by his grandfather Kishi Nobusuke and his father Abe Shintarō. His destiny was not simply to rule. From his forebears, he had inherited a mission: he would carry out Japan's return to the world of power politics.

The Meiji Restoration had made Japan a great power and a protagonist in the scramble for empire in Asia. The Second World War had left the country in ruins, and the US occupation had stripped it of its pretensions to great power, saddling it with constraints—particularly a US-authored constitution in which Japan "[renounced] war as a sovereign right of the nation and the threat or use of force as means of settling international disputes"—that would render it dependent on the US for its security. Kishi, a member of the cabinet that had declared war on America, never accepted that Japan should be anything less than a great power and spent his postwar career—which included three years as prime minister—battling the constraints the US had imposed after the war.

His grandson inherited this vision of a strong, independent Japan that could shed the vestiges of defeat and occupation. From Kishi, Abe also inherited a particular idea of statecraft: leadership means pursuing bold measures in the national interest. A strong leader must do whatever is necessary to surmount the challenges of the age. As Abe said in January 2007, "In order to realize 'a beautiful country, Japan,' my mission is none other than to draw a new vision of a nation which can withstand the raging waves for the next 50 to 100 years to come."[5]

* * *

From the moment he returned to power in 2012, Abe aspired to close the book on the Heisei era as an age of national failure.

The Heisei era had been characterized by the utter failure of Japan's leaders to overcome a decade and a half of deflation; ever-growing national debt; vanishing opportunities for young Japanese; the emergence of a strong and confident China; North Korea's increasingly potent nuclear arsenal; and the increasingly visible signs of an aging, shrinking population. Japan's leaders were a problem in their own right. Until Abe returned, since the Heisei era began in 1989 Japan had had sixteen prime ministers, who lasted only 538 days in office on average. The nation seemed resigned to a steady, inexorable decline in influence.

Abe was determined to banish that thinking. The nation must not surrender to malaise. "The most important thing is to restore pride and confidence in yourself, is it not?" he said in his first policy speech in January 2013. "We, and indeed Japan as well, can surely grow every day in the future by uncovering new capabilities lying dormant within us."[6] He was determined to be the strong leader of a confident country eager to regain its rightful place as a world leader, not the prime minister of a demoralized nation resigned to steady decline.

Abe would get Japan moving again. One by one, the fetters that had hindered Japanese leaders since 1945—a weak premiership forced to share power with bureaucrats, backbenchers, and opposition parties, a constitution that had limited Japan's armed forces strictly to territorial defense, and economic policies more interested in protecting Japan's markets than opening new markets overseas—would be broken by Japan's iconoclastic prime minister. Postwar institutions that had prevented the emergence of a strong, activist state would come tumbling down. He would end the acute national crises that had paralyzed his predecessors. He would introduce policies that would get Japan's economy growing again and reclaim an international leadership role for what was still the world's third-largest economy. He would pilot Japan through an "age of entropy," as US power declined and China and other non-western powers rose, as emerging technologies created new threats and opportunities, and as humanity began to cope with the cataclysmic effects of climate change.[7] In the process, he would dominate the country, marginalizing the opposition and breaking a fragile two-party system, while leading his party to victory in six consecutive national elections.

* * *

It is only natural that Abe would be interested in the choice of a name for the new era. And it soon emerged that he had strongly influenced the panel's deliberations, suggesting that the group should look to the *Manyōshū* for a name.[8] *Reiwa*, as explained by Abe, was the symbolic capstone for what he had sought to achieve.

The name clearly resonated with Abe. He had experienced a bleak personal winter, having been forced from office in 2007 only one year after taking power, and endured public humiliation. But his political career had blossomed again—sooner than anyone had expected—and the lesson for Japan was clear. "I am back, and so Japan shall be," he told an audience in Washington, DC, in February 2013.[9] After the hardships of the Heisei era, the Japanese people could still hope to enjoy the renewal of springtime. "Defeatism about Japan is now defeated," he said in Davos in January 2019.[10]

But as Abe led Japan into the *Reiwa* era, he may have taught his countrymen that the challenges of the new era—and all mature democracies—will not be solved by strong leaders alone. While he has broken taboos, shattered constraints, and thrust Japan back into power politics, when Abe leaves office, he will bequeath to his successors a country that might be wealthier and more open to the world but is increasingly vulnerable to climate change, unprecedented foreign policy challenge as US global leadership recedes and China rushes to fill the vacuum, and a population crisis that has profound implications for the nation's economy.

This book is the story of Abe Shinzō's place in history. Abe, the latest in a long line of Japanese leaders seeking a "restoration" for their own times, will be remembered for having girded Japan for global competition, yet his legacy will be increasingly shaped by missed opportunities and postponed decisions to tackle the "troubles at home and dangers from abroad" that beset Japan in the twenty-first century.[11]

2

THE BIRTH OF A DYNASTY

The dynasty began with a strategic decision. "This is the age of the newspaper reporter," Kishi Nobusuke said after the US military released the accused war criminal from Tokyo's Sugamo prison in 1948.[1] The former minister of munitions in the wartime government of Prime Minister Tōjō Hideki, he would be barred from politics until the end of the occupation as part of a purge of wartime leaders, yet he was already plotting his return to power. Nobusuke would have to adapt to life in a democratic Japan where mass politics was ascendant, so he decided that his daughter Yōko should marry a journalist.[2]

In June 1950, an acquaintance at the *Mainichi Shimbun*, one of Japan's oldest dailies, said he knew just the man. A young colleague, Abe Shintarō, was, like Kishi, a graduate of Tokyo Imperial University who hailed from Yamaguchi prefecture. He was not only a political reporter but the son of a politician, the late Abe Kan, who had died in 1946. Shintarō called on the elder statesman, who was satisfied. A date was scheduled with Yōko. They began courting, with Shintarō "visiting the Kishi residence at odd hours because of his grueling" journalist's schedule.[3]

On 5 May 1951, Yōko and Shintarō married. It was not obvious that this marked the birth of a political dynasty that would extend into the next century. Kishi was still prowling the margins of Japan's nascent democracy. As Shintarō was fond of saying, "I did not marry a prime minister's daughter. I got married to a war criminal's daughter."[4] Shintarō, meanwhile, was an orphaned journalist whose late father won respect for defying the militarist government—but fading memories of his father would not win him a parliamentary seat.

In the meantime, Yōko and Shintarō started a family. Their first son, Abe Hironobu, was born on 30 May 1952, one month after the US occupation ended. In April 1953, Kishi returned to the Diet. The following year, on 21 September 1954, Yōko and Shintarō's second son, Shinzō, was born in Tokyo.

* * *

The young family lived literally in Kishi's shadow, near his compound in the Nampeidai neighborhood in Shibuya. During the early years of Shinzō's life, Kishi returned from exile and accumulated ever greater power. His political recovery was not entirely surprising. His life had been characterized by an indomitable determination to overcome the impoverished circumstances of his childhood and rise to the top of the Japanese state.

Kishi was born in Yamaguchi prefecture on 13 November 1896. Although he would, like many children of the generation following the Meiji Restoration, admire the heroes of the restoration from the prefecture, his family had at best only distant connections to the movement that overthrew the shogunate. His family was downwardly mobile. He was the fifth child and second son of Satō Hidesuke and Moyo, who ultimately had ten children: three sons and seven daughters. Hidesuke's surname at birth had been Kishi, but he was adopted into his wife's family and assumed her name, a practice not uncommon in Japanese families, particularly when there is a difference in social status.[5] Hidesuke was a minor prefecture official and, when Nobusuke was three, quit his job to run a sake brewery in his hometown of Tabuse—needing a loan from his wife's family for a license.

The Satō-Kishi clan recognized Nobusuke's abilities and made sure he got advanced schooling. The Meiji state, determined to modernize Japan to fend off the threat of western imperialism, was building an education system to inculcate the skills and knowledge needed for national survival.[6] There were ample opportunities for an ambitious child, even one of modest means.

Nobusuke's education was supported by a series of patrons, including his paternal uncle Kishi Nobumasa, who would become his father-in-law when he married his cousin Ryōko in 1919. Nobusuke eventually attended the First Higher School in Tokyo, a secondary school established in 1886 to develop leaders for the rapidly modernizing nation. Like many of the school's graduates, he went on to Tokyo Imperial University, Japan's premier academic institution, enrolling in its law faculty in 1917.

Kishi arrived in Tokyo amidst political, economic, and intellectual upheaval. The Meiji era had ended in 1912, giving way to the brief flourishing of party democracy known as the Taishō Democracy.[7] Increasingly vibrant opposition to rule by oligarchs and military elites resulted in Japan's first party-led cabinet in 1918. Japan joined the Allies in the First World War, and participated in the Paris peace talks as a victorious power but chafed at western racism—while deepening its own imperial commitments on mainland Asia in response to the Russian Revolution, the decline of the European empires in Asia, and the birth pangs of post-imperial China.[8] The war's end also triggered a recession, accompanied by rice riots and labor strife, which for the besieged elites were haunted by the specter of Bolshevism.

Kishi plunged into the battle of ideas at Tokyo Imperial and flirted with radicalism, being especially drawn to Kita Ikki, a far-right thinker who sought to throw out corrupt politicians and business leaders, reclaim the emperor for the people, radically redistribute wealth, and pursue pan-Asian imperial expansion.[9] "I was simply overwhelmed by the revolutionary spirit of Ikki Kita," Kishi recalled.[10] Kita's call for a "Shōwa Restoration" won a following among junior military officers who eventually launched a coup in 1936, assassinating civilian and military leaders before being quashed by loyal army units—and resulting in Kita's execution as a ringleader. At the time, however, Kita's ideas were just one of many responses to the political tumult of the early interwar period—and it may not have been the only radical ideology that piqued Kishi's interest.[11]

Kishi would shed some of his radicalism as he graduated from university and entered the ranks of the national bureaucracy. But he retained a bedrock commitment to the idea that, in a turbulent and dangerous world, the state must defend the nation from external threats and that Japan ought to assume a leadership role in Asia as it struggled against western domination.

Despite performing well enough on the civil service exams to have his choice of ministry, in 1920 he joined the ministry of agriculture and commerce instead of the more prestigious finance or home ministries. This ministry—from 1925 the ministry of commerce and industry (MCI) following creation of an independent agriculture ministry—enabled Kishi to harness his vision of a powerful state to emerging tools for the direction of economic activity.

As Japan coped with the postwar recession, the devastation of the 1923 earthquake, and the Great Depression, its government became increasingly interested in economic planning and industrial rationalization that would let producers reduce their costs and compete with other industrial powers in the face of mounting protectionism. The MCI sought to curb "excess" competition and promote cartelization, and to focus state resources on the growth of critical industrial sectors, often generating conflict with Japan's prewar industrial conglomerates, the *zaibatsu*. Japan's commitment to state-led industrialization deepened as the Depression worsened and Japan invaded Manchuria in 1931, establishing the puppet state of Manchukuo the following year. Manchukuo became a laboratory for experiments with planning, and an indispensable source of raw materials needed for self-sufficiency in the event of war with the great powers.[12]

Manchuria offered a tremendous opportunity for an ambitious official like Kishi. As one of a cadre of "reform bureaucrats" who wanted the state to articulate national goals and shape economic activity according to them, Kishi made himself indispensable and acquired a powerful patron within the ministry, Yoshino Shinji, a pioneer of Japanese industrial policy.[13] Yoshino brought Kishi along to ever-higher posts, and by 1935, he had become director-general of MCI's powerful industrial affairs bureau. However, Kishi's talents also attracted the attention of the military, which sought to bring him to Manchukuo to plan its industrialization.[14]

Reluctant to leave Tokyo, in 1936 he nevertheless accepted the post of deputy minister for industrial development in Manchukuo, wielding power under a titular Manchu minister. Kishi had the opportunity to implement a five-year plan drafted by MCI, which would enable Japan to mobilize the quasi-colony's resources more effectively.

The crash industrialization of Manchukuo was not successful. Kishi had to contend with the imperial army as well as the Kwantung army, a garrison in Manchuria that often acted independent of (and against) Tokyo's orders, as well as with the South Manchuria Railway Company, which had enjoyed a preeminent role in Manchuria ever since Japan gained a foothold after the end of the Russo–Japanese war in 1905. He struggled to secure new sources of capital needed to develop Manchukuo's resources. The outbreak of the Second Sino–Japanese War simultaneously intensified Tokyo's need for Manchuria's strategic resources and dried up external sources of capital. Industrial planning would have to wait. While the client state did achieve some sharp increases in the production of critical resources, this was less the result of capital-intensive industrialization than the brutal exploitation of Chinese workers.[15]

But Kishi's career benefited from his three-year stint on the continent.[16] He became part of a five-man clique that dominated Manchurian affairs in the late 1930s—a clique that included General Tōjō Hideki, commander of the Kwantung army's military police from 1935 and chief of staff of the Kwantung army from 1937—whose members would return to Japan to assume positions of power and influence, and achieve greater notoriety in the process. All five were arrested as suspected Class A war criminals after the war and only two—including Kishi—escaped charges.[17]

Kishi returned to Japan in 1939 and became MCI's vice minister, its highest-ranking bureaucrat. He resigned after a feud with the minister but returned to MCI as minister in October 1941 after Tōjō was named prime minister—ensuring that Kishi's name would be on the imperial rescript declaring war on the US after the attack on Pearl Harbor. He served Tōjō loyally as commerce minister and, when the MCI was folded into a new munitions ministry headed by Tōjō himself, Kishi would serve as vice minister, organizing production as the war hit Japan hard. In the early months of the Second World War, Kishi launched his political career, comfortably winning a Diet seat as a candidate of the government's Imperial Rule Assistance Association (IRAA) in the 1942 general election.

But the war's endgame threatened Kishi's future. On 9 July 1944, the US took Saipan, an island in the Northern Mariana Islands. As a result, Japan's home islands were well within range of US B-29 bombers. The implications for Japan's ability to prosecute the war were dire. Within days, Kishi joined a movement within the cabinet to unseat Tōjō and seek an early end to the hostilities. Kishi used cabinet procedures to force the resignation of the entire cabinet, ending Tōjō's premiership and Kishi's war.[18]

Kishi was not a principled opponent of the war effort after Tōjō's resignation. He was planning for life after the war, when participation in a plot to remove Tōjō could be an asset, a hedge to distance himself from Tōjō in the likely event that Japan was defeated.[19] This turn against Tōjō throws Kishi's talent for survival—his willingness to shed political commitments as the situation required—into relief.

Kishi spent the last year of the war advocating for greater state control of the economy. He used his parliamentary seat to pull together a group of thirty-two right-wing lawmakers into a proto-party, the Association for Defense of the Fatherland. This group sought to organize a nationwide movement to agitate in support of centralizing control of the nation's war industries and mobilizing the people as a "productive army" to resist invasion.[20] He also created a local association in Yamaguchi prefecture devoted to his "productive defense" platform and delivered speeches on its behalf.[21] In the final months of the war, Kishi's association actually tried to topple Prime Minister Suzuki Kantarō as he negotiated Japan's surrender.[22]

But the end came. Okinawa fell. Tokyo and other major cities were burned to cinders. The US dropped atomic bombs on Hiroshima and Nagasaki. The Soviet Union entered the war. Kishi had, like his 70 million compatriots, to "[endure] the unendurable and suffer what is unsufferable" as Emperor Hirohito announced Japan's surrender on 15 August 1945. On 17 September, Kishi received word at home in Tabuse that he must report to US military authorities in Yokohama immediately. He would spend the next three years and three months in American custody, mostly in Sugamo, as a "Class A" war criminal accused of "crimes against peace" for his role in the war effort.

* * *

But even as Kishi languished in prison—stewing over his treatment by his American jailers and nursing resentments of America—world events gave him a second chance. The Truman administration came to see that a rebuilt Japan, firmly anchored to the US, could help resist Soviet expansionism in Asia.[23] Occupation authorities abandoned efforts to create space for left-wing parties and organized labor as part of a program of "demilitarization and democratization" and, in the words of historian John Dower, "aligned themselves more and more openly with the conservative and even right-wing elements in Japanese society, including individuals who had been closely identified with the lost war."[24] Kishi, who followed the news inside Sugamo, quickly recognized that tensions between the US and the USSR were a "golden opportunity" for Japan to rebuild itself as a fully independent US ally, united in opposition to Soviet communism.[25]

The "reverse course" in US policy in Japan meant Kishi got off more lightly than the twenty-eight wartime leaders who were tried by the International Military Tribunal for the Far East—six of whom, including Tōjō, were hanged. Although prosecutors had intended to try all accused war criminals, the exigencies of the early Cold War ensured that Kishi and others left Sugamo as free men.[26] As the Truman administration threw its weight behind the reconstruction and reindustrialization of its defeated enemy, it seemed there would be room for Kishi in the new Japan.[27] In fact, even before Kishi was released, US officials consulted with him regarding postwar reconstruction.[28]

When Kishi was released on 24 December 1948, his first stop was the official residence of Japan's chief cabinet secretary—who, at the time, was his younger brother Satō Eisaku, previously a transport ministry official who had become close to Prime Minister Yoshida Shigeru. There may be no more poignant illustration of the reverse course than, Kishi, after three years in prison, being delivered in an American jeep to his brother, a senior official in the postwar government, who plied him with sashimi. "The sashimi was tastier in Sugamo," joked Kishi.[29]

* * *

Political rehabilitation would take longer. He was banned from electoral politics thanks to the influence of Yoshida, an old adversary who intervened with US authorities to prevent Kishi being de-purged.[30] Kishi was on the sidelines, helpless to intervene as Yoshida erected the pillars of a postwar regime that Kishi would detest.

Yoshida dominated the first postwar decade, serving as prime minister for all but one year from 1946 to 1954 and navigating Japan through the occupation, the start of the Cold War, and the Korean War. Under his leadership, Japan introduced a new constitution, which included, among other innovations, Article 9, renouncing Japan's right to wage war or maintain "war potential." On this anti-militarist foundation, Yoshida signed a peace treaty and security treaty with the US and its allies, and committed to anchoring Japan to the US, abjuring rearmament, relying on the superpower for its defense, and focusing on trade and reconstruction. "Yoshida," writes historian Michael Schaller, "hoped to ease Japan back into the world community without incurring the costs of rearmament or alienating the United States. In exchange for the grant of bases, Japan would secure protection and access to the world's largest market."[31] This strategy, known as the Yoshida Doctrine, would remain the dominant political tendency among Japanese conservatives for the duration of the Cold War.[32]

These choices were anathema to Kishi, who thought that anti-communism should justify Japan's return to its rightful place in Asia and the world order, with all the trappings of a great power. His critique of Yoshida's compromises was not groundless. The alliance concluded with the US in 1951 not only allowed the US military to keep bases in Japan indefinitely but also gave Tokyo no veto over how those bases were used. American forces could also be used to quell domestic disturbances at the request of the Japanese government. Under the terms of the San Francisco Treaty, Okinawa became a US colony and hub for US military activities in Asia until reversion in 1972, with long-reaching consequences. The sovereignty Yoshida secured was partial and constrained. Japan, said US negotiator John Foster Dulles, had accepted "a voluntary continuation of the Occupation."[33]

Yoshida and his acolytes enjoyed a first-mover advantage in building postwar institutions. Once Kishi could enter electoral politics, he would face an increasingly durable status quo as he agitated for constitutional revision, building an equal alliance with the US and restoring commercial relations with Southeast Asia, rolling back occupation-era reforms, and pursuing political reforms to strengthen national leadership. A realist, Kishi accepted that he would have to advance these ideas in the rough-and-tumble world of democratic politics. "Strange, isn't it? We're all democrats now," he said, following his release.[34]

Kishi worked to build a revisionist political movement even before the occupation ended, calling upon a wide network of friends to bankroll his activities and advance his prospects. In the final years of the occupation, he built up the Japan Reconstruction Federation, that drew together reform-minded conservatives and right-wing socialists into a movement that would serve as the nucleus of a new political party.[35] Despite Kishi's reservations, the federation fielded candidates in the October 1952 general election, the first following the end of the occupation. Kishi did not run, and only one candidate won, destroying the federation as a political party.

Having failed to create a new party, Kishi turned to the existing parties. He flirted with joining the Rightist Socialist Party—triggering a rebellion from the party's members—but was then admitted to Yoshida's Liberal Party with the help of his brother, who had become its secretary-general, despite the antipathy between Yoshida and Kishi.[36] He was admitted just in time to run in the April 1953 general election and win a seat in the House of Representatives. His stay in the Liberal Party was short-lived: hostility to the Yoshida Doctrine led to his expulsion the following year. But that freed Kishi to resume his efforts to build a conservative party that would seek "true independence"—a new constitution, an equal alliance with the US as part of an autonomous foreign policy, a robust trade policy, and a new military—from within the halls of the parliament.

Kishi found a willing partner in Hatoyama Ichirō. A veteran of the prewar political system, Hatoyama was banned from political participation by the occupying US on dubious grounds when he was on the brink of election as prime minister in 1946, clearing the way for Yoshida to become prime minister. When he reentered politics after the occupation, he had become a strident opponent of Yoshida's "subordinate independence" and worked to topple his "one man" rule.[37]

Kishi and Hatoyama had to unify a right wing divided not only between Yoshida's supporters and opponents, but also among factions centered on strong, ambitious personalities. As a result, 1953 and 1954 saw a bewildering wave of political realignment as Yoshida's rivals sought to oust him and unify conservatives into a single party. Eventually in November 1954 they pulled together the Japan Democratic Party—led by Hatoyama, with Kishi as secretary-general. This was the end for Yoshida. His popularity waning due to a corruption scandal, he now faced a conservative opposition party with enough votes to pass a no-confidence motion.

By December, Hatoyama was prime minister. Although he enjoyed an initial surge of popularity with his calls for constitutional revision and an independent foreign policy focused on normalizing ties with the Soviet Union and communist China, his popularity failed to translate into a majority in the February 1955 general election. The result was another round of realignment.

After negotiations that lasted for much of the year between the Liberals, now led by Satō and Yoshida's right-hand man Ikeda Hayato, and Hatoyama's Democrats, the two parties merged in November 1955—achieving a breakthrough thanks largely to the formation of a reunified Japan Socialist Party (JSP) in October, which raised the specter of a Socialist majority. The Liberal Democratic Party (LDP) was born. Its charter called for economic planning to achieve "economic independence"; a robust social safety net; "peace diplomacy" to conclude peace treaties and normalize relations with former adversaries and colonies and join the UN; and revision of the constitution and other occupation-era laws, the redevelopment of Japan's armed forces, and the removal of foreign troops from Japanese territory.[38] Hatoyama would be its first leader, Kishi its first secretary-general. Kishi had not been the only protagonist in bringing about the LDP's formation but he was one of the most important, and the process moved forward in part due to his insistence that Japan needed a stable conservative party to truly regain its independence.[39] The new LDP was deeply fractured and full of ambitious rivals for the premiership, but it endured.

As luck would have it—and it took luck, since his rivals had to retire, fall ill, or die—Kishi had his chance to deliver those policies less than eighteen months later. Hatoyama exited in December 1956, after realizing his dream of restoring relations with the Soviet Union. Ishibashi Tanzan, a prominent prewar intellectual who had also been purged, succeeded him after narrowly defeating Kishi. Kishi received the deputy premiership and the foreign affairs portfolio as a consolation prize. When Ishibashi was sidelined, he stepped in as acting prime minister before being elected prime minister in February 1957 and

LDP president in March. Less than a decade after he arrived at his brother's doorstep, clad in prison uniform, he had reached the pinnacle of power.

* * *

Shinzō was two-and-a-half years old when his grandfather became prime minister. Kishi's progress would have a profound influence on the young boy's life. Most immediately, his grandfather's rise drew his father Shintarō into politics. After Kishi was named foreign minister in 1956, Shintarō resigned from *Mainichi* to become his father-in-law's private secretary. When Kishi moved into the premiership, Shintarō stayed on.

In 1958, however, Shintarō announced he wanted a Diet seat of his own. Both Kishi and Satō were opposed to his running after less than two years as Kishi's secretary. Kishi was also skeptical about his chances in Yamaguchi's first district. But Shintarō would not relent. "I will run even if I have to run as an independent," he told his father-in-law. "I will run even if I have to get divorced."[40] Kishi yielded, and Shintarō launched his bid, campaigning as "Abe Kan's son"—although the presence of Kishi's daughter by his side did not hurt his chances.[41] In the April 1958 general election, thirty-four-year-old Shintarō finished second and earned a seat as part of his father-in-law's majority. Shintarō's dogged pursuit of a parliamentary seat over his father-in-law's objections showed a stubborn streak that had also shaped his father's career and would in time influence his son Shinzō, as well.

Life forced Kan and Shintarō to be resilient. Kan was born in Yamaguchi and graduated from Tokyo Imperial in 1921. He established a bicycle business, but was forced back to Yamaguchi when the Great Kantō earthquake of 1923 destroyed it.[42] Then, eighty days after Shintarō was born in 1924, Kan's wife Shizuko abandoned him and left him to raise the child alone. Shintarō was largely raised by a great-aunt as Kan built a political career in Yamaguchi even as he battled tuberculosis.

Kan won reelection to the Diet in 1942 as one of eighty-five anti-war independents not endorsed by the pro-regime IRAA, overcoming harassment by government authorities to win. Kan's conduct made a deep impression on Shintarō. Kan was a consistent opponent of the war: when Shintarō told his father that he intended to become a kamikaze pilot, Kan told his son not to throw his life away because Japan would need its young people after the war.[43]

Shintarō struggled to overcome the impression that he owed his career to Kishi, even though as a freshman Diet member he could not help but be drawn into his faction and inner circle. He would be deeply entrenched in his father-in-law's political tribe, the Abe line becoming ever more deeply subsumed by the Kishi line—literally so, when, in 1959, he and Yōko obeyed a promise to his father-in-law to have Nobuo, their newly born third son, adopted by Yōko's brother Nobukazu, so the Kishi name would continue.

For Shinzō, his father's political career meant he would not know "normal" family life. Although when he married, Shintarō hoped to raise a family under circumstances more normal than his own childhood, his political ambitions made that impossible.[44] The life of an ambitious lawmaker, representing a constituency far from Tokyo, left Shintarō with little time for family, while the burdens placed on a politician's wife meant Yōko was also often away too. The family, Yōko would say later, was a "community of independent states."[45]

Shinzō and his older brother Hironobu were raised by a nanny, Kubo Ume, a Yamaguchi native who had known Shintarō and his father. When older, they also had a tutor, Hirasawa Katsuei, a Tokyo University student who would later become an LDP lawmaker.[46] Hirasawa recalled that, although he dined with the family three nights a week, Shintarō was never there.[47]

Just a toddler when Kishi became prime minister, Shinzō and his family were firmly in Kishi's orbit. Kishi delighted in visits by his grandsons to his private residence or at an inn in the resort town of Hakone on weekends, welcoming play with them as relief from the pressures of office.[48] Kubo would later describe Shinzō as a spoiled but headstrong child with a talent for mischief. He was, said Kubo, a boy who did not cry. Once, when Shinzō was only two, he went with his family to Haneda Airport to see Kishi off for his June 1957 trip to the United States. He wandered off from his family but did not scream or cry and eventually came back on his own.[49] Hirasawa recalled that while Hironobu was teachable, Shinzō was stubborn and it was impossible to get him to change his opinions.[50] As a baby boomer from an elite family with parents who by necessity were laxer than others, Abe's childhood was carefree. In Shinzō's only cameo in Daniel Kurzman's biography of Kishi, he and his brother "insist on watching American cowboys swear vengeance on each other in perfect dubbed-in Japanese."[51]

* * *

While Shinzō spent his days at play, his grandfather was struggling to remake Japan. The reverse course had laid the groundwork for a culture war. It had liberalized Japan in important ways—demilitarization, decentralization of the education system, and democratization of the political system—but then, in the name of enlisting Japan in the Cold War, rehabilitated and financed conservatives who were determined to undo the postwar reforms.[52] Although the US had cleared the way for the return of Kishi and other wartime elites, the devastation of war, the reforms and dashed hopes of the occupation, the Cold War and mounting fears of global nuclear annihilation had changed Japan in ways with which Kishi had not reckoned. The Japanese people had by and large come to cherish their democracy and value the "peace constitution." They did not want Japan to remilitarize or partner with the US in waging war, even as Kishi wanted Japan to reclaim its place among the world's great powers. Ultimately, they would take to the streets in the name of democracy and antimilitarism, in a display of mass mobilization that had profound implications for Japan's future.[53]

More than any other postwar politician, Kishi was a living symbol of the culture war. As he moved to uproot the institutions that he believed had reduced Japan to a humiliating dependence on the US, he provoked a fierce reaction from many Japanese. As George Packard writes, "No matter how much of a 'democratic statesman' Kishi had become, the pain and fear of the past could not be erased so soon."[54] But Kishi proceeded headlong to reclaim Japan's independence. With the JSP able to deny the LDP supermajorities needed to amend the constitution, he focused on revising the US–Japan security treaty instead.

The Eisenhower administration initially rebuffed Kishi's request for treaty revision. But the administration viewed Kishi as a reliable partner in the fight against communism, who would keep Japan from "drifting" into nonalignment—so much so that after Kishi's 1957 trip to the

US, the CIA began secret payments to the LDP, especially Kishi's faction, of up to $10 million a year.[55]

Kishi gained strength, winning a new electoral mandate in 1958. He began to bolster Japan's defense capabilities—Yoshida had established Japan's Self-Defense Forces (SDF) in 1954, but these were limited in size and funding, under strict civilian control, and restricted to a purely defensive role—so that the US began to soften its opposition when Kishi and his foreign minister approached them again in 1958.[56] However, despite widespread dissatisfaction with the 1951 treaty, Kishi had to tread carefully, since there was little consensus even within the LDP over its revision.

After a year of negotiations, Washington and Tokyo concluded a new treaty that addressed many, if not all, Japanese concerns about the 1951 version. The new mutual security treaty, commonly known as *anpo*, embedded the alliance in the UN collective security system; removed provisions permitting the US military to put down domestic disturbances; included a sunset clause that allowed either ally to abrogate the treaty after ten years; imposed some obligations for mutual consultations—if not a Japanese veto—over the activities of US forces in Japan; and strengthened US commitments to aid Japan.[57] Kishi flew to Washington to sign the treaty in January 1960, and returned confident that the Diet would ratify it ahead of a valedictory visit by Eisenhower in June.[58]

His confidence was misplaced. The LDP was divided over Kishi's renegotiated treaty and although left-wing parties and activists rarely agreed on much, they united to oppose Kishi and a closer alliance with the US. A culture of protest, frequently directed at US bases, had grown during the 1950s—Kishi became a target when, in 1958, he tried to ram a revision of the Police Duties Law through the Diet, that would have strengthened police powers to act against suspected lawbreakers. Pushed by a prime minister already tainted by his prewar past, the bill was highly redolent of the oppressive 1925 Peace Preservation Law.[59] Amidst delaying tactics by Socialists, strikes and demonstrations by unions and activists, and open dissent by LDP members, Kishi shelved the bill.

Despite these warning signs, he forged ahead with ratification. Kishi could not revise the treaty; it would be all or nothing, and Kishi could not back down without crippling his premiership.[60] LDP rivals were scheming so that Kishi would have to resign even if the treaty was ratified, while the JSP called for "total opposition" and vowed to use every parliamentary stalling tactic to prevent a vote before the parliamentary session ended on 26 May. As the debate, which began in February, dragged into the spring, mass demonstrations outside the Diet grew, increasing pressure on Kishi to act decisively.

On 19 May the LDP's parliamentary leadership rushed through a motion to extend the session by fifty days even as Socialist lawmakers attempted to block the vote physically. Then, in a stroke that took even LDP members by surprise, the lower house voted on the treaty itself, without opposition lawmakers. One critic likened this maneuver to Pearl Harbor—"a surprise political attack against the nation and against democracy."[61] Kishi would have his victory, since, according to the constitution, a treaty passed by the lower house would be automatically ratified after thirty days if the upper house did not act.

But it was a pyrrhic victory. His strong-arm tactics provoked ever-larger protests outside the Diet and his residence, three nationwide general strikes, and mounting pressure from within the LDP to resign. The protests were increasingly anti-Kishi, since the parliamentary vote appeared to confirm the public's worst fears about his anti-democratic tendencies.[62] The embattled prime minister stood his ground for several weeks. But when Kamba Michiko, a Tokyo University undergraduate, was trampled to death during a battle between protestors and police at the Diet on 15 June, he was finished. Eisenhower's visit was scrapped, the treaty came into force at midnight on 19 June, and on 23 June, Kishi announced his resignation, effective 15 July. In a grim coda to the crisis, on 14 July, shortly after Ikeda was chosen as his successor, a right-wing activist stabbed him in the leg during a reception at his home.

There would be more to Kishi's tenure than *anpo*. He pursued a coherent program of national revival that included both political and diplomatic measures to reassert Japan's sovereignty and economic policies to build the material basis for national independence.[63] Even as he pushed for a more equal partnership with the US, his foreign ministry articulated new principles for Japanese foreign policy—UN-centrism, maintaining a position as an Asian nation, and cooperating with the nations of the free world—that expanded Japan's diplomatic autonomy.[64] He undertook two landmark trips to South and Southeast Asia, rebuilding Japan's relations with former colonies and adversaries via apologies and reparations; the latter not only helped restore access to important sources of raw materials and markets for Japanese exports, also but bolstered Japan's efforts to counter communism in post-colonial Asia.[65] "It is my firm conviction that Japan, as a faithful member of the free world," Kishi told members of the US Congress in 1957, "has a useful and constructive role to play, particularly in Asia, where the free world faces the challenge of international communism."[66]

Kishi believed that Japan had become too dependent on the US for its growth—symbolized by the boom spurred by the Korean War—and that new sources were required for sustainable growth. His industrial policy program—which laid the foundation for the subsequent "income doubling plan" pursued by Ikeda[67]—recognized the need for investment in new technology that would boost productivity, which would in turn raise wages and boost consumption. Japan would also need to develop new markets to export surplus production, which meant working with the US to deepen their bilateral trade relationship and rebuilding links with Southeast Asian countries and Australia. Increasing national wealth would be the foundation for shared prosperity based on redistribution, and Kishi made creation of a welfare state a fundamental goal for his government.

* * *

But *anpo* would have an outsized impact on his legacy. For Shintarō, his father-in-law's downfall would have a devastating effect on his own prospects. As a junior backbencher, Shintarō had virtually no influence on Kishi—although when Kishi was determined to forge ahead with revisions to the Police Duties law, Shintarō asked whether it would be better for him to grapple with economic issues—and he had no major part in the *anpo* drama, other than reluctantly drafting Kishi's resignation letter.[68] But his fortunes were tied to Kishi's.

In the October 1960 general election, Ikeda, wishing to distance himself from his predecessor by promising to govern with "tolerance and patience," sought a new mandate for LDP rule. Although the LDP won, Kishi allies like Shintarō suffered. He fell to fourth in his district, barely holding his seat—and in 1963, with Kishi's faction splintered and frozen out of power by Ikeda, Shintarō lost his seat outright. It was, according to Yōko, the first time he cried in front of his sons.[69] Losing his parliamentary seat was a descent into a personal hell for the proud and ambitious Shintarō, particularly since, it turned out, he would have to wait until 1967 for the next general election. In the meantime, he and Yōko spent long stretches in Yamaguchi, canvassing voters and trying to sow the seeds of a comeback. This separated both parents from their sons for long stretches.

For Shinzō, meanwhile, *anpo* and its aftermath would be the touchstone of his political identity. He and his brother continued to visit their grandfather when demonstrators surrounded Kishi's house during the security treaty protests. In his 2006 book, Shinzō tells how once he and his brother, to the amusement of his parents and his grandfather, stamped their feet and shouted, "Down with the security treaty!" in imitation of the protestors outside. In a moment that he suggests was portentous, Shinzō asked his grandfather, "What's *anpo?*" To which Kishi replied, "The security treaty is a treaty for Japan to be defended by America. I don't understand why everyone is opposed."[70] Kishi, virtually housebound due to the demonstrations, desired the company of his grandchildren in order to weather the storm, and gave Shinzō and Hironobu piggyback rides as protestors hurled epithets just outside the house.[71]

* * *

This whole episode—the loud, raucous demonstrations through which Shinzō had to pass to enter Kishi's house, the contrast between his image of Kishi as a kindly grandfather and the public's vilification, his grandfather's commonsense explanation for the treaty, and his grandfather's stabbing shortly after having resigned—left an indelible impression on Shinzō.[72]

* * *

Kishi served in the Diet until 1979, and remained influential as a faction boss and elder statesman, using his personal connections overseas to, for example, help his brother negotiate the 1965 basic treaty with South Korea and the Okinawa reversion agreement with the United States. He continued to wield influence until his death in 1987.

His daughter Yōko became the guardian of his legacy. Dubbed the "godmother" by tabloids for her longtime public role, she assumed responsibility for transmitting her father's historical mission to her children. "The LDP of the present was made by my father Kishi Nobusuke," she told Shinzō, "and you must never forget those great footprints."[73] There may be no better symbol of his grandfather's influence than the fact that, even as prime minister, Shinzō continues to live in an apartment building with his mother in Tokyo's Tomigaya neighborhood. Usually he breakfasts with his mother and first lady Abe Akie before commuting to his office.[74]

Japan is hardly the only democracy with hereditary political families—and the Abe–Kishi clan is not Japan's only political dynasty.[75] For an entire decade, from 2001–2010, every Japanese prime minister was a dynastic politician and all but one—Koizumi Junichirō—the son or grandson of a prime minister. But Kishi's legacy—both his determination to overturn the postwar order and return to great power politics, and the spectacular collapse of his premiership—created a dynasty whose relationship with the political status quo was ambivalent.

3

THE WORLD THAT MADE SHINZŌ

Shinzō was ten years old in October 1964, when the Olympics came to Tokyo. He was swept up in the pageantry of an event that would change the face of the capital and show the world a rebuilt, peaceful Japan in the early stages of an economic miracle.

The government spent extraordinary sums of money on Tange Kenzō's new Olympic stadium and athletic facilities, but these expenditures were only the beginning. Haneda Airport was upgraded. New highways and subway lines opened. The Tokyo games, framed as the "Science Olympics," were used to showcase Japan's technological prowess. A new domestically produced airliner transported the Olympic torch. Japan and the US jointly deployed a satellite transmission system allowing the games to be broadcast simultaneously around the world. And on 1 October, nine days before the Olympics opened, Japan's first *shinkansen* line—the high-speed "bullet train"—commenced operations between Tokyo and Osaka.[1]

The games also celebrated Japan's rebirth as a peaceful, internationalist democracy. The Self-Defense Forces (SDF), ten years old and still controversial, participated in the spectacle. Jets from an Air Self-Defense Forces acrobatic team formed the five Olympic rings in the sky at the end of the closing ceremony; Abe remembered the sense of wonder it awoke in "a child's heart" and the premonition it gave him that "from this something brilliant would awaken" in Japan.[2] But the use of the SDF was part of a broader "redeployment" of national symbols, including the flag and the emperor, to signal that Japan had been reborn as a peaceful country.[3] As Abe later wrote, "Nineteen years after the defeat. Our country, starting from burnt-out ruins, had achieved reconstruction until we could finally hold the Olympics."[4]

Shinzō's memories of the Olympics are part of his broader nostalgia for the world of his childhood, a nostalgia shared by many of his generation. As historian Laura Neitzel writes, "Looking back from the 1990s, people felt nostalgia for the feeling of 'looking forward.'"[5] This sense of nostalgia for a time when Japanese people could feel pride in their country's achievements and optimistic for its future permeates Shinzō's political thought.[6] In his 2006 memoir, he expresses his appreciation for the award-winning 2005 film *ALWAYS: San-chōme no yūhi*, a popular work of Shōwa nostalgia that depicts life in a "low city" Tokyo neighborhood in the late 1950s and early 1960s. "Everyone is poor," he writes, "but the people in the neighborhood are depicted as living with dreams of acquiring wealth amidst warm connections with each other."[7]

Shinzō, however, was a child of plenty, both his family's personal wealth and the broader prosperity of a rapidly growing economy. From his starting school in 1960 until 1977, when he graduated from university, Japan's per-capita gross domestic product grew from $479 to $6,335. Life expectancy rose from roughly 67 years to nearly 77 years. In 1968, Japan's gross national product surpassed West Germany's and it became the world's second-largest economy.[8] Japan became an exporting powerhouse, running perpetual trade surpluses with the United States and other trading partners. This period also marked the reemergence of a society of mass consumption as households sought the "three sacred treasures"—washing machine, refrigerator, and vacuum cleaner—then the "three Cs"—cooler, car, color television—and then the "three Vs"—villa, *vacansu*, and visit (vacation home, overseas travel, and guests for dinner).[9]

But Shinzō's recollections mask an ambivalent relationship with the Japan of his youth. The prosperity and social peace after 1960 came from a decisive rejection of his grandfather's politics, as the LDP tightened its embrace of the Yoshida consensus and the politics of "tolerance and moderation" trumpeted by Ikeda. The 1964 Olympics celebrated Yoshida's Japan, not Kishi's.

During this period, as Shinzō entered school, he began making sense of what he had witnessed as a child in 1960. The boy's sense of wonder curdled into resentment of and reaction against the compromises that his father's generation of conservative leaders made to wield power, instead of admiration for their accomplishments. Shinzō would come to see the post-1960 consensus as an enemy that had to be defeated for Japan to be great again. He entered politics as a fervent devotee to his grandfather's cause, decisively winning the culture war that resulted from the stillborn transformation of postwar Japan in favor of a "national greatness" conservatism that would let the country act as a great power.

* * *

Shintarō, meanwhile, was in many respects an archetypal participant in the "1955 system," the term used to describe the LDP's stable, long-term dominance of Japanese politics during the Cold War. The LDP, working with bureaucracy and business, invested in high-speed growth and redistributed its fruits to disadvantaged regions and sectors, while clinging to the lightly armed, US-dependent foreign policy of the Yoshida Doctrine. The rejection of Kishi's vision for Japan became even more decisive with the rise of Tanaka Kakuei, a political prodigy from Niigata prefecture in Japan's snow country, who left school at fifteen, made a fortune in the construction business during the Second World War, and, despite his lack of formal education, won a Diet seat in 1947. Tanaka and his protégés built a third tendency in the LDP to compete with the Yoshida school and Kishi's revisionists, and dominated the party from Tanaka's election as LDP leader in 1972 until 1993.[10]

For Tanaka, politics came down to money. "Politics equals power; power equals numbers; numbers come from money," he famously said. His followers would extract money for interest groups and other constituents and triangulate between interest groups and central government ministries to deliver benefits to the interest groups as well as to constituents. Many of these benefits manifested as concrete, as the LDP's "construction state" channeled government funds into grandiose projects even in Japan's remote countryside. The LDP parliamentarians were increasingly organized into "policy tribes" as well as factions, focusing their efforts on the distribution of benefits in areas besides infrastructure. This approach extended to foreign policy, where Tanaka, who rushed to normalize relations with the People's Republic of China (PRC) after Nixon's surprise opening to Beijing, encouraged a transactional approach to the PRC that would also shape his faction's approach to North Korea.

Tanaka's rise came at the expense of Kishi's heirs. He bested Fukuda Takeo, the ex-MOF official who was Kishi's handpicked successor, in the LDP's 1972 presidential election, marking the triumph of Tanaka's machine politics over Kishi's revisionism. Tanaka, Fukuda and their partisans continued to wage the so-called "Kaku–Fuku war" for decades after their 1972 contest, but in reality Tanaka won the war early on, remaking the LDP in his image and reducing Kishi's acolytes to the LDP's "anti-mainstream," an internal opposition within the ruling party. Tanaka's premiership was brief—he resigned in 1974 when faced with allegations of corruption by LDP candidates in the 1974 upper house elections—but he continued to dominate the party as a "shadow shogun." He ruled from the shadows even after 1976, when he was charged with accepting bribes from the Lockheed Corporation during his premiership—charges he spent much of the following decade contesting.

Shintarō, who had lost his parliamentary seat in 1963, regained it in 1967. By then, Kishi's brother Satō had been prime minister for three years, some of the bitterness from Kishi's tenure had faded, and Japan's economic miracle was well advanced. Shintarō finished first and would continue to do so for the rest of his career. He would remain a member of his father-in-law's faction even as it lost ground to Tanaka, but Shintarō did not evince a particularly strong commitment to his father-in-law's agenda for overturning the legacies of Japan's defeat. His watchword was "balance," his conservatism dispositional rather than ideological.[11]

Despite being part of the anti-mainstream, he steadily climbed the party hierarchy, serving in party offices under Satō before becoming agriculture minister in the cabinet of Miki Takeo, who, like Shintarō's father, had won a Diet seat in 1942 as an independent anti-militarist candidate. Shintarō built a lengthy résumé in the 1970s, serving as the LDP's parliamentary affairs chairman in 1976, coordinating with opposition parties when the LDP's majority receded; chief cabinet secretary in 1977 during Fukuda's premiership; and chairman of the LDP's policy affairs research council, a key agenda-setting institution, under Prime Minister Ohira Masayoshi, another Yoshida protégé.

During his rise to the LDP's top ranks, Shintarō was a conciliator, softening the divisions between mainstream factions—Tanaka's as well as those led by Yoshida's onetime lieutenants—and right-wing anti-mainstream groups. He worked closely with one of those lieutenants, Ohira, as the LDP's policy chief, and became a close friend of Takeshita Noburu, Tanaka's chief lieutenant. Shintarō, along with future prime ministers Takeshita and Miyazawa Kiichi, was considered one of the LDP's "new leaders" as the party faced a generational changing of the guard in the 1980s. "In a political world that swirled with trickery, he did not make full use of wiles. Nor was he the possessor of an indecently fierce individualism. This existence as the opposite of a 'stubborn politician' was neither a merit nor a demerit."[12]

Perhaps because of his temperament, he was not an outspoken standard bearer of his father-in-law's revisionist conservatism. Indeed, as a member of the generation that fought and died in the Pacific War—almost perishing himself—there is good evidence to suggest that Shintarō supported the postwar constitution, including Article 9. As Shinzō writes, "My father's pre-college education was prewar, but after that it was postwar. Then, because he had an extremely tragic experience of the war, that casts a very large shadow on the form of his thought. Why did we go to war? There was quite a lot of generational reflection on this and other such skeptical points."[13] Even having reached the heights of power as one of his father-in-law's heirs, Shintarō remained the son of Abe Kan.

* * *

The prime years of Shintarō's career, as he fought to regain his seat and then scrambled for power, were the years in which Shinzō grew from a mischievous boy playing at his grandfather's house to a privileged but aimless young man. During these years, particularly after 1963, when Shintarō was absent for long stretches in his constituency, Shinzō drew closer to Kishi. His nanny suggested that it was around this time—perhaps when he was as young as six—that Shinzō first said he wanted to follow his father into politics.[14] But with an older brother, as well as a younger brother who would inherit the Kishi name and perhaps the Kishi legacy, it was not guaranteed that Shinzō would win his parents' blessing to succeed his father.

There was little about Shinzō's adolescence that marked him for political leadership. He loved movies—particularly action movies—and his great ambition as a child was to become a director, so much so that it may have factored in his parents' decision not to push Shinzō on to a more ambitious academic track.[15] As a child, he would sometimes play director, barking orders to friends as he pretended to shoot a film.[16] His classmates from primary school through university remembered him as "innocent" and "kind," a good friend who wanted for little and did not boast about his family. But he also made little impression on his classmates. He was "very ordinary."[17] At best a mediocre student, neither his classmates nor his teachers remembered him as an excellent scholar or athlete.[18]

Shinzō and his older brother Hironobu had unexceptional educations. Both attended Seikei, a middling private school for elite children in suburban Tokyo that had been part of the Mitsubishi *zaibatsu* before the war, starting from the lower elementary school all the way through university. Whereas many of his peers were subjected to "examination hell" and "cram schools" as they raced for admission to top schools and, eventually, leading companies and elite government ministries, both Shinzō and Hironobu opted out of the high-stakes competition that would so profoundly shape the lives of many in their generation.[19] Shinzō's decision to stay at Seikei and "escalate" into the university instead of seeking admission to Tokyo University—the alma mater of Shintarō and both of Shinzō's grandfathers—was particularly vexing to Shintarō. Kishi was disappointed by his lack of interest in civil service examinations.[20]

Shinzō was not active in student politics or vocal about national issues. This set him apart from much of his generation, since by the time he was in high school in the late 1960s, radical student politics had spread from the universities to secondary schools as protests erupted against the US–Japan relationship against the backdrop of the Vietnam War and Japan's postwar state and economy.[21] For the teenaged Abe, politics was a family matter. Aoyama Kazuhiro, a journalist who has covered Abe for years, suggests Shinzō came to identify with his grandfather's politics at least in part because he saw his grandfather as an underdog and Japan's conservatives as a persecuted minority deserving of his admiration. Shinzō told him, "During my adolescence, when I was in middle school and high school, an anti-LDP mood was dominant. Amid these circumstances, I of course felt that I had to protect my father and grandfather, who were being abused by society, in school."[22] He may have felt especially protective of Kishi because he was able to enjoy intimate moments with his grandfather that he had been unable to share with his often-absent father[23]—and also to please his mother, who appeared to favor his older brother and whose approval Shinzō sought.[24]

In his memoirs Abe recalls an episode from high school, when, as Japan was rocked by battles between left and right over the renewal of the US–Japan security treaty in 1970, he defended the treaty against a teacher who was advocating for its abrogation. But Abe recounts this story to illustrate the left-wing conformism that prevailed in his youth, admitting, "at the time I knew little about what the treaty is supposed to do."[25] This episode is "at most only a glimpse at his respect towards his grandfather."[26] None of Abe's classmates has described Shinzō as voicing strong political opinions as a student.[27]

There is little to suggest that he changed after April 1974, when he escalated from Seikei's preparatory school to the university, where he joined the law faculty as a major in political science.[28] At university, he continued to give the impression of a pampered rich kid. He was an indifferent student, not atypical for a Japanese university student. He drove around in a red Alfa Romeo and played mahjong obsessively.[29] But while he was in university, it became increasingly possible that Shinzō could one day succeed his father.

His older brother, who had graduated from Seikei's economics faculty en route to a successful career at the Mitsubishi Corporation, was uninterested in following in Shintarō's footsteps. From a young age, Hironobu and Shinzō had helped with their father's campaigns. Even today campaigning is arduous, long hours spent distributing leaflets outside train stations or going door-to-door to speak with voters. Hironobu detested campaigning, and when he fell ill on a campaign one winter, requiring three months of hospitalization, he decided that he could never become a politician.[30] With his brother uninterested,

Shinzō began to dream of following his father—and became increasingly open about his political ambitions, to his classmates' surprise. When he told a friend in the Seikei archery club of his dream, his friend thought he was "too nice" to become a politician.[31]

The problem was that unlike other members of his generation, who, as they approached the end of schooling were engaged in arduous exams and interviews to land good jobs out of college, there was no exam for Shinzō to take. Many politicians have used bureaucratic careers as stepping-stones to elected office, but Shinzō's academic record and lack of interest in civil service exams foreclosed that option. His brother had taken a graduate degree at Tokyo University, but Shinzō had no interest in that. He was unprepared for a private-sector job search, too callow for his father to employ as a secretary.[32] He had spent sixteen years at the same academic institution, never having risked failure by taking the entrance exams for another school, and, as the end of his schooling approached in 1977, it was not immediately clear what he could do.

Having shunned the standard pathways of a Japanese university graduate, he took a less conventional path. After graduating in March, he left Japan for the first time to study in California. His first stop was Hayward, California, south of Oakland on the eastern shore of San Francisco Bay. He enrolled in a language school, intending to improve his English before enrolling in a graduate program. But there were too many other Japanese students in Hayward, making it impossible for him to focus on English.

Shinzō relocated to Southern California, where an old friend of his mother's family introduced him to an Italian–American widow who took him in as a boarder while he studied English.[33] Years later, addressing the US Congress, he praised his hostess's cooking and recalled his amazement at the visitors to her house. "They were so diverse," he said. "I was amazed and said to myself, 'America is an awesome country.'"[34]

After spending most of 1977 studying English, in January 1978 Shinzō enrolled in a political science course at the University of Southern California. He never took a degree. He quickly succumbed to homesickness, placing collect calls to his family costing hundreds of thousands of yen, prompting his father to bellow, "It's time for Shinzō to return to Japan!"[35] In the spring of 1979, he gave in to his father's demands and returned home. He would not be away from America for long.

At home, he needed a job and ultimately landed a position with Kobe Steel. It was an unconventional hire, entirely the result of Shintarō's political maneuvering.

Shintarō, his eye firmly on winning the premiership, was anxious about his position in his district. His seat was safe, but to be taken seriously as a contender he had to finish first consistently in the four-seat district. When former MITI official Hayashi Yoshirō, won a seat as an LDP candidate in 1969, Shintarō not only gained a rival but lost a key supporter, Hayashi's father.[36]

To safeguard his position as the district's top vote-getter, Shintarō sought an alliance with Kobe Steel, the district's largest employer. Hayashi had secured the company's support, increasing his threat to Shintarō. After a series of negotiations with the company's executives—Kishi was also enlisted to woo the company—Shinzō's employment at Kobe Steel was presented as a token of the partnership between Shintarō and the firm. Shintarō's gambit worked—his advantage over Hayashi grew in subsequent elections—and Shinzō entered the world of the salaryman.

But he had missed the window for training and indoctrination as part of a new cohort of employees, so Kobe Steel decided to put Shinzō's English to use and dispatched him to its office in New York, after which he could return and join the next cohort of new hires. Shinzō protested, but by May 1979, only two months after returning from California, he moved to New York City.[37]

His stay in New York was more successful than his time in California. Kobe's New York office was small. When they learned that they would be hosting the son of a politician for a year, Shinzō's colleagues were dismayed at the prospect of having to "babysit" a political princeling. But he disarmed the office staff with his shy, humble demeanor and it did not take long for Shinzō to fit in comfortably. Working alongside Japanese dispatched to America with their families, Shinzō was virtually adopted by his colleagues, who took him along for mahjong or karaoke after work, hosted him at their homes, and invited him on golf outings, thus sparing him from homesickness.[38]

His time in New York also gave Shinzō opportunities to interact with Americans in more formal settings. In his memoirs, he recounts a senior colleague explaining how to negotiate with Americans: "Do not be arrogant, but never be subservient. Even if you think your counterpart is older or higher ranked or in the same position, you should treat them equally."[39] However, he also describes a visit to an American steel plant, and his shock at how dirty it was compared with Japanese plants, with parts strewn about: "There was no sign that the workers cared about this at all."[40]

By April 1980, he was back in Japan, undergoing formal indoctrination into Kobe Steel at its headquarters and trading a comfortable life in New York for a dorm room, a roommate, and long hours at work in a steel plant. Although his work mainly involved writing orders to manage the plant's production process, like most white-collar workers employed by Japan Inc.'s leading manufacturers, he was still expected to learn the business from the bottom up. He neither asked for nor received special treatment as Shintarō's son—even as Shintarō drew his son closer into the family business. For example, when Japan had a "double election" in June 1980—a snap election for the lower house timed to coincide with fixed-term upper house elections—on the basis of an agreement between Shintarō and Kobe Steel's management Shinzō took a sleeper car to Yamaguchi after work on Friday, spent the weekend campaigning with his father, and then took another sleeper on Sunday night, going straight to the mill from the train.[41]

His professional life improved in February 1981, when he was transferred to Kobe's headquarters in Tokyo and worked strictly in an office capacity, managing exports of cold-rolled steel to customers in Southeast Asia.[42] Shinzō was regarded as a diligent worker and his boss, Yano Shinji, took the young man under his wing.

Shinzō was working in this office in November 1982, when his father's career took a major leap forward. Having served as MITI minister from 1981 to 1982, Shintarō contested the LDP's 1982 leadership election, against the guidance of his father-in-law. Kishi was concerned that Nakasone Yasuhirō enjoyed the backing of Tanaka's faction—which still dominated the LDP—and he feared a poor showing would cripple Shintarō's chances in future elections.[43] Kishi was not entirely wrong: Shintarō finished third of four candidates. But the victorious Nakasone—who would describe Kishi as "Japan's greatest postwar leader"—rewarded Shintarō with the ministry of foreign affairs (MOFA), marking him as a potential successor.[44] Much as Shintarō entered politics when Kishi became foreign minister, so too would his father's new job be Shinzō's chance to enter the political world. "If you want to be my secretary, do it. Start on Monday," said his father.

* * *

But the stubborn child reappeared. Shinzō was reluctant to abandon his colleagues when there were major deals in the works. He may also have harbored doubts about a life in politics and resented the brusque manner in which his father delivered the message.[45] He was still hesitant the following day when his father's principal secretary visited him. A week later, he still had not answered.

* * *

His father grew increasingly frustrated, sputtering that when Kishi had called upon him to leave the *Mainichi Shimbun* and become his secretary at the foreign ministry, he quit the following day. Frustrated with his son's reluctance, Shintarō called Kobe Steel's executives. Just fire him, he suggested. The union won't allow it, they replied.

Ultimately, it fell to his boss, Yano, to persuade Shinzō. He gave him his blessing to leave, stating that if Shinzō wanted to become a politician, he should take the opportunity presented to him. At a farewell party Shinzō, usually a teetotaler, drank a little and apologized for quitting at short notice. On 6 December, ten days after Nakasone's election, he began working as his father's private secretary. He later described the decision as realizing his destiny.[46]

Shinzō's appointment put him close to a father with whom he had not had the easiest relationship. According to his memoirs, "For the first time, when I became his secretary, my father and I came to have extremely close time together not just as politician and secretary but also as father and child."[47] He was not necessarily given substantive work, but would shadow his father as he fulfilled the duties of office, including overseas trips and long hours of parliamentary deliberations, as well as domestic trips in support of LDP candidates, which became more frequent as Shintarō came to the brink of inheriting the leadership of his faction from Fukuda.

It was a crucial moment for Shintarō, who would serve nearly four years at MOFA, noteworthy at the time given the high turnover rate in ministerial posts under LDP dominance.[48] He pursued an active style of diplomacy that he called "creative diplomacy," which he characterized as Japan's pursuing initiatives to promote peace that neither the US nor the USSR could pursue[49]—and visited eighty-one countries as foreign minister. He forged a close relationship with his American counterpart George Shultz that complemented Nakasone's friendship with Ronald Reagan.[50]

Nakasone was the most vocal advocate of Kishi's revisionist conservatism to have won the premiership since Kishi's resignation. Nakasone sought to forge Japan into an assertive great power when Japanese were already feeling confident after decades of high-speed growth. He fervently supported constitutional revision, opposed the Yoshida Doctrine, and was an ardent defense hawk who favored a more independent security policy. As prime minister, he would "settle the accounts of postwar politics" by revising the constitution, lessening Japan's dependence on the US for its security and reforming the education system. He visited the controversial Yasukuni shrine, which honors those who have died for the emperor in wars since 1868, but which prime ministers had shunned since 1978 when fourteen Class A war criminals (including Tōjō) were enshrined, triggering disputes with China and South Korea. Like Kishi, Nakasone promoted administrative reforms that strengthened the prime minister's leadership and advocated for the direct election of prime ministers.[51]

Shinzō, meanwhile, continued learning on the job, which offered him innumerable opportunities to work the smoke-filled rooms where decisions were made. His father's globe-trotting personal diplomacy impressed upon his son the importance of building trust with foreign leaders.[52] He also took his first foray into diplomacy. For years, local activists in Yamaguchi had sought the return of a cannon that France had seized in 1864 following the besieging of Chōshū by France, Britain, the US, and the Netherlands in the Shimonoseki campaign. Shintarō asked President François Mitterrand to intervene, but he said that the cannon could only be returned by an act of the National Assembly, which was not forthcoming. So Shintarō entrusted Shinzō to devise a solution. After pressuring MOFA officials, he crafted an arrangement whereby France lent the cannon to Yamaguchi, with an option for extending the loan indefinitely.[53]

In 1984, a friend introduced Shinzō to Matsuzaki Akie, the daughter of a president of confectioner Morinaga & Company. Almost eight years younger than Shinzō, she was working at public relations giant Dentsu and showed up a half hour late for their first date. They married in June 1987 in a joint ceremony with Shinzō's brother Hironobu and his bride, because Kishi was by that time hospitalized and nearing death, and their mother wanted him to see his grandsons marry.[54] As his death approached, Kishi also sought to influence Shinzō's political career, suggesting that when one of Yamaguchi's delegates to the upper house passed away suddenly in 1986, Shinzō should run in the by-election. Shintarō, however, thought he was not ready to run for office and blocked the idea.[55]

* * *

Towards the end of Nakasone's premiership in 1987, the question of who would succeed him was open. Shintarō had continued his pursuit of the top job, moving from MOFA to become chairman of the LDP's general affairs council in 1986, when he also inherited factional leadership from Fukuda. Nakasone left it to Takeshita, Abe, and Miyazawa to determine the successor. These new leaders represented the three dominant tendencies in the LDP: Miyazawa was Yoshida's heir, Abe was Kishi's, and Takeshita was Tanaka's.

Ultimately, the decision came down to face-to-face negotiations between Shintarō and Takeshita, who were rivals but also friends. They and their lieutenants gathered in a room at Tokyo's Akasaka Prince Hotel, when, after more than nine hours of talks, Abe bowed out to Takeshita, who not only led the largest faction but also could count on the support of others.[56] After an internal rebellion in 1985, Takeshita had wrested control of the faction from Tanaka, who suffered a debilitating stroke soon after. Takeshita also had an advantage in the LDP, having won more electoral victories, a consequence of Shintarō's 1963 defeat.

Shintarō accepted a compromise whereby he would serve as secretary-general under Takeshita and be next in line to lead.[57] After his death, his wife Yōko criticized her late husband for his idealism. "There is more to the world than ideals," she told the *Mainichi Shimbun*. "Meanwhile, I guess you can say to a certain extent, 'strength'—I think it would have been better if he had had that. But that was his personality…"[58] Given that the balance of power within the party favored Takeshita, this post-mortem judgment seems cruel and is likely colored by the reality that Shintarō's time never came. But it also suggests that Yōko may have encouraged Shinzō to idealize strength in politics, using his father's failure of nerve as an example to avoid.

Almost immediately after Takeshita inherited the premiership, the Japanese political system was rocked by a scandal that disrupted the cozy world of the new leaders and set the stage for the LDP's eventual ouster in 1993.

In the mid-1980s, Recruit, a job placement company, had offered pre-flotation shares at favorable prices to leading politicians, bureaucrats, business leaders, and media who would profit when the share price rose after listing. The scandal implicated a long list of LDP politicians and forced Takeshita to resign in April 1989, when he admitted to having received sizable political contributions from Recruit.[59] Despite the backroom deal he made with Takeshita, Shintarō could not succeed him: one of his secretaries had accepted shares from Recruit. Facing a widening crisis, with upper house elections only months away, the LDP opted for a prime minister untainted by the scandal, the hapless Uno Sōsuke, who took office in June 1989 and resigned in August after leading the LDP to a historic defeat.[60]

As the LDP grappled with this crisis, Shintarō, who as secretary-general was expected to lead its campaign, was missing. On 18 April, he had been hospitalized. Following surgery, his doctors told Shinzō that Shintarō had pancreatic cancer and probably had only two more years to live. Upon the advice of doctors, Shinzō concealed the diagnosis from his father, who after his hospitalization appeared to have regained his strength and threw himself back into work to strengthen his faction's position in the approaching 1990 general election. He also led an LDP delegation to the USSR in January 1990. In a meeting with Mikhail Gorbachev, Shintarō expressed a strong desire to settle the longstanding dispute between Japan and the Soviet Union over the South Kuril Islands, and formally conclude a peace treaty, inviting Gorbachev to visit Japan the next year. But after a year at breakneck speed as he prepared another bid for the LDP's leadership, he was hospitalized again in September—at which point Shinzō told him that he had cancer.

Shintarō stoically accepted the diagnosis—and the rapidly closing window of time before he succumbed to the disease. From his sickbed he began preparations for Shinzō to succeed him, urging him to make regular visits to his constituency. Shintarō would conduct one last act of diplomacy, rising from his sickbed in April 1991 to attend a reception for Gorbachev, who had accepted his invitation. Shintarō's weight had dropped from seventy-two to fifty-seven kilograms. Shinzō notes in his memoirs that his father was wearing multiple layers of clothing beneath his suit, to pad out his appearance. "Although it was a meeting of just five minutes," he writes, "my father smiled at me brightly."[61] It was his last public appearance. The following month, on 15 May, Shintarō died at the age of sixty-seven.

The postwar world that nurtured Shintarō's career was passing, too. The Shōwa emperor had died in 1989, ushering in the Heisei era. The financial bubble popped in early 1991. The Berlin Wall fell in 1989 and the USSR would dissolve at the end of 1991. The US–Japan relationship was marred by trade friction as Americans came to fear Japan's economic prowess.

Shinzō would make his way in a world dramatically different from that which had allowed Shintarō to reach the highest levels of power.

4

THE ICONOCLAST

Abe Shinzō had never lived in Yamaguchi's first electoral district, the constituency he sought to represent. His life had been spent far from Yamaguchi, which sits at the western tip of Honshū, closer to Pusan in South Korea than to Tokyo. As Shinzō prepared to run for office, he knew Yamaguchi largely as the driver of the Meiji Restoration, and his constituency's links to the restoration would become critical to his political identity.[1]

The prefecture has an undeniable role in the political history of modern Japan. Then known as the Choshū domain, it played a central role in the shogun's downfall in the 1860s. After Commodore Matthew Perry's "black ships" opened Japan and forced the shogunate to sign "unequal treaties" giving foreigners extraterritorial rights and control over Japan's commercial policies, anti-regime activism spread. Choshū was a hotbed of resistance, as the domain's young samurai lamented the national government's ineffectual response to the western powers.

Yoshida Shōin, a samurai intellectual, gathered activists at his academy in Hagi, Choshū's capital, where they fervently studied how to build a modern Japanese state. They also pressured Choshū's leaders to launch attacks against foreign navies in 1863, and the imperial palace in Kyoto in 1864. But Yoshida and his acolytes were not mere idealistic hotheads. To preserve Japan's independence, the nation had to adapt and learn from America and Europe. Japan needed to study western science and technology and government in order to resist western imperialism.[2]

Yoshida was executed in 1859, but his students included Itō Hirobumi, the author of Meiji Japan's constitution and its first prime minister, and Yamagata Aritomo, the father of the imperial Japanese military. Choshū was not alone in its campaign against the shogunate—its alliance with Satsuma, another western domain, was a decisive moment heralding the central government's overthrow—but the domain, reorganized as Yamaguchi in 1871, would nevertheless dominate government well into the twentieth century. The political vision of a strong state, led by statesmen willing to do whatever it took to defend their nation, remained a powerful idea in Japanese politics, imparting to Japanese conservatism in particular a statist tendency whose object was top-down reform to strengthen the state and mobilize the nation.

Abe felt strong attachment to this legacy. "In my fundamental views of life and death," he wrote in a 2005 essay, "one common thread—from my native land—is the Choshū Bakumatsu-era thinker Yoshida Shōin's *Ryūkonroku*."[3] Throughout his career, he would draw on Meiji thinkers in his remarks to argue for reformist conservatism. Abe said in 2017, "150 years ago, Iwakura Tomomi, who led the modernization process, said of the just-born Meiji state, if all the people are made of one heart and if national power is vigorous, it will absolutely not be difficult to become a country that is active in the world. There is no reason that the Japanese people of today cannot do what the Japanese people of Meiji could."[4]

* * *

On 8 July 1991, after a period of mourning his father, Abe formally announced his candidacy in Hagi. He could not know when an election would be called, so he threw himself into converting his political inheritance into a parliamentary seat.[5] Abe could rely on powerful supporters from the upper echelons of the LDP, eager to aid the son of their fallen comrade. Shintarō's old friend and rival Takeshita visited his friend's grave and pledged to campaign ten times on Shinzō's behalf.[6]

But Abe and his wife Akie still had to visit voters door-to-door, an arduous feat in the large, semi-rural, and partly mountainous constituency. He had also to appeal to the support groups that had generated volunteers and money for his father. To the chagrin of some of the latter's long-time supporters, he seemed eager to distance himself from his father. "I am of course Abe Shintarō's second son," he said. "However, I am determined to live as a politician myself from now on."[7]

He got his chance to bid for his father's seat two years after declaring his candidacy. On 18 June 1993, defections from the LDP led to a successful no-confidence vote aimed at Prime Minister Miyazawa Kiichi. In response, Miyazawa dissolved the lower house and called an election for 18 July.

It was an inauspicious time for an LDP newcomer. The defections that forced Miyazawa's hand were the culmination of five years of conflict over "political reform"—calls for sweeping change to the electoral system and campaign finance laws, after scandals revealed widespread graft and eroded public confidence in LDP rule. The party's old guard resisted and was especially reluctant to embrace a proposal to replace the postwar era's multiple-member electoral districts with single-member districts, which reformers argued would encourage the creation of a competitive two-party system and weaken the grip of faction leaders.

But the emergence of another major scandal emboldened the reformers. A shipping company paid off leading politicians, including Takeshita's lieutenant Kanemaru Shin, who, when he was arrested in March 1993, was found to have millions of dollars' worth of gold and bearer bonds stashed in his house. The reformers had also gained a charismatic leader, Ozawa Ichirō, another Takeshita lieutenant who was an articulate advocate for reforms that would let Japan become a "normal nation" able to carry its weight in international society. When the debate over political reform resumed in the Diet, Miyazawa's inability to advance reform led Ozawa's group to rebel.

Within days of the no-confidence motion, Ozawa and forty-five other LDP members formed two new political groups, Ozawa's Japan Renewal Party (JRP) and the New Party Sakigake (NPS) led by former Abe faction member Takemura Masayoshi. These parties joined another reformist party, the Japan New Party (JNP), led by Hosokawa Morihiro, a former LDP upper house member and governor of Kumamoto prefecture. These parties were not liberal; they were committed to reform conservatism that would clean out the rot in Japanese politics to make Japan strong again.

The emergence of the reform conservative movement was partly a response to—and facilitated by—wide-reaching changes facing Japan in the last decade of the century. The pillars of Japan's postwar order—LDP dominance, a stable alliance with the US, and a growth model that had made Japan an economic superpower—were crumbling.

The end of the Cold War meant anti-communism would no longer serve as a unifying force for the LDP. At the same time, Japan's economic convergence with the US rattled their alliance. Presidential candidates from both American parties accused Japan of unfair trade practices and members of Congress competed to "bash Japan," literally smashing Japanese electronics on the front lawn of the US Capitol.[8] The US-led campaign to expel Iraqi forces from Kuwait prompted more soul-searching, since the government could not overcome resistance to participation in the multinational coalition, and sent money instead. This caused Japan's omission from a Kuwaiti advertisement thanking the coalition.[9] The Yoshida consensus appeared increasingly outmoded.

This situation was exacerbated by the end of "the Bubble," a six-year boom in asset prices that saw the Nikkei 225 index rise from around 7,000 in the mid-1980s to an all-time high of 38,916 at the end of 1989. Land prices, particularly in Tokyo, surged to dizzying heights.[10] In 1991, as the Bank of Japan (BOJ) raised interest rates to tame markets, prices collapsed, saddling financial institutions and corporations—which had borrowed against inflated assets—with debts they could not service.

What followed was a deep recession, the failure of venerable financial institutions, the complete reorganization of the banking sector, decades of slow growth, and the eventual onset of deflation. Overnight, Japan went from being a juggernaut that could dream of vying with the US for global leadership, to an economic basket case.

Abe's first campaign unfolded against this backdrop. The splintering of the LDP meant he faced seven other candidates for the district's four seats. He could depend on the support of LDP heavyweights, particularly from his late father's faction, who trooped down to Yamaguchi to campaign for him. But there were concerns in his camp that Abe, as an establishment candidate, might struggle against the new reform parties. Abe tried to use his youth to his advantage, campaigning on the slogan, "Change, Challenge!" In the end, he prevailed, finishing comfortably in first place. He was two months shy of his thirty-eighth birthday. The following day he visited his father's grave and exclaimed, "Papa, I did it."[11]

But the LDP failed to secure a majority. Its splintering created an opening for new government. Heated bargaining produced an eight-party "non-LDP, non-communist" coalition that included the Japan Socialist Party (JSP) and an offshoot on the left, the three LDP splinter parties on the right, and the Democratic Socialist Party (DSP), the Buddhist party Komeitō, and the Democratic Reform Party in the center. Hosokawa was prime minister. He took office on 9 August with approval ratings above seventy percent, among the highest ever for a new prime minister. Abe began his political career in opposition.

* * *

Abe was undaunted by the changes sweeping Japan and soon emerged as a leader of a new generation of conservatives, who used the vacuum created by the breakdown of postwar institutions to agitate for change.

Before his first election, there is little evidence of his political beliefs beyond his strong identification with Kishi. His brother Hironobu suggested that his views coalesced after entering politics. Meanwhile, his boss at Kobe Steel, when asked if he had any sense that Abe had harbored right-wing beliefs, said, "No, no, absolutely not. Before that, I did not feel at all that he was hardcore right. He was a normal, good kid. I think that [his right-wing ideology] is definitely something he acquired."[12]

But Abe's conservative views took shape almost immediately. His relationship with his grandfather, and complicated relationship with his late father, clearly inclined him towards Kishi's strident conservatism. He was also reacting to fast-changing circumstances within the LDP and in Japanese society.

Nakasone failed to achieve a final reckoning with the unfinished business of the postwar era, but he had eroded taboos regarding constitutional revision and the veneration of war dead at the Yasukuni shrine, and had backed the adoption of nationalistic history textbooks.

He also ramped up defense spending (in 1987 breaking an informal ceiling of one percent of gross national product for defense spending), and carved out new roles for the Self-Defense Forces (SDF), including patrolling sea lanes far from Japan.[13] Abe had witnessed these developments as his father's secretary during the Nakasone years.

By the 1990s, some of the most significant constraints on the right had eroded. Scandals, political reform, and the 1993 "defeat" had weakened the LDP's two mainstream camps, Tanaka's money politics and Yoshida's dovish mercantilism. Reformers like Ozawa lamented the consensus politics of the LDP's golden age and pushed for changes—particularly single-member constituencies and first-past-the-post voting—that would privilege more strident candidates.[14] Ironically, given his later battles with Abe, it was Ozawa's activism and eventual departure from the LDP that made room for Abe's brand of conservatism.

Ozawa not only undermined the ability of the LDP's center-right to constrain the right wing, he also mortally wounded the JSP. The JSP had, after all, been a useful partner in the Yoshida consensus, helping to block constitutional revision and remilitarization.[15] Although the JSP was included in the new coalition, Ozawa's maneuvers as the mastermind behind the coalition would so alienate the JSP that in less than a year it left the coalition and joined forces with the LDP, ushering it back into power after less than a year in opposition.

Despite being the junior partner to the LDP, JSP leader Murayama Tomiichi was tapped as prime minister. But the LDP exacted significant concessions. The JSP reversed longstanding opposition to the SDF—which it claimed was unconstitutional—and the US–Japan alliance, and even endorsed the SDF's participation in UN peacekeeping operations. These compromises crippled the Socialists, who were abandoned by their base. Thereafter, Japan's leading opposition party, first the Ozawa-led New Frontier Party (NFP) and subsequently the Democratic Party of Japan (DPJ), would be centrist or even center-right, marking a rightward shift.

The LDP–JSP coalition was useful for the LDP's insurgent right wing. Abe and others supported the Murayama-led coalition to save the LDP from opposition. But they also used the blatantly opportunistic arrangement to condemn the LDP's old guard for its unprincipled compromises. As Abe later wrote, "By making the leader of a party with public approval of only five or six percent prime minister, naturally the dissatisfaction within the party [the LDP] was amplified. The opposition was especially large from people who had become representatives who approved of the LDP's ideas, who, if I had to say, belonged to the conservative mainstream."[16]

Meanwhile, when Murayama offered a strong apology for Japan's wartime behavior on the fiftieth anniversary of the end of the Second World War, the right wing protested fiercely. His statement became a new bête noire in their opposition to the "masochistic" interpretation of history favored by the postwar establishment. It appears, for example, that the statement was a major impetus in the creation of the right-wing pressure group *Nippon Kaigi* (the Japan Conference), which formed from a merger of older right-wing groups in 1997.[17] Other events during Murayama's eighteen months in office—the government's poor handling of the January 1995 Hanshin-Awaji earthquake and the March 1995 sarin gas attack on the Tokyo subway by the "new religion" Aum Shinrikyo—bolstered right-wing arguments about the failures of the postwar state and the need for radical change to the national government.

* * *

Despite beginning in opposition, Abe's first term would coincide with an extraordinary window of opportunity for the LDP's new conservatives.

As a freshman Diet member in opposition, there was little for Abe to do immediately after his first election. He was the only LDP freshman named to the foreign affairs committee, but still had more time than an LDP lawmaker normally would have.[18] He used it to read extensively on the constitution and national security, and deepened his understanding of political ideas, becoming captivated by the writing of conservative critic Nishibe Susumu and Spanish theorist José Ortega y Gasset's *The Revolt of the Masses*.[19]

In a 1996 book that he co-wrote with two other young lawmakers, it is clear that Abe was grappling with Kishi's legacy and how to adapt Kishi's ideals for a new era. Abe explicitly identifies his grandfather as the source of his conservatism, but the reasons he gives are noteworthy.

Abe describes how as a child he was especially attracted to Kishi's confidence. Whereas his father's generation was tormented by its experiences of the war, his grandfather was born in the Meiji era and his career flowered before the war. Like many of his generation Kishi was extremely self-confident, leading Abe to wonder what explained this, and writing—with a note of envy—that they had lived in a "shining era" when Japan was advancing. This may be Abe's most fundamental ambition: remaking Japan into the kind of country whose people are once again able to feel that same sense of confidence.[20] Journalist Kakizaki Meiji writes that when Abe speaks of "taking back Japan," it is "the politics of taking back the values and pride that were lost in the occupation period."[21]

The broad contours of Abe's political project—recapturing the national pride lost when Japan was defeated and restoring it to great power—were plainly visible. This project generated a grand unifying theme, a thread running through his beliefs about how a politician should conduct himself in the arena, his ideas about the role of the state in public life, his idea of the Japanese nation and its past and future, and his vision for Japan's foreign relations and its place in the world.

In this period, Abe was focused on the duties of a politician hungry for change. In his earlier writings and his 2006 memoir, he idealizes the "politician who fights." It is the duty of a politician, he argues, to voice unpopular opinions that he knows are right for the state and the nation even in the face of public criticism. Politicians should explain what they want to do directly to the public.[22] Abe embraced what journalist Kikuchi Masashi describes as Kishi's elitist strain in postwar Japanese conservatism. As Kishi says in his memoirs, "I have strongly emphasized leadership in democratic politics as the heart of politics. I do not think that democratic politics is the politics of following the masses and being dragged around by the masses. I think that true democratic political leadership is whether you stand two or three steps ahead of the people and lead the people."[23]

The idea that a democratic politician must stand apart from the people and lead the nation in the direction he thinks best would profoundly impact Abe. The only way to smash the postwar shackles that had prevented Japan from competing for global power was to attack them—and their defenders—directly. A leader must explain what he is doing, rather than engage in endless deliberations about the means and ends of government. Naturally, this view has little patience with freewheeling parliamentary debate, aggressive questioning from the press, or mass demonstrations.

This vision of leadership was at odds with postwar Japanese democracy and had been the undoing of Kishi in 1960.[24] Postwar Japanese democracy depended on consensus forged between rival factions, ministries, and parties that safeguarded the rights of political minorities despite the LDP's dominance. The LDP's divisions were a constraint on executive power, and over time the LDP had developed procedures for informal consultations with opposition parties to include them in policymaking while minimizing conflict within the Diet.[25] Despite a cozy relationship with lawmakers through the so-called *kisha* club system, the press still played an important role uncovering scandals and otherwise restraining leaders. This style of politics was a major part of the postwar regime that the new conservatives wanted to leave behind.

Even as a young lawmaker, Abe was thinking not just how to advance his ideals, but also how to wield power effectively. While he explored and articulated a radical new conservatism, he also made the case for a pragmatic approach to government that takes into consideration what is possible as well as what is right.[26] Writing in 1996, he looked to Max Weber for a way to think about pragmatism and the balance between ideals and outcomes.

In *Politics as a Vocation*, Weber argues that political leaders must navigate two competing impulses, the "ethic of conviction"[27] and the "ethic of responsibility." The former is a politician's raison d'être, the ideals that a politician hopes to realize in the world. However, idealism alone can lead to a disregard for consequences, and excesses that can discredit a cause. The "ethic of responsibility" requires acceptance of responsibility for the likely consequences of one's actions, a willingness to grapple with the world as it is and not as it should be. "Surely, politics is made with the head," writes Weber, "but it is certainly not made with the head alone."[28]

In the 1996 book, Abe cites Weber explicitly and explains that his grandfather Kishi was thoroughly imbued with the ethic of responsibility: "With regard to what one should do as a politician, my grandfather consistently acted according to 'responsibility for consequences.' That is, Max Weber's 'ethic of responsibility.'"[29] In Abe's eyes, Kishi was made great by his ability to use power in the service of his ideals, even if at times that meant compromising in the service of the broader goal. Far from being a romantic idealist, early in his career Abe was drawn to pragmatic statecraft. As a politician, he would not always successfully strike a balance between his ideals and reality, but this theme—the tension between his self-conscious participation in a conservative movement seeking dramatic change in Japan and his sensitivity to the constraints of reality—would endure. His admiration for the Meiji Restoration and for his grandfather shaped him into a conservative statist who sought strong leadership to guide Japan in a dangerous world.[30]

Abe and the new conservatives saw a model in the Meiji-era "founding fathers," who had opposed a national government that had accepted constraints on Japan's independence and left the country vulnerable to foreign threats. Abe recounts in *Towards a Beautiful Country* how external threats led to the Meiji Restoration and the creation of a modern state.[31] "A strong state is not a potential threat to political liberty that must be restrained by constitutionalism and civil society. It is the ultimate guarantor of national independence in a dangerous world governed by the law of the jungle."[32] While Abe admits that the state could oppress its own people, he suggests that oppression is not inherent to strong states but is instead attributable to "closed governments" in which power is dominated by a small number of rulers.[33]

The new conservatives foregrounded the strength of arms, impatience with deliberative democracy, and strong leadership, believing the state's leaders should be free to act as required to safeguard the national survival, regardless of prevailing ideological or political commitments. Abe notes, for example, that Kishi's allies, who strongly opposed the US and objected to an alliance with Japan's former adversary, were puzzled by his willingness to preserve and strengthen that relationship.

Thus, Abe and the new conservatives pursued fundamental political reform to consolidate a two-party, majoritarian democracy, with ideologically coherent political parties leading to stronger prime ministers perched atop an executive able to articulate a national vision.[34] Ozawa, although he would over time drift away from some of his more conservative views, made the strongest case for political reform as crucial to the generation of government that could, for example, pursue a more assertive foreign policy as a "normal nation."[35]

The new conservatives above all sought to fortify the Japanese state to withstand and overcome the challenges of the coming century, as the Cold War gave way to concerns about the reliability of the US, questions about what China's increasingly inevitable rise would mean for Japan, and anxieties about the Korean Peninsula. A strong state was also needed to grapple with economic stagnation. To the extent that the right wing had sought to strengthen Japan since the occupation, Abe and the new conservatives were "policy entrepreneurs" exploiting the political chaos and policy failures of the early 1990s to advance goals that had been stymied by the Cold War consensus.

When Abe and the new conservatives talked of ending the postwar regime, they wanted to remove constraints on the Japanese state that had been imposed by the US occupation. The most significant, of course, was the postwar constitution, especially Article 9, which, as Abe noted in 1999, has meant that debates about how to defend Japan have "not been policy debates but have instead concentrated solely on constitution or legal arguments."[36] The SDF's legitimacy was still questioned, its ability to support allied operations curtailed by the prohibition on its ability to exercise its right of collective self-defense, and its capabilities limited by limitations on its budget, multiple layers of civilian control, and a broader "culture of anti-militarism."[37] Abe has expressed many reasons for wanting to revise the constitution—lamenting the role played by "New Dealer" liberals in drafting the document and the humiliation of Japan's basic law arising from a period of national humiliation—but his most fundamental reason is that Article 9 is the most enduring symbolic and practical constraint upon the Japanese state's ability to fulfill its duties to defend the Japanese people.[38]

* * *

The rest of Abe's ambitions fall into place around this vision of decisive leaders commanding a strong state liberated from its postwar bonds. For example, Abe's nationalism—the subject of considerable debate within and outside Japan—appears secondary to his focus on rebuilding the Japanese state. His nationalism—and, relatedly, his conservatism—have served two functions.

First, as a young conservative, he wanted to use nationalism to make Japan a country worth defending, by which he meant not Japan as it was, but rather a kind of "essential Japan." This vision of a "deep Japan" was also part of his inheritance from Kishi. "As for our country's form," he writes, "my grandfather firmly believed that Japan, as an Asian nation, should exist as a country in which a tradition centered on the imperial household is maintained and as an agricultural people who strongly help each other while having a mutual sense of unity. Hence, he himself was always overflowing with a feeling of 'we can do even that considerable thing.' The truth is that I remember this left a deep impression on me."[39] This idea would crystallize into what he would later call his vision for a "beautiful country."

As the title of his 2006 book suggests, Abe's goal was to move "towards" a beautiful country. In his first press conference after being elected as prime minister in September 2006, he explained what he meant by this phrase. "First," he said, "I think one part of this image is to make a country that cherishes its beautiful nature and Japan's culture and history, as well as its traditions." He added that it is necessary to pursue education reform in order to "aim for a reliably independent and courageous country on the basis of a free society" and to make Japan a country whose leadership "is respected and loved by the countries of the world."[40] In other words, the Japanese nation must be able to feel proud of itself.

For Abe, nationalism began with a sense of place. In his memoirs, he rejects the notion of a "citizen of the world," arguing that the country of one's birth exerts an exceptionally powerful influence on an individual's identity that cannot easily be cast aside. "Wanting to take pride in the history, tradition, and culture that has been spun by the country to which we belong is, no matter what people say, essentially a quite natural feeling."[41] But, he argued, postwar Japan has sought to "bypass" these feelings, encouraging Japanese citizens to feel attached to their communities and the international community while rejecting their nation.[42] He rejects the progressive argument that nationalism is "intolerant" and argues that it is not just about attachment to the modern nation-state and its symbols—although he expresses his love for Japan's national anthem and flag—but rather a love for the "deep Japan" that precedes the nation-state.

But building a "beautiful country" was a political agenda—and perhaps no aspect of this agenda would be as controversial as Abe's position on the imperial household.

After the occupation, the survival and status of the emperor became an important front in Japan's culture war. US authorities allowed Hirohito to remain on the throne but remade him into a "symbolic" emperor. As Article 1 of the Japanese constitution says, "The Emperor shall be the symbol of the State and of the unity of the People, deriving his position from the will of the people with whom resides sovereign power." Neither Japanese left-wingers, some of whom wanted to do away with the imperial household altogether, nor Japanese right-wingers, many of whom continued to uphold the emperor's divinity and treat him as the embodiment of the timelessness of Japanese culture, were satisfied with this compromise.

To a certain extent, for Abe, upholding the imperial household as the center of the nation is what it means to be a Japanese conservative. "Japan's conservatism," he writes, "is firmly based on our history. For this backbone, in the case of Japan, I think that the existence of the imperial family has a very important meaning."[43] In practical terms, Abe and the new conservatives supported loosening the constraints on the emperor's role included in the postwar constitution, formally making the emperor head of state and not just its symbol, which, Abe argues, the emperor has always been anyway. In this vein, they would build upon efforts made by LDP governments to interpret Article 1 as permitting some head of state functions.[44]

But more than that, the new conservatives wanted the emperor, whom they see as the heir of an unbroken line stretching back to 660 BCE, to be a bulwark against social change. As the right-wing group Nippon Kaigi says in its mission statement, "We believe that an understanding of history derived from the sense that we share the same history, culture, and tradition—centered on the imperial household—can not only foster a feeling of 'we are all Japanese' compatriotism and promote social stability, but also can greatly increase national power."[45]

The conservative view of the emperor is that he is an organic symbol of the union between state and nation that stretches from the distant past into centuries yet to come, a seeming flirtation with a revival of the state Shinto uprooted by the US occupation.[46] At times, reverence for the imperial household has set new conservatives against the living occupant of the throne. After all, Akihito fully embraced his role as what historian Kenneth Ruoff has called the "people's emperor," a symbolic monarch who derives his position from the popular will. As the former emperor said when he declared his intention to abdicate, "I think that…there is need for the emperor to have a deep awareness of his own role as the emperor, deep understanding of the people and willingness to nurture within himself the awareness of being with the people."[47]

Another source of tension between the imperial household and the new right has been the debate over how to honor the war dead. As part of a desire to elevate the status of the emperor, Abe and others sought to normalize the status of Yasukuni, the Tokyo shrine established in 1869 to honor soldiers killed during the Restoration wars but which over time became "the central shrine for divinization and memorialization of the war dead in Shinto form."[48] The shrine's status became especially controversial after 1978, when its priests honored fourteen Class A war criminals—including Tōjō—as "martyrs of Shōwa."

Thereafter, visits by prime ministers and other cabinet ministers to Yasukuni would inflame tensions with Japan's neighbors. Abe, however, would argue that visits to Yasukuni should be no more controversial than visits by US presidents to Arlington National Cemetery, where, after all, Confederate soldiers are also buried.[49] As a result, conservatives have resisted calls to make Chidorigafuchi National Cemetery, which houses the remains of unknown soldiers from the Second World War, a national war memorial or to establish an entirely new secular memorial.[50] But, in the forty years since the "martyrs of Shōwa" were enshrined, no emperor has visited Yasukuni.

The focus on Yasukuni shows that Abe's nationalism has served his statism, and not vice versa. In his thinking, nationalism is a unifying force that will strengthen the state's ability to surmount obstacles and navigate a perilous world. Arguably this is in keeping with Abe's Meiji forebears who not only forged a modern state but also encouraged the emergence of a Japanese national consciousness. As Doak writes, "Prior to 1853, there was no Japan."[51] This explains why when Abe and other new conservatives articulated their program they identified the national education system as a pillar of the postwar regime that had to be transformed. The postwar education system was a constraint on state power: "Postwar Japan was set on pursuing statism as the cause of the war sixty years past and the reason for defeat. As a result, the equation 'state=bad' was built in somewhere in the minds of postwar Japanese people. Therefore, they are quite incapable of conceiving things from the perspective of the state. No, there is a strong tendency to avoid it. It is one of the failures of postwar education."[52]

Education was one area in which the US did not deviate from its aims of uprooting militarism and promoting democracy despite the "reverse course." The education ministry was pressed to promote decentralization, democratization, and pacifism. The teachers themselves, radicalized by the war's bloodletting, were enthusiastic promoters of the occupation's education agenda and their union, Nikkyōso, was among the most fervently left-wing and anti-militarist labor unions.[53]

The effective target of these reforms was the 1890 Imperial Rescript on Education, which called upon subjects to "advance the public good" and "should emergency arise, offer yourselves courageously to the State."[54] The rescript provided the basis for "moral education" that would instruct students in the virtues needed to fulfill their duties.[55] The US occupation, via 1947's Fundamental Law on Education and School Education Law, decentralized control of the country's schools, promoted individualism, and introduced coeducation.[56] The new conservatives would identify the education system—what they saw as left-wing teachers instructing future generations along lines imposed by a foreign power—as a core institution of the postwar regime that had to be replaced.[57]

Education was the most active front in Japan's culture war early in Abe's political career. Much of his and the new conservatives' activism during the mid-1990s was directed at education reform to restore "moral education" to the national curriculum, while combating the influence of the teachers and inculcating national pride in the hearts of young Japanese. This activism was conducted against the backdrop of the "textbook wars," which had been waged between the Japanese left and right for much of the postwar era and which from the early 1980s onward had increasingly pitted Japan against China and South Korea in a battle over apologies, contrition, and the historical narratives taught in their nations' classrooms.

Abe was quickly drawn into these battles. He was one of 105 LDP parliamentarians invited to join the party's investigative committee on history issues, which in 1996 published an account of the "Greater East Asia War" that, in the contemporary summation of a lawmaker from Kōmeitō, claimed Japan did not wage a war of aggression; that its military saved Asia from Russian invasion; that Manchuria was not historically viewed as part of China and therefore the 1931 "Manchurian incident" was not an invasion of China; and that Japan's annexation of Korea in 1910 and the post-1931 military campaigns were acts of self-defense.[58] The new conservatives sought to replace the "masochistic" view of history that, they argued, made it impossible for Japanese to feel proud of their country by painting imperial Japan entirely as an aggressor that invaded Asian countries and committed unspeakable atrocities.

At times, this effort has engaged in outright historical revisionism, particularly regarding the imperial military's use of "comfort women" in military brothels and events like the Nanjing Massacre of 1937. Other times, the new conservatives would seek to "relativize" imperial Japan's behavior, comparing it to the behavior of the western empires in Asia or to other states in other places and at other times. This activism was directed not only at Japan's history textbooks, but the full spectrum of apologies and understandings that forced Japan to accept the "victor's narrative" of the war, dating back to Article 11 of the San Francisco Treaty in 1951, in which Japan accepted the judgments of postwar war crime trials.

In addition to the LDP's investigative committee, Abe joined established right-wing parliamentary leagues like the Diet members' league of the Shinto Association of Spiritual Leadership, which had long advocated for the reintroduction of Shinto to public life, as well as new groups that emerged during the 1990s. These groups included the Parliamentary Alliance on the 50th Anniversary of the End of the War, which convened in 1994 and mobilized against Murayama's apology the following year; the Junior Parliamentarian Group to Consider Education and the Way Forward for Japan, established in 1997 by Diet members with fewer than five election victories; and the Nippon Kaigi Parliamentarian Association, also established in 1997 as a liaison group between parliamentarians and the national "grassroots conservative" movement established that year.

Abe was particularly active in the junior parliamentarian group, serving as the director of its secretariat. An interim report by the group criticizes Nikkyōso's dominance of the textbook approval process; challenges claims that Japan had coerced women into serving as "comfort women" (in short, disputing that imperial Japan engaged in sexual slavery); and rejects "apology diplomacy" with Japan's neighbors.[59] Most of the allies who would populate his first and second governments belonged to the same parliamentarians' leagues, and Abe formed some close political friendships in these study groups, particularly with Nakagawa Shōichi, another hereditary LDP lawmaker who would become his closest ally.[60]

Abe and Nakagawa would be particularly focused on combating the "masochistic" narrative on the comfort women, opposing not just the inclusion of the comfort women in history textbooks but also the 1993 statement by Chief Cabinet Secretary Kōno Yōhei, whereby the Japanese government acknowledged that the imperial military had been involved in establishing and managing "comfort stations" and that many comfort women were forcibly recruited. The statement cleared the way for the issue to be taught in schools as well as for the Murayama government to establish the Asian Women's Fund, a nominally private fund to which the Japanese government contributed ¥4.8 billion that distributed compensation and a signed apology from Japan's prime minister to former comfort women in South Korea, Taiwan, the Netherlands, Indonesia, and the Philippines.

The new conservatives were incensed by this admission of guilt, and argued that there was insufficient evidence to prove that the Japanese military had been involved, and that an important source for allegations about the military's involvement in forcibly recruiting comfort women, the recollections of a former soldier named Yoshida Seiji, had been thoroughly discredited. In their eyes, the issue had been politicized by China and Korea and by the "anti-Japanese" left at home, justifying an uncompromising campaign against the claims.[61]

The new conservatives' historical revisionism was problematic—and it had consequences domestically—well into the twenty-first century, periodically leading right-wing politicians to resign from cabinet posts for politically insensitive remarks, and internationally, complicating relations not just with Japan's Asian neighbors but also with the US and Australia—but the new conservatives were not gratuitously provoking domestic enemies and foreign governments. Their arguments about Japan's education system and its history curriculum matched their broader agenda. In his memoirs Abe refers to a poll that found that just half of Japanese high school students felt proud of their country. "The purpose of education is to foster a nation that has will and make a state that has dignity. Moreover, the revival of education is the duty of the state. The replies of Japan's high school students show that bold structural reform of our country's education, especially compulsory education, is necessary."[62]

Education reform was the base upon which the conservative revolution depended. Moral instruction and banishing "masochistic" history from textbooks would make future generations feel proud of their country; national pride would foster support for sweeping changes to the postwar regime, particularly revision of the constitution, which would enable Japan to realize true independence and assume its place as a great power in Asia and globally. Of course, they pursued these goals simultaneously, and focused on the media and other institutions of the "intellectual commanding heights" as targets for reform as far as Japan's historical narratives were concerned. Education reform would be a top priority for the new conservatives as they sought to unseat the LDP's older generation and claim national leadership. With an illustrious pedigree and a penchant for attracting loyal friends, Abe would soon find himself at the vanguard of the LDP's young iconoclasts. But it would take his embrace of another, more emotional issue to put him on the path to higher office.

5

CHAMPION OF THE ABDUCTEES

In September 1988, a man named Arimoto Akihiro visited Abe Shintarō's office seeking help. Five years earlier, his daughter Keiko went missing in Europe. Several years later, her parents learned she was alive in Pyongyang. Upon learning that their daughter was in North Korea, Akihiro visited with his own representatives as well as Socialist leader Doi Takako. Eventually, he came to Abe, then the Liberal Democratic Party's (LDP) secretary-general.[1] He explained the situation to one of Abe's secretaries, who brought Arimoto first to the ministry of foreign affairs (MOFA) and then to the national police agency (NPA), neither of which could help.[2] But the secretary later briefed Shintarō and Shinzō about the visit, and both took an interest.

Shinzō met Arimoto the following spring and impressed him with his sincerity. Shintarō, meanwhile, raised the issue with Hirasawa Katsuei—his sons' former tutor and now an NPA official—but they faced an uncooperative bureaucracy. The LDP was little better. Kanemaru Shin, Takeshita's right-hand man, made a high-profile trip to Pyongyang in September 1990 in pursuit of diplomatic normalization. He enjoyed a close relationship with Kim Il Sung and may have received kickbacks from Pyongyang, as the Stalinist state schemed for the diplomatic recognition that would generate economic assistance.[3]

The DPRK began abducting Japanese in the 1970s, expanding a program initially aimed at South Korea. Kim Jong Il, who was being groomed as his father's successor, took command of the DPRK's intelligence services and used abductions not only to kidnap foreigners who could provide language and cultural training for North Korea's spies, but also to steal their passports and other papers.[4] There was an element of state terror—which, as a series of bombings and hijackings in the 1970s and 1980s indicated, was part of the DPRK's toolkit. Pyongyang abducted mostly young adults from beaches and European cities far from Japan, but also at least one child, Yokota Megumi, a thirteen-year-old girl who disappeared in 1977 from a coastal town in Niigata prefecture. However, in the years following the abductions, there was little more than rumor to link North Korea to what seemed unrelated missing persons' cases. The issue lingered on the margins of Japan's political system, the allegations dismissed as paranoid not only by left-wing politicians friendly to North Korea but also in the LDP.

Shinzō did little to raise awareness during his first term. "In the environment at that time," he writes, "the main issue for diplomacy towards North Korea was how to provide rice relief, as Diet members who insisted on rescuing the abductees were a small minority even in the LDP."[5]

But the issue suited the new conservative agenda; the abductions were the ultimate indictment of the postwar regime. The state was so feeble that not only could it not protect its own citizens from kidnap by a hostile power, but also, when rumors of the abductions surfaced, its politicians, bureaucrats, and other elites refused to verify the rumors and recover their fellow citizens. North Korea's abductions—including a childlike Yokota, who would become the face of the movement to bring abductees home—strengthened the emotional power of Abe's indictment. In a parliamentary committee hearing on 16 May 1997, the first time he raised the issue in the Diet, Abe said, "Of course the human lives and human rights that our country's government must protect have clearly been violated—especially those of a young girl—but in response to this the government can do nothing, which I think is equivalent to abdicating the duties of the state."[6] While he and his colleagues were undoubtedly sincere in their concern for the abductees, the issue was to prove critical in helping the new conservatives strengthen the state and fortify it with a new spirit of nationalism.

* * *

By 1997 the taboos that had prevented activists from calling public attention to the plight of the abductees were eroding. In February, Ahn Myong Jin, a former North Korean agent who had defected to South Korea in 1993, told reporters that he had seen Yokota alive in Pyongyang. Ahn's account confirmed an earlier reference to Yokota in an academic journal article and lent more substance to suspicions of North Korean abductions, leading to a public outcry.

Abe was involved in the creation of the Association of the Families of Victims Kidnapped by North Korea—the *Kazoku-kai* or Family Association—which was headed by Yokota's father Shigeru and grew into a nationwide network of activists. He was also a leader of the Parliamentarians' League to Rescue Japanese Citizens Suspected of Being Abducted by North Korea, formed with support across party lines. Thereafter, conservative lawmakers began questioning government officials about the abductees and pressuring the cabinet to take a more strident position towards North Korea, including by withholding humanitarian relief promised as part of ongoing talks. On 1 May, a police official confirmed the government suspected that ten people had been abducted by North Korea.

Abe too began using his membership of the lower house foreign affairs committee to attack how his own party, the bureaucracy (especially MOFA), and the media handled the abductee issue—as well as against North Korea, which he accused of carrying out an act of state terrorism.[7] His strident approach made party elders uncomfortable; they preferred more patient, diplomatic methods as part of broader normalization talks with Pyongyang and felt uncomfortable with the young conservative's iconoclasm.[8]

But Abe and the new conservatives had an opportunity to transform Japan's North Korea policy. With the 1994 Agreed Framework in place and South Korean President Kim Dae-Jung's introduction of the "sunshine policy" towards the North in 1998, Japan faced pressure from both Washington and Seoul to pursue normalization. Senior politicians and MOFA officials were amenable, but they increasingly had to contend with new conservatives like Abe pressing for prioritization of the abductee issue, but also with North Korea itself. North Korea's August 1998 launch of a Taepodong I intermediate-range ballistic missile over Japan was a "Sputnik moment" for Japan's leaders, who fretted about their vulnerability and Japan's ability to face the changing security environment in Northeast Asia. The following year, Japanese Coast Guard and Maritime Self-Defense Forces (MSDF) vessels encountered two mysterious ships, which resulted in the coast guard firing warning shots for the first time in nearly fifty years, and the MSDF dispatching destroyers to give chase for the first time ever.[9]

The new conservatives' activism did not have immediate results—the LDP's leaders were still interested in diplomatic normalization with Pyongyang and willing to offer substantial financial assistance to achieve it—but even a moderate politician like foreign minister Obuchi Keizō was forced to concede that the abductions should be on the agenda in negotiations with North Korea.[10] The new conservatives also had to confront turmoil within their own ranks when Nakayama Masaaki, the head of the Japan–North Korea friendship parliamentarians' league, after a surprise visit to Pyongyang, denied the abductions. Nakayama's about-face prompted Abe—with the support of the Arimoto family and other abductee families—to attack the Nakayama-led league as too soft on North Korea and to launch a new group that would push for a hardline approach.

When in 1998 a new nationwide activist network was established—the National Association for the Rescue of Japanese Abducted by North Korea, more commonly known as the Rescue Association—Abe and other conservative lawmakers dissolved Nakayama's league and established a league that would coordinate with both the Rescue Association and the Family Association to pressure LDP leaders on the abductees. This new group was chaired by Ishiba Shigeru, a leading defense hawk and included Nakagawa Shōichi, Hirasawa, and other new conservatives. After years of fruitless door-knocking in Nagatachō, the seat of political power, the abductee families now had powerful LDP allies, two pressure groups mobilizing voters, media organizations trying to make up for years of ignoring the issue, and a public increasingly incensed by North Korea's actions.[11]

When for the first time, MOFA, in its annual survey of public opinion regarding Japan's foreign policy, asked citizens to state their level of concern about North Korea as well as issues of greatest concern, sixty-three percent of respondents said they were concerned about North Korea, nearly seventy percent of whom cited the abductions as a concern compared with only 52.1 percent who mentioned North Korea's missiles.[12] Conservative mobilization had profoundly impacted public opinion. Despite North Korea having fired a missile over Japan, the abductions, which ended more than a decade prior, ranked as a greater concern than any other issue.

While Abe was not alone in advocating for the abductees and their families, few would become as strongly associated with the cause. Arimoto described him as the only politician the abductee families could trust, a trust shared by other families with rare exceptions.[13] This status gave him the freedom to pressure not only LDP moderates he viewed as unwilling to stand up for Japan's national interests, but also other conservatives. These included Mori Yoshirō, a protégé of Kishi and his father who had become the head of the *Seiwa-kai*—the faction once led by Fukuda Takeo and then Shintarō—and increasingly appeared to be a kingmaker and potential prime minister. When Mori was preparing to lead a delegation to North Korea in November 1997, Abe, still a junior parliamentarian, told Mori he should be prepared to leave if the North Koreans refused to discuss the abductees.[14]

* * *

But the new conservatives' abduction-related activism occurred slightly off stage. It was not the highest priority for a political system preoccupied with reforms needed to adapt to the post-Cold War world and the post-bubble economy. And, with Washington and Seoul committed to reducing tensions with North Korea, it would be difficult for Japan's leaders to prioritize confronting North Korea over the abductees even if they had wanted to do so.

The LDP's strange alliance with Murayama's Socialists finally ended in January 1996 when Hashimoto Ryutarō was chosen as prime minister. Hashimoto, who had won a landslide victory over Koizumi Junichirō in the LDP's leadership election in September 1995, was an unlikely savior for the LDP. After all, Hashimoto had spent his career as a follower of Tanaka and Takeshita, whose brand of money politics had done so much to lead the LDP to disaster in the 1990s. However, it seemed momentarily as if Hashimoto could stabilize LDP rule. Enjoying a surge of popularity after making a name for himself as MITI minister under Murayama, when he resisted the Clinton administration in automobile trade talks, Hashimoto portended the arrival of a new style of top-down leadership.[15] The shift from the postwar era's multimember electoral constituencies to single-member districts meant that whereas LDP candidates could often win their seats regardless of who led the party, now a popular, telegenic leader could be indispensable for reelection—and an unpopular leader could prove fatal.[16]

Hashimoto pledged an ambitious agenda to overcome economic stagnation and stabilize the financial system, reform Japan's bureaucracy, and strengthen Japan's relationship with the US.[17] Seeking a mandate for this agenda and for a consumption tax increase planned for 1997, he called a snap election for October 1996, Japan's first under a new electoral system.

The LDP again fell short of an absolute majority, forcing it to maintain its coalition with the Japan Socialist Party (JSP), but the LDP gained twenty-eight seats and comfortably outperformed the new leading opposition party, Ozawa's New Frontier Party (NFP). Abe fared well in the vote and was reelected by a comfortable majority in what had become Yamaguchi's fourth district, ensuring a stable electoral base under the new system.

Hashimoto was determined to make significant progress on his reform agenda. In April 1996, he had signed a joint security declaration with Bill Clinton renewing the bilateral alliance for the post-Cold War era and launching a review of the guidelines for security cooperation that defined allied roles and missions. The two governments also reached an agreement to close the controversial Futenma Marine air station in Okinawa and consolidate the US military presence in the prefecture, a contentious issue after three US servicemen raped a twelve-year-old girl in 1995.

After winning a new electoral mandate, he launched what would be his most durable legacy, central government reorganization. The "Hashimoto reforms" not only consolidated twenty-two ministries and agencies into twelve—they made the executive supreme in the political system. The Hashimoto government's legislation established a cabinet office and a cabinet secretariat with enlarged staffs and more political appointees tasked with coordinating policy across ministerial lines; increased the number of special advisers and private secretaries working directly for the prime minister; established new advisory councils to enable the cabinet to draw upon outside expertise to control the policy agenda and the budgetary process; and increased the number of political appointees in each ministry.[18] These reforms, which took effect in January 2001, reinforced the trend towards a stronger prime minister who could dominate policymaking.[19]

A separate set of reforms reduced the influence of the ministry of finance (MOF). A new Bank of Japan (BOJ) law in 1997 guaranteed the central bank's independence, while another law spun off MOF's financial supervisory functions into a new, independent agency, the financial services agency (FSA). Hashimoto also launched "big bang" financial reforms that broadly deregulated Japan's financial sector.[20] These changes set the Hashimoto government apart as the decade's most effective administration.

* * *

But economic stagnation continued. The economy had enjoyed a modest recovery in the mid-1990s, but financial institutions continued to struggle with non-performing loans from the end of the bubble, loans which by 1998 were estimated to have totaled twenty-five percent of gross domestic product.[21] The unstable and short-lived governments of the mid-1990s struggled to overcome opposition to using public funds to restore the financial system. Stopgap measures utilized by MOF were unsuccessful, and in November 1997, major financial institutions—including the nation's oldest brokerage, Yamaichi Securities—collapsed, triggering a bank run that rippled through the economy.[22] Other venerable institutions would fail in 1998.

The financial panic occurred not only as Asia grappled with financial contagion but also as Japan's economy stumbled. In April 1997, Hashimoto's government raised Japan's consumption tax rate from three percent to five percent, part of a package of fiscal reforms that increased the tax burden on households as part of a premature effort to rein in deficits that had resulted from the post-bubble slowdown. Consumer demand cratered, shrinking GDP by nearly one percent in 1997, Japan's worst year for growth in a quarter century.

Instead of delivering fiscal sustainability, the tax hike led in 1998 and 1999 to some of the largest stimulus packages to combat economic stagnation.[23] In retrospect, 1997 was a turning point for post-bubble

Japan. The nation's leaders had to grapple with non-performing loans, persistent slow growth, growing national debt, and, from 1998, relentless deflation.

Economic turmoil wrought havoc on the political system. The LDP suffered its worst-ever performance in the 1998 upper house elections, failing to recover the absolute majority it lost in 1989 and losing thirteen seats to the newborn Democratic Party of Japan (DPJ), which emerged as the leading opposition party. The DPJ's surprising performance reflected not only defections by LDP voters but also a surge in turnout by a growing bloc of mostly urban and suburban "floating voters."[24]

Hashimoto was replaced by Obuchi, another veteran of the Tanaka–Takeshita faction. Obuchi was unassuming and, thanks to a foreign commentator, gained an unfair reputation for dullness after being described as "having all the pizzazz of cold pizza."[25] Nakasone called him a "vacuum prime minister" for having virtually no policy agenda—in stark contrast to his predecessor—freeing him to "vacuum up" ideas from those around him.[26] In order to stabilize the LDP's control of the Diet, Obuchi entered coalition negotiations with Ozawa's Liberal Party, an offshoot of his broken New Frontier Party, and Kōmeitō, a centrist party affiliated with the Buddhist "new religion" Sōka Gakkai.

Neither coalition partner was particularly desired by the LDP. Many LDP members had never forgiven Ozawa for leaving in 1993, and feared that he could hold the government hostage.[27] They also distrusted Kōmeitō: the LDP had viewed Kōmeitō and its relationship with Sōka Gakkai as a violation of the constitution's separation of church and state, and, after the 1995 Aum Shinrikyo attack, had pushed for a new law that would enable the state to monitor new religions—including Sōka Gakkai—more closely.[28] Nevertheless, political expediency again prevailed over principle. By the end of 1998 the LDP joined forces with Ozawa. Kōmeitō joined the coalition in October 1999. The partnership with Ozawa would be short-lived, but the coalition with Kōmeitō would, surprisingly, endure.

* * *

The instability that followed the financial crisis made room for young politicians to raise their profiles. At the time the most pressing issue facing Japan's lawmakers was whether and how to save financial institutions burdened with non-performing loans. A new group of young lawmakers known as the *seisaku shinjinrui*—the "policy new breed"—emerged in late 1998 as they helped forge a multi-party consensus on financial stabilization during the so-called "finance Diet."

Abe, by virtue of his lack of interest and knowledge in economic and financial affairs, was not part of the new breed, which included lawmakers like former BOJ staffer Shiozaki Yasuhisa and Ishihara Nobuteru, who were involved with new conservative policy groups but who also used the financial crisis to burnish reputations as experts.[29] Their work led to a financial stabilization law, based largely on DPJ-drafted legislation, which enabled the government to nationalize distressed institutions. Their policy expertise and willingness to work across party lines in an increasingly two-party system suggested they could be the wave of the future—and save Japan from its economic crisis.[30]

With the public, the political system, and financial markets focused squarely on economic challenges, the "new breed" had gained an edge in the race to lead the rising generation of political leaders. For example, in a virtual LDP election conducted in December 1999 Shiozaki prevailed over Abe and three others in a vote that included politicians and journalists as well as ordinary Internet users.[31]

Although Abe had received his first position in the LDP's hierarchy—deputy chairman of the party's parliamentary affairs committee, responsible for the legislative agenda—his progress appeared sluggish next to the "new breed" lawmakers. Other members of his cohort were already being appointed to government posts—including Tanaka Kakuei's daughter Makiko, who was appointed director-general of the science and technology agency as a first-term Diet member in 1994, and Noda Seiko, who became the youngest-ever cabinet minister when Obuchi appointed her postal minister in 1998 when she was thirty-seven.[32]

During his second term, Abe expanded his policy repertoire from foreign policy to social security, forming a study group on social security reform in April 1999 with Shiozaki, Ishihara, and Nemoto Takumi that drew on their English initials to become known as the "NAIS club" (pronounced "nice"). Japan's social safety net was not a new interest for

Abe. Kishi had passed some of the key legislation to build the postwar social security system and Abe reportedly told a friend at university, "If I become a politician, I want to do welfare." Later that year he was appointed chairman of the social security committee of the LDP's policy affairs research council, a rare distinction for a junior parliamentarian that confirmed his status as one of the party's future leaders.[33]

Despite this honor, it did little to help him accumulate legislative achievements. Abe struggled to manage the main task facing the committee—the introduction of a long-term care insurance system. He was frustrated by the resistance of Kamei Shizuka, a truculent senior lawmaker who had split with the faction once led by Abe's father the previous year. Kamei's opposition ultimately delayed the scheme's rollout, which Abe was powerless to stop.[34]

Even as Abe struggled in the race to the LDP's highest ranks, a medical crisis left him wondering whether he could even persist in his political career.

At seventeen, he had suffered a bout of stomach cramps, bloody diarrhea, and frequent trips to the bathroom. Doctors could not name the disease, but the attacks continued, roughly once a year for two weeks at a time but occasionally for as long as a month. Eventually he was diagnosed with ulcerative colitis, an autoimmune inflammatory bowel disease.[35]

This illness was a closely guarded secret when he first campaigned for his father's seat, even as a side effect of his medication caused pressure to build up in his eyeballs, requiring multiple trips to hospital. Key supporters wondered whether he would have the stamina for a successful political career.[36]

Abe's illness had had minimal impact on his career through 1998, but after receiving his first party post he suffered a severe attack that led to his being hospitalized for three months. It was, he later said, "the greatest crisis" of his career, one that he had to conceal completely, given what he later described as a "taboo" regarding discussions of illness by public figures. While hospitalized, his weight dropped sharply, from sixty-five kilos to fifty-three. Akie, in tears, urged him to abandon politics. Eventually, he found a treatment that maintained remission and let him continue his career.

But the attack was an untimely reminder of his physical frailty and also that, although he was still only a second-term Diet member, his peers were accumulating policymaking experience, whether in government posts or as "new breed" lawmakers, while in Abe was in hospital, fighting for a chance to continue his career.

* * *

The unspectacular Obuchi chugged along as prime minister, leading Japan into a new century. His record proved remarkably conservative for a prime minister from the less ideological Tanaka wing. His government passed legislation in 1999 that formally recognized Japan's "rising sun" flag as the national flag and the song "Kimigayo" as the national anthem. Obuchi also updated Japan's national security laws to reflect the 1997 revision of the US–Japan Guidelines for Security Cooperation, legislation to enable a more active role in allied activities in "situations in areas surrounding Japan," albeit not a full combat role alongside US forces. In the final months of his premiership, his government also established constitutional commissions for the two houses of the Diet, a necessary step for constitutional revision.

But, by the spring of 2000, Obuchi's coalition was fraying. Ozawa was making ever-more grandiose demands and with a general election due that year, proposed that the LDP and his Liberal Party should dissolve and form a new party. This was dismissed as "nonsense" by Obuchi.[37] Talks between Obuchi and Ozawa finally broke down on 1 April 2000, so Ozawa left the coalition, although more than half of his members stayed and launched a new party, the Conservative Party. In the early hours of 2 April, Obuchi suffered a stroke and fell into a coma. He died on 14 May.

Obuchi's death was the death knell for the LDP's machine politics. After Obuchi, control of the party would shift to the new conservatives. In the twenty years since Obuchi died, other than for the LDP's three years in opposition, Japan has been governed by the *Seiwa-kai*, the descendant of Kishi's old faction for all but one year—and that one exception was Asō Tarō, although older, a new conservative fellow-traveler.

The vanguard of the new wave was Mori Yoshirō, LDP secretary-general at the time of Obuchi's stroke. Mori was elevated to the LDP presidency after a series of closed-door meetings between a "gang of five," a group of senior party leaders—including Mori himself—who moved quickly to manage the transition once it became clear Obuchi would not recover. It was Mori who proposed that the party forego a full election, while the others proposed that Mori should succeed Obuchi in the premiership. By midnight on 3 April, the group had decided on Mori. The choice was confirmed by the LDP's parliamentarians on 5 April. Reports of the secret meetings soon surfaced, undermining Mori's legitimacy and harming his approval ratings, which had already been below fifty percent.[38] But despite Mori's inauspicious beginnings, he was the first prime minister drawn from the *Seiwa-kai* since Fukuda, a two-decade drought during which Tanaka and his successors had controlled the party.

Mori's conservative bona fides were impeccable. Son of a local politician, he sought national office after a brief stint as a journalist and then as the secretary to an ally of Kishi. But when he decided to run in 1969, the LDP had already backed two candidates in his constituency and then-secretary-general Tanaka Kakuei was unwilling to endorse him, forcing Mori to run as an independent. But Kishi embraced him and campaigned on his behalf; Mori joined his faction after pulling off a surprising victory.[39] As a young lawmaker, he joined the *Seirankai*, a group of anti-Tanaka conservative firebrands. The group was an antecedent of the new conservative groups of the 1990s, albeit with some eccentric touches.[40] Its members, for example, signed its statement of principles in blood.

The group demanded constitutional revision, education reform, and a strong national defense based on an equal partnership with the US. This manifesto also attacked inequality and "unearned income," giving the group a populist flavor.[41] Mori, meanwhile, focused on education, lamenting the "masochistic" education of the postwar era as well as the baleful influence of the left-wing teachers' union, *Nikkyōso*. He argued that children should be taught the nation's founding myths, that "long ago there were gods and they made Japan."[42]

The rise of Tanaka's machine blunted the *Seirankai*'s influence. However, it denied LDP prime ministers easy political victories, organizing mass resistance to shifting diplomatic recognition from the Republic of China to the PRC, delaying the ratification of the Nuclear Non-Proliferation Treaty, and eroding taboos on defense policy debates.[43] Mori would pursue his vision of education reform under Nakasone, serving as his education minister from 1983–1984.

As Abe Shintarō inherited the *Seiwa-kai* from Fukuda Takeo, Mori emerged as one of the faction's "big four," poised to become one of the faction's and the party's next generation of leaders. During the 1990s, he served two stints as secretary-general, and in 1998 assumed the *Seiwa-kai*'s leadership. While his relationship with the elder Abe was not frictionless, they worked closely together, particularly as Shintarō sought to resolve Japan's territorial dispute with Russia and build a new relationship as the Cold War ended. Mori inherited a personal interest in Russia from his father, who is buried in Siberia, and has cultivated personal ties with Vladimir Putin and other Russian leaders. Mori facilitated Shintarō's attendance at the April 1991 reception for Gorbachev that was his final public appearance.[44] As a sign of the significance of Mori's becoming prime minister, eight days after his selection, he visited Shinzō's home to kneel before the household altar—where deceased ancestors are honored—and report to Shintarō on his election.[45]

Almost immediately, Mori signaled a break with the past. As a sign of his commitment to improving ties with Russia and resolving the territorial dispute—a dream of the LDP's right wing dating back to Hatoyama Ichirō at the party's founding—his first foreign trip was to Russia, not the US, where he conferred with Putin on 29 April, shortly before he was sworn in as Russia's president.[46]

On 15 May, he openly declared his sympathies with the new conservatives at a party for the Shinto Association of Spiritual Leadership, a venerable conservative pressure group.[47] In a rambling toast to the group's efforts, one line stood out: "Now that I am on the government side...we will firmly make all of the Japanese people aware of the fact that the country of Japan is surely an emperor-centered land of the gods."[48] This line prompted an immediate and furious backlash. In Japan, this remark was particularly maligned since it came amidst a discussion of education reform and suggested that Mori would erode constitutional guarantees of the separation of church and state.

He soon faced calls for his resignation from opposition lawmakers, but, more importantly, he faced criticism from Kōmeitō, whose support the LDP needed. Finally, on 26 May, Mori apologized in a press conference but also took another opportunity to explain, saying, "The people of Japan have been distracted by material wealth, and it seems to me that at times we have not paid enough attention to such spiritual values as the respect for life, consideration for others, and appreciation of the traditional culture of our nation."[49]

Already viewed with suspicion for the backroom deal that brought him to power, the 15 May speech exposed Mori as out of step with public sentiments. It also led to a snap election, since, after opposition parties submitted a no-confidence motion in the House of Representatives on 2 June, Mori responded by dissolving the house and calling an election for 25 June.

The vote was a firm rebuke of Mori and the LDP: the party not only lost thirty-eight seats and failed to win an absolute majority but also dragged down its coalition partners. The implication of this outcome was that even as the new conservatives consolidated their control of the LDP, they became dependent on a pacifist, centrist party to contest elections and to govern, enabling Kōmeitō to function as a brake on their ambitions. The LDP would need Kōmeitō not only for parliamentary votes but also for its support at the ballot box and from its well-organized volunteers.

Meanwhile, the DPJ, contesting its first general election, made great strides, gaining thirty-two seats but, more importantly, trailing the LDP by fewer than two million votes out of nearly sixty million cast in proportional representation voting. The Democratic gains reflected the stirring of Japan's urban and suburban floating voters, who roused themselves despite Mori's suggestion, days before the vote, that it would be fine if undecided voters stayed in bed instead of voting.[50]

Mori limped on for another nine months, and survived a party rebellion by Katō Kōichi, one of the LDP's last liberal lions, overseeing the implementation of Hashimoto's reorganization of the central government on 1 January 2001. He also gave Abe his first government post. Mori was finally driven to resign in February 2001, when he faced universal opprobrium for his decision to continue playing a round of golf even after receiving word that the *Ehime Maru*, a high school training ship, had been struck by a US Navy submarine near Hawaii and sunk, causing nine deaths.[51]

* * *

On 13 May 2000, Mori was with Abe, attending a memorial event for Shintarō that doubled as a political event for Shinzō in light of the general election that would be held that year.[52] The event, coming shortly after Mori went to Abe's home to deliver the news of his premiership to Shintarō, highlights how Abe was being pulled into Mori's orbit. Mori was prepared to boost the prospects of his faction's rising star and the heir of his patrons.

In the June general election, Abe won with more than seventy percent of the vote for the first time. With three electoral victories under his belt, he was still relatively junior, and, according to the LDP's seniority conventions, would have been in line for a chairmanship of one of the party's policy committees—a job he had already held. Instead, when Mori reshuffled his cabinet on 4 July, he brought Abe into government as one of three deputy chief cabinet secretaries, a position likened to being the government's appendix.[53] According to at least one report, Koizumi Junichirō took credit for recommending Abe for the post and described him as the "feature attraction" in the new cabinet lineup.[54]

But Abe's appointment in July 2000 meant he would likely be in office as Hashimoto's administrative reforms took effect on 1 January 2001, at which point significant power would accrue to the prime minister's office, cabinet office, and cabinet secretariat, raising the importance of the deputy chief cabinet secretary's role. Perhaps more importantly, it meant that when Mori finally resigned and was succeeded by Koizumi Junichirō in April 2001, Abe was well positioned to stay in his post. He would then have the opportunity to serve not only under a fellow member of Mori's faction but also under a prime minister who was determined to revolutionize the Japanese political system and, if perhaps not as committed a patron as Mori had been, was sympathetic to many new conservative goals.

Thanks to the transition from Obuchi to Mori, and then from Mori to Koizumi, Abe raced to the head of the pack and found himself at the heart of a dynamic administration that would end up being Japan's most enduring and stable since Nakasone.

6

THE WEIRDO

Koizumi Junichirō took his first overseas trip as prime minister in June 2001. His first stop was the US, where he joined George W. Bush, who had been inaugurated as president in January, at Camp David.

Bush and his most senior advisers wanted a closer relationship with Japan. Several of the new administration's foreign policy officials had helped draft what became known as the Armitage-Nye Report.[1] The report, released shortly before the 2000 election by a bipartisan group of experts led by veteran Republican official Richard Armitage and former assistant secretary of defense and Harvard professor Joseph Nye, recommended that the next administration treat Japan as an equal partner in crafting regional and global policies and pursue closer security, diplomatic, and economic cooperation. The report, building on work done by Nye and his onetime deputy Kurt Campbell during the Clinton administration, outlined a bipartisan blueprint for the post-Cold War relationship.

Koizumi's emergence as prime minister was a stroke of luck. Shortly after taking office, the Bush administration had a Japanese prime minister who was a willing partner in building a new kind of bilateral relationship.

It helped that Koizumi was eager to strike up a friendship with Bush. At Camp David, they tossed a baseball, bonded over their love of *High Noon*, and, according to Koizumi, had a "heart-to-heart meeting" that exceeded his expectations for "[establishing] a relationship of trust." Bush for his part gave his full endorsement of Koizumi's reform agenda and praised his good humor and his courage as a leader "who recognizes that his duty is not to avoid, but to lead."[2]

Koizumi's visit also marked Abe's arrival on a bigger stage. As deputy chief cabinet secretary, he accompanied the prime minister, and it was there, Michael Green recalls, that Koizumi introduced his young deputy to the Americans as the next prime minister. From his earliest days in office, Koizumi—who had recommended Abe to Mori for the deputy chief cabinet secretary post—saw Abe as a future leader. Thanks to Koizumi, there would be no doubt about Abe's stature as the most promising of the LDP's young leaders.

During his five years and five months in power, Koizumi promoted Abe to ever-higher government and party posts, ensuring that when he yielded power Abe was well placed to succeed him. Koizumi's eagerness to advance his protégé's prospects had wide-reaching effects for Abe, the LDP, and Japan.

* * *

Koizumi was an unlikely prime minister. Born in 1942 in Yokosuka, a port southwest of Tokyo where Matthew Perry arrived and which would later become an important hub for the imperial Japanese navy and the US navy, Koizumi, like Abe, was the son and grandson of politicians. His maternal grandfather had been a prewar politician and wartime cabinet minister known for his extensive tattoos. His father, Junya, was adopted by his wife's family after marriage and began his political career before the war when elected to the Diet in 1937. Purged during the occupation, Junya returned to the Diet in 1952 and eventually became defense agency chief under Ikeda and Satō, dying in August 1969. But in the December 1969 general election, Junichirō failed to win his father's seat; he had been studying economics at University College London and had barely three months to prepare to run in his father's place.

Instead, his entry into politics was aided by Fukuda Takeo, Kishi's top lieutenant who became prime minister and a power broker in his own right. After his failed campaign, Koizumi worked as Fukuda's secretary, a title that does not convey the extent to which Koizumi shadowed and learned from his boss. He won a Diet seat in 1972 and joined the *Seiwa-kai*, becoming a loyal retainer in Fukuda's battles against Tanaka and Ohira during what came to be known as the Liberal Democratic Party's (LDP) "warring states period."[3]

Despite winning his first election before he turned thirty-one, there was little in Koizumi's early career to suggest that he would ever become prime minister. He did not receive his first ministerial post until 1988, and his subsequent cabinet appointments were lower-tier ministries, including a brief stint as postal minister under Miyazawa and another as health minister under Hashimoto. His résumé included none of the party and cabinet posts that would mark out an LDP law-maker as a future party leader. Although he mounted leadership bids in 1995 and 1998, he ran more to ensure that his faction was represented in the field than as a serious contender. His 1998 leadership bid against Obuchi and Kajiyama Seiroku was memorable mostly for producing a durable nickname: Tanaka Makiko, daughter of Kakuei, referred to the election as a contest between "a mediocrity [Obuchi], a soldier [Kajiyama], and a weirdo [Koizumi]."

In a word, Tanaka captured that there was something different about Koizumi. With his wavy mane—which earned him the nickname "Lionheart"—he stood out from just about every other Japanese politician. He was a divorcé, who had taken sole custody of two of his three sons but was also unabashed about his penchant for Tokyo's nightlife.[4] He wore his passions on his sleeve, especially his love of music, including Japanese pop music, opera, and, most famously, Elvis Presley, going so far as to release a "mix tape" of his favorite Elvis songs.[5] During the LDP's golden era, it is unlikely that he would have ever had the chance of becoming party leader and prime minister.[6]

But the golden age was over. The LDP needed to think differently about its leaders. In April 2001, when Mori finally resigned after reaching record-low approval, the LDP was in crisis. Deprived of majorities in both houses and forced to govern in coalition, it also faced an increasingly serious threat from the Democratic Party of Japan (DPJ), which was consolidating strongholds in urban and suburban constituencies. The LDP was mere months away from an upper house election, which, if the party failed to undo the impact of Mori's tenure, could result in another disaster.

* * *

In these circumstances, Koizumi's eccentricities became assets. He drew adoring crowds and had a talent for controlling media coverage through his use of simple, clearly articulated phrases that could easily be repeated on television and in the tabloid press. But people were not just attracted to Koizumi's style. He also attracted voters, particularly urban and suburban voters, with a populist appeal that tapped into public frustrations after a decade of slow growth, financial instability, and political turbulence.

After all, if populism is about identifying entrenched elites as the enemy and mobilizing public anger to wield power, Koizumi was a populist.[7] He had an enemy: the Tanaka machine and its allies in the bureaucracy and the private sector. "I will destroy the LDP," he said as he campaigned for the LDP's leadership. He would destroy the old party of factions and policy tribes that above all worked to transfer wealth from metropolitan Japan to the depopulating provinces—usually in the form of extravagant, unnecessary infrastructure projects that created jobs for rural voters.[8] He replaced it with a new party controlled by a strong leader, able to compete for the increasingly dominant urban independent voters.

This was the right message at the right time, and Koizumi deployed it magisterially, helped by a rule change introduced shortly before Mori's resignation. The LDP's rules had previously given each parliamentarian one vote, and each of the party's forty-seven prefectural chapters one vote, ensuring the LDP's faction bosses controlled the election of party leaders, since they controlled the votes of their parliamentarians. However, in the name of openness and legitimacy—lessons learned from his own troubled accession—Mori prevailed upon the party to change the rules so that each prefectural chapter would have three votes. All but two prefectural chapters decided that they would award their votes winner-take-all, based on a vote held for the party's rank-and-file members. This rule change neutralized Hashimoto Ryutarō's advantages—the former prime minister had launched a comeback bid and his faction was still the LDP's largest—and amplified Koizumi's strengths.

Koizumi launched a campaign that exploited this advantage. Defying the conventional approach to LDP leadership campaigns, he worked from the outside in. Campaigning on a shoestring budget, he made speeches in plazas in large and medium-sized cities across the country to generate a surge of support from the electorate. This attracted favorable press coverage and swayed the party's rank-and-file members, whose support for the underdog led LDP lawmakers to rally to his standard.[9]

He won comfortably, receiving 298 votes to Hashimoto's 155, with another thirty-one going to Asō Tarō. Koizumi's victory in the rank-and-file voting was particularly lopsided, as he won forty-one out of forty-six prefectures.[10]

While Koizumi told voters he was running against factional politics, in reality he was mainly running against the Tanaka school's domination. He may have attracted voters disgusted by the LDP machine, but he wanted to end once and for all the "Kaku–Fuku war," the conflict between Fukuda and Tanaka dating from the early 1970s, in favor of Fukuda's political descendants.[11] Mori's role in Koizumi's victory and guiding Abe's career suggests that his role in cementing the new right's domination of the LDP has been underappreciated.[12]

Mori's influence was visible in Koizumi's first cabinet. While it is mostly remembered for his willingness to name non-politicians to ministerial posts and his choice of Tanaka Makiko as foreign minister, Koizumi also retained seven members of Mori's second cabinet and favored the Mori faction. The faction was not just overrepresented in the cabinet, but also dominated the executive branch, since the prime minister retained Fukuda Yasuo as chief cabinet secretary, Abe as the deputy chief cabinet secretary from the lower house, and Ueno Kōsei as the deputy chief cabinet secretary from the upper house.

* * *

Abe helped lead the campaign for Koizumi who was, after all, his faction's candidate. But it was not obvious that Abe and Koizumi would forge a close relationship, or that Koizumi would gamble on Abe and advance his career.

For Abe, Koizumi was not a natural patron. He was not a fervent partisan in the culture war, paying relatively little attention to issues of greatest concern to the new conservatives. These included defense and foreign policy, and fights over the constitution, education, Japan's wartime past, and reverence for the imperial household. In fact Koizumi would battle with the new conservatives when, later in his term, he signaled his willingness to change succession laws to allow female inheritance of the throne.[13] He was not particularly close to Abe's father or grandfather, despite having risen through the ranks in their faction. Koizumi and Abe were an odd couple, the junior lawmaker determined to make his own name even as he fought for his family's legacy and the unlikely prime minister who, above all else, brought a sense of fun to Japan's democracy that it had never had before.

But thanks in part to Koizumi's commitment to advancing his faction's interests, the two men forged an effective partnership during Koizumi's five-and-a-half years in office. With the prime minister preoccupied with political and economic reform, Abe battled with bureaucrats and even LDP members to push the Koizumi government in a more hawkish direction and erode longstanding constraints on Japan's defense policies. As Abe said later, "Because Mr. Koizumi's foreign and security policies were a blank slate, I imbued them [with my views]."[14]

Koizumi, whose constituency had hosted a US aircraft carrier since he was a freshman lawmaker, likely had more appreciation of the realities of Japan's national defense than the average Diet member, but from the beginning of his premiership he listened to arguments from Abe and other new conservatives regarding the need to build a stronger alliance with the US and undo constitutional, legal, and political constraints on the SDF. Abe and his own informal foreign policy adviser, retired diplomat Okazaki Hisahiko, impressed upon Koizumi before taking office that he should prioritize strengthening the US–Japan alliance, for example by loosening restrictions on Japan's exercise of its right of collective self-defense and should also visit Yasukuni shrine despite past protests from China and South Korea. During the LDP campaign, Koizumi pledged to visit Yasukuni on 15 August, the anniversary of the end of the Second World War, and from his first press conference on 27 April 2001, he took a hawkish approach to the US–Japan alliance, stressing Japan's relationship with the US as the "largest foundation for Japan's prosperity" and embracing the logic of reinterpreting the constitution to permit collective self-defense.[15]

Koizumi's willingness to trust Abe's judgment on foreign affairs was important, but Koizumi and Abe were ultimately united by a shared commitment to top-down political leadership. In a note published in the inaugural issue of Koizumi's "mail magazine"—the email newsletter, edited by Abe, that was regarded as a revolutionary means for communicating directly with voters—Abe likened Koizumi to the Choshū heroes Yoshida Shōin and Takasugi Shinsaku for his strong determination to change Japan.[16] While Koizumi frequently, although not continuously, enjoyed strong approval ratings as prime minister and would use all the tools available to shift public opinion in his favor on controversial issues, he nevertheless pursued Kishi's vision of democratic statesmanship that "stands two or three steps ahead of the people." He entered office with a vision of how Japan should be governed, and determined to sweep aside all obstacles to realize it.

Serving under Koizumi, Abe saw what a strong-willed politician could do with the powers that the prime minister acquired during the 1990s. The Hashimoto reforms, which came into effect on 1 January 2001, and little-noted changes to Japan's Cabinet Law in 1999 that formally recognized the prime minister's ability to control the cabinet's agenda and strengthened the cabinet secretariat's ability to draft legislation, meant that by the time Koizumi won the premiership, the prime minister's office had become a potent weapon for a determined leader.

Abe, as deputy chief cabinet secretary, was also a beneficiary of administrative reforms. The cabinet secretariat and the cabinet office, under the leadership of the chief cabinet secretary, served the prime minister directly to oversee the policy coordination process across central government ministries, imposing the prime minister's will on the bureaucracy. The chief cabinet secretary, once a relatively minor cabinet post, became the equivalent of the US vice president, White House chief of staff, and communications director rolled into one, an indispensable player whose ability to gather information, manage the prime minister's time, and control the policy- and decision-making processes could make or break governments. The status of the three deputy chief cabinet secretaries grew in tandem.[17]

* * *

What made Koizumi's embrace of Abe puzzling is that, while Koizumi's and Abe's projects for institutional change and national renewal occasionally overlapped, they were not identical. Koizumi's tenure was strongly influenced by the decisions made in Washington after the 9/11 terrorist attacks, but throughout his administration he sought to change Japan's political economy fundamentally. As deputy chief secretary until 2003, Abe was effectively a bystander to some of Koizumi's most consequential decisions. He did not, for example, participate in Council on Economic and Fiscal Policy (CEFP) meetings, where some key decisions were made.

For Koizumi, "destroying the old LDP" was not just about winning a power struggle. He wanted to use the prime minister's new powers to uproot the entire system of "convoy capitalism," whereby LDP backbenchers, bureaucrats, and special interests used various channels to funnel resources to noncompetitive regions and industries, and used the power of the state to protect them from new competitors.[18]

Accordingly, "destroying the LDP" was just one slogan among several that conveyed Koizumi's zeal for reform. "No growth without reform." "Structural reform without sanctuary." "Reforms accompanied by pain." "From public to private." And his sobriquet for the LDP's old guard that mobilized to block his agenda: the "resistance forces."[19] These slogans were the packaging for what amounted to Japanese-style neoliberalism, a sweeping program of deregulation, privatization, decentralization, and fiscal consolidation along with political reform that would amount to—as Koizumi stated in his first policy speech as prime minister—"a restoration for the new century."[20]

Koizumi was not just promising reform. Notwithstanding his preference for appointees from his own faction, by rejecting the advice of faction bosses and the very notion of factional balance in distributing ministerial posts and instead appointing three "civilians" to key jobs—most notably economist Takenaka Heizō as minister of state for economic and fiscal policy—Koizumi showed he would emphasize ability and loyalty over factional affiliation, seniority, or other conventions. He meant to make good on his promises.[21]

Despite the surge of popular support that propelled him into government, it took time for the Koizumi's policies to coalesce, not least because he first had to lead the LDP to victory in the July upper house elections. In the event, the LDP won sixty-four of 121 seats up for election and improved its vote total in proportional representation voting by fifty percent over the party's dismal 1998 performance. Although the LDP still needed coalition partners, the party significantly outpaced the DPJ, suggesting that under Koizumi the LDP might be able to blunt its inroads among urban voters.

The elections gave Koizumi a popular mandate, but first he had to overcome another recession. In the first three quarters after Koizumi became prime minister, Japan fell into its second recession in five years. Unemployment spiked, reaching a postwar high of 5.5 percent by the end of 2001. Prices continued to fall, exacerbating the financial sector's lingering debt problem, as it became clear that earlier efforts to clean up bank balance sheets were inadequate. There was still substantial work to do, to shore up financial institutions while they reduced the number of non-performing loans.[22] As a result, even before Koizumi's election, the Bank of Japan (BOJ) had gifted the world a new term: quantitative easing. The bank launched its program of money supply targeting via long-term bond purchases in March, a program that would by the end of the decade become known around the world.

The Koizumi government was especially dependent on the BOJ's willingness to launch what were then unconventional monetary policies, largely because Koizumi wanted to end the fiscal pump priming, that had swollen the government's debt to 135 percent of GDP by 2001, and begin the process of consolidating the government's debt. Unlike many LDP deficit hawks, Koizumi was not an ex-ministry of finance (MOF) official, but his patron Fukuda had been, and after entering politics Koizumi had joined the LDP's fiscal policy "tribe."[23] During his leadership campaign, he identified fiscal consolidation as a top priority, pledging to cap new debt issued by the government in FY2002 to below ¥30 trillion, a target Koizumi's predecessors had blown past. In June, despite growing signs of a recession, the CEFP had formally adopted the target as part of its basic policy for the budgeting process and Koizumi would defend this pledge even as economic conditions deteriorated. Abe later praised him for his stubborn refusal to change course: "Despite the deterioration of the unemployment rate, stock prices, and other indicators, the Koizumi cabinet persistently adhered to its original intention and did not revert to the fiscal stimulus line—such as expanding public investment—as in the past."[24]

But, at the time, it seemed his bid for a political and economic revolution would fail. The recession meant that Koizumi had to wait until 2002, when Japan's economy began to grow again, before he could begin work on more ambitious reforms. It was not until September 2002, for example, that Koizumi expanded his economy czar Takenaka's portfolio to include leadership of the financial services agency (FSA) and tasked him with resolving the bad loan problem once and for all. Within a month of his appointment, Takenaka had overcome resistance from within the LDP to launch a financial stabilization plan that commanded the FSA to more rigorously evaluate financial sector balance sheets, order banks to improve their capital adequacy, and use government tools to improve the governance of major banks. The Koizumi administration also used new vehicles to purchase bad loans and inject public funds into financial institutions with inadequate holdings.[25] The financial stabilization plan was both helped by and reinforced a broader macroeconomic recovery, which improved the balance sheets of major lenders.

As the recovery accelerated—fueled by a global recovery as the Federal Reserve eased after the bursting of the dot-com bubble and the effects of China's 2001 accession to the WTO began to be felt—Koizumi had more room to pursue reforms that targeted economically inefficient but politically connected sectors of the economy. With the CEFP increasingly directing the budgetary process, Koizumi sharply slashed public works spending, which shrank by nearly twenty-five percent during his tenure. He privatized four highway construction corporations—semi-public entities that directed resources to building under-utilized roads in rural constituencies represented by powerful Diet members. And, after 2003, he could pursue his long-standing ambition to privatize Japan's postal system, whose bank turned the deposits of millions of Japanese into a piggy bank for pork barrel spending.

* * *

However, as Koizumi grappled with recession, financial instability, and structural reform, his government also embarked upon a momentous transformation of Japan's relationship with the United States—and in this case, Abe would be closer to the action.

Building a more equal alliance in which Japan could bear a greater burden, not only for its own defense but also for assisting US forces, was part of Abe's inheritance, an ambition he had imbibed as a six-year-old boy watching his grandfather battle for the revised security treaty.

As a junior Diet member thinking about Japan's position in post-Cold War Asia, while he recognized the importance of establishing close ties, particularly economic ties, with all of the region's powers, he also knew there was no substitute for the US–Japan alliance. Abe was explicit about the need to change the constitution to let Japan exercise its right of collective self-defense and deploy Japanese forces to at least provide rear-area logistical support for the US military, if not to assume a frontline combat role. Given the risks of conflict on the Korean Peninsula or in the Taiwan Straits that could require US forces to mobilize for Japan's defense, Abe worried that if Japan failed to assist in a crisis in which American lives were at stake, it could prove fatal for the alliance and therefore for Japan's national security.[26] These views, which Abe increasingly expressed as the Diet debated legislation to implement the updated guidelines for bilateral security cooperation negotiated by Hashimoto and Obuchi, dovetailed neatly with bipartisan consensus on the future of the US–Japan alliance that was comfortably ensconced in the Bush administration.

Abe became particularly close with Michael Green, who was handling the Japan portfolio at Bush's National Security Council. They eventually exchanged private mobile numbers—against protocol—ensuring a direct line of communication between the White House and the Kantei.[27] While Green, a young scholar who early in his career had worked as a journalist for a Japanese newspaper and a secretary to a Diet member, had not known Abe before joining the administration, he found him a useful partner for managing the bilateral relationship, and Green and others over time saw Abe much as Koizumi saw him, as a future leader of a more dynamic Japan.

The emerging affinities between Bush and Koizumi and their administrations assumed higher stakes on 11 September, when four hijacked airliners shattered the illusion of an impregnable superpower. As the Bush administration mobilized for what the president described on 20 September as a "lengthy campaign, unlike any other we have ever seen," Washington called upon allies and friends to join "civilization's fight" against terrorism. Bush would not be satisfied with the checkbook diplomacy that Japan used when his father organized an international coalition to reverse Iraq's invasion of Kuwait. The Bush administration, wanting Tokyo to assume a greater role in the alliance, were determined to enlist Japan in the fight—and they found a willing partner in the Koizumi administration.

Koizumi himself condemned the attacks swiftly and showed Japan "is resolved to spare no effort in providing necessary assistance and cooperation." His support was not merely rhetorical: within hours of the attacks, he used the executive's expanded powers to establish an emergency headquarters to manage the inter-ministerial response to the crisis, and by 19 September he announced that Japan would dispatch Maritime Self-Defense Forces (MSDF) vessels to provide logistical support and gather intelligence in the Indian Ocean in support of US operations. Five days later, Koizumi was in the US, where he visited Ground Zero in New York City and then went to Washington to meet with Bush, who voiced his appreciation of the visit and Koizumi's expression of support in person.

As news of the attacks on the World Trade Center and Pentagon reached Tokyo on the evening of 11 September, Abe, along with Chief Cabinet Secretary Fukuda, LDP policy chief Asō Tarō, and Abe's fellow Deputy Chief Secretary Ueno rushed to the prime minister's office.[28] As the scale of the crisis widened, it was the administrative deputy chief secretary—Furukawa Tetsujirō, a career health ministry official who had served in the post since 1995—who spearheaded the Koizumi administration's response. Furukawa organized a project team that included senior bureaucrats from MOFA (including future national security adviser Yachi Shotarō) and what was then Japan's defense agency (JDA) to coordinate the policymaking process.[29] This team's work enabled the Koizumi government to move quickly and enact a special anti-terrorism act that allowed Japan to satisfy US Deputy Secretary of State Armitage's call for Japan to "show the flag" in support of US military operations in Afghanistan. By 5 October, the bill had secured the support of the ruling coalition and was submitted to the Diet; by 29 October, it had become law.[30]

While Abe was more involved in these debates than in deliberations about the administration's economic program, he was still a junior deputy tasked with supporting the work of principals. And while he enjoyed a good relationship with Koizumi, his relationship with Fukuda Yasuo—his direct boss—was chillier.

* * *

Fukuda, like Abe, was the Tokyo-born child of a prominent conservative politician. He, like Abe, had a career in the private sector before becoming his father's secretary and then inheriting his father's parliamentary seat. But Fukuda was almost twenty years older than Abe, had worked for seventeen years for Maruzen Oil, and then another fourteen years as his father's secretary before winning a seat in the LDP stronghold of Gunma in 1990. He was nearly fifty-four by the time he succeeded his father, and therefore enjoyed a truly accelerated rise through the LDP's ranks to become chief cabinet secretary only a decade after his first election.

He joined his father's former faction, and served as chief cabinet secretary under Mori and Koizumi as they consolidated the *Seiwa-kai*'s power. However, Fukuda was a notable exception to the faction's reputation as a right-wing bastion; he was very much his father's son. Despite being Kishi's political heir, Fukuda Takeo had not shared his ambitions to undo the postwar regime, replace the constitution, or remilitarize Japan. He emphatically objected to being called a hawk and is now best remembered for the Fukuda Doctrine, which, articulated while on a tour of Southeast Asia, declared that Japan "rejects the role of a military power" and embraces establishing relations based on trust and equality with Southeast Asian nations, by which Japan would assist their economic development.

Yasuo pursued similar ideas in his own career. He cultivated close relationships with MOFA officials and, as chief cabinet secretary and later as prime minister, he emphasized the importance of peaceful relations with Japan's neighbors, including China and North Korea, and the development of closer economic links with the continent. Not a culture warrior like Abe or a neoliberal crusader like Koizumi, he harkened back to an older, more balanced era of LDP rule.

After taking over as chief cabinet secretary in October 2000, Fukuda found himself at odds with Abe. Lee Teng-hui, the former president of Taiwan, sought a visa to travel to Japan for a conference in late October, but MOFA demurred. The following spring, Lee sought another visa, to receive treatment for a heart condition. This request, which came in the midst of the LDP leadership election and occasioned grandstanding by candidates regarding the need to support Taiwan, was granted.[31] But the circumstances surrounding Lee's visit led to open conflict between the ministry and pro-China and pro-Taiwan lawmakers in the LDP and within the Koizumi government itself, pitting the pro-Taiwan Abe against Fukuda, a leading member of the LDP's China school. Abe, with Mori's backing, had maneuvered to secure a visa for Lee, enraging the usually placid chief cabinet secretary, who thought Abe was overstepping his authority. Abe, for his part, said in Diet hearings that although there were differences of opinion, the government made its decision based on assessment of Japan's national interests.[32] While Abe was not alone in supporting a visa for Lee, he had defied Fukuda, who would not look favorably upon his deputy.

It was not the only time Abe drew Fukuda's ire. In May 2002, Abe triggered a minor tempest when news leaked that, in an off-the-record speech at Tokyo's Waseda University, he reminded the audience that Japan was not prohibited from possessing nuclear weapons. Fukuda, reportedly, reacted sourly to his deputy's remarks as well as his attempts to dodge criticism by claiming that he was merely making a legal claim, not advancing a policy position.[33]

The uproar died down and Abe kept his job. But for Fukuda, it was another argument against Abe's reliability, suggesting that he would not willingly back Abe's advancement in the LDP hierarchy. Their earlier clashes, however, would pale in comparison with what was to come, as Koizumi pursued diplomatic normalization with North Korea. This time, Abe would not only prevail over Fukuda, but emerge with significantly greater national renown and an edge in the race to succeed Koizumi as prime minister.

7

ABE'S RISE

Koizumi and his entourage arrived at Haneda airport on the morning of 17 September 2002, for a two-hour flight to Pyongyang. Koizumi would be the first postwar prime minister to visit North Korea, and the first to meet with a North Korean leader. His traveling party included Iijima Isao, his principal private secretary; three senior officials from the ministry of foreign affairs (MOFA), including Tanaka Hitoshi, chief negotiator with Pyongyang; two administrative private secretaries; and Abe, still a deputy chief cabinet secretary.

Although Koizumi and Kim Jong Il were expected to sign a declaration providing a roadmap for diplomatic normalization, there was little fanfare. Koizumi wanted answers from Kim about the fate of Japan's abductees, and so refused to schedule even a working lunch. His entourage carried their own meals.[1]

The stakes were high. Diplomatic normalization could mean billions of dollars in aid and reparations. Yet, simply visiting Pyongyang risked fraying ties with Washington. In January that year, George W. Bush had referred to North Korea as part of the "axis of evil." At that very moment the Bush administration was marshaling evidence of a North Korean uranium enrichment program that violated the terms of the 1994 Agreed Framework, which had resolved the nuclear crisis that had brought the US and North Korea to the brink of war. The Bush administration was determined to prove its failure to curtail Pyongyang's nuclear ambitions.[2]

Therefore, as Japanese officials conducted secret negotiations with North Koreans ahead of the Pyongyang summit, the Koizumi government was careful to keep the Americans, who were increasingly determined to ratchet up pressure on Pyongyang to prevent its development of a nuclear arsenal, briefed on the talks.[3]

While Koizumi's historic trip appealed to his penchant for drama and fulfilled his need to shore up his approval ratings, it was the product of careful diplomacy. Public attention to the plight of the abductees had stymied normalization talks in the late 1990s, but by late 2001, the North Koreans seemed more open to discussions that would address all issues, including the "humanitarian issue," their euphemism for the abductions.

The talks became serious when an apparently high-ranking North Korean official known only as "Mr. X" began meeting with Japanese officials. Japan's representative in these talks was Tanaka Hitoshi, MOFA's director-general for Asian affairs. A veteran diplomat who had managed the nuclear crisis and then worked with US counterparts to strengthen bilateral cooperation, he was uniquely capable of managing the sensitive issues surrounding diplomacy with Pyongyang. Koizumi and Fukuda directly tasked him to negotiate with North Korea, ensuring that the prime minister's office would ultimately be responsible. According to Tanaka, in order to preserve the secrecy of the negotiations, knowledge of the talks was limited to Koizumi, Fukuda, Deputy Chief Cabinet Secretary Furukawa, and the minister and administrative vice minister of foreign affairs. Tanaka met regularly with Koizumi, visits logged in the prime minister's schedule published in daily newspapers, in part to signal to Mr. X that he was working closely with the prime minister.[4]

But Tanaka needed assurances that Pyongyang would address Japan's concerns about the abductions, without which normalization would be impossible. Tanaka and his backers were not fixated on the issue, at least not to the exclusion of other issues like North Korea's nuclear ambitions and its growing stockpile of missiles. In October 2001, for example, Fukuda sought to discourage treatment of North Korea's abductions as terrorism.[5] But Koizumi had assured abductee families in March 2002 that normalization would not proceed without resolution of the abductee issue. He also placed Abe at the head of an inter-ministerial team, giving him a formal role advocating for the abductees within the administration, although he was absent from the small group overseeing Tanaka's negotiations.[6]

As North Korea gestured towards a proper accounting of its abductions, the possibility of Koizumi's traveling to Pyongyang grew. Koizumi increasingly recognized that meeting Kim might be required, to settle the issue and facilitate constructive discussions of normalization. After more than six months of meetings and numerous obstacles, in early June Koizumi accepted that traveling to North Korea for a summit with Kim was the best option.[7]

The negotiations over the wording of a declaration continued into the summer, but Koizumi instructed Tanaka to carry on. The joint declaration was a roadmap for normalization, merely identifying issues that would have to be addressed to establish diplomatic ties—historical reconciliation and the provision of reparations, security issues like the nuclear and missile programs, and the abductees. Crucially, at North Korea's urging, the final text of the declaration did not explicitly refer to the abductees but to "outstanding issues of concern related to the lives and security of Japanese nationals."[8]

By late August, a draft was ready and plans for Koizumi's trip were sufficiently advanced that the leadership team began to brief others—starting with Tanaka's senior colleagues—about Koizumi's plans.[9] Yachi Shotarō, then the director-general of MOFA's foreign policy bureau, wondered why the draft did not explicitly mention the abductees.[10] Nevertheless, the ministry had little choice but to cooperate and notified regional powers of the imminent summit. Before announcing publicly that Koizumi would go to Pyongyang, the government gave the Bush administration notice, first to Armitage and Assistant Secretary of State James Kelly, and then to Bush via a direct call from Koizumi.[11]

Having also informed the South Korean, Chinese, and Russian governments, the stage was set. The prime minister, said Fukuda on 30 August, would travel to Pyongyang the following month to "make the utmost efforts to break through the situation."[12]

* * *

Abe boarded the prime minister's plane on 17 September, at a considerable disadvantage having been entirely out of the loop until just before

Fukuda's announcement. Koizumi picked him to join his traveling party, but Abe had been unable to schedule time with MOFA for a briefing on the declaration. He did not see the draft until he was en route to Pyongyang and was taken aback when he saw that it did not explicitly mention the abductees, and included a Japanese apology to North Korea for historic wrongs that echoed the Murayama statement.[13]

Unlike a typical summit, in which advanced work by diplomats ensures little is left to chance, Koizumi could not be sure what awaited him. As Fukuda later said, "We were prepared for a situation in which, depending on the fate of the abductees, the prime minister might come home without signing the Pyongyang Declaration."[14] They expected to receive some information from the North Koreans regarding the abductees but even Tanaka—who had traveled to Pyongyang in late August—had no idea what they would hear. Would North Korea be forthright about the number of abductees and their fates? If any survived, would they be able to return home? Would Kim apologize?

Upon arrival at 9:15am, Koizumi and his entourage traveled to the lavish Paekhwawon state guest house. Shortly before Koizumi's first meeting with Kim, the North Korean government delivered the results of an investigation into Japan's "missing." Ma Chol-su, Tanaka's counterpart at North Korea's foreign ministry, delivered two sheets of paper, written in Hangul script, to Tanaka. It was a list of fourteen names: five living, eight dead, one whereabouts unknown, together with their birthdays and—where necessary—their dates of death.

Tanaka, stunned by the number of dead, told Ma that it would be necessary for Kim to speak clearly about the abductees in the meeting. He then hurried back, to report back to Koizumi and the delegation before the summit began at eleven o'clock. Tanaka first spoke with Abe, who asked for information about Yokota Megumi and Arimoto Keiko.

"Those other than the five [on the list] have died," said Tanaka.

Abe later told reporters of the great shock he felt upon receiving the news: "I felt like my heart was shaking."[15]

They hurried to bring the news to Koizumi, who was speechless at the death toll. After Kim opened the summit with cordial remarks welcoming Koizumi and praising the joint declaration, Koizumi responded harshly, describing himself as "utterly distressed" by the information from the North Koreans. Over the course of the hour-long meeting, Koizumi told Kim of his shock and demanded that Pyongyang continue its investigation, return the survivors, and guarantee that such acts would never happen again. As the session adjourned shortly after noon, he demanded an "outright apology" from Kim. But Kim ignored Koizumi's demands and made no mention of the abductees.

The meeting adjourned and the Japanese delegation huddled over lunch. It was at this moment, as Koizumi and his advisers considered how to approach the afternoon session with Kim that, in Abe's own telling, he strode on to the stage of history.

As the discussion proceeded, Abe, speaking at full volume to ensure that his advice would be picked up by North Korean listening devices assumed to be in the room, counseled Koizumi that he should be prepared to leave without signing if Kim failed to apologize in the afternoon session. As Abe tells it, he was the one who urged Koizumi to take this approach.[16]

Other accounts suggest more consensus. Tanaka says that he and other diplomats shared Abe's view that, if Kim refused to acknowledge the abductions, Japan would have to scrap the joint declaration.[17] Iijima similarly notes the delegation was largely in agreement that the prime minister should walk if there was no apology: "Strong opinions were expressed that, if there were no apology by Chairman Kim regarding the abductions, we should return home without announcing the Pyongyang Declaration and the like."[18] Koizumi himself was silent.

We may never know for certain what happened in that room, but following events were critical for Abe's rise to power, the culmination not just of his years advocating on behalf of the abductees but of arguing that the postwar Japanese state had failed its people and that a new approach was necessary. When the summit reconvened at two o'clock, Kim opened the session by reading a statement acknowledging the "appalling incident [sic]," recognizing that the abductions had been carried out by North Korean agents acting out of "misguided heroism," apologizing for the conduct of the agents, and pledging that such incidents would never recur.[19] The meeting concluded at half past three. At four o'clock, Fukuda conveyed the news to the families of the abductees back in Tokyo. At half past five, Koizumi and Kim signed the joint declaration. The delegation immediately departed.

While Koizumi's personal diplomacy in Pyongyang gave him the bump in approval that he sought, Abe ultimately won the day. Kim's admission that North Korea had abducted at least a dozen Japanese and that at least eight had died—including Yokota and Arimoto—prompted a shift in Abe's favor. Koizumi's trip was a pivotal moment in the new right's path to power, serving to both discredit the political and bureaucratic old guard that had sought to accommodate the North Koreans and embolden the new conservatives.

The Japanese public did not necessarily embrace Abe and his critique of the postwar state wholesale, but he had been right to point the finger at Pyongyang, and citizens turned against the Japanese government for uncritically accepting the information provided by North Korea. Koizumi was not immune from criticism, having signed the declaration despite being told that eight abductees had died in North Korea.

But MOFA was singled out for the strongest criticism, for its eagerness to normalize relations with a state that not only kidnapped Japanese citizens but was also—as the US would clarify weeks later—determined to build a nuclear arsenal that could directly threaten Japan. Tanaka bore the brunt of the public's anger, at one point weeping in response to questioning in the Diet.[20] The vitriol was not wholly innocent: in 2003, a right-wing group planted explosives in his garage.[21]

After the summit, Abe lobbied successfully within the administration for a hardline approach. Koizumi continued to follow Abe's lead. Notwithstanding Koizumi's intentions in signing the Pyongyang Declaration, subsequently it would be difficult for the Japanese government to pursue normalization with North Korea or even to prioritize other issues over the abductees in North Korea policy. Within ten days of Koizumi's trip, a cabinet committee on normalization affirmed that ministries and agencies would "exert all their power to resolve the abductee issue as a matter of the highest priority."[22]

Upon return from Pyongyang, Abe conferred with leaders of the abductee advocacy groups to brief them on the trip. In the meeting, he helped fuel further activism on the abductees, by giving reason to doubt North Korea's claims about which abductees had died.[23]

Meanwhile, the Koizumi government was trying to secure at least temporary visits to Japan for the five survivors, an increasingly urgent matter as the US prepared to confront Pyongyang on uranium enrichment. Tanaka notified Pyongyang that Japan would accept temporary returns by the five survivors, lasting seven to ten days. They arrived in Tokyo on 15 October, ten days after James Kelly visited Pyongyang to confront North Korea about uranium enrichment and two days before Washington announced that North Korea had admitted to its enrichment program.[24]

The Koizumi government was divided over how to treat the five abductees and the spouses and children they had left back in North Korea. Abe, together with Nakayama Kyōko, a former ambassador named as a special advisor to Koizumi on the abductees, and backed by the abductee families and the public, argued that the government could not possibly allow them to return to the DPRK. It was a matter of sovereignty. Japan's citizens had been kidnapped, and now, having been returned to their families and their homeland, the government could not possibly send them back.[25]

Fukuda, however, argued that the government had to honor the terms of the deal, after which it could negotiate for their safe return along with their families. Otherwise, he argued, North Korea could use the families left behind as hostages.[26] Tanaka worried about the impact breaking the agreement might have on his ability to negotiate with the North Koreans.[27] But he also worried what the domestic reaction would be if they sent the abductees back to North Korea and were then unable to negotiate their return.

As the end of the ten-day period approached, Koizumi's advisers debated. Finally, Abe's argument won the day and they told the prime minister that his government's policy should be to not return the abductees as the "will of the state." On 24 October, the Japanese government informed Pyongyang.

It was a personal victory for Abe, who had marshaled support to win a policy fight against members of the political and bureaucratic establishments. It was also a demonstration of his conviction that, to be truly independent, Japan must stand up and be willing to defend the lives of its people, including at the negotiating table. As Abe later wrote, "That day [24 October], I remember clearly that a newspaper reporter said to me, 'Abe-san, it seems that for the first time Japan has taken the initiative in diplomacy.' It was exactly that."[28] It took another eighteen months of negotiations and a further trip by Koizumi to Pyongyang in

May 2004 before the eight family members of the abductees were free to leave for Japan, but Abe took their arrival as vindication of his stance.

* * *

The drama in Pyongyang and the fate of the surviving abductees and their families transformed Abe. He was no longer just a junior lawmaker in a sub-cabinet post trying to raise awareness of a secondary political issue. Now, he was the courageous activist who had fought the indifference of Japan's establishment from within the halls of government on behalf of Japan's missing, and the parents and siblings who suffered from their absence. He was in high demand as a speaker and as a guest on leading television programs. He would keep fighting for a hardline approach to North Korea, via what journalist Funabashi Yoichi called the "pressure school," which argued that the government must be prepared to impose sanctions and take other coercive measures even while negotiating with Pyongyang. He again clashed with Tanaka, who wanted the administration to downplay its willingness to apply pressure. Again, Abe prevailed, and Koizumi embraced "dialogue and pressure" as his post-2002 approach to North Korea.[29] Abe's stock rose as North Korea dominated national attention and recession gave way to a sustained recovery.

* * *

Koizumi noticed Abe's new public image. In 2003, the prime minister's first term as LDP leader would close and he would face a party leadership election in September. He was beginning to think about the timing of a general election, which would have to be held by June 2004. Koizumi wanted to use his cabinet and LDP leadership team to strengthen his position heading into a campaign. Abe, still riding a wave of popularity, would be an asset. The question was how best to use him.

After three years in the same post, Abe was prepared to leave government and spend time in a party leadership role, to bolster his résumé. Shortly before the LDP's leadership election on 20 September, he spoke with Mori, who suggested that Abe could be a deputy secretary-general. Abe agreed, but asked Mori if he could persuade Koizumi to establish an LDP headquarters on abductee issues and make Abe its chief. Mori said he would, and it seemed the matter was settled.[30]

But Koizumi had other plans. Fresh from a party reelection fight that he won overwhelmingly, he wanted to surprise voters and remind them of his willingness to subvert the unwritten rules of Japanese politics. He looked to Abe, the young iconoclast, who would turn forty-nine the day after the LDP election and had just three electoral victories to his name.

The night of the LDP election, the prime minister called Abe at eleven o'clock. Abe was already in bed. After apologizing for calling late, Koizumi told Abe that he would "probably be asked to carry a heavy burden." Abe thought Koizumi was planning to name him as deputy secretary-general, but when Koizumi told him to forget that, he wondered if he would be remaining in government after all, perhaps as foreign minister. In fact, Koizumi asked Abe to become secretary-general.[31]

This request stunned Abe. He would not be the LDP's youngest-ever secretary-general—Tanaka Kakuei was appointed at forty-seven—but he would equal his grandfather's record of becoming secretary-general after just three electoral victories (and Kishi, after all, had enjoyed a long career by that time). Having been his father's secretary when Shintarō was secretary-general, he knew what the job entailed—and was sensible enough to recognize that it might be beyond him. It was not a matter of having had a short career. It was what a short career implied for his ability to perform the tasks required.

Second in the LDP hierarchy, the secretary-general is, historically, responsible for mobilizing resources for elections and managing the parliamentary party, as well as controlling party funds and advising the party leader on the distribution of appointments.[32] The LDP's secretaries-general have therefore been heavyweights with extensive networks and broad support from across the party. The office holds awesome institutional power, but the occupant needs extensive personal power to wield it. Its occupants have tended to be at the sweet spot between having had a distinguished career and having a promising future: of the thirty-one men in the post before Abe, ten went on to become prime minister, and the remaining twenty included luminaries like Abe's father and Ozawa Ichirō.[33]

While Abe had acquired fame during his time as deputy chief cabinet secretary, it was questionable whether he had the skills to carry out these duties. He had not, after all, been appointed to a single cabinet post when Koizumi called him. If he accepted Koizumi's offer, he would not only have to deal with Koizumi's enemies in the party—and, having just won a second term, the prime minister was determined to reenergize his campaign to "destroy" the old LDP, ensuring more internal conflict—but he would have to do so in the face of resentment from senior politicians for having jumped the queue.

The following day, Mori called Abe to confirm Koizumi's offer and convince him to accept. "This is what it is to be a politician. If you refuse, as a politician, the chance probably won't come again," he said. "This is destiny."[34]

When Koizumi called again, Abe accepted.

* * *

Abe's appointment was genuinely surprising, not least to his mother who recognized how unusual it was for such an inexperienced politician to serve as secretary-general and worried that he would not be equal to the task.[35]

Koizumi was unconcerned. After all, destroying the old LDP meant destroying old conventions, like those that mandated that the secretary-general must be sufficiently experienced or, according to a convention that emerged after the strife of the 1970s, never from the same faction as the prime minister. What Koizumi wanted most from Abe was his youthful vigor and national following, to help him lead the LDP into elections.

Koizumi inherited from Mori the diminished ruling coalition that emerged from the 2000 election. The LDP went into the 2003 election with a slim majority of 247 seats in the 480-seat lower house, and still governed in coalition with Kōmeitō and the Conservative Party. The Democratic Party of Japan (DPJ) had continued to cement its status as the LDP's main rival, seemingly marking the arrival of a competitive two-party system. In July 2003, the DPJ leadership, sensing a snap election was imminent, joined ranks with Ozawa. A minority disliked him, but his arrival not only boosted the DPJ's numbers, it brought a shrewd strategist into the party's leadership. The DPJ was a significantly more potent threat to the LDP with Ozawa than without him.

Facing elections for both houses of the Diet in the coming year—the upper house would hold its triennial elections in July 2004—Koizumi all but admitted that he tapped Abe as secretary-general to use his post-Pyongyang popularity against the DPJ's rise. In fact, Mori, who remembered his debts to Abe's father and grandfather, was wary of Koizumi's plans, feeling especially protective of the younger Abe, who was also a key player in his plans to ensure his faction's dominance continued after Koizumi—although Mori wanted Fukuda, not Abe, to succeed Koizumi.[36]

But Koizumi's bid to leverage Abe's reputation failed. As had been widely anticipated, Koizumi dissolved the lower house on 11 October. The election would be held on 9 November. Abe worked hard on Koizumi's behalf, but there was little he could do to halt the DPJ's rise. While the Democrats fell short of a lofty goal of 200 seats, they still took 177, the most of any postwar challenger. The LDP, meanwhile, lost ten seats and fell short of an absolute majority, which it only recovered when the Conservatives merged with the LDP after the election.

Koizumi remained in power, but the DPJ had won. For a growing number of voters, it was a plausible alternative, and got two million more votes than the LDP in proportional representation voting. Exit polls suggested that the DPJ had become the preferred choice of most floating voters, precisely the bloc Koizumi had hoped to attract with his campaign against the LDP's old guard.[37]

The upcoming upper house elections would therefore be a crucial test for Koizumi—and for Abe. At first, it seemed Koizumi and Abe would be campaigning under more favorable circumstances. Early in 2004, the Diet was gripped by a debate over Koizumi's determination to send a Self-Defense Forces (SDF) detachment to support the reconstruction of US-occupied Iraq. However, that debate gave way to scandal when it was discovered that leading politicians across the political spectrum had neglected to pay public pension premiums.[38] The scandal led both Fukuda and DPJ leader Kan Naoto to resign in May. Ozawa succeeded Kan, but promptly resigned when it emerged that he too had failed to pay. Okada Katsuya, a colorless former MITI official, took over.

The DPJ's leadership carousel dented the trust it had gained in 2003, and Koizumi's second visit to Pyongyang in May—which led to the arrival in Japan of eight family members of the previously recovered abductees—meant North Korea was back in the headlines, playing to Abe's strengths. By the time of the upper house campaign, Abe had been in office nearly a year and could wield more control over the LDP's election apparatus. The LDP therefore set an optimistic goal, to win at least fifty-one seats in the 242-seat upper house and strive to win the fifty-six needed to secure an absolute majority for the first time since 1989. But the LDP not only missed its target, it lost to the DPJ, which won larger shares in both constituency and proportional representation (PR) voting (in the case of the latter, by a nearly eight-point margin) and edged out the LDP with fifty seats to the ruling party's forty-nine. The ruling coalition still had a majority, but the DPJ was rapidly winning the confidence of the public and could entertain thoughts of taking power.

Abe was finished as secretary-general. With Mori's help, when Koizumi changed his cabinet in September, Abe was not dismissed entirely, but rather was demoted to acting secretary-general, one step down from the secretary-general but higher than the post Abe had been prepared to accept in 2003. Koizumi's bid to borrow Abe's popularity to survive the elections failed. With the Democrats ascendant, there may not have been much Abe could have done to change these outcomes, but someone had to take responsibility—and Abe was a natural scapegoat.

It was unhelpful that he also struggled with what was the most important parliamentary issue he had to manage, Diet ratification for the dispatch of SDF personnel to Iraq.

* * *

Koizumi had supported Bush's decision to invade Iraq and his administration planned to support postwar reconstruction by sending Japan's armed forces months before the war began. Based on the 1992 International Peace Cooperation law, which had enabled Japan to participate in UN-sponsored peacekeeping operations, Koizumi dispatched SDF transport planes to deliver humanitarian relief from the start of the war.

But Koizumi wanted to do more to support international efforts to rebuild Iraq after Bush declared an end to major combat operations on 1 May, and so—when a UN resolution called for international cooperation on reconstruction—his administration drafted an Iraq special measures law that would enable Japan to contribute with "boots on the ground." The bill was largely uncontroversial and passed on 26 July 2003.[39]

But sending troops was not a simple process. As the security situation worsened, it was unclear whether any part of the country would be secure enough for the SDF to be deployed in a non-combat role, satisfying restrictions on its overseas activities. Koizumi downplayed the issue as he sought a new term as LDP leader in September and contested the general election in November, but the DPJ and other opposition parties were increasingly against an SDF deployment and the public also soured on the idea, particularly after two Japanese diplomats were murdered in November.[40] A poll conducted by NHK in December 2003 found that just seventeen percent supported a prompt dispatch of troops. Fifty-three percent wanted the government to wait until order was restored and another twenty-eight percent thought troops should not be sent at all.[41]

Abe naturally supported dispatch of the SDF to Iraq. As he later explained, he believed Japan needed to deploy its forces not because of the alliance with the US, but because as a rich democracy it had a responsibility to work with the international community to rebuild Iraq—and because Japan's dependence on Middle Eastern fossil fuels gave it an interest in the region's stability.[42] As LDP secretary-general, he had to marshal support within the party for a decision by Koizumi to send soldiers.

Koizumi was determined to deliver on his commitment, even after the public turned against an Iraq mission. By 9 December the cabinet had approved the deployment. But the special measures law mandated that the Diet would also have to authorize the mission. Abe would have to manage the legislative process as the parliament considered a high-profile issue of grave significance, a debate that not only would attract vocal opposition from the DPJ, but could also face dissent from within the ruling coalition, since Kōmeitō and some LDP lawmakers were concerned for the safety of Japan's service personnel.

Despite its official pacifism, Kōmeitō signed off on the mission after its chief visited the town of Samawah, near Basra, where the SDF would provide basic services, including healthcare and water. With Kōmeitō on board, Koizumi could proceed and in January 2004, an advance team was dispatched to Iraq. It soon reported that Samawah was secure enough for the SDF detachment. The Diet's approval was not necessary in advance—it could be finalized after the troops had departed—and the outcome was never in doubt. However, the debate could influence the mission's domestic legitimacy. Opposition lawmakers challenged the government's account of conditions on the ground and argued that if the deployment were in fact to a conflict zone, it would violate the constitution. But their efforts to delay a vote failed, and the resolution cleared the Diet on 9 February.

Abe still had to quell a small but embarrassing parliamentary rebellion. Three senior LDP members of the lower house—Katō Kōichi, a former secretary-general and defense agency chief; Koga Makoto, another former secretary-general; and Kamei Shizuka, who had just been defeated by Koizumi in the September leadership race—were not in favor of the SDF's dispatch to Iraq. They were significantly more senior than Abe, who had only won his fourth term in November. The three lawmakers questioned the wisdom of dispatching the SDF when the security situation in Iraq was so uncertain. They also argued that the SDF was being sent mainly to satisfy US demands for "boots on the ground."[43]

Abe pleaded with the three elders to support Koizumi's decision, but when the House of Representatives voted on 30 January, Katō and Koga were present but abstained and Kamei absented himself entirely. Abe then had to decide how to deal with the rebels, since some LDP members wanted them punished for embarrassing the government in a high-profile vote. After deliberation, Abe issued a formal reprimand to the three rebels, a slap on the wrist according to the party's by-laws, which was taken as a sign of his inability to maintain discipline and command the respect of more senior lawmakers.[44]

If Abe struggled with two of the secretary-general's most important roles—managing elections and maintaining parliamentary discipline—his brief tenure as secretary-general was enormously successful in one respect: it raised his profile in Washington immensely.

In late April 2004, during Japan's "Golden Week" holidays—when many Japanese parliamentarians use the recess to travel to the US and other destinations—Abe received a red-carpet reception in Washington. While there, he delivered an address at American Enterprise Institute, the Bush administration's favored think tank, in which he touted Koizumi's efforts to make the US–Japan alliance more equal, argued against the Japanese people's "allergy" to discussions of national security, and for revision of Japan's constitution. "It has now become clear that the safety and security of the country cannot be preserved under the present Constitution," he said.[45]

He also met a series of high-level administration officials, including Secretary of Defense Donald Rumsfeld, national security adviser Condoleeza Rice, and Armitage, as well as senior congressional Republicans. Rice was particularly impressed by him. Their meeting was scheduled to last fifteen minutes but ran for forty-five. Afterwards, Rice said to Japan's ambassador to the US of Abe, "I like him. He's tough."[46]

The esteem in which Abe was held by the Bush administration was demonstrated the following year, when he returned and met again with Rice (now the secretary of state), Rumsfeld, treasury secretary John Snow, new national security adviser Stephen Hadley, and Federal Reserve chairman Alan Greenspan. He also met with Vice President Dick Cheney at the White House, which led to an unplanned discussion with the president himself, an extraordinary itinerary for a politician who had recently been demoted.[47] Whatever doubts members of his own party harbored about his prospects, high-ranking US officials saw Abe as an emerging leader who would remake Japan into a more capable ally.

* * *

As it turned out, Abe's demotion was a blessing in disguise. With fewer responsibilities, he could rejoin the ranks of the new conservatives and agitate on issues like North Korea, historical memory and education, and constitutional revision. His reputation as a conservative firebrand may, ironically, have been helped by a report by the *Asahi Shimbun* in January 2005 that claimed in January 2001, Abe, then the deputy chief cabinet secretary, and Nakagawa Shōichi had pressured NHK to edit a documentary that featured a mock trial focused on imperial Japan's use of the sex slaves known as "comfort women" across Asia during the Second World War. The two conservatives had met with NHK executives before the film aired, and thereafter references to the emperor's culpability were removed, commentary critical of the claims in the mock trial added, and portions of the testimony of the former comfort women who participated in the mock trial were cut.

Far from being cowed by claims he had interfered with press freedom, Abe hit back at his critics. He disputed the paper's account—the documentary, he said, had come up in the context of a meeting regarding the broadcaster's budget, not in a meeting convened to discuss the film—and argued that the mock trial and the documentary were pro-North Korea propaganda intended to silence their increasingly effective activism on behalf of the abductees.[48] Four years in positions of responsibility had done little to temper Abe's ideological fervor. If anything, having emerged from his tenure as secretary-general with his pride bruised but his future still bright, Abe seemed more willing than ever to fight for a new Japan.

He remained the most prominent advocate for the abductees, agitating for sanctions and leading the charge to castigate North Korea, when an examination of what Pyongyang claimed were Yokota Megumi's remains yielded no trace of her DNA, leading the Koizumi government to accuse North Korea of defrauding Japan.[49] This led to a new wave of public outrage, and both houses of the Diet called upon the administration to impose unilateral sanctions, even as Japan participated in the six-party nuclear talks and despite a promise made by Koizumi during his second trip to Pyongyang that he would not impose sanctions.[50]

* * *

The demotion also made Abe mostly a spectator of the climactic battle between Koizumi and the "resistance forces" in the LDP to privatize Japan's postal system.

The postal system was intimately linked with Tanaka's machine. Tanaka, serving as postal minister under Kishi, had given the LDP's backing to the nation's postmasters, who became a quasi-formal arm of the party's electoral machine. The postal system gathered enormous sums of money through its savings and insurance arms, which then financed pork-barrel projects that benefited other LDP constituencies. Koizumi wanted to destroy this system root and branch, breaking up and privatizing the postal system's divisions and forcing them to compete with private parcel carriers, insurers, and banks. In the process, he aimed to destroy an interest group that he believed had sapped the LDP's dynamism.[51]

Koizumi had made no secret of this ambition; it featured in every one of his leadership bids. It was never far from his mind during his premiership, and, as the end of his second term as LDP leader approached, he decided that it was finally time to act. The challenge was enormous, given the wide reach of the postal system and the extensive relationships between postmasters and both LDP and opposition lawmakers. "It would literally be the world's biggest privatization project," wrote Takenaka Heizō.[52]

Once again, Koizumi turned to Takenaka. In September 2003, Koizumi tasked Takenaka to use the CEFP to develop a privatization plan. The basic policy on privatization was approved by the cabinet a year later, at which point Takenaka—who had been elected to the House of Councillors that summer—received a new portfolio for postal privatization.[53]

In 2005, the spring session of the Diet was dedicated to postal privatization. Koizumi's proposals faced pitched resistance from the LDP at each stage in the process, first in the LDP's policy committees and then in its general affairs council, which customarily signs off on all legislation to be submitted to the Diet by the cabinet. Resistance in the council was so intense that its chairman had to break with the council's tradition of unanimous consent to force the reform bills through by simple majority vote.

In early May, the fight shifted to the Diet. In the lower house, Koizumi overcame weeks of opposition boycotts, and then, once the special committee on the bills could sit, he faced withering criticism from opposition and LDP lawmakers. He had to extend the parliamentary session, originally scheduled to close on 17 June, to 13 August. After more than 100 hours of debate, Koizumi and the LDP agreed to revisions, which sent the bills back to the LDP's general affairs council, which again forced the bills through by majority vote on 28 June. The bills went back to the Diet, where they finally went before the whole house on 5 July. They passed by a 233-to-228 margin, with thirty-seven LDP members—including four sub-cabinet officials—voting against the reform package, and another fourteen abstaining.

The odds were longer in the upper house. The ruling coalition's margin for error was smaller, and the LDP's upper house caucus was more dependent on traditional constituencies like the postmasters. If eighteen or more LDP members defected, his bills would fail. Koizumi threatened to dissolve the lower house and call a snap election if they were defeated. A snap election would not directly impact the upper house, but it would scramble the LDP's internal dynamics and could even risk the party's majority—and forestall a possible no-confidence motion following a legislative defeat.

Koizumi prepared quietly for a snap election as the upper house debated, secretly recruiting candidates to challenge the lower house lawmakers who had opposed the reforms.[54] As the parliamentary session neared its climax, Mori, convinced that the LDP would lose a snap election, visited Koizumi on 6 August to advise him against playing his trump card. Koizumi disagreed.[55]

Finally, on 8 August, the House of Councillors voted, defeating privatization by 108 for and 125 against, with eight absences and abstentions. Twenty-two upper house LDP members voted against the reforms, another eight abstained. That evening, Koizumi told the LDP that he would call a snap election and withhold the party's endorsement from any lawmaker who opposed privatization. To dissolve the Diet, he had to overcome objections raised by his cabinet, including conservatives like Nakagawa Shōichi and Asō Tarō, but ultimately the only obstacle to unanimous consent was the agriculture minister, who was forced to resign.[56] A general election was called for 11 September.

Despite his reform's defeat by his own party's lawmakers, Koizumi was defiant. That evening, he oddly but memorably invoked Galileo's defiance in the face of heresy charges to demonstrate his faith in the rightness of his cause. He would prevail, winning a majority for the ruling coalition despite the expulsion of dozens of LDP members, or he would resign.[57]

* * *

Abe was quiet as the privatization debate reached its climax. Even as Koizumi battled to move his legislation, Abe, judging by his contributions to the *Yūkan Fuji* evening paper, was focused mostly on hot-button cultural issues like the Yasukuni shrine and the continuing debate regarding his involvement in changes to the NHK documentary. He addressed the impending upper house vote and the possibility of a snap election in a 30 July contribution, but was cautiously optimistic about the bills' passage and incredulous that the thirty-seven postal rebels—whose ranks included some of his closest allies among the new conservatives—would be expelled from the party.[58] Many of these new conservatives had been skeptical about the Koizumi–Takenaka neoliberal program from the beginning, as they feared the impact "market fundamentalism" would have on traditional communities and values and worried that it would leave Japan vulnerable to predation by Wall Street.[59]

Abe was ambivalent, torn between loyalty to his patron and loyalty to his fellow new conservatives. On 12 August, he dutifully made the case for Koizumi's aggressive approach to reform but lamented having to campaign against his friends. "As an official responsible for elections," he wrote, "It is not easy to arrange candidates in such a short time. Moreover, I am pained that my friends are among the rebels."[60] Abe was more critical in private but felt unable to speak out. Even after the election, when asked how he differed from Koizumi, Abe only mildly rebuked his patron, suggesting that his was a more "cooperative" style.[61]

Koizumi's postal privatization crusade had exposed a fault line among the LDP's conservatives. Koizumi, in his willingness to visit Yasukuni shrine and to push the envelope on Japan's security policies, was a useful partner but he was ultimately different from the new conservatives. He was a neo-liberal reformer who wanted small government, decentralization, and privatization. As he proved in 2005, everything else was secondary. These differences between Koizumi's neo-liberalism and the new conservatives had been managed for much of Koizumi's tenure, but after the fight over postal privatization it became difficult to rebuild the alliance.

* * *

It quickly became clear that Koizumi had achieved something remarkable. While it initially seemed the DPJ could exploit the schism, both the DPJ and the postal rebels were overwhelmed by Koizumi's political prowess. To challenge the rebels, Koizumi sent new LDP candidates—

many of them young, charismatic women—who quickly became known as "Koizumi's assassins." Koizumi barnstormed the country, giving rousing stump speeches before adoring crowds. His visits, carefully targeted at marginal seats, were a crucial and perhaps even decisive factor in the outcome.[62] The battles between the assassins and the postal rebels were made-for-TV drama, making it virtually impossible for the Democrats to be heard above the din.

The vote would be a referendum on Koizumi's reform politics. Koizumi was asking the people whether they supported his vision of a strong prime minister who would do battle with the entrenched interests and would reshape the LDP into a reform party rooted in Japan's metropolises rather than its rapidly depopulating hinterlands.

Turnout surged and Koizumi won in a landslide. The LDP took 296 seats—its most ever—and, with Kōmeitō's 31 seats, the ruling coalition had a supermajority in the lower house for the first time, enabling it to overrule the upper house. The DPJ suffered a devastating loss of seats, its total falling to 113. Okada resigned, and the party entered a period of soul searching. If Koizumi's new LDP was here to stay—and, having defied his critics to lead the LDP to its best performance ever and ushered into office a bloc of reform-minded newcomers known as the "Koizumi children," it seemed it was—the DPJ faced an existential crisis.

As it turned out, however, the birth of the new LDP was far from complete—and Abe would pay the price for the schism of 2005.

8

THE SUCCESSOR

On the morning of 12 August 2006, Abe addressed his supporters in Shimonoseki. "At the time of my first election, I declared that I would inherit the ambitions of my father. I have firmly held on to these ambitions. I am determined that in early September, that I want to explain this ambition to all the people."[1]

With this announcement, Abe effectively declared his candidacy for the Liberal Democratic Party (LDP) presidential election just over a month away. On 1 September, he made his candidacy official: "There has been advice that I am too young, and it would be better if I waited a little longer, but, sincerely and directly taking the hopes of many people, I have decided to run." If elected, he would be Japan's youngest postwar prime minister and its first born after 1945. He would run as an unabashed new conservative, promising—under the slogan of "a beautiful country, Japan"—to revise the constitution, build an equal partnership with the US, and exercise top-down political leadership to "leave behind the postwar regime."

By the time he declared his candidacy, the race was all but won. While Mori hoped to persuade him to defer to Fukuda Yasuo, Abe rejected his entreaties. Mori had, after all, advised him in 2003 that when an opportunity presented itself, he should take it because it might not come again. In July, Fukuda declared he would not seek the party's leadership. With Fukuda out, Abe could count on the undivided support of his own faction—now the LDP's largest—and was increasingly attracting support from other factions. Fukuda's decision was a green light for uncommitted members to embrace Abe, as lawmakers sought to be on good terms with Koizumi's heir apparent. As the LDP looked for a leader who could be the face of a national campaign, neither foreign minister Asō Tarō nor finance minister Tanigaki Sadakazu proved able to match Abe's appeal. Polls conducted in August and September showed that majorities of fifty-three and fifty-four percent respectively identified Abe as the best choice to succeed Koizumi. His rivals lagged far behind.[2]

Despite his frontrunner status, he did not provide a detailed program for government. Abe issued a four-page manifesto, paltry compared with Asō and Tanigaki, whose manifestos each ran for more than twenty pages. He had already published a best-selling campaign book, but it was more memoir and credo than manifesto. The pamphlet mostly contained slogans that were thinly veiled imitations of Koizumi's. "No fiscal reconstruction without growth." "A strong Japan, a Japan that can be relied upon." "Establishing political leadership."[3]

But the pamphlet showed that while Abe was presenting himself as an iconoclastic new conservative, he would also approach governing cautiously. He had not forgotten his Weber. While he highlighted conservative ambitions like constitutional revision and education reform, in this document, Abe carefully avoided commitments on the most significant and controversial issues.[4] He proposed that a consumption tax hike should be studied by a commission as part of a broader review of tax reform. Similarly, an advisory council should study reinterpretation of the constitution to let Japan exercise its right of collective self-defense. He refused to say whether he would worship at Yasukuni shrine. And, in his first press conference as prime minister, he said of constitutional revision, "As I have already stated several times during the presidential election, I would like to exercise leadership as the LDP's president in order to put [constitutional revision] firmly on the political schedule. However, I think that henceforth it will be fundamentally party-centered and we will proceed with discussion with other parties."[5] He wanted to fulfill his political mission, but to do that he had to wield power.

In the end, it was less an election than a coronation, fitting for a political prince who began his campaign reminding voters of his late father's unrealized dreams. When the LDP gathered on the ninth floor of the LDP's headquarters to vote on 20 September, Abe crushed his rivals, winning 464 of 702 total votes, which included 267 of the 402 votes cast by his fellow lawmakers. Six days later, he was elected as Japan's ninetieth prime minister.

But, despite a mandate from the LDP and robust public support—in the first polls after his election, his approval ratings reached as high as seventy percent, with disapproval under twenty percent across the board—he inherited a divided party that had spent Koizumi's last year in office grappling with his legacy and an anxious nation.[6] Despite his desire to sidestep controversy, his honeymoon would be short-lived.

* * *

By the time the postal privatization passed on 14 October 2005, Koizumi had less than a year left in office. Having spent most of his tenure in bitter conflict with adversaries and with his career-long ambition realized, Koizumi turned to the selection of an heir who would safeguard the achievements of his political revolution.

The stakes of his final cabinet reshuffle were, therefore, unusually high, his last chance to groom a handpicked successor. When he announced a new government on 31 October, it included three of his most plausible successors. As foreign minister he tapped Asō, a grandson of Prime Minister Yoshida who was the same generation as Koizumi but traveled in new conservative circles. As finance minister he retained Tanigaki, a moderate whose faction descended from those formed by Yoshida's lieutenants and who had already served as finance minister for two years.

Finally, he appointed Abe as his chief cabinet secretary, giving him a central role in coordinating the government's policies across the bureaucracy, communicating with the press, and laying the groundwork for the transition to a new prime minister. Notably absent was Fukuda, who had been out of government but remained Mori's choice to succeed Koizumi.

Abe's appointment to a cabinet-level position suggested the premiership was his to lose. Polls showed he was the overwhelming favorite. As chief cabinet secretary, Abe spent Koizumi's last year in a highly visible role, cementing his status as frontrunner. The post also served as a crash course in economic policymaking, since, as he admitted to a biographer in 2004, "I am not very familiar with the economy, finance, and fiscal issues."[7]

After the drama of postal privatization, the hardest work of the Koizumi government was finished. The administration had to prepare the groundwork for postal privatization but otherwise Koizumi did not seem prepared to launch major new initiatives.[8] Having driven the postal rebels out of the party, Koizumi enjoyed unchallenged dominance of the LDP for the first time since he took power and he sought to use his last year to improve the machinery of government.[9] His advisers were left to debate how to grapple with his legacy.

* * *

By 2006, the Koizumi boom was on the track to become the longest in postwar Japanese history. Japan's real GDP had grown by more than seven percent over the previous five years. The boom depended heavily on trade with China after it joined the World Trade Organization in 2001, when China became an important market for both Japanese finished goods and components for manufacturing goods for export to the US and other markets.[10]

But recovery changed the public's expectations of what the government's priorities should be. Voters might have tolerated Koizumi's hard-charging reforms when Japan was still in the post-bubble doldrums, but the Japanese people were increasingly worried by the price of Koizumi's policies. What impact had the recovery had on a society that had experienced a decade of slow growth and deflation? As Koizumi entered his final year in office, the emergence of an unequal society in a country that once prided itself on being universally middle-class became a national obsession.[11]

Japanese people saw inequality all around them. They saw it in the swelling ranks of "non-regular" workers, the part-timers, temps, and other workers who enjoyed few of the usual protections and benefits. They saw it in the creation of a new vocabulary for disaffected youth, as "NEET" and "Freeter" became commonplace terms.[12] They saw it in a growing homeless population. They saw it in the dramatic rise in suicides, particularly among those in their prime working years.[13] And they saw it in the vanishing names of their towns, as depopulating villages and towns across the country merged into new municipalities in order to provide services for their increasingly elderly inhabitants.[14] These anecdotal impressions, of a society in which many—including the young, the growing population of retirees, and the inhabitants of depopulating regions—were being left behind, were reflected in data.[15]

Japan may have been recovering, but the society that emerged from the "lost decade" was different. In 2006, seventy-four percent of respondents told the *Asahi Shimbun* that income inequality was growing, and of those respondents, seventy percent said it was a problem.[16] Despite having just led the LDP to its largest parliamentary victory ever, Koizumi was blamed for growing inequality, since he not only promoted reforms that enabled employers to reduce their wage bills by hiring non-regular workers, in his zeal for "small government" he also curbed spending on Japan's safety net. But in parliamentary questioning, Koizumi both disputed reports of widening inequality and welcomed inequality as the healthy result of a more competitive society.[17]

* * *

The men jockeying to replace him could not be so cavalier. It was particularly awkward for Abe, who had to uphold the official line but as the presumptive favorite had to communicate some comprehension of the issues he would confront in office.

In parliamentary proceedings, he too downplayed economic data that pointed to widening inequality, but admitted that the government had to address the emergent "lost generation" of underemployed young Japanese who had missed their one shot of landing stable, secure jobs.[18] He began using a new term—再チャレンジ, "re-challenge"—to describe the need to give all Japanese second chances to succeed, whether in the job market or as entrepreneurs, and began to distance himself from Koizumi's dogmatic pursuit of "small government."[19]

"For those who cannot do it alone, it is necessary to extend a helping hand as mutual aid," Abe said in a Diet debate in March 2006. "And for this reason, we are completely committed to maintaining a safety net for employment and small- and medium-sized businesses and have also been working on social security reform for the creation of a more dynamic system."[20]

"Re-challenge" would be his pet project. He convened an advisory council, staffed with officials from across the government, to draft reforms to promote new opportunities for the disadvantaged. Its recommendations were ineffectual. But it showed that while Abe would carry on Koizumi's reforms, he would take a gentler approach and focus on improving the quality of life for those Japanese at risk of being left behind.

The term was more useful as political marketing. In June, a group of LDP lawmakers close to Abe established the Parliamentary League in Support of Re-Challenge. Ostensibly intended to address concerns about inequality, the group—organized mainly by Suga Yoshihide, a lawmaker who had risen from local politics in Yokohama—soon became the nucleus of Abe's campaign. Its initial membership included ninety-four legislators from both houses, spanning factional lines and including many veterans of the new conservative activist groups.[21]

Abe's interest in the structural barriers that denied many Japanese second chances and discouraged risk-taking seemed sincere. Around the time that the parliamentary league formed, Abe's memoir 『美しい国へ』 [*Towards a Beautiful Country*] was published and quickly became a best-seller.[22] While the book focused predominantly on his beliefs, his history with the abductee movement, and his vision for foreign policy, it closed with an appeal to build a "re-challenge" society. As he wrote, portentously, in the book's penultimate paragraph, "I would like to change from a single-track society in which a person's life can be determined by a single failure to a society in which ways of working, ways of learning, and ways of living have become multi-tracked."[23]

Abe's focus on inequality was part of a process of articulating an economic philosophy for the first time. He was careful not to criticize Koizumi directly—his book contains surprisingly few mentions of his patron—but Abe nevertheless distanced himself from Koizumi's more controversial views. Whereas Koizumi touted small government and "[leaving] to the private sector what the private sector can do," Abe drew a distinction between the "night watchman state" and a "super high welfare state" like Sweden, and situated Japan and his own views somewhere in between. He viewed the state as having an essential role to play in national life, explicitly citing not only Kishi's role in building a social safety net but also the influence of socialist ideas on his grandfather's thinking. Comparing Kishi with his grandfather's friend, Socialist Party lawmaker Miwa Jūso, Abe writes: "Miwa gave counsel and was active as a lawyer and as a politician in order to save the needy people before his eyes. However, in the case of my grandfather, he tried to restructure the state that brought forth that poverty."[24]

His emerging philosophy, which he called "open conservatism," contained contradictions. In an interview published shortly before the LDP's leadership election, for example, he said that his "re-challenge" policies would not simply distribute subsidies to the unfortunate but would rather use tax incentives and other regulatory policies to promote entrepreneurial activity and more market-based solutions.[25]

The result was a syncretic—or, less charitably, opportunistic—mix. He did not share Koizumi's neo-liberalism but wanted Japanese companies to be more competitive. He rejected Kamei's and Hiranuma's hostility to "market fundamentalism" but shared their concerns about preserving Japan's uniqueness in the age of globalization. There were hints of the pragmatic philosophy that would guide his economic program after 2012. But in 2006 his philosophy was inchoate, and, while many of the LDP members would welcome retrenchment after Koizumi's relentless reform drive, the party's leaders were sharply divided over where to go after Koizumi. Abe's "Koizumi-lite" approach would also be a feeble challenger for the more full-throated big government populism that the Democratic Party of Japan (DPJ) would advocate once Ozawa Ichirō became its leader in April 2006.

* * *

Despite being the frontrunner, Abe was a bystander to the most significant debate of Koizumi's valedictory year. In the spring and summer of 2006, leading LDP policymakers were preoccupied with cleaning up the government's finances. Japan's debt-to-GDP ratio, which had been only thirty-nine percent when the financial bubble burst in the early 1990s, was 131 percent by 2006. Koizumi, who had campaigned on a pledge to slow the growth of the national debt by limiting the annual issuance of new bonds to ¥30 trillion, had stabilized the ratio by the end of his tenure. He steadfastly refused to consider another consumption tax hike and therefore relied on spending caps, discretionary spending cuts (particularly for public works but also for defense), premium hikes, and less-visible tax increases to curb deficits.

However, with the government facing greater outlays as baby boomers approached retirement, the next prime minister would have to do more to reform the tax, social security, healthcare, and welfare systems. Even as Koizumi strengthened his grip on the LDP after postal privatization, the party was soon divided again over how his successor should address the national debt.

Abe could have been more active, by dint of having a seat on the Council on Economic and Fiscal Policy (CEFP). The CEFP, its stewardship of the postal privatization process complete, was the main arena for the debate, as the main prize was the blueprint for the following year's budget, which the council drafted every spring. But the council's minutes show that in the nineteen meetings from January until the basic policy's release on 7 July, Abe was virtually silent in the debate over how the Japanese government should raise and spend its revenues.

The fight was between Yosano Kaoru, who succeeded Takenaka as minister for state for economic and fiscal policy and therefore oversaw the CEFP, and Nakagawa Hidenao, a veteran Mori faction lawmaker from Hiroshima who Koizumi named as the LDP's policy chief after the 2005 election.

Yosano, a diplomat's son and devout Christian of nearly seventy, was a fiscal hawk who wanted the government to adopt a medium-term target to eliminate Japan's primary budget deficit, reform government taxation and spending, and introduce another consumption tax hike. Tanigaki, the finance minister and aspirant for the LDP's leadership, backed him, as well as to other fiscal hawks in the LDP, bureaucracy, BOJ, and the business community. The fiscal hawks were generally not interested in deficit reduction for its own sake. They wanted to reduce anxiety about the sustainability of the social security system and raise revenue to better support younger Japanese citizens.

Nakagawa cut a more colorful figure. He had resigned as Mori's chief cabinet secretary in 2000 when television networks broadcasted audio recordings of him with a mistress. There were also rumors of yakuza connections.[26] Nakagawa was a full-throated supporter of the Koizumi–Takenaka line and wanted an aggressive response to the postal rebels. He had also become the de facto leader of the Club of 83, the name given to the "Koizumi children" elected in 2005. Under

Nakagawa's leadership, the group was poised to serve as the shock troops for carrying on Koizumi's revolution.

Nakagawa, together with Takenaka and other advisers in Koizumi's circle, articulated what became known as the "rising tide" view, arguing that Japan could grow its way out of the government's fiscal difficulties via monetary easing, spending cuts via administrative reform, and deregulation and other supply-side policies to jumpstart faster growth, instead of raising taxes.[27]

Both partisans recognized that policies adopted in Koizumi's final year could shape the succession fight. They sparred publicly over the dangers of reflation, the importance of fiscal prudence, and the costs of financing a safety net. In their first press conferences following the October 2005 reshuffle, both Yosano and Tanigaki said the next government should increase the consumption tax in its first budget. Nakagawa pushed back, arguing that any consumption tax hike would have to wait until after deflation was conquered, excessive spending was cut, and state assets privatized. Takenaka referred to those who were calling for a tax hike as "the resistance forces in changed form."[28]

Yosano, the minister responsible for the CEFP, had an edge as the council began its deliberations on the 2006 basic policy. Takenaka was still on the council, but Nakagawa was only a party official. But Takenaka—and Koizumi, who formally chaired the CEFP—resisted Yosano. Yosano, incredulous at the "rising tide" camp's belief that spending cuts and economic growth alone could reduce the deficit, challenged Nakagawa to identify spending cuts that could be included in the basic policy, a role that he gladly embraced, prompting ministry of finance (MOF) officials to joke that he was "Budget Bureau Director Nakagawa."[29]

In the end, the two camps fought to a draw when the basic policy was finalized in July 2006.[30] Yosano's main accomplishment was including a target for bringing the primary fiscal balance—the balance of current spending and current revenue excluding interest payments—into surplus by 2011. The government would also "safely reduce" the debt-to-GDP ratio. Tax hikes remained an option—although to "the minimum extent possible"—but in the near term, the government would commit to trying the rising tide's preference for budget cuts and supply-side reforms. The plan envisioned more than ¥11 trillion in spending cuts over five years. It was an unsatisfactory compromise, ensuring that the struggle between the fiscal hawks and the rising tide faction would continue after Koizumi's departure.

Despite his reticence in CEFP meetings, as the LDP election approached, it became clear that Abe broadly shared the "Rising Tide" school's approach. "I cannot agree with the way of thinking that says from the start, 'a such and such percent consumption tax hike is inevitable,'" he told business executive Fujita Tsutomu. "It weakens efforts to cut spending by any means necessary."[31]

Abe shared another belief with Nakagawa's camp, namely opposition to the Bank of Japan (BOJ) curbing its zero interest rate policy (ZIRP). The BOJ had introduced a ZIRP for the second time in 2001. In November 2005, however, BOJ Governor Fukui Toshihiko hinted at raising interest rates, even though inflation was barely positive. Nakagawa and Takenaka, already arguing that Japan could grow its way to fiscal sustainability, knew that for their approach to work, inflation had to rise to at least two percent, as inflation would erode the value of the government's debt and also boost tax revenues as incomes drifted into higher brackets. That required the BOJ to continue providing easy credit.

* * *

Nakagawa and Takenaka both publicly challenged Fukui and warned that it might be necessary to revise the BOJ law, to curb its independence and require it to pursue a two-percent inflation target. Here too they were at odds with Yosano, who backed Fukui and publicly suggested that Japan no longer faced a deflationary spiral and was perhaps seeing signs of an asset bubble.[32]

Abe was less reticent in the monetary policy debate. In early March 2006, an unnamed senior government official—widely believed to be Abe—told reporters that the BOJ was being too hasty. Koizumi too said that the BOJ should be cautious about raising rates prematurely. Abe reportedly wanted Koizumi to exercise the government's right to send a representative to the BOJ's policy board meeting to submit a motion to postpone a vote until the next meeting, but was dissuaded by MOF officials who feared the market fallout from heavy-handed government intervention in rate-setting.[33]

The BOJ and its fiscal hawk allies prevailed. On 9 March, the bank voted to raise interest rates. Nevertheless, the debate left a strong impression on Abe, who continued to wonder whether the BOJ's independence should enable it to work at cross purposes with the national government.

* * *

Koizumi's foreign policy legacy was also ambiguous. On the one hand, the US–Japan relationship was stronger than ever, thanks to his investment in personal ties with Bush, willingness to commit the SDF to allied operations, and effective shelving of the trade disputes that once threatened bilateral amity.[34] In his final trip to the US in June 2006, Bush and Koizumi celebrated their relationship with a trip to Graceland, Elvis Presley's mansion in Memphis, Tennessee, where the flamboyant prime minister donned the King's oversized sunglasses, gyrated his hips, and crooned "Love Me Tender" to an amused Bush.[35]

But within Asia, Koizumi left his successor an increasingly challenging environment. The second North Korean nuclear crisis continued, and the region's powers were engaged in an ultimately futile effort to convince Pyongyang to curb its nuclear ambitions. The six-party talks had begun in August 2003, bringing together North Korea, South Korea, the US, Japan, China, and Russia to defuse the crisis even as North Korea moved ever closer to building its own nuclear weapons. The talks yielded a statement in September 2005 in which Pyongyang acknowledged that it had nuclear weapons and agreed to "verifiable denuclearization," while the US assured Pyongyang of its non-hostile intent and, along with Japan, agreed to engage in bilateral talks that would address outstanding obstacles to normalization.[36]

The joint statement took a heroic effort on the part of the six parties, with long gaps between meetings amidst stonewalling by Pyongyang. Once the joint statement was concluded, the process broke down completely, when the US imposed sanctions on North Korea and Banco Delta Asia in Macau in response to money laundering operations, freezing $25 million in North Korean accounts. Pyongyang left the talks pending the return of its frozen assets.[37] This time, walking away led to a series of gestures demonstrating its increasingly lethal capabilities, including a barrage of ballistic missile tests in July 2006 and, finally, a small nuclear test—its first ever—on 9 October 2006, two weeks after Koizumi left office.

There was little Koizumi could have done to advance normalization with North Korea, though domestic fury over the abductees meant Japan was more inflexible than other parties. Abe, still the leading advocate for the abductees, would face unique challenges in trying to reboot Japan's relations with North Korea, not least a gap with the US. Although the Bush administration had its share of hawks who wanted to scuttle any deal with North Korea, its representative at the talks was Ambassador Christopher Hill, who wanted a diplomatic settlement if at all possible.

Koizumi left his successor with similarly fraught relationships with China and South Korea. Koizumi's annual visits to Yasukuni had enraged both governments, and by 2005, not only had the Chinese government told Tokyo that it could not schedule bilateral meetings with the prime minister but Beijing had also become increasingly tolerant of anti-Japanese protests. This was at least partly a tool for pressuring Japan to change its behavior on history issues, but also a means to block Japan on unrelated issues like its bid for a permanent seat on the UN Security Council.[38] China could still rely on friends in the Diet, the bureaucracy, and the business community who were interested in a constructive relationship, but the relationship was attenuated at the highest levels.

Japan's relations with South Korea were not quite as deeply frozen as its relations with China, but the pursuit of bilateral cooperation on North Korea and other issues was still marred by Koizumi's Yasukuni visits, South Korean protests regarding Japanese history textbooks, outstanding issues related to compensation for wartime comfort women and forced laborers, and the active dispute over the Liancourt Rocks (Takeshima in Japanese, Dokdo in Korean). While South Korean President Roh Moo-hyun was initially willing to meet with Koizumi, eventually he too withdrew, amidst deepening mistrust in both countries.

This was especially the case after Koizumi fulfilled his promise to visit Yasukuni on 15 August 2006. The visit led to strenuous protests from governments across Asia—although China, looking ahead to a new prime minister, was relatively muted—but Koizumi was defiant, castigating Chinese and South Korean leaders for their immaturity in refusing to meet with him. Koizumi's visit to Yasukuni increased pressure on Abe, since his reputation as a conservative hawk who visited the shrine regularly sparked fears that as prime minister, he could prolong the deep freezes in Tokyo's ties with Beijing and Seoul.

Whoever succeeded Koizumi would not govern freely. He would have little choice but to grapple with the outgoing prime minister's legacy. Abe, publicly focused on his job as chief cabinet secretary, said little of what he would do if he succeeded Koizumi. Privately, he was deep into preparations for his leadership bid, conferring with informal advisers and supporters to plan his administration.

He consulted with two very different groups of advisers. One, nicknamed the "gang of five," included new conservative intellectuals Itō Tetsuo, Nakanishi Terumasa, Nishioka Tsutomu, Shimada Yōichi, and Yagi Hidetsugu. They were involved with Nippon Kaigi and other right-wing organizations, and primarily focused on the new conservatives' culture war: constitutional revision, historical memory, and education. This group, which met three times during the summer of 2006, worked on a policy program for the prime minister-in-waiting and devised some of the slogans—perhaps most notably, "breaking free of the postwar regime"—that Abe would unveil after assuming the premiership.

He also met, separately, with a group that involved some of his closest allies in the LDP, including Shiozaki Yasuhisa, then a vice minister of foreign affairs, and Seko Hiroshige, an upper house member with a background in corporate PR who was working in the LDP's public affairs office. This group focused more on political reform, devising plans for building on Koizumi's efforts to strengthen the prime minister's office and modernize the LDP.[39]

Abe had also begun to refine his image. Yajima Hisashi, the head of public relations firm PRAP Japan, wanted to highlight Abe's youth and present his candidacy as a symbol of generational change in the LDP. He provided extensive speech and media training, working to change Abe's tendency to speak too quickly, particularly when excited.[40]

* * *

Marx suggested that no leader can choose the conditions he faces, and this was true for Abe in September 2006. He took power thanks to

Koizumi's patronage, and to the historic parliamentary majority that Koizumi had won in 2005. The public expected Abe to govern as Koizumi's successor, perhaps making some adjustments to the economic program but carrying on his predecessor's fight against entrenched interests. He could not claim to have a mandate for constitutional revision, "patriotic education" reforms, or the other fights that the new conservatives were spoiling for.

Also, Abe could not ignore Kōmeitō, whose votes the government needed to control a supermajority in the lower house and a majority in the upper house. Kōmeitō had already functioned as a brake on Koizumi, for example, by constraining his government's actions in support of US wars in the greater Middle East and stalling debate on education reform that would make fostering patriotism a goal of the education system.[41] The relationship had not always been easy but both the LDP and Kōmeitō were willing to preserve their coalition. Abe, more conservative than Koizumi, had to work even harder to win his coalition partner's trust, not least because Kōmeitō's leaders were particularly nervous about party morale ahead of nationwide local elections in April 2007 and upper house elections in July.

He also faced challenges within the LDP itself. Despite his victory on a "rising tide" platform, the party was divided on taxation, social security, and deficit reduction. The party was not of one mind on Koizumi's legacy. Koizumi may have won the battle for postal privatization and expelled the rebels, but not all LDP members were happy about it. At the same time, the Club of 83 was still a formidable bloc, and well represented at the highest levels when Abe named its de facto boss Nakagawa as the LDP's secretary-general. Abe had also to manage a party full of big egos and big personalities—which he had struggled to do as the LDP's secretary-general—and many of the more senior party leaders resented Abe not only for his hawkishness but perhaps more importantly for his impudence at having leapt to the premiership without having paid his dues. In short, the scale of Abe's victory concealed a restive party that could agree on who should lead it but could otherwise agree on little else.

Meanwhile, by the time Abe took power, the DPJ had recovered from the existential crisis it faced after its landslide defeat in 2005. When Okada resigned to take responsibility for the defeat, the party turned to Maehara Seiji, a forty-three-year-old technocrat many hoped would show the DPJ to be the party of generational change and new ideas. But Maehara was distrusted by the DPJ's ex-socialists, and, when he tried to attack the LDP's secretary-general with corruption allegations based on fake emails, Maehara's position quickly became untenable. He resigned in March 2006 after just six months as leader.

But the DPJ soon recovered, largely because of one man—Ozawa. On 7 April 2006, he defeated Kan Naoto, one of the party's founding fathers, then brought Kan and fellow party founder Hatoyama Yukio into a leadership troika to stabilize the party. Ozawa was not entirely trusted, but he was far more adroit than Maehara, adept at forging alliances and an astute campaigner and election strategist. He knew how to wield power and to attract important electoral constituencies and was as hungry as ever to drive the LDP from power. His clash with Abe was veritably Shakespearean: the former LDP wunderkind-turned-opposition leader doing battle with the LDP's newest star, who happened to be the son of one of Ozawa's former patrons.[42]

As leader, Ozawa forced compromises on the issues that most divided the party; strengthened the DPJ's headquarters so it could exercise more control over election campaigning, finance, and policy; and, in contrast with Maehara, with whom Koizumi considered forming a grand coalition to divide the DPJ, sought to sharpen distinctions with the LDP to appeal to independents. From the moment he became opposition leader, Ozawa was fixated on the 2007 upper house elections as a chance to strike the LDP—which would have to defend seats it had won in 2001 thanks to the surge in support for Koizumi—and lay the groundwork for an upset at the next general election. Abe would face a DPJ very different to the party so easily outmaneuvered by Koizumi in 2005.[43]

Managing these circumstances demanded deft leadership by Abe. It also required a capable cabinet and LDP leadership team around the prime minister, not least because of his relative youth and inexperience. However, Abe relied heavily upon the young new conservatives who had long been his closest friends and allies rather than opting for more experienced, senior LDP members who might not share Abe's ideological commitments, but would keep the prime minister's attention on what should have been his primary focus from the moment he was elected—winning the upper house elections.

Instead, the group that was quickly derided as Abe's "cabinet of friends" reinforced the prime minister's ideological preoccupations and generally struggled to read the public mood, maintain message discipline, and control the LDP's backbenches. His cabinet included Suga, who was minister of internal affairs; Yamamoto Yuji as minister of state for financial services; Takaichi Sanae as minister of state for science and technology policy; and Amari Akira, who became the minister of economy, trade, and industry. He also retained Asō, his rival for the leadership, who sympathized with the new conservatives on many issues but was older and had his own power base. The cabinet was dominated by Abe's own faction—now the Machimura faction, once Mori passed control to veteran lawmaker Machimura Nobutaka—which had seven of seventeen cabinet posts, with the rest divided primarily among factions that had backed Abe's campaign from early on.

While the "cabinet of friends" became shorthand for Abe's questionable personnel choices, the problem was most acute at the prime minister's office. The reforms of the 1990s had dramatically expanded the prime minister's ability to set the policy agenda and to control the bureaucracy and the ruling party. But Abe would show that stronger institutions alone do not guarantee stronger leadership. The prime minister had to be capable of using the bolstered premiership.

Abe lacked a strong gatekeeper. He filled key executive posts with longtime friends, who vied to dominate Abe's staff, but none had the stature to dominate the policymaking process or control access to the prime minister. One deputy chief cabinet secretary was Shimomura Hakubun, an education specialist who had worked with Abe on history textbooks and the fight against a "masochistic" view of history since the 1990s. Of his five special advisers, four came from the Machimura faction, including Yamatani Eriko and Nakayama Kyōko, who had worked with Abe on the abductee issue; Seko, who advised Abe on public relations; and Koike Yuriko, an Arabic-language specialist who had been a favorite of Koizumi's and who served as Abe's de facto national security adviser, pending the creation of a US-style national security council.

* * *

Managing Abe's executive team was the responsibility of Inoue Yoshiyuki, his executive secretary, and, most importantly, Shiozaki Yasuhisa, the chief cabinet secretary. Both were unconventional choices.

Inoue was ill suited to serve as executive secretary. The post had become particularly essential as the prime minister accumulated power. A former Japan National Railways employee on a technical, non-elite career track, Inoue transferred to the prime minister's office in 1988 when the railways were privatized. At the time, there was little prestige being an official permanently attached to the prime minister's office. But in this capacity Inoue became Abe's secretary in 2000, working closely with him on the abductee issue. When Abe became chief cabinet secretary, Inoue became his secretary and stayed on when he was elected prime minister.

However, the qualities that Abe liked in Inoue—particularly that he was not an elite bureaucrat who would put his ministry's interests ahead of the prime minister's—hindered Inoue in his new role. He lacked the network and the gravitas to serve Abe effectively. He was particularly inept at vetting prospective cabinet appointees, an essential task.

On paper, Shiozaki seemed a more inspired choice. Like Abe, he came to the post without having served as a cabinet minister, but he had a successful career as a BOJ official and was still viewed as a likely future leader of the LDP and highly regarded as a policy wonk. He had a long acquaintance with Abe: they first met while working as their fathers' secretaries when both were members of Nakasone's cabinet in the early 1980s. But Shiozaki's reputation as a policy wonk was a liability in the chief cabinet secretary's job—whose work mainly concerns coordinating the policymaking process among different and often competing actors—and he was seen as arrogant and aloof by the officials he had to manage. As a relatively junior lawmaker, he also lacked the relationships and eminence that would have strengthened the prime minister's grip over his own party, compounding Abe's problems as a relatively junior prime minister.

The party leadership itself was in better hands, particularly through Abe's appointments of the two Nakagawas (no relation), Hidenao as secretary-general and Shōichi as chief of the policy research council. Hidenao was amply qualified for the post, being older, wiser, and more experienced than Abe. His appointment also signaled further erosion of the norm that the prime minister and the secretary-general should come from different factions, since—although Abe had nominally left the Machimura faction upon becoming prime minister—Nakagawa belonged to the faction. Meanwhile, Shōichi had served in senior posts, but, more importantly, he shared Abe's new conservative beliefs and was perhaps Abe's single closest friend in politics, limiting the potential for friction between the government and its backbenchers.

Notwithstanding the relatively capable picks for the LDP's leadership posts—and the strong approval ratings that Abe enjoyed after taking office—there was uneasiness even from Abe's supporters about his cabinet, particularly Shiozaki's appointment as chief cabinet secretary. "I do not think," concluded Mori, "that this administration will go smoothly."[44]

* * *

Despite these anxieties, Abe's administration enjoyed a successful launch. Ten days after his inauguration as prime minister, he made his first overseas trip on 8 and 9 October, traveling to Beijing and Seoul for meetings with Chinese President Hu Jintao and South Korean President Roh. Working through administrative vice foreign minister Yachi Shōtarō, with whom Abe had worked closely on the abductee issue, he communicated his desire to stabilize Japan's relations with both countries and convinced them to accept Abe's deliberately ambiguous approach to Yasukuni as a sincere declaration of his determination not to provoke either government. The trip was punctuated by North Korea's first-ever nuclear test on 9 October, which played to Abe's favor: he was not just committed to fixing relationships that had been damaged by Koizumi's insouciance, he was expanding Japan's freedom of maneuver by improving its ties with its neighbors at the very moment the North Korean nuclear crisis entered a new, more dangerous phase. It seemed the young prime minister was more capable of pragmatic statecraft than his critics had feared.

However, Abe's honeymoon did not last. On 23 October, Abe suggested that he was looking into clearing the way for some of the postal rebels to return to the LDP. He was uncomfortable with Koizumi's excommunication of his friends for their opposition to postal privatization, and immediately after taking control of the party had begun to work towards rehabilitation of some of the rebels, including Hiranuma Takeo, Furuya Keiji, and Etō Seiichi, who had been among his closest political compatriots.

It was a disaster. Just over a year after Koizumi had expelled them, Abe was scheming to readmit "resistance forces" to the LDP. The public might not have been particularly enthused about postal privatization, but Koizumi's determination to "destroy the old LDP" had resonated with voters. Now his handpicked successor was betraying his work. The issue publicly divided Abe's advisers: Nakagawa Hidenao, the Koizumi loyalist, warned Abe against readmitting the rebels, while Nakagawa Shōichi, who shared his affection for many of the ousted, favored their unconditional readmission. The rift embarrassed the prime minister and confirmed fears that his administration could not handle the divisions that Koizumi had been able to manage. The situation was made worse by Abe's indecisiveness, particularly after internal polling showed that readmitting the rebels would result in a significant blow to his approval ratings.

Eventually, he tried to find a compromise. The rebels seeking to rejoin the LDP would have to sign a loyalty oath, pledging their approval of the postal privatization bills, their support for Abe's governing agenda, obedience to the party's rules, and their contrition for acts of disloyalty to the party. Hiranuma categorically rejected these conditions and never returned. Abe's new conservative allies, including many in the government, also opposed these conditions and the result was a free-for-all that continued for much of November, as the LDP divided into warring camps between those who opposed the rebels' readmission, those who wanted their unconditional readmission, and those who favored conditional return. It was an entirely self-inflicted wound that exposed party divisions, pitted the prime minister against his own secretary-general, and inaugurated the steady erosion of his support that would continue for months. By the start of 2007, his approval ratings were well below fifty percent, a steep fall from the seventy-percent support he had upon taking office.

The loyalty oath was finally presented to twelve postal rebels on 27 November, even as Koizumi loyalists continued to protest their return. All but Hiranuma signed the oath and were readmitted. But the damage was done. Abe had not only failed to manage the LDP's internal divisions but had actively enflamed them and then, when faced with the consequences of his actions, he struggled to decide as the party's factions battled publicly. Doubts about Abe's management skills were deepened by the resignation of two minor political appointees in December, which, as it turned out, marked the beginning of a torrent of personnel issues in the following year.

Yet Abe's first months in office were not without durable achievements. In December, the Diet replaced the 1947 Basic Act on Education with a revised law and elevated Japan's defense agency, the civilian organ responsible for managing the SDF, from an agency attached to the prime minister's office into a full-fledged ministry. The former had been sought by conservatives since before the occupation ended in 1952. The new act simply outlined the fundamental principles that would guide the national education system and therefore did not have immediate policy implications, but the new conservatives in Nippon Kaigi and other organizations welcomed a law that made the promotion of patriotism and instruction in ethics basic goals for the education system. By the same token, critics charged the Abe administration with wanting to return to the statist principles enshrined in the Meiji-era Imperial Rescript on Education. But even this legislation, a genuine victory for the new conservatives, was marred by scandal: the Abe administration had to fend off accusations that it and the Koizumi administration overstated and misrepresented public support for the new education law.

Thus, as 2006 ended, the basic contours of Abe's government were apparent. He had shown a capacity for pragmatic statecraft, but was prepared to use his historic parliamentary majority in the service of a deeply conservative agenda, even as he faced a growing loss of public trust. It was a volatile mixture, and it was only a matter of time before it would spark a crisis of public trust, triggering a vicious cycle that would eventually prove fatal to his government.

9

INFERNO

"Nowadays," the *Asahi Shimbun* reported in August 2007, "it seems that among middle and high school students the phrase 'KY' is being used. 'K' means *kuuki* [air] and 'Y' means *yomenai* [cannot read]. If there is a classmate who, among close friends, acts selfishly without considering the surrounding environment, 'That kid is KY' is how it is used."

"This young person's slang is also being used when commenting on Prime Minister Abe," the paper noted.[1]

Less than a year into his premiership, Abe had become the "KY Prime Minister." In 2007, he struggled to retain cabinet ministers, who repeatedly made inappropriate public comments or faced corruption allegations. He angered even Republicans in the US with hair-splitting comments about imperial Japan's treatment of wartime sex slaves and mishandled a scandal involving the mismanagement of public pension records. And, when faced with a Democratic Party of Japan (DPJ) campaigning on quality-of-life issues, he campaigned on constitutional revision at a time when citizens were afraid that they would not receive their pensions.

By the time the *Asahi*'s item ran, Abe was still failing to "read the air," clinging to power with grim determination amidst calls to take responsibility for an electoral defeat and resign.

* * *

As 2007 began, however, it seemed Abe might have turned a corner. In his New Year's message, Abe highlighted his achievements, noting his trip to Beijing and Seoul, international coordination to pressure North Korea following missile and nuclear tests, the creation of the defense ministry, and the first-ever revision of the postwar Basic Law on Education.[2] Several days later, he struck an aggressive note. "Although upper house elections are planned for this year," he said, "I am determined to do my best to squarely and steadily build a record of achievements." He would not leave difficult issues for after the elections.

He promised more substantive changes to the education system. The administration would formulate a new strategy to encourage young Japanese to start families. A new growth strategy would deliver more equitable growth. He would move constitutional revision forward by establishing a process for conducting national referenda, necessary to ratify amendments but for which no process had ever been established. Finally, to restore confidence in the social security system, he would break up the social insurance agency (SIA).[3]

After the New Year holiday, Abe traveled, visiting Belgium, France, and Germany for consultations with European leaders as well as senior EU and NATO officials to articulate his vision for a more globally active Japan that would work with like-minded countries to "support a free and prosperous world based on the fundamental values of freedom, democracy, basic human rights, and the rule of law."[4] Foreign Minister Asō had already begun articulating a vision for "values-based diplomacy" and an "arc of freedom and prosperity" along the maritime rim of the Eurasian continent, which would serve as the basis both for a more global alliance with the US and a more autonomous Japanese foreign policy.[5]

Ten days later, a new parliamentary session opened. In his policy address, Abe not only restated his agenda, but also laid out a grandiose political vision. Looking back at the postwar institutions that had produced the prosperity enjoyed by his generation and subsequent generations, Abe declared that the institutions were no longer effective. "Now the time has come to boldly review these post-war regimes all the way back to their origins, and set sail on a new course," he argued. "In order to realize 'a beautiful country, Japan,' my mission is none other than to draw a new vision of a nation which can withstand the raging waves for the next 50 to 100 years to come." In making this case for sweeping, top-down change he recalled the Meiji Restoration—citing Meiji-era scholar Fukuzawa Yukichi on the Meiji spirit of "[taking] on difficult tasks optimistically"—situating his vision of a state-led conservative revolution in Japan's past. And he subtly referenced his grandfather's vision of democratic leadership, stressing that he would "stand at the fore and lead the way."[6]

But the Japanese public was not eager for a twenty-first-century restoration. Most voters, grappling with widening inequality and demographic change, wanted assurances that their livelihoods were secure, not the grandeur of taking part in a project to build a new Japan.

Even as he articulated this vision, cracks began to grow in his government's foundation. Abe would spend the year focused not on advancing a new restoration but on defending his cabinet ministers—and his premiership—from scandal allegations and accusations of insensitivity to public sentiment. In fact, on 29 January, three days after Abe's policy address, Ozawa blasted Abe for hypocritically discussing greater opportunities for working women in his address while employing a cabinet minister—Health, Labor, and Welfare Minister Yanagisawa Hakuo—who, in a gaffe heard around the world, referred to women as "baby-making machines" the day after Abe's speech.[7]

Meanwhile, in early January, the communist newspaper *Akahata* and then other, more mainstream publications reported that the political support groups of Ibuki Bunmei, the education minister, and Matsuoka Toshikatsu, the agriculture minister had reported suspicious office expenses. Ibuki stonewalled and said the questionable expense arose from irregular but legal accounting practices.[8] Matsuoka's own claim that unusually large "office expenses" were an expensive water filtration system was soon exposed as a lie. The sums of money involved were relatively minor—in 2005, Matsuoka's main support group claimed roughly ¥40 million, or $368,000 in current dollars—but the absurd lie, a history of suspected corruption, and Abe's decision to close ranks around his agriculture minister made Matsuoka an inviting target.[9] Abe insisted that the minister had broken no law, which only attracted further questioning from the opposition. Opposition lawmakers lambasted Matsuoka and Abe, hoping to force Matsuoka's resignation.

* * *

Even as the Diet was preoccupied with Matsuoka's office expenses, Abe was grappling with the consequences of his own rhetoric, which would blacken his reputation not only across Asia but also in the US.

In November 2006, the Democratic Party had won control of both houses of the US Congress for the first time since 1994. In early 2007, the impact of this would be felt in Tokyo. In January, Mike Honda, a Democratic congressman and third-generation Japanese-American, introduced H.Res. 121.[10] Honda's resolution, though nonbinding, called upon the Japanese government to "formally acknowledge, apologize, and accept historical responsibility in a clear and unequivocal manner for its Imperial Armed Force's coercion of young women into sexual slavery," particularly by having the prime minister offer an official apology, reject attempts to deny the "sexual enslavement and trafficking" of the comfort women, and commit to educate present and future generations about this shameful history.[11]

Honda's resolution reflected concerns about the new conservatives and their mobilization against the Kōno statement, particularly as the mandate of the Asian Women's Fund, the semi-public entity established by the Japanese government to distribute compensation to former comfort women, would expire on 31 March. To support the resolution, three former comfort women—Lee Yong-soo, Jan Ruff O'Herne, and Kim Koon-ja—testified about their treatment at the hands of Japanese military on 15 February.[12] However, the resolution languished after the hearing.

* * *

Thanks to Abe, its fortunes were revived. The ministry of foreign affairs (MOFA) and the Kantei had initially ignored it, but in February, new conservatives pressured Abe to respond more forcefully. After an internal debate in which Shiozaki—well connected in Washington—advised caution and in which his deputy Shimomura called for a more confrontational response, Abe sided with Shimomura. He dispatched Seko, his special adviser on strategic communications, to consult with US officials, some of whom told Seko that the administration could not get involved in a minor legislative matter. Importantly, he did not meet with leading figures on Capitol Hill. It is unlikely that Seko changed any minds in Washington and, through his meetings with news organizations, he may have directed their attention to the Honda resolution and the possibility of a standoff between Congress and a major US ally.[13]

The new conservatives then forced Abe's hand. On 28 February, the Parliamentarian Group to Consider Education and the Way Forward for Japan petitioned Abe demanding that the government drop the Kōno statement's claim that Japanese military and civilian authorities had forcibly taken women to serve in brothels.[14] Despite having indicated that he would continue to abide by the Kōno statement, Abe decided to endorse the substance of the petition without necessarily changing government policy: "The fact is, there is no evidence to prove there was coercion."[15]

Abe was trying to satisfy his beliefs while doing what was necessary to safeguard the national interest, steering a middle course between the new conservatives, who would have preferred that Abe scrap the Kōno statement entirely, and Japan's allies and neighbors, who wanted Japan to adhere to a more humble approach to historical wrongdoing.[16] In this instance, however, his middle course—adhering to the letter of the Kōno statement while undermining its substance—was folly. There was no acceptable middle course. His approach triggered a swift global backlash that gave the DPJ another issue with which to attack him.

Instead of retreating, Abe reaffirmed his initial statement. On 5 March, questioned by a DPJ lawmaker, Abe stood by his position that there was no evidence of coercion by Japanese authorities and attacked the *Asahi Shimbun* for relying on the discredited account of comfort women "hunting" by former soldier Yoshida Seiji. When pressed, he admitted that there might have been coercion "broadly interpreted" but claimed it was the fault of contractors, not the Japanese government. Perhaps even more damaging than his words was his attitude. Abe reacted petulantly, described the Honda resolution as not based on objective facts, suggested his questioner was showing contempt for Japan's postwar achievements, and said the line of questioning was a waste of time.[17]

This fueled another round of critical press coverage and guaranteed that other lawmakers would press him for his views, hoping to goad him into embarrassing sound bites. Abe's comments breathed new life into the Honda resolution, which had only twenty-five co-sponsors at the end of February but had picked up fifty-two from both parties by the end of March.[18] It also led to a scathing editorial from the *Washington Post*, calling out Abe's hypocrisy for demanding answers from North Korea on the abductees while evading responsibility for imperial Japan's own abductions. "If Mr. Abe seeks international support in learning the fate of Japan's kidnapped citizens," the paper noted, "he should straightforwardly accept responsibility for Japan's own crimes—and apologize to the victims he has slandered."[19] The Japanese embassy in Washington challenged the editorial, but Abe had already lost control of the narrative.

Increasingly, the issue threatened the US–Japan relationship. The risks became apparent when J. Thomas Schieffer, the US ambassador, expressed his hope that Abe would continue to abide by the Kōno statement and sharply disagreed with the prime minister's position on the meaning of coercion. "I take the word of the women that testified," he said.[20]

Abe was in a hopeless position. Even American conservatives struggled to defend a prime minister engaged in an arcane discourse on the meaning of coercion in order to evade responsibility for a shameful episode from his country's past, particularly after hearing the testimony of three deeply sympathetic, elderly women in February. For many Americans, Abe was effectively calling the former comfort women liars, which alienated even his friends in Washington.[21]

Finally, at the end of March Abe began to back down and offer token words of apology to former comfort women. His first official visit to Washington—scheduled for late April—was rapidly approaching and if he were unable to defuse the issue, it could overshadow the trip. On 11 April, Yachi met with Schieffer and confirmed that Bush was still uneasy about the toxic atmosphere that could surround Abe's visit. This led his administration to relocate much of the summit to Camp David, limiting the potential for disruptive protests.[22]

While Yachi did much of the legwork to ease Washington's concerns, it was only after meeting with Bush, and with members of Congress, on 26 and 27 April that Abe finally calmed tensions. In a joint press conference with the president, Abe expressed his apologies that the comfort women "were placed in that sort of circumstance" and Bush effectively exonerated him: "He told me what was on his heart about the issue, and I appreciated his candor. And our jobs are to, obviously, learn lessons from the past. All of us need to learn lessons from the past and lead our nations forward."[23] This statement hardly qualifed as the apology the Honda resolution sought, but was sufficient to blunt the resolution's momentum.[24]

Abe's trip to Washington was a rare moment when it seemed he might be able to persevere, despite scandals and falling approval ratings. Bush and Abe did not have the same easy rapport Bush and Koizumi had enjoyed, but Abe could nevertheless retake control of the agenda and demonstrate his ability to manage Japan's relationship with its most important ally, at a particularly sensitive moment for the alliance due to denuclearization talks with North Korea.

The Bush administration had been willing to take a more flexible approach in order to restart the six-party talks, resulting in an announcement in February that the US would return funds that had been frozen. With the Abe administration unwilling to compromise without more progress on the abductees, a rift between Washington and Tokyo was possible, and there was in fact little love lost between Abe and Assistant Secretary of State Christopher Hill, the point man for the six-party talks.[25] Nevertheless, both Abe and Bush sought to smooth over these issues—"We expect North Korea to meet all its commitments under the February 13th agreement, and we will continue working closely with our partners," said Bush—and it appeared that Abe could continue to rely on statecraft to improve his position at difficult moments at home.

Indeed, by the end of April, it appeared that Japan's relationships with both the US and China were on a stable footing, as earlier in the month Abe had hosted Chinese Premier Wen Jiabao for meetings that strengthened the foundation for building what Abe called a "mutually beneficial relationship based on common strategic interests."[26] He was even on track for a substantial domestic achievement: the lower house had passed a bill establishing procedures for holding national referenda and it was on track to move smoothly through the upper house.

* * *

The calm that followed April's diplomacy was short-lived. In the final two months of the Diet session, Abe went from crisis to crisis, limping to the start of the upper house election campaign in July. The most significant blow was the "vanishing pensions" scandal.

Political reformers had targeted the SIA for years. They saw the agency as notoriously ineffectual stewards of a service that would become increasingly essential as the country aged and as growing numbers of Japanese moved into non-regular employment that increased their dependence on the national basic pension system. The agency's reputation had been damaged irreparably by the 2004 non-payment scandal, and by revelations in 2005 that more than 1,500 agency officials had viewed private information in pension records, particularly those of politicians and celebrities.[27] There was a growing consensus across the political spectrum that significant reforms were needed. Abe had hoped to use this consensus to move a reform bill through the Diet ahead of the upper house elections.

However, Abe would soon have to grapple with a scandal decades in the making that would simultaneously guarantee that the agency would be broken up and that Abe would find it difficult to take credit for reforms. Since the SIA had begun digitizing pension records in the 1970s, its officials had been sitting on an enormous problem. A growing number of records were not connected to any worker or pensioner, due to errors in transcribing names, missing addresses, or multiple numbers assigned to individuals who changed jobs. The problem became increasingly evident after 1997, when the agency began to merge records for the three major pensions systems into a unified system. By 2007, the agency had a massive problem, but its efforts to solve it—sending postcards to verify information—were woefully inadequate. Due to the error, pensioners failed to receive benefits they were owed, a serious issue in a country already uneasy about widening inequality and growing poverty.

The Abe administration seemed blindsided when, in the spring of 2007, the public became alarmed about the missing pensions. Abe, however, had been warned of the issue; a report was delivered to the prime minister's office soon after he took office, although it may not have properly accounted for the scale of the missing records.[28] Abe—with his background as a member of the LDP's social security policy "tribe"—should have been more sensitive to the risks. Pension reform was in fact one of a handful of concrete policy proposals that Abe included in his 2006 book.[29]

Meanwhile, well before the business reporter-turned-DPJ-lawmaker Nagatsuma Akira first questioned the administration about the missing records on 14 February 2007, he had already raised the issue in Diet proceedings, in June 2006.[30] When the SIA and the ministry of health, labor, and welfare (MHLW) submitted reports in February that showed the scale of the problem they were quietly working to fix, Nagatsuma already appeared to have a clear idea of what was being covered up, even as Abe assumed the matter could be addressed without public outcry. In fact, Nagatsuma all but pleaded with the prime minister to declare a state of emergency and provide workers with a simple accounting of their pension accounts, to hasten the process of identifying the owners of the unidentified records. Abe replied that declaring an emergency would unduly alarm the public and that the government's verification process was managing the task. It was perhaps the single greatest error of his first premiership.

While Nagatsuma did not appear to get much traction at first, major newspapers reported on the issue for the first time thanks to his questioning, noting that an internal agency investigation suggested there could be issues with as many as 50 million pension records.[31] There was little immediate reaction. The Abe government said the problem was being addressed appropriately and proceeded with plans to reform the SIA by semi-privatizing the agency, making it into a public corporation and stripping its officials of their status as central government bureaucrats.

The reform plan, however, gave the DPJ—which opposed this status change, preferring instead to create a revenue agency that would manage the government's collection of tax revenues and premiums—an opportunity to keep the public's attention on the missing pensions. Why did the government think, asked Nagatsuma, that it could restore public trust in the pension system by taking responsibility for managing that system out of the public sector?[32] To call attention to the issue, the DPJ submitted legislation in early May to aid the "victims of missing pensions records," and public awareness began to grow.

Finally, on 25 May, the SIA finally admitted the full scale of the problem: at least 50 million pension records could not be linked to any individual, while another 14 million records remained only in hard copy because they could not be digitized.[33] It was only at that point that Abe began to appreciate that the missing pensions had become a serious liability, as millions overwhelmed government helplines with questions about pension accounts. Abe and the LDP tried to go on the offensive, noting that the DPJ's Kan had been health minister when the SIA began consolidating its databases and therefore the scandal was his responsibility. But this claim was so absurd, the LDP was forced to withdraw a flyer that named Kan as the culprit.[34] While Abe was not wrong to point the finger at earlier governments and generations of SIA officials, his attempts to shift the blame were the worst possible response to a situation that demanded steady reassurance from national leadership.[35] Having ignored the warning signs, Abe scrambled to show that his government had the situation under control as public panic grew. Abe said that the problem would be completely resolved within a year or else he would "take political responsibility," implying that he would resign if the government's efforts failed.

At precisely the moment the pensions scandal exploded, Abe was floored by another shocking development. Matsuoka had limped along as agriculture minister for months, hounded by critics but protected—and prevented from resigning—by the prime minister. The Matsuoka scandal reached a grim denouement on 28 May 2007, when he committed suicide in his room at a dormitory for Diet members. He was the first sitting cabinet minister to commit suicide during the postwar era.[36]

Now wholly preoccupied with the pensions crisis, Abe moved to put Matsuoka's scandal behind him, declaring that there would be no investigation into the office funds scandal or a separate scandal regarding kickbacks that the late minister had allegedly received from companies that had contracts with his ministry. Neither Abe's attitude nor Matsuoka's suicide would prevent the DPJ from making "money and politics" a high-profile issue ahead of the July elections. It did not help that almost immediately after his appointment, Matsuoka's successor faced questions over irregularities in his political funding accounts, allowing the Democrats to keep up the pressure during the final weeks of the legislative session.[37]

On the morning of Matsuoka's death, the *Mainichi Shimbun* published a poll showing a massive drop in the cabinet's approval rating, an eleven-point fall to thirty-two percent. After lingering in the forties—well below where Abe started but not dangerous to his prospects—for most of 2007, the public was finally wearying of the Abe administration's chaos. Other polls recorded similarly dismal numbers. Even the center-right *Yomiuri Shimbun*, whose polls (and editorials) had been most favorable to Abe, found that he had fallen into a deep hole.[38] Even more distressing for Abe, the DPJ pulled ahead of the LDP in the upper house race. The elections were approaching rapidly—although slightly less rapidly after the government extended the Diet session by twelve days, bumping the upper house elections back a week from 22 July to 29 July.

Abe seemed powerless to reverse the plunge. His legislative achievements, including the passage of the bill that would dissolve the SIA and replace it with the Japan Pension Service in 2010, were overshadowed by the ongoing panic over the missing pensions and the latest corruption allegations. He would lose another cabinet minister before the session finally ended on 5 July, when Defense Minister Kyuma Fumio—who hailed from Nagasaki prefecture—opined that the US atomic bombing of Nagasaki "could not be helped." His indiscretion, condemned by his home prefecture's legislature, led to his prompt replacement with Koike, Abe's de facto national security adviser.[39] He would suffer one last defeat when a group of new conservatives (including several lawmakers) signed their names to a full-page ad in the *Washington Post* on 14 June that purported to offer—as the title read—"THE FACTS" about the comfort women. The ad was wholly unappreciated on Capitol Hill and shattered the understanding Abe had reached with Bush in April, opening the door for the passage of the Honda resolution on 30 July.[40]

* * *

By the end of the Diet session on 5 July, Abe's government was in shambles. The Japanese people had turned against him. Increasingly, the LDP took falling approval ratings as a cue for mobilizing against Abe. The prime minister had to fend off murmurs from within his own party that he should prepare to take responsibility for an electoral defeat and resign. While some of his allies remained by his side, the LDP knew that it might be choosing a new leader within weeks.

The DPJ, meanwhile, entered the campaign energized. While there was still a significant number of undecided voters, the party's leaders felt confident enough they would break for the DPJ that they raised their target for the upper house election to fifty-five seats, which would make it virtually impossible for Abe to reach his own "victory line" of fifty.

In the 2000s, upper house elections increasingly turned several dozen prefectures that elected only a single representative per election cycle, and these battleground prefectures became increasingly competitive as Japan's nascent two-party democracy matured. In 2007, there were twenty-nine single-member districts (SMDs). The LDP and DPJ would likely split the twelve districts that elected two members per cycle and fight pitched battles for marginal seats in the five districts that elected three and the one (Tokyo) that elected five. Forty-eight would be decided by proportional representation from national lists, but proportional representation makes it difficult for one party to win an overwhelming number of seats. Winning single-member constituencies was the easiest way for the DPJ to win.

Ozawa's campaign strategy focused on these races. The DPJ fielded candidates in all twenty-nine, and Ozawa prioritized campaign stops in these predominantly rural prefectures. Even as other senior party leaders were preoccupied with attacking Abe in the Diet, Ozawa was often absent from Tokyo, taking the DPJ's message to the voters who would decide the elections.[41]

The party's platform stressed lifestyle issues—the DPJ's slogan was "livelihoods first," an implicit rebuke to a prime minister who repeatedly said that he wanted the campaign to focus on constitutional revision—and used the missing pensions to claim that Abe could not be trusted to safeguard the economic security of all Japanese. Memories of Koizumi were fresh, and Ozawa hammered on fears of widening inequality and a "winner-take-all" society to argue for change. "We do not necessarily reject free competition and market principles," Ozawa told a crowd in Okayama prefecture in western Japan, "but if we accept unchecked freedom, we will become a survival-of-the-fittest society, in which case neither nation nor society is viable."[42] In a bid to peel off disaffected LDP voters, the DPJ's manifesto included among its three most prominent proposals an expansive new system to subsidize farmers growing rice and other staple crops.[43] Other planks offered new benefits that would appeal to urban middle- and working-class voters. It was a new form of populist politics, aimed squarely at Koizumi's legacy, and Ozawa was even willing to make common cause with some of Koizumi's bitterest rivals to advance the DPJ's prospects.[44] It was a strategy perfectly designed to exploit Abe's critical weaknesses. He was simultaneously too close to Koizumi and his legacy to be appealing to rural voters—who resented postal privatization and Koizumi's cuts to pork-barrel spending and other budget items that favored the countryside—but, thanks to his readmission of the postal rebels and otherwise weak commitment to structural reform, appeared to be too "old LDP" for many of the urban and suburban independents that Koizumi had attracted.

Abe was outmatched. He had taken office promising to continue Koizumi's reforms, but quickly readmitted lawmakers who openly defied Koizumi. He had highlighted growing inequality ahead of his leadership bid but had devoted much of his first year to laying the groundwork for constitutional revision and other longstanding conservative goals. More importantly, he undercut his own allies—who had argued that Abe should not have to resign in the wake of an electoral defeat since the upper house was not responsible for selecting the prime minister—when he told voters that the election was a choice between Abe and Ozawa.[45] Even LDP candidates tried to distance themselves from Abe. An LDP incumbent from a hotly contested single-member district frankly stated that he did not understand what Abe meant by "beautiful country."[46]

It became apparent that the LDP would lose in a landslide. Undecided voters were breaking for the DPJ. Voter interest was running high, suggesting that the Democrats might bring out the floating voters they needed to seize control of the upper house.[47] As the campaign entered its final days, Abe and his leadership team grew increasingly desperate, with Shiozaki telling voters in his home prefecture of Ehime—another battleground—that North Korea would be pleased with an LDP defeat.[48]

In the end, the LDP won only thirty-seven seats, including six of the twenty-nine SMDs. For the first time, it was no longer the largest party in the upper house. Although turnout rose only slightly, it was more than enough to seal the victory for the DPJ, since the party's vote totals in both proportional representation and constituency voting both grew by roughly two million votes over 2004. The DPJ won sixty seats and held more seats than the LDP and Kōmeitō combined. Exit polls suggested that the DPJ had not only won large numbers of independents—roughly fifty-one percent compared with only fourteen percent for the LDP—but also attracted sizable numbers of LDP and Kōmeitō supporters. It may not have been an explicit endorsement of Ozawa and his program, but it was a stunning rebuke of Abe.

The "twisted Diet" had arrived. While the lower house would have precedence on budgets, treaties, and selecting a prime minister, control of the upper house would give the DPJ power to block most legislation and could only be overruled by a supermajority vote in the lower house. Abe would have little choice but to work with the Democrats. Abe's control of his own ruling coalition, meanwhile, would be more tenuous. LDP members already dissatisfied with Abe's leadership before the election had every reason to push for his resignation. Kōmeitō's voice would also be louder, giving it a virtual veto over the government's agenda.

Despite this bleak outlook—and most of the public wanted him to resign—Abe did not hesitate to declare that he would stay. "My nation building has only just begun," he said on election night.[49] Instead, Nakagawa Hidenao resigned as secretary-general. Although some of his closest allies suggested that quitting immediately could save his career, and both senior LDP members and junior backbenchers called openly for his resignation, Abe refused. He would not yield the post that his grandfather had been forced from prematurely, and which his father had never been able to occupy.[50] No one—not Ozawa, not his own party, and not the millions of voters who opted for the DPJ—would force him out. He gritted his teeth, looked to a silent majority among the LDP's rank-and-file members, and persevered through the hardest days immediately after the election.[51] By the time the nation began its summer holidays it did in fact appear that Abe would defy the odds, cling to power and fight on.[52]

* * *

On 10 September 2007, Abe delivered his policy speech to open a new session of the Diet. The dust had settled, and he had survived. He had been chastened, however, and when he reshuffled his cabinet in late August its ranks were filled with party elders who would focus on reaching a modus vivendi with Ozawa and the DPJ. Yosano Kaoru had prepared a memo for Abe recommending how he could pivot to pocketbook without necessarily abandoning his core principles.[53] The prime minister took his recommendations to heart and began preparing his government to focus more on economic policy and the social security system, downgrading the "beautiful country" rhetoric that had confused his own party and led his foes to tar him as an arch-nationalist.[54]

In the August reshuffle, Yosano, marginalized while Nakagawa led the party, replaced Shiozaki as chief cabinet secretary. Machimura, head of Abe's faction and a former foreign minister, returned for another stint as foreign minister. Masuzoe Yoichi, a telegenic Tokyo University professor previously a vigorous critic of Abe's decision to stay in office, was tapped as health minister, so responsible for cleaning up the missing pensions. Inoue stayed as principal executive secretary, but most of the loyalists—Shiozaki, Seko, and Shimomura among them—were out. Out too was Suga, who despite having been considered as a possible replacement for Shiozaki during 2007, was denied the job in August due to the whiff of a political finance scandal of his own.[55] Koike, having sparred with bureaucrats during her vanishingly brief tenure as defense minister, was out. Abe also named Asō as the LDP's secretary-general, keeping the ambitious politician on his side but also placing him in a position to expand his power base such that the reshuffled leadership team was quickly dubbed the "Abe–Asō system."

Abe had taken the defeat to heart. But the pivot came too late. His approval ratings continued to plummet, dropping to twenty-nine percent approval in NHK's August poll even as his disapproval rating rose to fifty-eight percent. And even this lineup was not free from scandal: a week after the reshuffle, Abe lost his third agriculture minister (his second had resigned in early August) when he admitted that his former agriculture cooperative had defrauded the government to receive subsidies.

Nevertheless, Abe continued to govern as if he intended to endure. In August, he took a foreign trip, visiting Indonesia, Malaysia, and India from 19–25 August, a trip capped off by a historic address before the Indian Parliament. While at the time Abe seemed like a dead man walking—politically speaking—this trip would prove hugely consequential over the long term, because it was then that Abe began fleshing out the concept of a group of Asian maritime democracies that would counter China's growing influence across the region, as well as the concept of treating the rim of the Indian Ocean and the Western Pacific as a single region. These concepts would be revived during Abe's second administration. Abe also planted the seeds of a stronger bilateral relationship between Japan and India, based on shared values and deepening economic ties, bolstered by Japanese official and private investment. This too would bear fruit later.

At the time, however, these gestures appeared more like a desperate ploy by a mortally wounded prime minister than a bid to articulate principles that could guide Japanese foreign policy for decades. In mid-August, it seemed unlikely that Abe would have the wherewithal to convince Ozawa to approve an extension to Japan's soon-to-expire mission providing maritime rear-area support for allied operations in Afghanistan, let alone advance a sweeping vision for regional competition with China.[56] But he soldiered on, returning from Southeast Asia to reshuffle his cabinet before taking another foreign trip to attend the Asia Pacific Economic Cooperation (APEC) summit in Sydney in early September. He returned just in time to open the autumn Diet session on 10 September.

While chastened by his electoral defeat and focused mostly on economic and social programs in his policy address, it appeared that Abe's faith in himself as a man of destiny was unshaken. "With a vision of how Japan should be in 50 years, and in 100 years, and never losing sight of our origins," he said, "I solemnly swear that I will give all my body and soul to fulfill the responsibilities of the Prime Minister."[57]

Little did the Japanese public know that Abe had in fact given his body to fulfilling the responsibilities of the premiership—and it was failing him.

* * *

After his protracted hospitalization in 1998, Abe had controlled his ulcerative colitis. However, he now faced stress at a level unlike anything he had encountered before, with few opportunities to escape from the duties of office.[58] The strains of office grew as he battled members of his own party to keep his job, and then embarked on his swing through three tropical countries at the height of summer.

Within a week of the elections, he experienced cramps and loss of appetite that worsened during his travels. In a confessional essay published in 2008, Abe described forcing down "ethnic cuisine" during his trip despite diarrhea and gastrointestinal pain. His condition worsened to the point that he lost nearly fifteen pounds over the course of a month and visited the bathroom upwards of thirty times a day. By the first week of September, he began to think about resigning.

His closest aides noticed that something was wrong. Yosano, for example, noticed that Abe was unusually subdued in a 6 September roundtable discussion with editorial writers.[59] His determination to resign was stiffened on 10 September when, while speaking before the upper house, his pain made it difficult to concentrate and he omitted three lines from his prepared text. As he later wrote, "Whether it is possible to fulfill the duties of the prime minister or whether it is possible to make the right judgment or whether it is possible to respond adequately to the Diet in this condition—considering myself, I am truly sorry to say but I had no choice but to recognize this as impossible."[60]

Finally, after medical exams and discussions with senior LDP officials, on Wednesday, 12 September, Abe shocked the nation by announcing his resignation. He did not reveal his illness, and instead blamed the DPJ's intractable opposition to a bill to extend the SDF's Indian Ocean operations. In his press conference, reporters were incredulous that, having defied precedent to cling to power after the electoral defeat, Abe would suddenly resign after the start of the new session. Their suspicions were confirmed the following day when Abe was admitted to Keio University Hospital to undergo treatment for what his physician called "functional dyspepsia." It was only eleven days later, on 24 September, on the eve of the transfer of power to his successor, that Abe admitted that he had "reached the limits of [his] physical wellness" and apologized for the sudden and inconvenient timing of his resignation, which had left Japan virtually leaderless for two weeks.[61] But, even then, neither he nor his physician identified his ailment as ulcerative colitis.

By the time Abe emerged from the hospital to give his farewell remarks, the LDP had moved on. Fukuda Yasuo had been chosen as its next leader, fulfilling Mori's wish for four straight prime ministers from his faction. Asō was perceived as overly eager to replace Abe and also too hostile to Koizumi's legacy, leading the former prime minister to mobilize his followers on Fukuda's behalf.[62] While Abe had introduced some changes that would outlast him—establishing the defense ministry, a national referendum process, and the Japan Pension Service—he left office broken in body and spirit.

* * *

At fifty-three—he had marked his birthday in the hospital—he truly tasted failure for the first time. He had avoided school entrance exams, the civil service exams and the grueling hiring process for blue-chip companies, joined a company thanks to his father's intervention, and then left—with some angst—when his father summoned him to be his secretary. When his father died, he easily won his parliamentary seat and then kept winning, in the process rising ever higher in the LDP. His prospects hardly suffered after failure to lead the LDP to electoral victories in 2003 and 2004, and he secured his place as Koizumi's successor with barely a fight from his would-be rivals.

Every step propelled him to the heights of power, but nothing had prepared him for what it would feel like to win the ultimate prize, but then watch it slip inexorably from his grasp over the course of a year, his life's work unfinished. By 2009, when the LDP had gone through three leadership changes in as many years, he was a footnote, one of the three bad leaders in the post-Koizumi carousel.

After leaving the hospital and returning to the backbenches, Abe had ample time to consider his government's failure, and filled notebooks with reflections on what had gone wrong. The causes of failure were numerous: the controversial legacy of Koizumi's tenure inside the LDP and in Japanese society; Abe's lack of ministerial experience and poor sense of economic policy; an inexperienced advisory team that failed to vet cabinet appointees properly, respond effectively to crises, stay on message, and protect the prime minister; the coalescence of the DPJ around Ozawa and Ozawa's pursuit of a strategy that exploited Abe's weaknesses. And then there was Abe's fundamental inability to "read the air" and adapt.

These factors doomed his first premiership. Moreover, it is highly likely that sooner or later he would have been tripped up by the battle within the LDP between fiscal hawks and the "Koizumi children" as the debate over fiscal consolidation intensified—or by the impact of the global financial crisis that was already looming.

Thus, by the end of 2007, he was postwar Japan's youngest ex-prime minister. Given that no LDP leader had ever received a second chance to lead, few expected Abe would ever have another opportunity.

"From throughout Japan, I was branded as useless," he later told the *Sankei Shimbun*, a conservative daily. "I looked into hell."[63]

10

ABE IN THE WILDERNESS

On 9 October 2009, more than two thousand mourners gathered at Zenpuku-ji, a Buddhist temple in Tokyo's Azabu neighborhood, to pay their respects to Nakagawa Shōichi. The memorial service drew colleagues from across the political spectrum, even from the recently victorious Democratic Party of Japan (DPJ), one of whose candidates had defeated him on 30 August when the DPJ swept into power. But foremost among the mourners was Abe.

"Shōichi-san and I had the privilege of fellowship that included our families as our fathers enjoyed a relationship as fellow politicians," he said in his eulogy. "It was my pleasure to have been able to deepen this long friendship from the moment I entered the political world until today."[1] He recounted their shared vision for Japan and their battles against the postwar regime, particularly against the education system they felt insulted national pride.

But he also used the eulogy to signal that he would once again lead the Liberal Democratic Party's (LDP) new conservatives. Nakagawa, significantly more experienced as a cabinet minister and party executive, had been the most promising choice to lead the demoralized right wing. In December 2007, he spearheaded the creation of the True Conservative Policy Study Group, which was committed to rebuilding the new conservative movement after Abe's tenure.[2] The task was vital because the new prime minister, Fukuda Yasuo, was determined to marginalize them—and the new conservatives had not forgotten that, as chief cabinet secretary, Fukuda had been more interested in normalization with North Korea than in pressing Pyongyang for answers about the abductees. Had Nakagawa lived, Abe would have gladly supported his ambitions.

But now, it fell to Abe to lead again. "We promise," he said on 9 October, "to grapple with all our energy towards a conservative rebirth that will make the Japan that has the pride that you [Nakagawa] had aimed for."

* * *

But Abe himself recognized the unlikelihood that he would ever govern again. "When I resigned as prime minister, I thought my political life was over," he said later.[3] No ousted LDP leader had reclaimed the party's leadership. The sheer magnitude of his humiliation would have deterred most people from making another bid.

Meanwhile, the LDP had a long history of former leaders acting as powerbrokers behind the scenes, and perhaps becoming even more powerful as ex-prime ministers. Tanaka Kakuei had a substantially longer tenure as a "shadow shogun" than he had as prime minister. Meanwhile, Mori Yoshirō had transitioned from being a historically unpopular prime minister to the power behind the LDP's largest faction and sponsor of prime ministers. There was a well-trodden path for Abe.

But he was Japan's youngest ex-prime minister. He knew nothing outside of politics. He needed to be in the arena. He had left too much unfinished. The sense of destiny that had propelled him would continue to sustain him. And there was his pride. He had not just resigned because of an electoral defeat. Instead, he lingered for another month—defying party elders—and then resigned, just as the new Diet session began—leaving the nation leaderless as he disappeared into the hospital. He had to redeem his name.

* * *

But before Abe could dream of a comeback, he had to get back on his feet. He finally left the hospital on 27 September 2007, two weeks after his admission. It would be another six weeks before he reappeared at the Diet.

After leaving the hospital, he began to tell his story. In January 2008, he published an account of the circumstances surrounding his resignation. In this essay, Abe pushed back against some of the myths that had emerged to explain what had happened—for example, he categorically rejected the argument advanced by Koizumi and his followers that Asō carried out a "coup" against Abe in the final days—and provided an account of his struggles with ulcerative colitis that was stunning for its raw honesty but also exposed him to public ridicule.

Having provided a frank description of his ailment, he would repeatedly have to answer for his physical condition. His ability to manage his condition would improve immeasurably in 2009, when a leading treatment for the condition became available in Japan.[4] He would also be more diligent about adhering to a fitness regimen to manage his stress.[5] By and large, the public was reassured.[6]

Healing his pride would take longer. He had become a punch line, disparaged even by those who had once supported him.[7] He was gradually returning to the public eye, sitting for print and television interviews in which he would always begin by apologizing for the chaos that his resignation had caused.[8] He was acutely aware of how the public and—perhaps more importantly—his peers in the political world saw him.

As he coped with defeat, Abe relied on friends and allies who supported him at his lowest ebb. Members of his first government checked in regularly with the former prime minister, including Suga, Seko, and Asō. Nakagawa Shōichi also communicated regularly with his longtime friend and ally. Suga, who had orchestrated the trans-factional movement that fueled Abe's election as LDP leader in 2006, was particularly dogged in his loyalty to the former prime minister. "I will absolutely restore Abe," Suga reportedly said on the day of Abe's resignation.[9]

Hasegawa Eiichi, an official at the ministry of economy, trade, and industry (METI) who had served in Abe's Kantei, orchestrated another step in his recovery. Hasegawa thought hiking would help Abe feel stronger and let him interact with voters in more casual settings.[10] On 2 December 2007, Abe, Hasegawa, some other associates, and a couple of security officers gathered to climb Mount Takao, an hour from central Tokyo. As Abe hiked, other climbers who saw him on the trail inquired about his health and wished him well. It was an important moment in his recovery. Not only did he manage the physical exertion, but ordinary citizens greeted him kindly within three months of his resignation.

With Hasegawa's encouragement, he continued to hike regularly, often with Hasegawa and other loyal friends from his first government, including Imai Takaya, another METI official who had been one of his administrative secretaries. Many of his hiking partners took key roles in his second administration.[11]

The presence in the upper reaches of the second Abe administration of many of those who stuck with him during the wilderness years is no accident. Abe had always attracted followers easily, but his time in the wilderness taught him who his true friends were. This sense of trust extended to whole ministries, since METI continued to provide him with high-level briefings—perhaps thanks to high-ranking friends like Imai—while MOF was colder. This reassembled Team Abe sustained him during the early wilderness years and became the nucleus of a movement to establish a second Abe premiership.

But even as he continued to attract loyal friends after his resignation, he faced a more immediate challenge: reelection in his constituency. In Japanese politics, it is an essential part of the rehabilitation process for a disgraced politician to seek purification at the ballot box—called *misogi* after a Shinto purification ritual.[12] After so spectacular a fall, Abe needed the absolution of his constituents in a general election. Given the headwinds facing the LDP, he could not assume they would grant it.

He began an "apology tour" in his constituency in December 2007, going home for the first time since his 2006 elevation to the premiership. After meeting Yamaguchi's governor—who encouraged him not to give up—he received a hero's welcome from a crowd of more than 1,000 people gathered outside Shimonoseki's main train station. In 2008 and 2009, Abe dedicated himself to canvassing his constituency with more zeal than ever since his first victory. He went door-to-door across his district, visiting not just LDP supporters but of all his constituents, including backers of the Communist Party, sometimes as many as 200 homes a day.[13] He endured jeers, too: some laughed at the spectacle of a former prime minister engaged in elementary retail politics.[14] He did it even though his wife Akie feared for his health and implored him to retire.[15] She had never been entirely happy as a political wife and, without children to raise—when Abe became prime minister, she gave an unusually frank interview in which she discussed the couple's difficulties conceiving, their use of fertility treatments, and their consideration of adoption—she was eager to pursue her own ambitions.[16]

Nevertheless, when the general election finally came in August 2009, Abe trounced his DPJ challenger, winning a sixth term by a robust, if slightly reduced, majority. Many of his colleagues did not fare so well.

* * *

When Abe stepped down, the political world was consumed with two questions. Could the "twisted Diet" effectively govern the country—and when would the government call an election to give the DPJ a chance to take power?

Fukuda recognized that the divided Diet imposed limitations on his power, and that he would need to be flexible. Although he had a trump card—the lower house could overrule the upper house with a two-thirds majority—he preferred to cooperate with the DPJ instead of forcing bills through the legislature. Fukuda wanted to draw a line between his government and his predecessor's.[17] He enjoyed a burst of public support after inauguration, with a sizable majority approving of his efforts to stabilize the government.

Nevertheless, he faltered. He could not convince the DPJ to back a bill to extend the MSDF mission, which required a lengthy extension of the parliamentary session. He held talks with Ozawa in November about a grand coalition, but the effort collapsed when Ozawa could not bring the DPJ, hungry for its chance to oust the LDP, along with the plan.[18] The situation did not improve in 2008, when the DPJ blocked the renewal of a gasoline tax tied to road construction, sparking a fierce debate within the LDP over using a lower-house supermajority to renew a tax that LDP reformists wanted to kill. The DPJ also used the upper house's veto over personnel appointments—certain posts required the approval of both houses—to block Fukuda's first choice for a new BOJ governor in March 2008, just as Bear Stearns failed.[19]

Despite his promise to govern patiently and cooperatively, by spring 2008 Fukuda was frustrated with having to fight pitched battles with both his party and the opposition on every issue. By April, his approval ratings had plummeted to roughly twenty percent, and disapproval had reached an astonishing and unsustainable seventy percent. He limped along, but his rivals—particularly Asō and Yosano—were already mobilizing to replace him. Fukuda competently guided Japan's foreign relations even as his ability to lead domestically evaporated, hosting the G8 summit in Hokkaido in July and a lengthy visit by Chinese President Hu Jintao in May that nudged Japan and China further along the path to a more constructive relationship. However, even in diplomacy Fukuda could not escape domestic turmoil: when, as part of denuclearization negotiations the Bush administration agreed to remove North Korea from its list of state sponsors of terrorism—over howls of disapproval from Tokyo—Fukuda could not shift the government's stance on the abductees, due to opposition from the LDP's new conservatives.[20] Finally, a few months after Fukuda admitted that he disliked the job—"It's not fun! It's like a painful lump," he said in June—he quit abruptly on 1 September, less than a year after Abe's resignation.[21]

After losing three of the four previous leadership elections, it would finally be Asō's chance. He won a landslide victory in a five-way race, burying not only Yosano but also Koike Yuriko, Koizumi's choice as the reform candidate. Reflecting the lingering divisions from the Koizumi years, Nakagawa Hidenao defied Mori and Machimura, the leaders of his faction, to back Koike.[22]

In different circumstances, Asō—a bon vivant who is a grandson of Yoshida Shigeru, a former Olympian (shooting, Montreal 1976), and an obsessive fan of *manga*—might have had more success connecting with the Japanese public. Indeed, he won in large part because, with a general election due sometime before September 2009, Asō's idiosyncrasies might fend off the DPJ threat. However, when he took the LDP's leadership, he inherited the wreckage left behind by two short-lived prime ministers, and the public was rapidly losing patience with the LDP.

By the time Asō took power there was only one issue to address: the global financial crisis. Between the start of the LDP leadership campaign on 10 September and the vote on 22 September, the Lehman Brothers rescue failed. What had begun as a slow-rolling crisis in the US housing sector had felled a venerable Wall Street institution—and gone global. By the end of September, the Nikkei 225 lost twelve percent of its value. The stock market continued to plummet in October, with almost ten percent of its value wiped out on 10 October alone. By the end of October, the index was a third smaller relative to the beginning of September. Whatever Asō had hoped to achieve in office would have to be shelved: his government had to prioritize macroeconomic policies to save Japan's economy and coordinate with others to save the global financial system. The snap election Asō wanted to call would have to wait.[23]

Japan's banks were relatively insulated from the panic, but Japan's real economy was hit harder than those of its peers in the developed world. Japan had become more dependent on exports for growth; many of those exports were critical inputs for manufactured goods produced in China and other emerging markets, for export to the US and Europe. As global growth slowed in late 2008 and early 2009, Japanese exports and industrial production collapsed sharply, and the country entered a deep recession.[24] In the first quarter of 2009, Japan's economy shrank at an annualized rate of 15.2 percent, the single worst quarter of the postwar era.[25]

On 16 October, Asō's government passed an ¥11 trillion supplemental budget that had been prepared under Fukuda. By the end of the month, his government unveiled a record-setting stimulus package that totaled ¥27 trillion, although it did not pass the Diet until the following January. Asō unveiled another ¥15 trillion stimulus package in April 2009. In the meantime, he pressed for a global, coordinated fiscal response to the financial crisis that would stabilize markets and international trade. Economist Richard Koo argues that Asō is an unheralded hero of the global financial crisis, for convincing other members of the G20 that "the global economic slump triggered by the Lehman failure could be reversed with the application of fiscal stimulus by the entire G20."[26] Koo also credits Asō with upholding a G20 pledge to avoid competitive devaluation even as other countries broke it, resulting in a de facto strong yen policy that continued after Asō left office (and would ironically become one of Abe's major grievances against the DPJ).[27]

This fiscal stimulus was not heralded at the time and did little to reverse Asō's sinking approval ratings, even after Ozawa, facing corruption allegations, resigned and was replaced by Hatoyama Yukio. Asō was also not helped by his appointment of Nakagawa Shōichi as finance minister. Nakagawa became a source of global embarrassment when, at a G7 finance ministers' meeting in Rome in February 2009, he appeared to be drunk, slurring his words at a joint press conference to announce a historically large Japanese loan to the IMF and falling asleep in a meeting. Nakagawa claimed his behavior was due to a combination of painkillers and cold medicine, not inebriation, but the incident revealed a drinking problem that was an open secret in political Tokyo, prompting questions about the wisdom of Asō's naming him as finance minister in the midst of the worst financial crisis since the Great Depression. Nakagawa resigned and was replaced by Yosano.[28]

Many Japanese found it difficult to credit Asō with success, with unemployment reaching a record-high of 5.5 percent by July 2009, the layoffs hitting temporary "dispatch" workers and other non-regular workers disproportionately as companies shuttered factories and production lines. Japan's Great Recession was symbolized by the creation of a "dispatch village" in Hibiya Park in central Tokyo, which, flanked by the financial district, the Imperial Palace, and the political and administrative nerve centers of Nagatachō and Kasumigaseki, has long served as Japan's public square. The "village," erected for a short time at the end of 2008 and the beginning of 2009 before being dispersed, provided food, shelter, and other services for only 505 laid-off workers and raised national awareness of the plight of newly unemployed temporary workers. The dispatch village, the missing pensions, the post-Lehman slump: these developments congealed into a consensus that the LDP had fundamentally failed to address the most pressing social and economic problems.[29]

By the time Asō dissolved the lower house on 21 July 2009 and called a general election for 30 August, his party was collapsing around him. The LDP lost control of Tokyo's metropolitan assembly in early July, and by mid-July an anti-Asō movement, led by Nakagawa Hidenao, tried to unseat him before he could call an election. Nakagawa's coup failed but revealed that the divisions exposed and deepened by Koizumi had rendered the party ungovernable. While most of the "Koizumi children" stayed in the LDP, a handful left before the election, joining Watanabe Yoshimi, formerly Abe's administrative reform minister, in the awkwardly named Your Party (YP), whose manifesto was committed to small-government neo-liberalism.

As the prospect of a DPJ-led government became real, the LDP tried to close ranks behind Asō, but it was too late. By the time the election arrived, it was merely a matter of how badly the LDP would lose. The Democrats, running on a populist platform promising sweeping administrative reform, monthly child allowances, and income support for farmers, overwhelmed the LDP. Days before the vote, at least one poll suggested that the DPJ could win an outright supermajority, a feat the LDP itself had never achieved.

Ultimately, fueled by turnout above sixty-nine percent, the highest since 1990, the DPJ won 308 of 480 seats—the most ever for a party during the postwar era—and reduced the LDP to just 109, a stunning rebuke considering it went into the election with 300. Rejection of the LDP was nearly total. The DPJ won in the urban and suburban districts that Koizumi had won for the LDP but also knocked off LDP heavyweights in rural strongholds. For the first time in its history, the LDP was not the largest party in the lower house. Japan had finally achieved an orderly alternation of power between parties at the ballot box.

However, while the emergence of a two-party system had led to the LDP's historic defeat in 2009, it contained the seeds of the party's renewal—and with it, Abe's resurrection.

* * *

As Asō grappled with the global financial crisis, Abe ramped up his political activities. As his physical condition—and his ego—recovered, he quietly resumed his involvement in the battles that roiled Tokyo after his resignation.

His resignation had not weakened his commitment to building a stronger state, free of postwar constraints. He was, as he told the *Sankei Shimbun* in December 2007, still committed to remaking the LDP into a "party of ideas," namely his vision of a strong, independent nation capable of defending its national interests and pursuing "assertive foreign policy." "I think that my mission," he said, "is the further broadening of a high-quality conservative base that is being consolidated bit by bit. Because the cultivation of a 'beautiful country' has only just begun..."[30]

As Abe reflected on his year as prime minister, recording notes in what became his "reflection notebooks," he focused mostly on tactical errors. He was determined to use failure as a teacher. In his reflections, he recognized that he should never have become prime minister in 2006; he was too inexperienced and should have resisted the forces pushing him to run.[31] His inexperience led to other mistakes. He had allowed his feelings to compromise his judgment regarding personnel matters, both when it came to appointments and when to cut loose a cabinet minister under fire for scandal.

Meanwhile, he had been clumsy in his relationship with the media. He had, for example, inherited a new model of prime ministerial communication from Koizumi, who instituted a practice of making twice-daily on-camera statements to the press pool gathered in the foyer of the Kantei. This practice had suited Koizumi's telegenic, "one phrase" politics, providing an endless stream of sound bites for use on the day-time shows. But it was less suited to Abe's more ponderous style, increasing the likelihood of gaffes. While he gained a reputation for a heavy-handed approach to the media during his second administration, the lesson Abe learned from his first was the need to shape the public narrative about his premiership, to push back against "hostile" news organizations, bestow favors on "friendly" organizations and journalists, and use social media to reach voters directly. Even in the political wilderness, he became a regular guest on popular TV programs, carefully rebuilding his image in the eyes of the public. His recovery was also aided by a conscious effort organized by TV political commentator Miyake Hisayuki who, along with LDP lawmaker Shimomura Hakubun, convened a study group of writers—the Abe Shinzō Revival Project, he called it—to help rehabilitate Abe's image in preparation for another leadership bid.[32] Abe's multi-pronged media strategy argued that Abe was uniquely suited to lead Japan out of the crises that emerged during the DPJ years.[33]

He also considered how to wield power more effectively. It was not only about being more cold-blooded in his cabinet appointments. He would also have to leverage more effectively the institutional power that had accumulated in the prime minister's office. His government had been undone in part because members of his inner circle in the Kantei were more preoccupied with battles amongst themselves than with the larger mission of protecting Abe and his pursuit of national transformation. With the prime minister's office divided, the administration struggled to control either the bureaucracy or the LDP, resulting in a vicious cycle that culminated in Abe's resignation. Fukuda's and Asō's short-lived administrations both ran aground between a fractured ruling party and the "twisted" Diet, which weakened the prime minister's grip on the legislative process, reinforcing the importance of a strong, unified executive.[34]

Abe also learned to appreciate what he had acknowledged was a problem before he had even become prime minister: his lack of experience as an economic policymaker made it difficult for him to speak confidently on the matters voters cared about most. He would need a coherent economic program as part of his vision of national renewal.

In the meantime, however, his political activities in the years immediately after his resignation were basically a continuation of the new conservative activism that marked his first decade as a backbencher. While in early 2008 he joined a parliamentarians' league to promote a plan to halve carbon emissions by 2050, he remained focused mainly on his "leaving behind the postwar regime" governing agenda. From February 2008, he attended meetings of Nakagawa Shōichi's True Conservative Policy Study Group, the group Nakagawa had established in December 2007.

For Abe, this was a safe venue to find his voice again. Surrounded by his oldest political friends, he would quickly reemerge as the most prominent new conservative. He had lost none of the fighting spirit—the willingness to confront party elders and other guardians of the established institutions in the name of what he believed was right—that had made him someone to watch early in his career. In the spring of 2008, Abe sparred in the media with Yamasaki Taku, one of the LDP's senior-most doves and once one of Koizumi's closest friends, who argued that prioritizing the abductees above all was isolating Japan in the region. The two had clashed over North Korea in the past, and Abe renewed the feud, slamming Yamasaki for advocating a return to failed policies.[35] Abe won the debate, as the Fukuda administration could not shift its approach to North Korea.

Abe would become even more visible after Nakagawa joined the Asō cabinet in September. With Asō in the premiership, he and his colleagues were acting not as an opposition bloc trying to keep a dovish prime minister in line, but as loyal supporters occasionally calling for Asō to move to the right. Thus, in 2009, even as he took a high-profile trip to Washington in April that included a meeting with Vice President Joe Biden and an address at the Brookings Institution, he was also arguing—after North Korea's 5 April satellite launch that highlighted its advances in developing long-range missiles and led to another breakdown in the six-party talks—for collective self-defense and the acquisition of conventional military capabilities that would enable Japan to strike targets in North Korea. The hawkish agitation went nowhere. But it did show that, having returned to the stage, Abe's belief in the need for a strong state capable of defending the Japanese people was undiminished.

These convictions were strengthened after Hatoyama Yukio formed the first DPJ-led government in September 2009.

* * *

It is one of the great accidents of Japanese political history that Hatoyama, not Ozawa, became the first DPJ prime minister. Ozawa, who had stepped down earlier that year after aides were indicted for failing to report questionable donations, knew what the DPJ had to do to take power and retain it. Hatoyama, meanwhile, was the privileged son of a leading political dynasty—his grandfather had been the first LDP prime minister—who founded the DPJ in the 1990s thanks largely to his mother's willingness to bankroll the party. He had several turns as party leader, but he was notoriously flaky—his nickname was "spaceman"—and lacked the Machiavellian instincts the DPJ needed to succeed when so many wanted it to fail. As a sign of things to come, party officials spent the weeks leading up to the general election trying to reassure Washington that, despite a fanciful essay proposing the creation of an Asian community, a DPJ-led government would not pose an imminent threat to the US–Japan alliance.[36]

The DPJ took power on 16 September with an enormous majority and ambitious plans to introduce Westminster-style cabinet government to Japan—but with a prime minister and cabinet not equal to the tasks before them. The DPJ's manifesto had made strengthening political leadership its top priority.[37] However, it was stymied in these efforts, in part because the DPJ had to cope with subterfuge by the bureaucracy, which, after all, had dense links to the now-opposition

LDP. But the Democrats, who quickly showed their inexperience, did not help matters. For example, Nagatsuma Akira, the "Mr. Pensions" who had played so instrumental a role in exposing the scandal that led to the LDP's 2007 defeat, became minister of health, labor, and welfare and, in his zeal to exercise political leadership, refused to delegate virtually anything to the senior officials in his super-ministry, resulting in his being chronically overworked.[38]

Hatoyama shared this zeal to introduce immediate sweeping changes. Most notably, he decided soon after taking office that he would try to make good on a pledge to scrap a 2006 agreement for realigning US forces in Japan that included a plan to close the controversial Futenma Marine Corps Air Station—located in a densely populated part of Okinawa—to a more remote location built on reclaimed land at Henoko Bay. Hatoyama had promised voters that he would relocate the base out of Okinawa, and out of Japan if possible, raising hopes in Okinawa even as DPJ national security specialists tried to warn him that it would not be easy to deliver. Despite upper house elections looming in 2010, Hatoyama spent his political capital on getting a better deal for Okinawa even as the Obama administration pressured him to recommit. Hatoyama infamously appealed to Obama to "just trust me" when the US president took his first trip to Japan as president in November, but his own administration soon concluded that there was no alternative and by May 2010 Hatoyama admitted defeat. He resigned in early June.[39]

Both Japanese and American foreign policy establishments feared that the DPJ sought "balance" between the US and China. Ozawa, as DPJ secretary-general the power behind Hatoyama, went to China for four days in December with a 500-person delegation that included 143 lawmakers and hundreds of business leaders. Immediately upon his return, he contravened administrative rules to arrange an audience with the emperor for the Chinese vice president, Xi Jinping, on 15 December. Ozawa's trip raised hackles in Washington, as it appeared to, in the words of Jeffrey Bader, senior director for Asia on Obama's National Security Council, "demonstrate the direction in which the DPJ wished to go."[40]

The new conservatives were apoplectic, particularly at Ozawa's use of the emperor, disregarding rules that palace officials said were intended to protect the emperor's health. Nippon Kaigi convened an emergency meeting to condemn the DPJ. Abe, sharing the stage with Hiranuma and fellow LDP lawmaker Ishiba Shigeru, warned attendees that the Hatoyama administration had revealed its character as a "socialist administration" and pledged that he would "exhaust all his strength to overthrow this arrogant administration that does whatever it wants."[41]

Abe, who had warned of the dangers of DPJ rule, felt vindicated.[42] The Democrats—with few exceptions—could not be trusted to safeguard national interests.[43] For Abe, the DPJ would become what he had lacked during his premiership: a tangible enemy, a more concrete target for his ire than the "postwar regime," a symbol of everything that was wrong with Japan and the reason why the new conservatives had to retake power and fundamentally transform the Japanese state and nation. Once in opposition, Abe seemed energized as never before.

After Nakagawa's death, leadership of the "true conservative" group passed to Abe in accordance with Nakagawa's wishes. Under Abe's leadership, the group—which changed its name to *Sōsei Nippon* (Japan Rebirth) in 2010—gave the former prime minister a platform for attacking the DPJ and a venue for gathering together his closest supporters. It would also be a pressure group within the LDP that could lean on the party's leadership—now headed by the dovish Tanigaki—to oppose the DPJ unflinchingly and to articulate a new conservative program.

Despite Tanigaki's leadership, the LDP in opposition differed greatly from the party that had crumbled beneath Asō. Koizumi had retired, his neo-liberal movement was dead. All but ten of the eighty-three "Koizumi children" had lost their seats. Meanwhile, by 2010, the liberal elder statesmen who had clashed with Abe were leaving politics altogether. Yamasaki lost his seat in 2009. Katō Kōichi, who had sparred with Abe over the Iraq war, retired in 2012, as did Koga Makoto, another senior liberal.

In the greatly reduced LDP, no group could match the clout of Japan Rebirth, whose ranks numbered more than seventy in 2010. Not only did the group include former prime ministers like Abe and Asō, it was also a remarkably deep collection of prime-aged party members from which Abe could draw to staff the most important jobs in his second administration.[44] This group would mobilize a national movement to resist the DPJ administration, linking up with other new conservative groups and prefectural and local politicians to "rouse across the country a national movement to create a new political current based on true conservatism."[45] Their cause was no less than the future of the nation, since, as the group's action plan stressed, the DPJ was not only actively harming national interests but also preventing the changes Japan needed to implement, to guarantee its independence.

The sense of urgency did not abate when Kan Naoto replaced Hatoyama in June 2010. Kan was a more formidable opponent than Hatoyama. Unlike the blue-blooded Hatoyama, he was the son of a middle-class family who had worked as a lawyer and left-wing activist and lost three elections before winning a parliamentary seat in 1980. He had become a household name when, as Hashimoto's health minister (the New Party Sakigake to which Kan belonged was a minor coalition partner), he admitted and apologized for the government's role in the distribution of HIV-tainted blood. He stood a better chance of connecting with voters than Hatoyama.

But he would hurt his cause when, a month before the upper house elections in July 2010, he suggested that he was willing to consider raising the consumption tax in the near term, which the DPJ's 2009 manifesto had explicitly ruled out—a reversal that was made worse when he immediately backtracked. This debacle led to a disappointing performance in the elections, depriving the DPJ of control of the upper house and creating another "twisted" Diet.

Despite this outcome, the new conservatives grew more alarmed at Japan's direction. While Kan stabilized the relationship with the US, the DPJ's leaders were effectively blindsided by a dramatic shift in Beijing's approach to the world that made the DPJ's musings about a "balanced" foreign policy look dangerously naïve—and out of step with a Japanese public increasingly alarmed by the dangers of China's rise.

The global financial crisis was an inflection point. With China's recovery hastened by a massive fiscal stimulus program and the US, Europe, and Japan mired in slow growth and political turmoil, it seemed China could abandon Deng Xiaopeng's admonition to "hide and abide" and approach its neighbors and the world more assertively.[46] This trend became more pronounced as the Chinese Communist Party underwent a generational transfer of power from Hu Jintao to Xi Jinping.

Notwithstanding the DPJ's efforts to foster goodwill, by late 2010 it was apparent that living next door to a stronger, wealthier, and more confident China would present new challenges for Japan's leaders. Over the course of six months, a relatively stable relationship with China gave way to something far more contentious and dangerous, which played into Abe's hands.

The most significant trigger for the deterioration of the bilateral relationship was the sudden flare-up of their dispute over the Senkaku Islands (or Diaoyu, in Chinese). Japan and China had sparred over the islands since the US transferred them to Japanese control as part of the reversion of Okinawa in 1972. But, more recently, the two governments had shelved the dispute in the interest of encouraging cooperation in other areas.

On 7 September 2010, a Chinese fishing trawler rammed two Japanese coast guard (JCG) ships that were attempting to interdict it in the waters around the islands. The JCG eventually arrested the crew, and, pressured by Beijing, released most of them on 13 September—but not the captain, who was charged with obstructing the work of public officials. The Kan government eventually released him on 24 September, but only after China suspended shipments of rare earth metals needed for high-tech manufacturing, arrested Japanese citizens on espionage charges, and warned that if the captain was not released, "Japan shall take full responsibilities for all dire consequences incurred."

The incident exposed Japan's vulnerability to Chinese economic pressure—although it would serve as a wake-up call that led Japan and other countries to diversify their sources of rare earths—and seemingly confirmed the new conservative accusation that the DPJ could not stand up for Japan. Kan's situation worsened in November when a JCG officer leaked footage of the incident, strongly suggesting that the trawler had deliberately rammed the JCG ships. The videos suggested that Kan had caved even though the government's own evidence showed the Chinese were at fault.

As an exclamation mark on the incident and a sign of how Japan's relationship had changed, in January 2011 China released its GDP data for 2010, showing that it had passed Japan to become the world's second-largest economy. That had been only a matter of time—China has ten times as many people—but was an important symbolic moment.

Would Japan ever be as wealthy, relative to China, again? Was the Senkaku incident—in which China deployed economic measures to bring Japan's government to heel—the shape of things to come? Could Japan's leaders rely on the US to help Japan against an increasingly powerful China?

For the new conservatives, the incident confirmed that the nation would be in crisis while the DPJ was in power. In November 2010, Abe and Japan Rebirth petitioned Tanigaki, calling for the immediate overthrow of the Kan/DPJ administration given its weakness in the face of "unjust pressure" by Chinese authorities and general inability to manage foreign and security policy. Abe was unsparing in his attack on Kan. "That day," he said, referring to 24 September when the trawler captain was released, "is the day when Japan received a historic humiliation."[47]

Increasingly, the public seemed to share Abe's sentiments. Kan's approval ratings plummeted, from sixty-five percent approval in September to twenty-five percent in December, with disapproval soaring from twenty-one percent to fifty-eight percent. Meanwhile, the LDP's support inched ahead of the DPJ's for the first time since the 2009 general election.

* * *

Only three years after his resignation, Abe had returned. Utterly convinced that it was his mission to deliver national salvation, he had stubbornly persevered. He was as confident as ever that he and his conservative allies were the only ones who could save Japan from misgovernment and remake the country, preserving its power and influence in a rapidly changing Asia.

But despite Abe's reemergence, it was still far from certain that he would get another chance to lead. Memories of his chaotic tenure and abrupt resignation were fresh, and he had done little to address what had been perhaps the most glaring deficiency of his premiership, his inability to speak competently and confidently on the nation's economic problems. It would take a historic crisis, but over the next two years Abe would learn how to include Japan's economy in his account of a nation in crisis and how to present himself as the man who could save Japan from seemingly irreversible decline.

11

THE COMEBACK

At 2:46pm on Friday, 11 March 2011, a tectonic plate off Japan's Pacific coast slipped by sixty feet, producing a massive earthquake reaching 9.2 on the Richter scale. It was the largest earthquake ever recorded in Japan, big enough to shift the tilt of Earth's axis.[1]

In Tokyo, more than 200 miles from the epicenter, the quake rattled buildings, caused fires along the shore of the Tokyo Bay, and suspended train service. In Tohoku, the expanse of Honshu north of Tokyo, the quake damaged tens of thousands of homes and buildings. Within an hour, Japan's northeast coast, from Hokkaido down to Chiba prefecture, was inundated by a tsunami that surged over sea walls. In Iwate, Miyagi, and Fukushima prefectures, closest to the epicenter, coastal towns were washed away. By March 2019, eight years after "3/11," the official death toll was 19,689, with another 2,563 listed as missing.

Had the destruction been limited to the earthquake and tsunami, it would still have been a transformative moment for Japan. But a third disaster made 3/11 a day of global historical importance. An hour after the earthquake, a tsunami struck the Fukushima Dai-ichi nuclear power plant—a facility with six reactors operated by the Tokyo Electric Power Company (TEPCO)—sweeping over its sea wall and knocking out backup generators needed to operate emergency cooling systems. Within twenty-four hours, reactors were melting down as TEPCO tried to keep their cores cool with injections of fresh water. By

Saturday evening, an evacuation zone had been established up to twenty kilometers, as the workers vented radioactive steam to relieve pressure, and the first of several explosions occurred. An army of plant workers and firefighters, supported by Japanese and US military personnel, toiled for weeks to keep the reactors cool and contain the disaster. It was the worst nuclear accident since Chernobyl.

The meltdown created more than 150,000 refugees, evacuated from a thirty-kilometer exclusion zone. Nearly a decade later, most had not returned. The release of radiation triggered panic not just in Japan but as far away as the Pacific coast of the United States.

Politically, the effects of the meltdown were far-reaching. Kan and his ministers struggled to contain the nuclear disaster even as they had to oversee the provision of humanitarian assistance to the devastated region and plan reconstruction. For the DPJ, having already lost the trust of much of the electorate, 3/11 was a death sentence.

The Fukushima disaster also shed light on the risks of nuclear power just as the international community was struggling to reach a global accord on carbon emissions. Japan took its reactors offline and the future of nuclear power became a contentious political issue, so much so that just nine of the sixty-one reactors operating or under construction in March 2011 had returned to permanent operation by mid-2019. The Fukushima disaster so alarmed European governments that Germany, Italy, and Switzerland abandoned nuclear power in its wake.[2]

While the disaster shed light on the cozy relationship between the nuclear industry, bureaucrats and regulators, and the LDP—the so-called "nuclear village"—the LDP nevertheless benefited from the disaster by virtue of not holding power. For Abe, 3/11 was an opportunity to prepare another bid for the LDP's leadership. The sense of national crisis played into his pitch that Japan needed renewal—and, as the debates about reconstruction proceeded, the former prime minister had his eyes opened to new policy ideas that would round out his appeal that he alone could fix Japan's problems.

* * *

In the immediate aftermath, Abe, like most of Japan and much of the world, focused on how to address the humanitarian crisis in Tohoku. In the weeks after 3/11, Abe personally gathered emergency supplies and in early April brought them in a rented truck to Tohoku, where he visited evacuation centers in Sendai, the region's largest city, and its surroundings. While he spoke mostly with survivors and listened to their stories, it was another step in his political rehabilitation.[3]

At the same time, the LDP sought to cripple Kan's administration and force him from power. He had been reeling when the disasters struck and, although in the earliest days of the crisis there was talk of setting aside politics as usual to focus on humanitarian relief and reconstruction, these sentiments were short-lived. The DPJ was still suffering blowback from its war on the bureaucracy, and the cabinet struggled to manage the crisis. As one senior ministry of finance (MOF) official lamented, "No matter how many countermeasures headquarters or councils they convene, the DPJ politicians cannot make any important decisions. The response to this earthquake and nuclear accident—without excessive interference in politics—can only be done by us [bureaucrats]."[4] Kan even tried to form a grand coalition, but Tanigaki demanded that the DPJ drop core pledges from its manifesto. It is unlikely that Tanigaki could have convinced the LDP to join a coalition, making this an empty gesture, but the prospect of Kan trading away the party's program in exchange for a potentially messy and temporary coalition with the LDP infuriated many DPJ backbenchers, including Ozawa, who hinted that he would support a censure motion in the upper house if the LDP were to introduce it.

Thus, as Kan struggled to manage a historic crisis, he could barely control his own party, let alone the legislative process. The only way Kan could implement his agenda was to offer his resignation in exchange for its passage and his tenure finally ended on 26 August 2011. He was replaced by Noda Yoshihiko, the self-effacing son of an SDF member who was more conservative than Hatoyama and Kan and therefore, the party hoped, more able to bargain with the LDP. Instead, Noda would be its undertaker.[5]

* * *

While the DPJ and the LDP battled over Kan's future, Abe was experiencing a personal epiphany that would pave the way for his return to power. And the man most responsible for this transformation was a MOF bureaucrat-turned-LDP parliamentarian named Yamamoto Kōzō.

In 2011, Yamamoto was a sixty-three-year-old lawmaker who in 2009 had won his fifth election as a member of the lower house. He won his first election in 1993, after quitting an eighteen-year career at MOF when it appeared that he was not on the fast track for the ministry's top jobs. His record as a politician was ordinary. While he ran and lost as an LDP candidate in 1990, he won as a candidate of Ozawa's new party in 1993 and remained outside the LDP until joining it after the 2000 election. He was not on the fast track in the LDP, either. He was the parliamentary vice-minister at METI during Abe's premiership, but otherwise his résumé was thin.

However, Yamamoto had a reputation as a maverick obsessed with pressuring MOF and the Bank of Japan (BOJ) to do more to combat deflation and revitalize Japan's economy. Yamamoto had fought a lonely battle against what he believed was the BOJ's risk-averse tolerance of deflation; called for the BOJ to introduce an inflation target; and argued for coordinated fiscal and monetary stimulus. In 1993, in his first parliamentary question as a freshman Diet member, for example, Yamamoto noted that the BOJ had not lowered real interest rates sufficiently and that, "This is the biggest cause bringing about the current recession."[6] He looked like an obsessive crank, marginalized in the LDP and unlikely to ever wield the kind of power needed to advance his ideas.

While reflationism, advocated by Yamamoto and some of his allies and friends on the margins of academia and finance, was a minority opinion in Japan's establishment, it had a distinguished pedigree. Takahashi Korekiyo, a finance minister in the 1920s and 1930s, had pioneered the use of government bond purchases to combat the Great Depression.[7] And outside Japan, it was practically the conventional wisdom among academic economists in North America and Europe in debates about what Japan should do to combat its "great stagnation."

In the 1990s and 2000s, leading macroeconomists diagnosed Japan as suffering from deflation due to the timidity and orthodox thinking of monetary authorities at the BOJ and, by extension, political leaders unwilling to confront the bank. As Paul Krugman repeatedly emphasized, standard analysis according to basic macroeconomic models dictated what Japan needed to do to overcome deflation, and, if Japan failed to do it, it was likely the result of a "bankers' orthodoxy [that] regards price stability as an excellent thing, not to be compromised."[8] Future Federal Reserve chairman Ben Bernanke identified the "self-induced paralysis" of monetary policymakers as a major cause of Japan's stagnation and called for "Rooseveltian resolve" regarding policy experimentation. Milton Friedman joined Krugman and Bernanke in attacking the BOJ, opening a 1998 op-ed with a stark accusation: "A decade of inept monetary policy by the Bank of Japan deserves much of the blame for the current parlous state of the Japanese economy." Friedman went on to recommend not an inflation target like Krugman, but rather purchases of government bonds by the BOJ to raise the money supply, i.e. quantitative easing.[9] Friedman repeated this argument, sharing with Krugman the diagnosis that Japan's real interest rates were still too high nearly a decade after the bubble burst.[10] The BOJ gave more ammunition to critics during the 2000s, when it prematurely ended quantitative easing and raised interest rates in 2006 and 2007.[11]

Other economists criticized Japan's fiscal policymakers for being unwilling to commit to Keynesian stimulus. For example, Adam Posen, of the Institute for International Economics and later of the Bank of England, argued that "fiscal policy works when it is tried"—and criticized the Japanese government for its inadequate use of fiscal policy, despite the impression that it had spent the 1990s engaged in futile pump priming.[12]

The arguments made by American and European economists informed the work of Japan's reflationists, giving them intellectual firepower for their battles with the guardians of economic orthodoxy. But while reflationists had a full arsenal of ideas, they lacked political power. As Ono writes, these thinkers were "losers," working largely on the margins of major public institutions and with little success to show for their efforts.[13]

Reflationists were not simply offering academic analysis of Japan's problems: they wanted political change. At first, they tried to convince the BOJ to abandon its anti-inflationary bias and defeat deflation. Yale economist Hamada Kōichi, for example, highlighted the role of "mistaken ideas"—ideas held by both the BOJ and the media that deviated from macroeconomic conventional wisdom—in Japan's long period of deflation.[14] Over time, however, reflationists became more strident and increasingly taken with the idea, developed by economists Thomas Sargent and Peter Temin to explain Franklin Roosevelt's launch of the New Deal, of "regime change." Reflationist Iwata Kikuo, a leading expert on Japan's response to the Great Depression, also saw Takahashi's program as an example of a reflationary regime change.

After so many false starts, the government and the BOJ had to deliver something new and bold to convince households, businesses, and investors that this time it really would be different. As Krugman had argued, the BOJ had to raise inflation expectations by "credibly [promising] to be irresponsible."[15] After the global financial crisis, which forced central banks to develop new tools, the BOJ had more options than ever, including conventional tools like inflation targeting and more unconventional tools including purchases of long-term government bonds, exchange-traded funds, and other financial assets. There was also the option, as Bernanke proposed in a 2003 speech to the Japan Society of Monetary Economics, of "greater cooperation, for a limited time, between the monetary and the fiscal authorities"—whereby MOF would limit the BOJ's exposure to losses on its bond holdings if interest rates were to rise, while the BOJ would increase its purchases of government bonds to finance new fiscal stimulus.

The bank had to signal an end to the old orthodoxy and deliver a dramatic shift in mass psychology.[16] By convincing the Japanese people that prices would begin to rise, they would start to spend and invest, allowing companies to pay more to shareholders and workers and the government to collect more in tax revenues.[17]

Deflation lingered under the DPJ, even as the economy recovered from the crash. For virtually all the DPJ's time in office, core-core inflation—which strips out volatile food and energy prices—declined between 0.5 percent and one percent monthly. Japan's deflation was not helped by the strength of the yen relative to the dollar and other major currencies, making imports cheaper but also encouraging manufacturers to continue offshore production. The yen strengthened as the global financial crisis worsened and remained at around ¥80 to the dollar—substantially stronger than historic levels—for most of the DPJ's tenure. The BOJ's inaction as other central banks experimented with ever-more-unconventional monetary policies only widened the gap.

Some DPJ backbenchers were alarmed and called for action, but the party's leaders were reluctant to challenge the BOJ's independence and relied upon former BOJ governor Shirakawa Masaaki to take the lead. Shirakawa was somewhat proactive, cutting interest rates to zero in October 2010 and introducing "comprehensive quantitative easing," which promised ¥5 trillion in asset purchases. But these measures failed. Shirakawa's heart was not in deflation fighting. He believed that demographics, not deflation, should be the focus of the government's efforts, since public expectations of deflation could come from the belief that a smaller population would retard long-term growth.[18]

Yamamoto immediately saw 3/11 as a window of opportunity, as the Kan government debated how to pay for rebuilding Tohoku.[19] But how could his mavericks, misfits, and outcasts attract enough attention to shift opinion in their favor? After 3/11, Yamamoto organized a parliamentarians' league to pressure the government to issue ¥20 trillion in reconstruction bonds for Tohoku instead of raising taxes, with the understanding that the BOJ would eventually buy these bonds. According to Yamamoto, as he sought a chairman, Tamura Norihisa, another LDP parliamentarian, directed him to Abe. Although he did not, as Yamamoto later noted, have a "special relationship" with the former prime minister, he had heard from Tamura that Abe had criticized the BOJ's decision to cancel its zero interest rate policy (ZIRP) when he was chief cabinet secretary. So, Yamamoto asked Abe to serve as the new group's chairman.

* * *

"At that time," said Yamamoto, "our opinions were not necessarily in complete agreement and he still had some doubts, but he took on the role of chairman."

That group—the Association Seeking Reconstruction Funds Not Coming From Tax Increases—was founded on 16 June 2011, and brought together 211 lawmakers from both government and opposition parties to argue that the government should use the reconstruction process to overcome deflation once and for all.[20] The association issued a statement that, citing risks to the recovery effort, Japan's economy, and the government's long-term fiscal health, called upon Kan and the BOJ to forge an agreement by which the government would issue "earthquake disaster" bonds and the BOJ would buy the full amount.

The statement shows the extent to which the global financial crisis and the unconventional monetary policies pursued by the Fed and other central banks had created new possibilities for reflationism in Japan, the birthplace of quantitative easing. The group cited the example of Bernanke's post-2008 easing policies—and quoted Bernanke directly to calm fears of hyperinflation—to press the case for unconventional monetary policy post-3/11.[21]

Abe and the reflationists were perfectly suited. The reflationists had a program, but no standard bearer. Abe still attracted attention but suffered from the perception that he was a conservative hawk with little to say about the economy. In fact, according to Yamamoto, this is precisely how he pitched Abe about the chairmanship. "You can do an inflation target policy. I would like you to be prime minister once more," Yamamoto told him. "Now that people's livelihoods are deteriorating, you should not just be about the Constitution and education but you should be the 'Economy Abe.'"

Under Yamamoto's tutelage, Abe learned to see Japan's economic performance as a crisis demanding an urgent response from the government. He acquired a policy program with coherent theoretical underpinnings and built relationships with experts who helped him refine policies, hone his message, and communicate with the public. It was a critical moment in Abe's road back to power.

It is tempting to view Abe's embrace of reflationism as a fundamentally cynical maneuver to regain power. While embracing the reflationists was useful for Abe, there is little to suggest that embrace was insincere or inconsistent with his underlying beliefs about the state's role in the economy in a time of crisis. There is evidence to suggest that he had previously been skeptical of BOJ and MOF orthodoxy, and Abe's economic instincts were statist. While some of the reflationists were part of Koizumi's neo-liberal movement, their proposals depended heavily on using a strong state to spend money and fundamentally alter economic behavior.

While the reconstruction association's immediate impact was limited, the association and its successor group—the Association to Eliminate Deflation and the Strong Yen by Revising the BOJ Law—

were where Abe was tutored in monetary policy by leading authorities, especially Hamada, Iwata, and economist Ito Takatoshi. Abe also turned to Honda Etsuro who, having been a MOF official until 2012, was less recognizable to the public than the others but had known Abe since 1978. Not a monetary economist, Honda, like Abe, was converted and committed to reflationism. This, and long association with Abe, drew him into Abe's circle.

These experts guided Abe's conversion and therefore laid the groundwork for what became the first stage of Abenomics. According to a list prepared by Yamamoto, between 19 May 2011, when he first approached Abe about chairing the association, and Abe's election as LDP president on 26 September 2012, Yamamoto met with Abe to discuss economic policy issues more than a dozen times. While some of these occasions were meetings of the association, at which experts like Hamada and Iwata lectured, sometimes Yamamoto would meet Abe one-on-one and, according to Yamamoto's characterization, lectured him on economic policy.

Within months of assuming the chairmanship, Abe had become a vocal proponent of reflationism. In a series of columns from November 2010 to November 2012, Abe barely mentioned economic policy in the eight columns published before 3/11 and did not mention deflation at all until his 18 May 2011 piece, in which he called for reconstruction to be financed by issuing ¥20 trillion in bonds instead of raising taxes.[22] Then, he devoted his 10 August column to a more comprehensive articulation of the association's argument, calling for a Bernanke-like accord between the then-DPJ-led government and the BOJ in which the government would issue reconstruction bonds that the bank would agree to purchase. From that point on, Abe, with the zeal of the convert, regularly used his column to attack the DPJ's handling of the economy.[23]

Abe's fervor played an increasingly dominant role in his political activities during the year leading up to the LDP leadership election in September 2012, and even spilled over into the work of Japan Rebirth. Japan Rebirth issued a manifesto in spring 2012 that included familiar calls for constitutional revision, education reform, and a strong national defense. But it also included several sections on economic revitalization that required the establishment of an economic revitalization headquarters, a new growth strategy, coordination between the BOJ and the government to end deflation and the strong yen, and corporate tax cuts—all policies that would be adopted when Abe returned to power.[24]

Abe was not solely focused on reflation. He played an important role in pressuring the LDP to issue a new draft constitution in 2012 that proposed—to the alarm of Japanese civil society groups—making the emperor the formal head of state, scrapping Article 9 and providing for the formal existence of a "national defense force," weakening protections for individual rights while emphasizing the people's duties and public order, granting the prime minister sweeping new emergency powers, and significantly lowering the threshold for revision of the constitution.[25] Nevertheless, the Japan Rebirth manifesto shows that Abe had melded his newfound embrace of reflationism with his long-standing pursuit of a strong, proud, independent Japan into a comprehensive program of national renewal, making him a more formidable contender than had seemed possible five years earlier.

* * *

Noda did little to arrest the precipitous decline in the public's trust of the DPJ. While he enjoyed a brief honeymoon—his government's support was initially sixty percent—by December 2011, disapproval topped approval for the first time and the gap between its disapproval and approval ratings only grew in 2012.

Noda tried to tackle the two problems that had contributed to his predecessors' downfalls, the DPJ's fractured ranks and the LDP's obstructionism. To address the former, he bolstered coordination between the government and the DPJ. He also walked back some of the DPJ's hostility towards the bureaucracy. Having served as the vice minister and minister of finance under Hatoyama and Kan, he had a better relationship with MOF. Meanwhile, in a bid to placate the LDP and Kōmeitō, Noda said he wanted to work with them to develop a comprehensive plan for social security and tax reform that would include a consumption tax increase.

Working in Noda's favor was that Tanigaki still led the LDP. Tanigaki was a fiscal hawk who believed raising Japan's consumption tax was a necessary step towards fiscal sustainability. But the LDP desperately wanted a snap election that seemed certain to go its way. Tanigaki wanted to negotiate with Noda on the tax hike, while securing a promise from him to call a snap election once it had passed.

As the leaders negotiated in the spring of 2012, Noda struggled to keep the DPJ united not only on fiscal policy, but also on his decision to resume nuclear power generation, which had virtually stopped after 3/11; his determination to join talks for the Trans-Pacific Partnership (TPP), an ambitious multilateral trade agreement that included the US; and new tensions with China and South Korea over disputed territories. With his party divided and the public abandoning him, Noda had limited bargaining power, particularly since Tanigaki knew that a consumption tax hike risked alienating a significant minority of the DPJ, notably Ozawa.

Finally, in June 2012, Noda made a deal with the LDP and Kōmeitō to raise the tax from five percent to ten percent and shelve some of the DPJ's plans for social security reform. When the three-party agreement came before the lower house on 26 June, fifty-seven DPJ lawmakers, including Ozawa, voted against it, and another sixteen abstained or were absent.

The vote marked the end of the DPJ as a ruling party. By 11 July, Ozawa and forty-eight other DPJ lawmakers had left the party and announced the formation of the People's Life First Party, which would stand on an anti-tax hike, anti-nuclear power, and anti-TPP platform. With Noda's leadership crumbling, Tanigaki tried to exact more concessions as the upper house deliberated on the tax hike. To fend off a no-confidence motion, Noda appealed to the LDP and Kōmeitō for support to defeat the motions and pass the tax plan. In exchange, he promised to call an election "sometime soon." The tax plan passed the upper house, at which point Tanigaki overplayed his hand.

Noda hesitated. The Diet would also have to pass legislation permitting the government to issue new deficit bonds to avoid Japan's answer to America's "fiscal cliff" later that year, he argued. Tanigaki then decided to back a censure motion in the upper house, which passed but which led Noda to break off negotiations. His failure to exact a concrete promise from Noda to call a snap election mortally wounded Tanigaki's standing as party leader weeks before the LDP's leadership election—creating an opening for Abe.[26]

* * *

Abe made little secret of his ambitions to lead again—his hunger to run was, he said, 1,000 times greater than in 2006—but he was also circumspect about whether he would challenge Tanigaki. He spent much of 2012 canvassing his closest friends about whether he should run and was far from certain that the time was right. Despite his efforts at rehabilitation, fewer than five years had passed since his resignation and he was still known mainly for his chaotic departure from office. Mori may have been nearing the end of his career—he would retire when the Diet term ended—but he remained a king-maker and wanted his faction's candidate to be Machimura Nobutaka, who had succeeded him as faction leader. It would be difficult for Abe to run in defiance of his own faction bosses. And there were others in Abe's camp—lawmakers who fully supported his political vision—who worried about his physical and mental fitness for a leadership bid, let alone the premiership and speculated that a losing campaign, particularly over objections of party elders, could truly mean the end of his political career. So, well into the summer Abe gave no indication that he was planning to run.

Nevertheless, in 2011, some of Abe's allies began laying the foundation for a leadership bid. As Etō Seiichi, the upper house lawmaker and one of Abe's closest collaborators since the start of his political career, said, "Although Abe himself did not openly show his ambitions until the very end, from after the summer of 2011, we—that is, Shimomura-san [Hakubun], Seko-san [Hiroshige], myself, and others—worked steadily thinking about a mass media strategy, a Diet strategy, a business world strategy, etc. for the leadership election. Abe-san did not stop this. It cannot be said that he would simply do it, because, at the same time, Mori-san and others were saying 'Cut it out.'"[27]

It looked increasingly certain that the LDP would soon return to power, but unclear who would lead it out of the wilderness. It is natural that Abe did not discourage his allies from preparing a campaign or dampen the impression that he was hungry for another chance. On the contrary, he was even willing to flirt with leaving the LDP to run as the head of a new party. In February 2012, he met with officials from the Osaka Restoration Association, a regional party led by then-Osaka mayor Hashimoto Tōru, that had ambitions to enter national politics as a conservative populist party. The Osakans, as well as Abe's friend, Your

Party leader Watanabe Yoshimi, hoped that joining forces with Abe would create a "dream team" that would give a new party instant credibility and enable it to make significant electoral gains.[28] It is unlikely that Abe was particularly serious about this plan, since the LDP was poised to retake power. But he was clearly determined to be an active player in the post-DPJ landscape.

The key figure in encouraging Abe to run was Suga Yoshihide, who had organized Abe's first leadership campaign in 2006, served as a minister in his cabinet, and remained a believer in Abe's political destiny even when it was unclear whether he would have a future in politics.

It would be hard to find two politicians as different as Abe and Suga. Unlike Abe, a political "thoroughbred" born to a political dynasty, Suga was older, lacked a distinguished political pedigree, and had toiled as a parliamentary private secretary and local politician for years before his first election to the Diet in 1996, when was forty-eight.

Suga was the son of a farmer and born in Akita prefecture, in Japan's remote "snow country." Like many of his peers, he left for Tokyo after high school and eventually matriculated at Hosei University. Through school ties he found a job as secretary to Okonogi Hikosaburō, an LDP lawmaker from Yokohama. After eleven years working for Okonogi, during which he developed a broad network in national politics, the business community, and Yokohama politics, he began climbing the political ladder, winning election to Yokohama's city council in 1987, where he earned a reputation as the city's "shadow mayor."

Nine years later he was elected to the Diet. Having served for more than a decade as Okonogi's secretary, he had considerable resources for a newly elected Diet member and enjoyed a swift rise through the LDP's ranks. After initially tying his fortunes to Kajiyama Seiroku, a faction boss and chief cabinet secretary in 1996, Suga drifted into Abe's orbit.

Through his long experience in some of the more thankless jobs in politics, Suga gained a reputation for achieving success by working harder than anyone else. His biographer Matsuda Kenya notes that he was hired as Okonogi's lowest-ranked secretary but quickly showed a talent for diligently addressing every request with little fanfare—"action before words," according to one of Okonogi's associates.

If the education of Abe Shinzō was in statist and nationalist ideology, the education of Suga Yoshihide was in power. While many members of

Abe's inner circle were drawn to him because of his commitment to waging a culture war, Suga appears to have been drawn as much to Abe's statist beliefs as to his new conservatism. He wanted the state to be able to solve big national problems.

While he shared Abe's principles, Suga was a far more astute student of how to wield power effectively, particularly the bureaucracy. In a book published in March 2012, Suga simultaneously criticized the DPJ's naïve "bureaucrat-bashing" approach to political leadership and articulated an approach that emphasized the need for political leaders to manipulate bureaucrats skillfully. "As we administer the Japanese state," he wrote, "the bureaucracy has an absolutely indispensable existence as a fount of wisdom and it is not an exaggeration to say that it is one of the world's leading think tanks. It is the skill of the politician to find out how to use that power. Politicians must draw out their ambitions and allow them to show their potential."

"True political leadership means maximizing the national interest to the maximum extent possible while mastering the bureaucracy and heeding the voice of the people as reflected in the National Diet," he added.[29]

If Abe brought to politics the ironclad conviction that the Japanese state had to make drastic changes to ensure national survival in a turbulent age, Suga brought a profound ability to manipulate the Japanese system of government. It was in large part thanks to Suga that Abe found the elusive balance between Weber's ethic of conviction and the ethic of responsibility and endurance in power.

As the LDP election approached, Suga persistently encouraged Abe to enter the race. Every month, he met with Abe and urged him to run, even as other friends and family members were circumspect.[30] Some thought that Abe's running again would be dismissed as another example of his inability to "read the air" and he would face certain defeat. For much of 2012, polls suggested that Ishiba Shigeru, a hawkish defense policy expert, or Ishihara Nobuteru, son of Tokyo's right-wing governor Ishihara Shintarō, were the favorites heading into the race, suggesting Abe might not even survive to compete in a runoff.[31]

Suga's persistence paid off. By August, polls suggested Abe might have a path to victory. It did not hurt that he had stayed aloof from the consumption tax debate that preoccupied much of the political establishment—or that, as the LDP's election approached, the Noda government was embroiled in disputes with South Korea and China that reinforced Abe's arguments about the need for strong leadership. Noda looked weak when on 10 August South Korean President Lee Myung-bak became the first Korean president to visit the disputed Liancourt Rocks. And he looked completely overmatched in August and September when, in response to his decision to "nationalize" the Senkaku Islands, anti-Japanese protests swept across China, Chinese activists tried to land on the islands, and Beijing began sailing coast guard vessels into the waters surrounding them. It was one more demonstration of what Abe said was the DPJ's bankrupt foreign policy, which he argued simply invited Japan's neighbors to exploit its weakness.[32]

On 15 August, the anniversary of Japan's surrender and the day protestors began gathering outside Japan's embassy in Beijing, Abe visited Yasukuni and then met Suga for a three-hour meeting over yakitori. It was on that day—a date so laden with historical significance—that Suga finally overcame Abe's doubts and convinced him that the time was right. No other leader but you could lead Japan out of the crises that had resulted from the DPJ's three years in power, Suga told him. "Abe-san," he said, "your chance has come. This is the time that I have been waiting for. If you run, I think you will win."[33]

Abe biographer Yamaguchi Noriyuki suggests that it was not just Suga's rhetoric that persuaded him to run. Suga also laid out how the electoral math could work in Abe's favor. He suggested that in a three-way race with Ishiba and Ishihara, Abe just had to do well enough to finish second to Ishiba, who had a strong following among the party's rank-and-file supporters and was likely to win the popular vote that determines the distribution of prefectural votes in the first round. But if Abe could finish second and force a runoff, he would have a strong chance of collecting Ishihara's support and knocking out Ishiba, whose independent streak did not endear him to his parliamentary colleagues.[34]

His path to victory was by no means assured—and he would have little time to convince skeptical colleagues to back him. On 31 August the LDP decided when the election would be held: the filing deadline was 14 September, and the vote would be on 26 September.[35] Mori still wanted Machimura to run, sparking fears that Abe would divide the party's largest faction. Asō thought it was premature for him to run and that perhaps it would be better if he served as a foreign or finance minister in another cabinet before seeking the premiership again. Asō also felt that Tanigaki merited a chance at the premiership after guiding the LDP in opposition.[36]

Abe also had not convinced his family of the wisdom of a leadership bid. His mother and his brother Kishi Nobuo were openly opposed.[37] His wife Akie, scarred from the experience of her husband's resignation, was unenthusiastic about his running but felt duty bound to support him—although she refused to let his candidacy scupper her plans to open an *izakaya* in Tokyo, for which preparations were well underway.[38]

Despite the trepidation of his family and some of his closest friends, it was clear that he would run. On 5 September, Abe launched a new study group focused on economic policy, which had sixty-seven members from across the LDP's factions, signaling that his base among the LDP's parliamentary caucus remained strong.[39] Japan Rebirth also gave him an ironclad base of support.[40] As the filing date approached, events broke in his favor.

On 10 September, Tanigaki, his support crumbling, announced that he would not seek another term. Tanigaki's exit freed his supporters to find new candidates to back, which, most importantly, brought faction leaders, including Asō and Komura Masahiko, a former foreign minister and a fellow lawmaker from Yamaguchi, into his camp.

On 14 September, five candidates declared, including Abe, Ishiba, Ishihara, Machimura, and Hayashi Yoshimasa, an upper house member from Yamaguchi whose father had been Abe Shintarō's bitter rival. Hayashi, as an upper house member, never stood much of a chance (the LDP has never been led by an upper house member). Despite high expectations for Ishihara, he proved to be an inept campaigner and faded rapidly. Perhaps the luckiest break for Abe came on 18 September, when Machimura felt ill during a campaign stop and was rushed to the hospital. He had suffered a stroke, and his campaign was over.

Machimura's exit was a gift of fortune for Abe. They would not split their faction's vote, and within a week it had become a two-man race between Abe and Ishiba.

On 26 September, the vote went as Suga had anticipated. In the first round, Ishiba received 199 of 498 votes—including 165 of the 300 awarded by prefectural chapters—defeating Abe by fifty-eight votes. Both finished well ahead of the others. But the makings of a come-from-behind victory were apparent. Ishiba had not only lost the vote among the 198 LDP parliamentarians, he finished behind both Abe and Ishihara, with the latter receiving the most backing. Ishiba was twenty votes behind Abe. In the second round, in which only lawmakers would vote, Ishiba picked up an additional fifty-five votes, but not enough to close the gap, since Abe gained fifty-four. By a vote of 108 to eighty-nine, Abe was again the leader of the LDP.

Having overcome long odds to win, Abe would likely get another opportunity to lead Japan. But first he had to accomplish what Tanigaki had failed to do: pressure Noda into calling a snap election, despite almost a year remaining in the lower house's four-year term. He also had to make his case to voters that this time would in fact be different, that he was older, healthier, and wiser than in 2007.

He moved quickly on both fronts, unveiling a leadership team—Ishiba as his secretary-general, Komura as the LDP's vice president, Amari Akira, a key economic adviser, as policy chief. Abe called upon Noda to uphold his promise and call an election promptly. He began using his status as the presumptive prime minister to sound the alarm about the wide-reaching crisis that Japan faced. "Now, Japan's territorial waters and territory are becoming threatened. And, at the same time, the economy is slumping due to prolonged deflation and the strong yen," he said in his first press conference after the LDP election. "We will overcome this difficult situation and we will create a strong Japan and a prosperous Japan. That is the mission that has been imposed on me."[41]

While he hammered Noda on his handling of territorial disputes, Abe signaled to voters, investors, and, perhaps most importantly, bureaucrats in the BOJ and government ministries that, if chosen as prime minister again, he would pursue aggressive measures to revitalize Japan's economy. Deflation fighting had been the top plank in his manifesto for the leadership election, and in the following weeks, Abe pledged that his government would seek an accord with the BOJ to introduce an inflation target of two or three percent (the LDP's manifesto ultimately called for a two percent target) and to institute "unlimited monetary easing" to achieve it. He also called for the BOJ to purchase so-called "construction bonds" to expand the monetary supply. He even threatened to revise the BOJ law to curtail the bank's independence. These proposals, eventually included in the LDP's manifesto, suggested that while Abe had not abandoned his conservative iconoclasm, he would return to power with a fuller vision for national revival that addressed some of the country's most urgent challenges.

Abe's reflationism was criticized by Shirakawa and Noda, who warned of the threat to the BOJ's independence. The chairman of Keidanren, Japan's most powerful business federation and a major supporter of the LDP, described Abe's reflationism as "reckless."[42] But the Noda government also conceded that Abe had shifted the debate on macroeconomic policy. The reflationists had won. Not only had they won Abe over to their cause and helped him achieve an unlikely victory, the Noda government, spearheaded by economy minister Maehara Seiji, shifted towards reflationism. Within days of Abe's victory, Maehara called for the BOJ to purchase foreign bonds to combat the strong yen and introduce other easing policies.[43]

This shift was not entirely due to Abe: Noda already knew that if the consumption tax was to be raised, the economy would have to be strong, and therefore the BOJ must tackle deflation more aggressively.[44] But Abe's election meant the BOJ would not be able to escape a more aggressive approach from political authorities. By late October, the BOJ began shifting towards an inflation target, lower interest rates, and a new quantitative easing program.[45]

Financial markets, meanwhile, received Abe's message, resulting in the birth of an "Abe trade" in the last months of 2012. Encouraged by the likelihood that Abe and the LDP would win power and Abe would follow through on his promises, the Nikkei 225 rose from 8,972.89 on 7 November, when Abe first promised "unlimited" easing, to 10,230.36 on 26 December, when he was inaugurated as prime minister, a gain of fourteen percent. Over the same period, the yen fell from ¥80 to the dollar to ¥85.64 to the dollar, a fall of 6.57 percent.

Even as Abe's power grew, Noda's vanished. The DPJ's majority was crumbing. The party hemorrhaged lawmakers to Ozawa's splinter party as well as the new Japan Restoration Party launched by Osaka

Mayor Hashimoto that autumn. Noda also faced the looming threat of a no-confidence motion that could topple his government before he could call a snap election. Threatened on all sides, Noda gave in. On 14 November, in his first party leaders' debate with Abe, Noda promised to dissolve the Diet on 16 November and call a snap election if the LDP and Kōmeitō would support the government's bills on debt issuance and lower house redistricting. To secure their cooperation, he even offered a compromise on debt issuance, agreeing to a bill that would provide for three years of debt issuance, depriving the DPJ of a weapon to use against the LDP if it went back into opposition.[46] Abe accepted, the bills were passed, and the Diet was dissolved. The general election would be held on Sunday, 16 December.

Campaigning on a slogan that promised a conservative revolution—"Taking Back Japan"—Abe and the LDP were heavy favorites. Abe stood at the head of a party more united than when he first led it, a party increasingly committed to the new conservatives' program and willing to follow Abe. The party's unity would only grow after the election, when scores of new conservative lawmakers were brought into the Diet.

In the general election, the restored ruling coalition won a supermajority in the lower house, as the LDP won 294 seats and Kōmeitō thirty-one. Just five years after experiencing the greatest failure of his life, Abe had returned to the premiership. The DPJ was humbled, and barely surpassed the JRP to become the lower house's largest opposition party.

It was not an unalloyed victory: turnout plummeted to a postwar record low of fifty-nine percent and the LDP received roughly two million fewer votes in its 2012 landslide victory than it had in its 2009 defeat, as the independents stayed home. Nevertheless, it was a robust parliamentary majority, and, as 2013 dawned, Abe set to work, using it to build a new Japan.

12

"THERE IS NO ALTERNATIVE"

When Abe addressed Guildhall in the City of London on 19 June 2013, he invoked the famous words of one of his predecessors at its rostrum. "This is a case of 'TINA,'" Abe explained. "There is no alternative."[1]

His leadership, he argued, was indispensable for realizing Japan's economic revitalization, part of a broader program of creating a "robust Japan." The world needed Japan to recover. Only he had the political will to deliver the sweeping changes promised by his government's economic program, which by then had become known around the world as Abenomics.

"I consider it both my role and my fate to restore and enrich the power of the nation of Japan," he told the audience.[2]

Abe's Guildhall speech was part of a sustained effort in the early months of his premiership to convince his fellow Japanese, as well as foreign governments and investors, that this time would be different. Through the power of his example, he sought to convince Japan that anything was possible. "I am back, and so shall Japan be," he told an audience in Washington, DC in February.[3] If the Japanese people could feel confident about their country and its future—even in the face of significant and intractable challenges—the country could achieve anything. "The most important thing is to restore pride and confidence in yourself, is it not?" he said in his first policy address in January. "We, and indeed Japan as well, can surely grow every day in the future by uncovering new capabilities lying dormant within us. Let us share a readiness to break through the crises confronting us here and now and carve out our future."[4]

When he was chosen as Japan's ninety-sixth prime minister on 26 December 2012, it was not inevitable that he would break the cycle of weak, short-lived governments, although he had advantages that his predecessors had not. His party was hungry to reclaim power. The process of losing in a landslide and then winning in a landslide with a predominantly new slate of candidates effectively ended the schisms of the Koizumi years and made it Abe's party. Meanwhile, having returned to power after the Democratic Party of Japan (DPJ) had spent their time in office uprooting old institutions, Abe had a virtually unprecedented opportunity to craft new institutions that would complete the process of building a stronger, executive-led state. For the time being, he also enjoyed strong support from the public.

But, as he learned in 2007, the public can be fickle—and he faced significant obstacles that could frustrate his leadership. To realize his plan for economic revitalization, Abe would have to grapple with administrative elites. The upper house—in which neither the ruling coalition nor the DPJ held a majority—could stymie his legislation. Meanwhile, Washington had not forgotten Abe's views on historical issues and the Obama White House was not overjoyed by his return. Daniel Russel, Obama's assistant secretary of state for East Asia in 2013, said in a private roundtable: "You would need a microscope to find one iota of an upside in the return of Shinzō Abe."[5] And he faced an increasingly assertive China that was prepared to use his historical views to drive a wedge between Japan and its friends in the region.

Abe therefore used his first months in office to set the stage for a durable administration, strengthening his grip on key institutions, reorganizing the prime minister's office, and articulating plans for what his government would do to deliver the salvation that Abe promised. By July, his ruling coalition had taken control of the upper house, and the "Abe system" seemed unstoppable.

* * *

The new cabinet—which Abe dubbed a "cabinet for breaking through crises"—featured lawmakers involved in both Japan Rebirth and the post-3/11 reflationist groups. Suga became the chief cabinet secretary. Asō was named deputy prime minister and finance minister. Tanigaki, his predecessor as LDP leader, and his rivals in the leadership contest received lesser ministerial portfolios, while Ishiba remained as LDP secretary-general.

His economic ministers were capable: Amari Akira, who led the ministry of economy, trade, and industry (METI) during Abe's first government and had been picked to lead a party economic revitalization headquarters established after Abe's election, received a wide-reaching portfolio that made him effectively "minister for Abenomics," and Motegi Toshimitsu, a onetime McKinsey consultant, received the METI portfolio. Meanwhile, the foreign and defense portfolios went to Kishida Fumio and Onodera Itsunori, both of whom belonged to what remained of Yoshida Shigeru's old faction and could be useful for softening Abe's image.

While Abe showed his new political savvy in striking a balance between ideological allies and LDP heavyweights in the distribution of government and party leadership posts, the real innovation was in Abe's recruitment of a leadership team for the Kantei and cabinet secretariat that would take control of the decision-making process. Power in the Abe government lay primarily with formal and informal advisers around the prime minister, rather than in the ministries or the government backbenches.

Abe and Suga crafted a pyramidal structure at the top of the government to ensure the infighting that plagued his first government would not recur. Under Abe was Suga, and under Suga was a new informal "council"—a daily meeting between the prime minister and the chief and deputy chief cabinet secretaries, as well as the prime minister's private secretary—to discuss the prime minister's goals and priorities and, at times, convince the prime minister of an alternative course of action. Proposed by Seko Hiroshige, who was one of the deputies, this informal group became the "highest decision-making body,"[6] responsible for setting the daily agenda for the entire administration. Abe's Kantei would speak with one voice. This informal committee was an embodiment of his determination to learn from 2007.[7]

From the beginning, its members included some of Abe's closest political allies. The two political deputy chief cabinet secretaries were

Kato Katsunobu, former secretary-general of Japan Rebirth, and Seko, who had been Abe's aide for strategic communications in 2006–2007. The administrative deputy chief cabinet secretary was Sugita Kazuhiro, a retired national police agency official who had served in the cabinet's intelligence and crisis management offices during the Koizumi years and came out of retirement to serve under Abe. Abe's principal private secretary, who also attended these meetings, was Imai Takaya, one of the METI officials who had served in the first Abe administration and remained close with Abe thereafter.

Below the leadership committee was the cabinet secretariat and cabinet office and a constellation of advisory councils, commissions, and headquarters that reported directly to the prime minister's office in a variety of policy areas, sidestepping cabinet ministries.[8]

In economic policy, Abe resuscitated the Council on Economic and Fiscal Policy (CEFP), which had spearheaded Koizumi's reforms but was disbanded by the DPJ. But the CEFP would be folded into a new Economic Revitalization Headquarters, which, helmed by Amari, oversaw the CEFP and a newly created Industrial Competitiveness Council. These groups brought together political leaders, bureaucrats, academics, and business leaders to fill in policy details. Abe's economic team was also backed by the reflationists. Hamada and Honda joined as special advisers, occupying offices on the fourth floor of the prime minister's office, one floor down from Abe, Suga, and the deputy chief cabinet secretaries. These posts were not full-time, but they gave the reflationists a seat at the table.

Abe also assembled a foreign policy team that would articulate a comprehensive national strategy. He—not the foreign or defense ministries—would conduct Japan's foreign policy.[9] At this team's heart was Yachi Shōtarō, who had been Abe's aide when he was the deputy chief cabinet secretary, and worked closely with him when Abe became prime minister for the first time. He was instrumental in the outreach to Beijing and Seoul and managed the fallout in Washington from Abe's remarks about the comfort women. Abe may have been generally distrustful of MOFA as insufficiently committed to the defense of Japan's national interests, but he knew and trusted Yachi, and so Abe brought him out of retirement to serve as a de facto national security adviser. Abe would rely on Yachi and his team to both articulate his government's strategy and conduct back-channel diplomacy that reduced his dependence on the bureaucracy, such that Yachi was called the "shadow foreign minister." Kanehara Nobukatsu, a younger diplomat appointed as an assistant chief cabinet secretary, would be a key member of Yachi's team. Kanehara, a highly respected strategic thinker, had worked together to articulate then-Foreign Minister Asō's vision of an "arc of freedom and prosperity," the main strategic concept of Abe's first premiership.[10]

Neither Abe's national security nor his economic policy teams were dominated by new conservatives from Japan Rebirth. This sprawling political executive, the product of decades of administrative reform, was staffed by bureaucrats seconded from the line ministries but who often had previous experience staffing the political executive and often enjoyed relationships with Abe and other principals. Whereas it was widely believed that earlier generations of bureaucrats were indoctrinated to put their ministry's interests first and the national interest second, the new breed of officials drawn to Abe's Kantei appeared committed to the new prime minister's vision for national rejuvenation.

His economic team was dominated by METI. The ministry, descendant of Kishi's MCI and the "mighty MITI" of Japan's high-speed growth period, had seen its influence wane but remained focused on using state power to shape Japan's economic development, especially the promotion of new, high-value-added sectors to enable Japan to compete with other manufacturing powers. Under Abe, METI wielded power thanks to a small group of METI officials close to the prime minister. This led Takenaka Heizo, Koizumi's economic reform czar, to call the Abe cabinet a "Cabinet of METI Officials."[11]

Hasegawa Eiichi, the METI official who had encouraged Abe to take up hiking, retired from METI and joined Abe as an adviser responsible for policy planning. Imai became his principal private secretary, an expansive role that includes political strategy, communications strategy, and parliamentary affairs management. Imai's role proved so significant that he was described as "Rasputin" or "shadow prime minister," becoming in time an adviser whose word was as good as Abe's.[12] METI officials assumed other roles, including as his principal domestic speechwriter. A young official named Saiki Kozo—nicknamed the "writing bureaucrat"—was responsible for crafting the prime minister's rhetoric. Saiki searched widely for phrases and anecdotes that precisely captured the prime minister's thoughts, going so far as to trawl through "prewar language and ethics textbooks" for examples.[13]

It was a mark of Abe's growth that in 2012 he tapped an experienced diplomat to serve as his national security adviser and a senior METI official as his chief private secretary. It was also a sign that the "new Abe" would, as he promised during the campaign, put economics first.

* * *

Nakagawa Hidenao had used the term "Abenomics" in 2006 but it never caught on. However, as Abe traveled the country in 2012 promising aggressive measures to combat deflation and the strong yen, the term was revived to describe Abe's new program and was soon widely embraced by domestic and foreign news outlets.[14] By late December, *Asahi* used "Abenomics" in the headline of an editorial that worried Abenomics could be "Danger-nomics."[15]

Although Abenomics made Abe a household name, he faced an uphill battle to deliver on his promise of quickly and thoroughly revitalizing Japan's economy. The Bank of Japan (BOJ) was still led by Shirakawa Masaaki, whose term as governor would not end until April. The upper house was deeply divided. While the ruling coalition could, thanks to their lower-house supermajority, overrule the upper house on certain issues, on others—including appointments to the BOJ's leadership—it needed the approval of both houses.

Nevertheless, Abe, drawing upon the guidance of the reflationists, developed a program of "shock and awe" that would force the public and markets to take notice.[16] To this end, Abe announced what he called the "three arrows" of Abenomics, a three-pronged program of "bold monetary policy," "flexible fiscal policy," and "a growth strategy to draw out private investment" that would defeat deflation, weaken the yen, and release the dormant animal spirits of the Japanese economy.[17] The government's argument was that to unseat the "deflationary mindset" that had depressed growth, the government's policies needed to work in sync. The first two arrows would raise inflationary expectations and spur consumption and investment, strengthening Abe's hand as he pursued a wide-reaching growth strategy that would lay the foundation for more robust growth. As Abe said in his policy speech on

28 January, "I have proposed a bold policy package that is from a different dimension than what has come before." Ten years after Ben Bernanke had urged Japan to pursue "combined monetary and fiscal ease" to overcome deflation, a Japanese prime minister was finally taking his advice.

The first task was regime change at the BOJ. Abe's desire to create a euphoric shift in public expectations meant he was impatient for Shirakawa's term to end so he could appoint a more pliable governor.

Shirakawa had begun to shift when the LDP returned to power. He wanted to resist political pressure that could jeopardize the bank's independence, since Abe had campaigned on revising the BOJ law if the bank resisted him. Shirakawa, a career BOJ official, wanted above all to protect the BOJ's statutory independence.[18]

Therefore, at a 20 December meeting, the bank expanded its asset purchases and announced it would study an inflation target ahead of its January meeting. In January, the BOJ formally adopted an inflation target of two percent and expanded its asset purchases.

More significantly, the bank agreed to an accord with the government that stipulated (1) political and monetary authorities would coordinate, (2) the bank would aim for a "price stability target" of two percent measured year-over-year, and (3) the government would "strive for flexible macroeconomic policy management" while using full policy mobilization to "strengthen the competitiveness and growth potential of the Japanese economy."[19] While the government respected the bank's independence in determining how to reach the inflation target, the accord meant that the BOJ had effectively become an arm of the Abe administration. Shirakawa had preserved the bank's de jure independence by yielding to Abe.

But Shirakawa remained out of step with the government. He was a reluctant partner for Abe, who wanted bigger and bolder actions than Shirakawa seemed temperamentally capable of. Therefore, on 5 February, he told Abe that he would leave office on 19 March, the same day as his two deputy governors and three weeks before the end of his own five-year term.[20] He wanted the new leadership team to commence all at once, he said.[21] Shirakawa's decision to hasten his exit led the Abe government to accelerate the process of naming the next governor and deputy governors.

Abe delegated the task to Honda, the reflationist ex-MOF official who had known him for more than thirty years.[22] Among the reflationists in Abe's orbit, perhaps none understood as well as Honda how reflationism fit into Abe's political program more broadly. "It was no exaggeration to say that Japan is surely being driven to the cliff's edge," he wrote in a book making the case for Abenomics published in April 2013. "Abenomics made its entrance in such a critical situation. The Japanese economy has been pulled back from the precipice just in the nick of time. We can truly say that this is 'economics of national salvation.'"[23] Honda wanted to ensure the BOJ's new leaders were reliable, willing not only to accept the straitjacketed independence that Shirakawa had begrudgingly accepted but also to do whatever it would take to escape deflation.

But there was another consideration: without an upper house majority Abe had to convince some opposition lawmakers to approve his choice. Despite the DPJ's longstanding objections to tapping an ex-MOFer for the BOJ's governorship, the administration included ex-MOF officials on its list. The search, which began early in the new year, soon produced a six-man shortlist: Mutō Toshirō, the ex-MOF vice minister and BOJ deputy governor who had been Fukuda's top choice in 2008; former deputy governor Iwata Kazumasa; Takenaka Heizō; Tokyo University economist Itō Takatoshi; Iwata Kikuo; and former MOFer and Asian Development Bank President Kuroda Haruhiko.[24]

Over the course of January and February, Honda and other advisers talked with candidates as well as with the key veto players whose support would be needed to ensure confirmation. Abe indicated that he wanted to appoint a cohesive team that would signal to markets that the BOJ was unquestionably committed to reflationism.[25]

One by one the shortlist shrank. Asō favored Mutō, but Abe did not view him as a reliable ally. Iwata Kikuo, who had impeccable credentials as a reflationary economist, was a strong contender but lacked international experience. That gave Kuroda an edge. He was the head of a major international development bank and had also served an unusually long stint as MOF's vice minister for international affairs under Mori and Koizumi. He was known to Abe, and had voiced his support for Abe's reflationist platform in a meeting in Tokyo in December 2012.[26] He also had a long record of advocating for the

BOJ to embrace reflationism.[27] With Abe's approval, Honda reached out to Kuroda about the possibility of his serving as the BOJ's governor. He accepted.

By late February, the Abe government had its slate. Kuroda would be governor, Iwata Kikuo a deputy governor, and Nakaso Hiroshi, a BOJ staffer who had served at the Bank for International Settlements in Basel, the other deputy. This lineup appeared to satisfy Abe's desire to signal the coming of a new policy regime.

But Abe still had to convince enough opposition lawmakers in the upper house to back his candidates. In confirmation hearings, the nominees began outlining what policies they would pursue—achieving two-percent inflation in two years emerged as a particularly salient mantra, with Iwata promising to quit if the target was not reached in two years—but as the debate moved to the upper house, it was still unclear whether Abe would have the votes. The opposition Your Party refused to back an ex-MOFer and some in the DPJ wanted to take the same line. But others in the party favored a more flexible approach to avoid leaving the governorship vacant at a sensitive moment. The pragmatists won and on 15 March, the upper house approved the new leadership team.

The reflationist movement's hopes for regime change were now in the hands of the sixty-eight-year-old Kuroda. Abe and Kuroda were an odd couple. Kuroda was an elite bureaucrat with degrees from Tokyo University and Oxford, a polished English speaker, widely respected in international financial circles as an expert on monetary and exchange rate policies. He was more intellectual than the typical bureaucrat, somehow finding the time as a young MOF official to publish a translation of Karl Popper's essay, "What is dialectic?"[28] Nevertheless, despite their differences, Kuroda and Abe forged a durable partnership that, while not without friction, enabled the prime minister to trust the BOJ regarding its pursuit of reflation.

After succeeding Shirakawa on 20 March, Kuroda signaled that a policy shift was imminent. With the bank's next meeting on 3–4 April, he had only a brief window to prepare a policy announcement that would communicate regime change. He did not disappoint. On 4 April, he announced what became known as "quantitative and qualitative easing" (QQE), a dramatic expansion of the BOJ's purchases of

Japanese government bonds (quantitative easing) and other financial assets, including exchange-traded funds and real estate investment trusts (qualitative easing). These purchases—which far exceeded what the BOJ had attempted before—were in pursuit of what Kuroda called the bank's "2–2–2" target, doubling the money supply in two years to achieve inflation of two percent. In practice, the BOJ expanded its purchases of government bonds to ¥60–70 trillion a year and bought bonds with significantly longer maturities than the BOJ had ever done, in order to slash interest rates all along Japan's yield curve. Kuroda argued that QQE would work through a variety of channels, boosting asset prices, inflation expectations, and encouraging more lending. It would also—although both Kuroda and the Abe government would deny this was anything but a side effect—drive down the yen, giving a much-needed boost to Japan's exporters.

This announcement, known as Kuroda's "bazooka," came as a major shock to investors used to being disappointed by the BOJ. The Nikkei 225, which at the start of April was at 12,371.34, rose more than thirty percent through the end of 2013 to close the year at 16,269.22. The yen, meanwhile, fell from 93.30 to the dollar on 1 April to 105 to the dollar at year's end, the weakest it had been since before the global financial crisis. Regime change had finally come to the BOJ and Abenomics had arrived, a seemingly inexorable force that would finally revive Japan. "The truth is that there was no alternative," opined the *Financial Times*.

* * *

Even as the Abe government was setting the stage for Kuroda, it was preparing the second arrow of Abenomics, which, in the early months of Abe's second government, mainly meant fiscal stimulus—and lots of it. The reflationists wanted greater coordination between fiscal and monetary authorities. The government should be prepared to ramp up spending and issue more bonds while the central bank was prepared to buy more debt.

On his first day in office, Abe had ordered MOF to prepare a supplemental budget that could be passed by the Diet in early 2013. By the time the government's accord with the BOJ was signed, MOF was finalizing a ¥13 trillion stimulus package—larded with public works spending that would help the newly elected LDP retain the support of voters—to be funded by issuing more than ¥5 trillion in new government bonds, breaking an informal limit on new debt issuance. The Abe government was determined to show that it would do whatever was required, even if it meant abandoning fiscal consolidation targets, a message reinforced on 28 February when a government estimate suggested that not only would the administration fail to achieve a target of halving the primary deficit by 2015, but the deficit would actually grow.

The same spirit guided the new government's budget for the next fiscal year, which began on 1 April. The government's draft called for more than ¥92 trillion in spending, which would require more than ¥40 trillion in new debt, the most in four years, and included significant increases in public works spending, which, with the exception of 2009, had been in decline since the Koizumi administration. Defense spending would also rise for the first time in eleven years.

But, just as the divided upper house almost held up Kuroda's nomination, both the stimulus package and the 2013 budget ran afoul of the divided Diet. The stimulus package, submitted to the Diet on 4 February and passed quickly by the lower house, was held up in the upper house and only passed on 26 February, by a one-vote margin. Although Japanese political convention dictates that the general budget should be passed before the start of a new fiscal year, the 2013 budget was entirely stalled, forcing MOF to assemble a temporary budget to cover the gap. In the end, the lower house did not pass the 2013 budget until 16 April and the upper house did not act until 15 May, the latest a budget had passed since 1996.

Nevertheless, despite the political roadblocks—which helped Abe make the case for a ruling coalition majority in the upper house elections—the first and second arrows were in place.

* * *

In foreign policy, Abe used his first months in office to signal that a strong, confident Japan would not hesitate to lead in East Asia. He virtually picked up where he left off in 2007, taking his first foreign trip in January 2013 to Southeast Asia, with stops in Vietnam, Thailand, and Indonesia. In Jakarta, he began articulating what would eventually become a comprehensive "Abe Doctrine." Picking up the theme of his last major foreign speech, in New Delhi in August 2007 when he spoke of the "confluence of the two seas," Abe again spoke of the confluence of the Indian and Pacific Oceans and of the need to maintain liberal values in the region's commons, keep the US engaged, and safeguard the deep integration of the region's economies.[29]

Notably, his Jakarta speech contained no mention of China. While portions of the address were clearly written with China in mind, Abe demonstrated an important principle that would guide his foreign policy. His goal would not be containing China. Rather, Japan would help Southeast Asian nations grow, integrate with the region and the global economy on the best possible terms, and support the development of robust political institutions. As Abe noted, referencing former Prime Minister Fukuda Takeo's "Fukuda Doctrine" of building peaceful economic ties with Southeast Asia with Japan as an equal partner for ASEAN, throughout the postwar era Japan had established deep roots in the region, first via compensation for the war's devastation and then as a source of investment and development aid. Japan, he implied, was well equipped to compete with China in shaping the region's future.

* * *

Abe started his new government by giving a clear statement of what was at stake in twenty-first-century Asia—and he would never lose sight of it. He began to act on it early in his administration, increasing incentives for private infrastructure investment in the region, sharply increasing development assistance, and increasing bilateral defense ties with ASEAN members engaged in territorial disputes with China in the South China Sea.[30] Abe returned to Southeast Asia in May, July, October for the ASEAN and East Asia summits, and November, managing to visit all ten ASEAN member states during his first year in office.

He anticipated this frenetic travel schedule in his Jakarta address. "If the Japanese need one thing now," he said, "that thing is confidence—the ability to turn our faces to the sun, like the sunflower does when it blooms at the height of summer. Japan once had tremendous confidence, but there is a shortage of it today." Abe was brimming with confidence and enthusiasm and determined to leverage it on Japan's behalf. His willingness to show up, with seemingly boundless energy, and put a personal touch on his relationship with other leaders, became a significant element in his pursuit of a new role for Japan.

* * *

But no relationship was as important as Japan's relationship with the US. While the relationship had improved under Noda, Abe knew that more was needed to repair the alliance. With China becoming an increasing threat to Japan, he had little choice but to draw closer to the US, which remained an indispensable partner for conventional and nuclear deterrence and a counterweight to China's attempts to supplant the US-led regional order. If the US were to pull back, it would force Japan to confront tough questions about its security, perhaps including whether it should turn its latent nuclear capability into a full-fledged deterrent.

On paper, the Obama administration was eager to reciprocate Abe's pursuit of a more robust partnership. Obama and his advisers had criticized the Bush administration for preoccupation with the Middle East and neglect of Asia.[31] The first principle of the administration's Asia-Pacific strategy, wrote Jeffrey Bader, senior director for Asia on the NSC, was "the Asia-Pacific region deserved higher priority in American foreign policy."[32] As part of this reorientation—later called the "pivot to Asia" and then the "rebalance"—Obama relied on traditional US allies like Japan, South Korea, and Australia, as well as new partners like India and Vietnam, to "[maintain] a framework of peace and stability" in the region and, in practice, counter if not contain China's growing power.

Therefore, Hillary Clinton was the first secretary of state in nearly fifty years to visit Asia for her first overseas trip, and she and other officials traveled regularly for bilateral meetings and multilateral summits, including the East Asia Summit, which Bush had declined to join.[33] Meanwhile, Asō was the first foreign leader to visit the White House after Obama's inauguration, a deliberate choice to signal Asia's status as a top priority.[34] But the rebalance would depend on allies—and for the entirety of Obama's first term, Japan was missing, consumed by political turmoil and unable to act as an effective "deputy" for the US as it sought to shore up a liberal order in the Asia-Pacific.

After dealing with four prime ministers during his first term alone, Obama had little reason to think that Japan would be different under

Abe. Washington appreciated what a stronger Japanese prime minister could mean for allied cooperation, but Obama, his new secretary of state John Kerry, Russel, and other officials had no idea whether Abe would be that leader. And they worried about Abe's baggage. Washington had not forgotten the dispute over the Honda resolution. Abe could be a loose cannon who might upset efforts to forge a united front to counter China. South Koreans, who parsed Abe's every word for signs of historical revisionism, especially loathed him, and South Korean antipathy could stymie the Obama administration's determination to strengthen trilateral cooperation to manage North Korea. Finally, Obama, known for his cool, cerebral leadership style and his aversion to personal diplomacy, seemed to appreciate the workmanlike Noda.[35]

Abe had his own reasons for being skeptical about Obama. He and his advisers chafed at the Obama administration's stern warnings about history issues. Abe, like many members of the LDP, also stubbornly believed that Republicans were friendlier to Japan than Democrats, although there was little evidence to suggest that this was true.[36] Most fundamentally, Abe's government took seriously the charges leveled against Obama that he was a weak, indecisive leader and watched closely for signs that the US commitment to Japan was wavering.

Ironically, Obama's determination to limit involvement in conflicts in Syria and Ukraine was indispensable for the success of a rebalance to Asia. Obama sought to avoid intractable conflicts that would constrain America's resources, waste American lives, and sap the will of the American people to support an active foreign policy in other parts of the world.[37] But Tokyo nevertheless worried that the credibility of the US security guarantee was at stake—and feared that even as US budget battles led to defense cuts that raised serious doubts about the US ability to meet its commitments in Asia, China's defense spending continued to outpace its still-impressive economic growth.[38]

Finally, from the earliest days of the Obama administration, the Japanese right in particular fretted that Obama would establish a "G2" relationship with China and even as the Obama administration ramped up its rebalance strategy, those fears lingered.[39] Some of these concerns were less about Obama than about the portents of the long-term decline of US leadership in Asia.

Despite these misgivings, the two leaders tried to establish an effective partnership. Their first meeting was delayed until February by Obama's second inauguration. Abe finally arrived in Washington on 22 February, where he tried to reassure Obama that he would not enflame Asia's history wars. In an interview with the *Washington Post* ahead of his first meeting with Obama, Abe indicated that he would not rescind earlier apologies—a major sticking point for Japan's neighbors—but that he would issue his own "future-oriented" statement at the appropriate time.[40]

Unfortunately, their first meeting would be the high point of 2013—and for the remainder of the year Abe's relationship with Obama was buffeted by challenges, quite a few of his own making, that made it difficult to argue the bilateral relationship had dramatically improved under his leadership.

Abe raised eyebrows on 12 March when he referred to the postwar Tokyo tribunals as "victor's justice."[41] On 23 April, he mused about the meaning of "invasion" and appeared to undercut the value of the 1995 Murayama statement—on the day that a record number of Diet members, including Asō and two other cabinet members, worshipped at Yasukuni shrine. The Yasukuni visits led both Beijing and Seoul to suspend scheduled meetings between senior officials, while Abe's remarks in the Diet were the subject of a scathing editorial in the *Wall Street Journal*, which warned, "Mr. Abe's disgraceful remark will make his country no more friends abroad."[42] This was perhaps one of the few occasions when the editorial lines of the *Wall Street Journal* and *Akahata*, the house organ of the Japanese Communist Party have overlapped.[43]

The fallout from the 23 April events seemed to confirm Washington's worst fears. As if to emphasize his defiance of the Obama administration's remonstrations on historical issues, on 28 April, Abe convened a ceremony—with the emperor and empress in attendance—to commemorate the end of the US occupation and the restoration of Japan's sovereignty sixty-one years prior, a date that had not conventionally been marked so ostentatiously.

* * *

While Abe and Obama would struggle to get their relationship started on the right foot, Obama would nevertheless provide Abe with an important gift when they met, the political cover he needed to bring Japan into the Trans-Pacific Partnership (TPP).

TPP began as an attempt by Chile, New Zealand, Singapore, and Brunei to salvage an early attempt in APEC to launch a trans-Pacific trade pact. In 2006, they launched the first iteration of TPP with virtually no fanfare. When the group restarted negotiations on some outstanding issues, the US became interested, and the Bush administration entered talks in the final months, leading Vietnam, Australia, and Peru also to seek accession.

The Obama administration decided early on to recommit to the talks as part of what would become the rebalance strategy. With the US now leading the process, ambitions for the agreement grew. The US sought not just aggressive cuts in trade barriers, but also substantial regulatory harmonization in new areas not included in other trade agreements (intellectual property rights, state-owned enterprises, e-commerce) and to upgrade trade rules to facilitate the operation of supply chains across borders. With global multilateral trade talks via the WTO stalled, TPP emerged as a promising approach to developing new trade and investment rules at the regional level.

While Kan and Noda were enthusiastic about TPP and trade liberalization, they struggled to commit Japan to the group. In November 2011, Noda began consultations with the eight countries negotiating TPP with a view to Japan formally joining. However, he lacked the wherewithal to achieve this. Japanese farmers were agitated by the high levels of market opening that the agreement was expected to achieve, and citizens were also concerned about the impact other chapters might have on Japan's public healthcare system and domestic institutions.

With talks entering their fourth year, Abe had to assume that Japan's window of opportunity was closing. Nevertheless, he and his advisers recognized the TPP's value and wanted to move quickly to join.[44] It could be an important lever for promoting the domestic reforms that would boost Japan's international competitiveness. The two allies would also be working together to craft trade and investment rules to counter a Chinese bid for economic leadership and could even pressure Beijing to undertake its own domestic reforms. If Japan joined, TPP would be a "megadeal," covering forty percent of global gross domestic product and functioning simultaneously as an upgrading of the North

America Free Trade Agreement (NAFTA) and a US–Japan bilateral free trade agreement.

But most importantly, joining TPP would be a strategic decision. It would bind Japan and the US closer together and keep the US politically and economically engaged in Asia. "Until now, Japan's diplomacy has succeeded when it has made a strategy using a Pacific rim and Asia-Pacific framework that draws in the United States, and it has failed when it has considered East Asian hegemony and the exclusion of the United States," wrote Yachi in 2010. "We must never forget this historical lesson. It is self-evident that if viewed from a strategic perspective, the Trans-Pacific free trade plan is a bus on which Japan should jump."[45]

But joining quickly risked a backlash from LDP supporters in rural Japan, who had helped the party win in December.[46] The LDP's victory depended in part on opposition to Noda's support for TPP participation, and the party's manifesto was virtually silent on it, noting only that the LDP opposed participating in the talks on the basis of "tariff elimination without sanctuary."[47] A group of LDP lawmakers opposed to Japan's participation was gaining in strength and included not just many of his new conservative allies—reminiscent of the 2005 postal privatization battle—but also members of his own cabinet.

To sidestep opposition from the LDP as well as from the bureaucracy, Abe centralized decision-making for TPP. In February, he spoke directly with Obama about the conditions regarding Japan's involvement in TPP. Their meeting resulted in a joint statement that fulfilled the LDP's most important precondition: "The two Governments confirm that, as the final outcome will be determined during the negotiations, it is not required to make a prior commitment to unilaterally eliminate all tariffs upon joining the TPP negotiations."[48] This statement was a critical step; Noda's government had done much of the preliminary work, but Abe needed a public commitment from the US to respect Japan's domestic sensitivities.

Abe could now move ahead. On 15 March, he announced that Japan would join—surprising even US officials with his haste, as the Obama administration assumed it would still be difficult for Abe to commit before the elections in July. "Now is our last chance," Abe said. "Losing this opportunity would simply leave Japan out from the rule-making in the world." Abe simultaneously pledged to defend his vision of Japan's collectivist capitalism—protecting the national interest in keeping with LDP demands that the prime minister defend five "sacred" agricultural products in negotiations—while committing Japan to participate in the formation of a new economic order that would "significantly contribute to the security of our country and also to the stability of the Asia-Pacific region."[49] It was an impassioned plea that decisively shifted the politics of TPP in Abe's favor.

The pact's opponents within the LDP shifted their focus to holding the prime minister accountable for his pledge to defend Japan's national interests in negotiations, but the public increasingly backed Japan's membership. Even before Abe's decision, most supported Japan's involvement; polls conducted after Abe's announcement showed that his decision to join TPP was popular, giving a bump to his already strong approval ratings.

As the Abe government began preparations to join talks later in the summer, the administration established a new headquarters attached to the cabinet secretariat that would be responsible for conducting talks on behalf of the whole government. Headed by Amari, the headquarters were Japan's answer to the US Trade Representative. The headquarters drew top negotiators and trade policy experts from MOF and MOFA but with Amari in charge, Abe could delegate responsibility to a single official who had his full backing, strengthening Japan's bargaining power.[50]

The Abe government still faced difficult talks with the US over what had long been the most challenging issues in the bilateral economic relationship—agriculture and automobiles—and also had to deal with periodic challenges from LDP lawmakers. Nevertheless, Abe's decisions to bring Japan into the talks and then to empower Amari to manage the process were momentous.

* * *

The excitement around Abe's TPP decision raised expectations for the growth strategy that was being drafted by the administration. But when the strategy was finally unveiled in June, it showed little of the boldness that had characterized Abe's decision to join TPP. Instead, it was a loose collection of targets and vague policy ideas that would be left to other advisory councils or ministries to flesh out into legislation.

The strategy included a raft of proposals to encourage more investment, risk-taking, and enter and exit in the private sector. Another pillar promised to remake the labor force by increasing female workforce participation (including expanding access to daycare to enable more mothers to work), creating new opportunities for the young, the elderly, and foreign workers, promoting more flexible work arrangements, and reforming higher education to develop a more globally competitive talent pool. Other proposals aimed to boost Japan's competitiveness in strategic sectors—particularly pharmaceuticals, robotics, information technology, and agriculture. The Abe government was especially committed to new strategic special economic zones and included a pledge that the government would not only conclude TPP but would also ensure that most of Japan's international trade was covered by trade agreements.[51]

The third arrow demonstrated a commitment to experimentation, but there was little sense of Abe's priorities. Whatever the Abe government's ambitions for Japan's economy, its growth strategy offered too few details of how it would achieve the ambitious targets. As journalist Richard Katz said, "It is a con game, in the sense that most of the so-called third arrow of structural reform is just nice-sounding targets with no strategies to realize them."[52] Perhaps the vagueness was the point, since it gave bureaucrats at the Kantei and METI more power to influence the final shape of policies.

However, it is likely that some of the disappointment felt by global investors reflected dashed hopes that Abe would be Japan's answer to Thatcher. To some extent, Abe encouraged these expectations. "Japan's regulatory regime is like solid bedrock," he told the audience at Guildhall. "I myself intend to serve as the drill bit that will break through that bedrock."

The reality, however, is that the third arrow's ambitions differed from Koizumi's neo-liberalism. If Koizumi's goals were "small government" and "leave to the private sector what it can do," Abe's goal was to leverage all the tools of state power to restore Japan's economic strength in what he called the "era of global megacompetition." To this end, the third arrow was intended to overcome three challenges: boosting productivity and shifting resources to higher-value-added sectors, to maintain high standards of living even with a smaller labor force; slowing the decline of the labor force in the near term by drawing more women, elderly, and foreigners into the workforce; and stabilizing the working-age population over the long term by fostering working conditions and a social safety net that encourage family formation and, to a lesser extent, attracted highly skilled immigrants to seek long-term residency. As Abe indicated in an April speech outlining what would become his government's first growth strategy—his government would issue a new growth strategy every June—the goal was to make Japan's economy more risk-tolerant, global, and innovative.[53]

The implication is that under Abe, the state would not leave it to private companies to enable Japan to compete for global markets, not when the leaders of other manufacturing powerhouses were developing their own plans to gain an edge in the industries of the future. To realize this transformation, the prime minister's office and the cabinet secretariat, together with METI's leadership, had to wrest power from other ministries and agencies and even apply pressure to big business and organized labor to move Japan in the right direction. If not as heavy handed as China's state capitalism, it was not laissez faire, either.

* * *

Despite the third arrow's disappointing reception, Abe entered the campaign for the upper house with a commanding lead. His approval ratings remained in the sixties, while the DPJ was mired in the single digits. There was little chance that the DPJ—defending seats it had won in its victory over Abe in 2007—would retain its status as the chamber's largest party.

On 21 July, the LDP won sixty-five out of 121 seats up for election. The party now held 115 seats in the 242-seat chamber, making it the largest party. But it fell short of a majority and needed Kōmeitō's twenty seats in the chamber. Turnout fell sharply again, cementing what would be the predominant feature of elections during Abe's tenure: with the opposition in disarray, there was no alternative for voters, leading many to stay home.

Nevertheless, Abe passed his first electoral test. His government now controlled the legislative process. The basic political and institutional framework of Abenomics was in place. Economic indicators suggested that Japan might finally be on the right track. And Abe could go another three years before he needed to face voters again. Now, it seemed, he could turn his attention to laying the groundwork for a new Japan that would be stronger and more assertive in Asia. But while foreign policy and defense policy would command much of Abe's attention for the subsequent two years, the battle for economic revitalization was far from over.

13

BUILDING A NEW JAPAN

On 6 September 2013, Abe boarded his jet in Saint Petersburg. He had been in Russia for the G20 summit—and was eager to build a rapport with his host, Russian President Vladimir Putin—but he had to leave the summit early. He traveled onwards to Buenos Aires, where the International Olympic Committee (IOC) would announce the host for the 2020 Summer Olympics.

Few Japanese leaders could match Abe's zeal for the Olympics. When Tokyo first hosted the summer games, in 1964, it was an indelible moment in his childhood, when the Japanese people could feel pride showcasing their rebuilt country and could look confidently to a prosperous future. He had backed Tokyo's bid for the 2016 games, and, when he returned to power, was personally committed to landing the 2020 games.

In 2013, Abe mobilized his government to drum up support for the Tokyo bid.[1] In Buenos Aires, he used his presence to convey his own and his country's enthusiasm for the games and made a presentation before the final vote in which he shared his memories of watching the 1964 opening ceremony as a ten-year-old boy. With memories of the Fukushima meltdown still fresh, Abe reassured the IOC that there would be no danger to athletes or spectators.[2]

Finally, on 8 September, IOC president Jacques Rogge opened an oversized envelope bearing the Olympic rings. "Tokyo," he announced.

Abe would have his Olympics. Hosting them would not just be about recreating the confident Japan of his youth—though he was undoubtedly animated by these feelings.[3] It would also serve as a "fourth arrow" of Abenomics, a lever for securing investments in infrastructure and services to prepare for an influx of tourists. It would be an opportunity for Japan to showcase itself as the kind of country Abe hoped it would be. "We will emphatically send out a message to people the world over," he said in a press conference following the announcement, "showing them a Japan that has accomplished laudably its reconstruction from the Great East Japan Earthquake and a Japan that is active on the world's center stage."[4]

The Olympic decision, coming little more than six weeks after Abe had regained control of the upper house, suggested that maybe this time Abe would have a chance to build a new Japan.

* * *

But first he would have to decide what to do about the consumption tax. On 1 April 2014, the tax would go from five percent to eight percent, as outlined by the tripartite agreement between Noda and the LDP and Kōmeitō in 2012.

Abe's fiscal inclinations were dovish. His government's slogan on fiscal policy was "no fiscal reconstruction without growth." And he wanted to maximize his freedom of maneuver. The compromise, after all, mandated that the prime minister could decide whether to proceed based on prevailing economic conditions.

Abe was not particularly wedded to the 2012 compromise. He was skeptical of the ministry of finance (MOF). The reflationists in the Kantei advised caution. Hamada, for example, said in a speech on 11 July, that given the potential impact on growth, the tax hike should either be postponed or, failing that, should be phased in gradually, increasing it from five percent to ten percent by a percentage point a year instead of in two stages in 2014 and 2015.[5] Finally, the LDP's manifesto that July made no reference to the tax hike.

And in the summer of 2013—as the "Abenomics boom" unfurled—Abe was reluctant. His biographer Yamaguchi Noriyuki relates a conversation with Abe in early summer in which he admitted to doubts about hiking the tax. Abe related that he was in a battle of nerves with the MOF and the bureaucracy as a whole. "If they knew that the option of 'not raising' [the tax] was in the prime minister's head," he told Yamaguchi, "Kasumigaseki's anxiety would increase instantly."[6]

But it would not be easy to delay. Despite the consumption tax's well-deserved reputation as a slayer of prime ministers, powerful forces favored fiscal consolidation.[7] MOF—with Asō dutifully defending his ministry's line in internal deliberations—was pressing Abe to respect the previous government's pledge to address public finances and warned that delaying could lead interest rates to spike if markets lost confidence in Abe's willingness to control spending.[8] MOF was not alone in its fight to preserve the tax hike. Fiscal hawks in the Liberal Democratic Party (LDP), the business establishment, and international financial institutions like the International Monetary Fund (IMF) and the Organization for Economic Cooperation and Development (OECD) leaned on Abe to raise the tax.[9] Kuroda also favored the tax hike, arguing that Japan's economy could withstand it.

Despite his early policy successes and his electoral victory, Abe's position was insecure. To inform his decision, in late August he convened meetings with sixty economists, business leaders, and advisers to weigh the potential impact of the tax hike. Forty-four recommended that he raise the tax as planned. He would not decide until early October, but by September, his administration seemed resigned to formulating policies to mitigate the effects of the tax increase.

On 1 October 2013, Abe formally decided that, pursuant to the goal of halving Japan's deficit by 2015 and eliminating it by 2020 and consolidating the national debt (which stood at –6.4 percent and 190 percent of GDP respectively in 2012), he would raise the tax the following April. To cushion the blow, the government would also introduce a stimulus package of roughly ¥5 trillion, while introducing tax reform to reduce Japan's world-leading thirty-eight-percent corporate tax to a rate more competitive with other developed countries. And, if necessary, the Bank of Japan (BOJ) could act to boost prices and growth. "Governor Kuroda and I are of exactly the same opinion when it comes to the necessity of escaping deflation," Abe said after he announced his decision. "The Bank of Japan will do what is needed to fulfill its mission."[10]

* * *

With the tax hike decision behind him, Abenomics was in place. The BOJ was purchasing bonds in huge numbers. The government would continue providing fiscal stimulus well into 2014 to offset the tax increase. Government advisory councils were busy translating the growth strategy's proposals into legislation.

Therefore, as the Diet reconvened in autumn, Abe's attention shifted to the machinery of state. In the final months of 2013, he advanced reforms that would complete the decades-long process of reorganizing the central government to enable the prime minister to wield state power more effectively. The Abe administration would strengthen its control of the bureaucracy, modernize the management of classified information, and establish a National Security Council that would enable the prime minister to command foreign policymaking. These reforms would not be without their critics—a state secrecy bill would inspire the first demonstrations against Abe—but once complete they amounted to a stunning consolidation of executive power.

* * *

The most important reform may have been the most innocuous.

In November 2013, the cabinet approved a bill to create a Cabinet Personnel Bureau (CPB) that would centralize in the cabinet personnel decision-making for the upper reaches of the bureaucracy across the central government's ministries and agencies. Reformists had argued for decades that the government had been plagued by "stovepiping." An official's career prospects depended on his ministry's personnel department, which decided who was on the fast track to leadership. An official might be seconded to other ministries, but his career would depend on defending his home ministry's interests.

Reformists believed that bureaucrats were unreliable servants of their political masters, less inclined to follow the will of the incumbent government or the national interest if doing so conflicted with ministerial prerogatives. But if political leaders could control personnel decisions, they could encourage a more national mindset in the bureaucracy, strengthen top-down policymaking, and discourage bureaucratic sabotage.

Both the LDP and DPJ had pursued this reform before Abe's return. Fukuda's government had passed legislation that would have created a personnel agency, but Fukuda resigned before it could be implemented and Asō scrapped it. The DPJ was even keener to control senior administrative personnel decisions. Its efforts went nowhere.

Abe had wanted to pass implementing legislation in his first months, signaling its importance to his broader agenda. Suga especially believed in the importance of personnel decisions as a source of power, and had a preternatural talent for matching people to positions.[11] In his first days in office, the chief cabinet secretary gathered together the government's highest-ranking officials and told them they should consult with him about all senior administrative personnel decisions.[12] He would command, in the words of Aurelia George Mulgan, "an intelligence network across the various ministries and was constantly gathering information on able bureaucrats so that the most capable bureaucrats are appointed."[13]

It was only in the autumn that Abe could line up support for plans to create a personnel bureau. His government's bill would create a 100-person cabinet agency under a deputy chief cabinet secretary, which would assume responsibility for personnel decisions regarding roughly 600 of the most senior bureaucratic posts. In a stroke, the career prospects of Japan's elite bureaucrats would be in the hands of the prime minister.

Opposition parties held up the bill during the autumn session, but it passed the following spring, and by 30 May 2014 the bureau had commenced work. The bureau was a key component of Abe's vision for a stronger Japan. "I want stovepiping to be completely swept away and for all to work always with the Japanese people and state in mind," he said at a ceremony inaugurating the bureau. "And while doing that, it is all of your work to put the right people in the right positions...who has the strategic thinking and tenacity as we move towards mid- to long-term goals?"[14]

The new bureau made its mark on the elite civil service immediately. In that summer's personnel shuffle, when officials received promotions and new assignments, fifteen women were appointed as bureau chiefs and deputy directors-general. Previously, only eight had risen to these posts in the entire history of Japan's bureaucracy. For the first time ever, METI and the justice ministry had female bureau chiefs. Abe had indicated that he wanted to create more opportunities for women in the civil service, as part of a broader agenda of creating greater opportunities for women in the workforce—and he would use his new statutory power to impose his will on the bureaucracy.[15]

This change affected every bureaucrat. A MOF official later told me that the creation of the CPB was more important than all the administrative reforms that had come before. While the reform left Abe vulnerable to the charge that he had politicized the bureaucracy—a charge that would gain more credence later in his tenure when allegations of influence peddling surfaced—it was an unmistakable step in his consolidation of power. Conflict between bureaucrats and politicians remained—and bureaucrats wielded power within the prime minister's office and cabinet secretariat—but the new bureau ensured that Abe could rely on the bureaucracy to implement his policies.

* * *

The personnel bureau's creation was delayed in large part because Abe decided to prioritize a new law to manage official secrets. The Specially Designated Secrets Act modernized the government's classification system and strengthened penalties for the unauthorized release of designated state secrets across a wider range of policy areas and more ministries and agencies than ever before. It also could lead to stiff fines and jail sentences for journalists who shared secrets. The bill, the government said, was intended to strengthen its ability to collect intelligence as part of its efforts to cope with an "increasingly complex international situation."[16]

The government's bill was immediately and vocally opposed by the Japan Federation of Bar Associations, which criticized the broad powers it would arrogate to the government to designate secrets, and the threat it posed to press freedom and the public's right to know what its government was doing.[17] Media organizations also voiced opposition.

As the bill worked its way through the Diet, the protests widened. Dozens of protestors became hundreds, and hundreds became thousands. By the time the upper house passed the bill in the early hours of 7 December—with opposition parties boycotting entirely—the protests were persistent in Tokyo and elsewhere. After a year in which Abe had managed to keep the public on his side, it seemed that citizens once again saw him as a dangerous reactionary and not the would-be savior of a weary nation. For the first time, his approval ratings fell sharply. But, with the legislation passed, the protests fizzled and Abe's approval ratings soon recovered. It was an important lesson: the early successes of Abenomics and the booming stock market had translated into uniquely strong public support, giving him political capital that he could then use to pursue other, more controversial ambitions.

In a sense, the protesters were correct: Abe's policies did portend the possibility of wide-reaching changes to Japanese democracy. However, the tone of the protests—in which protesters warned darkly of the secrecy bill's similarities with the notorious prewar Peace Preservation Law—suggests that much of the opposition was to Abe himself.[18] Some Japanese would always see him as eager to return to a prewar era.

However, Abe's policies were not quite as far from the mainstream as the protests would suggest. Kan, for example, angered by the leak of video of the 2010 Senkaku incident, pushed for legislation that would strengthen the government's ability to control state secrets.[19] The bill was also intended to strengthen cooperation with the US. Few Japanese saw the need to strengthen the state's ability to protect secrets, but the US government had long been concerned about how freely Tokyo leaked—and hailed the move.[20]

* * *

The protestors were wrong to think Abe simply wanted to take Japan back to the prewar era. Rather, he was looking to a more dangerous future. The secrecy law was part of a broader project of building a national security state.

As part of the constitution's antimilitarist legacy, Japan had resisted building an executive dominated by uniformed military personnel prepared to do whatever necessary to maintain national security, even at the expense of democratic oversight and accountability. Japan was not necessarily pacifist. It had established the Self-Defense Forces (SDF) within a decade of the promulgation of the "peace" constitution and hosted thousands of US military personnel. And through the US–Japan alliance, Japan imported some of the clandestine practices of the US national security state.[21]

But part of the Yoshida Doctrine's vision of a lightly armed Japan dependent on the US was that the uniformed services would be kept at arm's length from civilian leaders and employed in a strictly defensive role. During the Cold War, SDF chiefs reported to the head of the defense agency, an adjunct of the prime minister's office (making the agency head a subordinate of the prime minister and not part of the collective decision-making apparatus of the cabinet). A thick layer of civilian bureaucracy—mainly officials seconded from MOFA and MOF—controlled the armed forces, meaning that, as Sheila Smith writes, "Japan's defense planning became dominated by fiscal and political goals rather than by debates over what constituted an effective means to defend the country."[22] Politicians paid little attention to defense, and the public was actively hostile to the SDF, to the point service members would change into civilian clothes whenever they were off base.[23]

Uprooting this legacy was critical to Abe's vision for the new Japan. Defense hawks had chipped away at these constraints since before the Cold War ended and this work had continued even under the DPJ, particularly under Noda. The Kan and Noda governments sought to transform the SDF from a "basic defense force" deployed across Japan to counter a Soviet threat that no longer existed, to a "dynamic defense force" that focused on defending Japan's outlying islands from China's advances and "gray zone" operations; relaxed long-standing restrictions on arms exports to permit joint development of ballistic missile defense and the F-35 fighter with the United States; and initiated a review of the bilateral guidelines for defense cooperation with the US, which had last been updated in 1997.[24]

Despite these antecedents, Abe was not just promising new policies. To be a great power, Japan had to act like one. He wanted to change how the state formulated and executed policy—and, as the secrecy law showed, to limit the ability of the public to oversee the national security establishment. Abe relished his status as the SDF's commander-in-chief more than any of his predecessors—making regular appearances at fleet and army reviews—and drew uniformed officers into his counsel to signal a shift to a system in which the SDF answers directly to the prime minister. By 2015, nine years after the creation of a new joint staff office headed by a chief of staff who became the commander of the entire SDF, the chief of staff had met with the prime minister 100 times—seventy-six of which followed Abe's return to power.[25] This figure likely understates the number of interactions between Abe and senior brass.

He did not just challenge norms through his personal conduct. His government institutionalized the prime minister's control over national security policymaking and eroded institutional barriers separating the prime minister from the SDF. As the Abe government was moving its secrecy bill through the Diet, it also submitted a bill to establish Japan's equivalent to the US National Security Council. Abe had intended to establish an NSC during his first premiership, and it was high on his list of unfinished business.

The NSC finally came into being at the start of 2014 and included not just a US-style committee of principals but also established a British-style secretariat, headed by a national security adviser (Yachi was promptly named the first) who led a staff of sixty bureaucrats and SDF officers working in six teams: administration, strategy, intelligence, friends and allies, China and North Korea, and other regions. The secretariat was a clearinghouse for intelligence gathered by Japan, and its staff formulated Japan's national security strategy, managed inter-agency coordination, and supported the prime minister and his ministers in national security decision-making.[26]

It also became an important conduit for coordination with foreign governments. As political scientist Adam Liff writes, "Its institutional fingerprints can be found on almost every major aspect of the Japanese strategic trajectory that has attracted so much global attention (and some controversy) in the post-2012 'Abe era.'"[27] It is fitting that as part of the process of building a national security state for the twenty-first century, Abe created Japan's answer to a central institution of the post-war US national security state.

* * *

Abe's return to power occurred during a generational transfer of power across Northeast Asia. Xi Jinping became general secretary of the CCP and chairman of China's Central Military Commission in November 2012. In February 2013, Park Geun-hye, daughter of the late dictator Park Chung-hee, who had served in Japan's army in Manchuria and been close with Kishi, became the first South Korean president born after South Korea's founding. Kim Jong Un was still consolidating power. The leaders of Japan's neighbors were also new to power and were using nationalist appeals and promises of national rejuvenation to strengthen their positions.[28]

The region was undergoing a historic transition. Under Hu, China had begun pressing its territorial claims in the East and South China Seas, investing heavily in a "blue water" navy and other new military capabilities, and using its economic clout to expand its political influence overseas. These efforts all intensified under Xi.[29] China's new assertiveness was fundamental to the legitimacy of a new leader who, thanks to his aggressive efforts to root out corruption in the CCP and consolidate policymaking power, would become China's strongest leader since Mao.

Abe had used the DPJ's weakness when confronted with China's advances in the East China Sea to argue that Japan faced a national emergency for which his leadership was the only remedy. But during his first year in office, the scale of the China challenge became apparent. Under Xi, Japan faced a China that saw itself as a "big power," that should use its political, economic, and military might to shape regional and global institutions. Among the institutions China wished to bury were the US-led hub-and-spoke system of alliances, which Chinese officials called "Cold War relics."[30] "It is for the people of Asia to run the affairs of Asia, solve the problems of Asia and uphold the security of Asia," Xi said in May 2014.[31]

The most immediate problem was that, in the immediate aftermath of the Noda government's purchase of the Senkakus, the security situation around the islands was fraught. China sharply increased its presence in the waters surrounding the islands. In January 2013, a Chinese frigate directed its fire-control radar at a Japanese destroyer, an incident Beijing denied but which the Abe administration proved. The encounter set the tone for that year. In April, Beijing labeled control of the islands a "core interest."[32] After several years with virtually no Chinese presence, month after month in 2013 dozens of Chinese coast guard vessels entered what Japan claimed as its territorial waters around the islands. The PLA's air force became significantly more active over the East China Sea, prompting a marked increase in scrambles by the JASDF.[33] With both air forces active, the risk of a mid-air collision or other incident that could trigger a spike in tensions increased sharply.

These fears crystallized in November 2013, when China announced the establishment of an air defense identification zone (ADIZ) extending over the East China Sea. The Chinese ADIZ, which covered the disputed islands, sparked fears that tensions could spiral out of control.

Despite China's pressure campaign, Abe was still interested in a constructive relationship with Xi. In late July, he dispatched Saiki Akitaka, MOFA's top-ranking bureaucrat, to Beijing for consultations with senior officials. To defuse the situation in the East China Sea, Abe was willing to meet Xi without preconditions. But Beijing was not interested while Tokyo asserted there was no dispute over the islands because they were inherently Japanese. Abe made matters worse in December, when, to mark his first year in office, he visited Yasukuni. A Chinese foreign ministry spokesman said Abe was attempting to "whitewash history" while China's ambassador to the UK reached for a more colorful condemnation, describing militarism as Japan's "Voldemort" and Yasukuni as a "horcrux." Japan's ambassador replied by suggesting that China threatened to become Asia's Voldemort.[34]

By the end of Abe's first year, the Sino–Japanese relationship was as tense as at any point since the 1970s—worse even than the "deep freeze" of the Koizumi years since now the air forces and coast guards were squaring off in the East China Sea. Abe caused alarm in January when, in Davos, he cited the centenary of the outbreak of the First World War that year to warn of similarities between tensions between Britain and Germany before 1914 and tensions between Japan and China.[35] Abe faced backlash for these comments—not least from China, which accused him of papering over Japan's history of aggression—but his larger point was not wrong. The jockeying in the East China Sea, playing out against a backdrop of nationalistic competition between an assertive rising power and a status quo power, could trigger a conflict that neither intended to start.[36]

Since the 1990s, China had loomed as a threat that Japanese officials dared not name. Abe and his government became increasingly explicit about crafting policies to protect Japan from an increasingly assertive China and counter its influence across the region, what political scientist Jeffrey Hornung calls a "hard hedge" against its powerful neighbor.[37]

Even as he sought to rejuvenate Japan's economy, Abe saw himself foremost as a global statesman who would guide Japan through a turbulent age. The single most important lesson he learned from his grandfather was that a national leader has no more important duty than safeguarding the security of the nation.[38] Thus, immediately upon taking office, Abe set to work articulating and implementing a new strategy that would leverage all sources of national power to compete with China in Asia.

Faced with a more assertive China—and a North Korea that continued to refine its nuclear arsenal and the missiles needed to deliver its weapons to targets across East Asia—Abe's foreign policy team identified what Japan had to do to ensure its national security. The agenda was extensive, and involved both upgrading Japan's defense capabilities and its diplomatic partnerships. This would enhance Japan's ability to counter not only China's efforts to become a proper maritime power that could deny the ability of US forces to operate along Asia's littoral in a crisis, but also China's efforts to extend its political and economic influence across the region. For Abe himself, it would also mean indulging in the symbolic politics of historical memory that he believed essential for fostering national pride and the confidence necessary for Japan to act more assertively.

Predictably, these gestures rankled not only China but also South Korea. Park, who was suspect when it came to relations with Japan due to her father's history, rejected Abe's requests for a one-on-one meeting and refused to visit Japan unless and until Abe apologized for Japan's treatment of the comfort women and other colonial-era wrongdoing. Instead, she courted Xi, who welcomed her to Beijing in June 2013.

It was this development—a fight between two US allies pushing one into China's embrace—that so vexed the Obama administration about Abe and his determination to "correct" the historical record. Obama and his new foreign policy team ought to have welcomed a Japanese prime minister who sought not only to strengthen the bilateral alliance and improve Japan's defense capabilities but also wanted to strengthen economic ties with the US. But the US and Japanese governments spent most of 2013 at odds over history.

Abe had his own reasons for being frustrated with Obama. On 8 June, Obama hosted Xi Jinping for a summit at the Sunnylands Estate in California, reviving Japan's fears of a "G2." Senior Japanese officials fretted about what the summit would mean for the standoff with China in the East China Sea and the crisis with North Korea—or, for that matter, the future of US leadership in Asia. Obama, meanwhile, also raised concerns about his commitment to the rebalance when a government shutdown forced him to skip the annual APEC summit and send John Kerry in his stead.[39]

But the single most vexing question was whether Abe would worship at Yasukuni. While 15 August passed without incident, the specter of Abe's worshipping at the shrine and enflaming the region kept Washington on edge. In an unsubtle message to Abe, when Kerry and Secretary of Defense Chuck Hagel visited Tokyo for meetings with their counterparts in October, they laid a wreath at Chidorigafuchi National Cemetery, where the remains of Japan's unidentified dead from the Second World War are interred. A short time later, former Deputy Secretary of State Armitage met with LDP officials and warned them that if Abe visited Yasukuni, it would "destroy everything we have built."[40] Abe, meanwhile, had dispatched his old friend Etō to sound out Americans on how the Obama administration would react if Abe were to visit. Not surprisingly, he was told that Abe should stay away.[41]

The Obama administration, still concerned, sent Biden to Japan, China, and South Korea in early December, hoping that he could heal the rift between Tokyo and its neighbors and dissuade Abe from visiting the shrine. Biden called Abe upon returning to Washington and again urged him not to go. Biden seemed to think that the threat had been averted.

However, having failed to make headway with either Park or Xi, Abe seemed inclined to play the Yasukuni card both to shake up Japan's relations with its neighbors and fulfill a pledge Abe made to visit the shrine as prime minister. Of course, it was also a direct rebuke of the Obama administration. Abe would not cave to foreign pressure even from the US, and felt worshipping at the shrine was as natural for a Japanese prime minister as a visit by a US president to Arlington National Cemetery.

At eleven o'clock on 26 December, the first anniversary of his second government, Abe became the first prime minister since Koizumi to worship at Yasukuni. Addressing the press, he stated that worshipping there strengthened his resolve that Japan must never go to war again. He lamented that the shrine had become a diplomatic issue. "It is not my intention at all to hurt the feelings of the Chinese and Korean people," he said. "It is my wish to respect each other's character, protect freedom and democracy, and build friendship with China and Korea with respect, as did all the previous prime ministers who visited Yasukuni shrine."[42]

Predictably, Beijing, Taipei, and Seoul immediately protested. "Deplorable," a South Korean minister called it. The EU condemned it. The Wiesenthal Center said it was "morally wrong."[43] Most notable, however, was the terse statement issued by the US Embassy in Tokyo, headed by the newly arrived ambassador, Caroline Kennedy. "Japan is a valued ally and friend," the statement began. "Nevertheless, the United States is disappointed that Japan's leadership has taken an action that will exacerbate tensions with Japan's neighbors."[44] After a year of diplomacy by the Obama administration to encourage Abe to find a way to leave the history wars behind, it was not surprising that the US administration expressed its frustration so openly. But for Abe, who had come to power promising to restore Japan's relationship with the US, it was a shocking moment.

Abe appeared to have made the decision to go. Suga opposed it: "The administration's most important job is economic revitalization. It will not be too late to worship at Yasukuni after economic revitalization is accomplished."[45] The timing was also questionable for Abe's position domestically. His approval ratings were suffering after the rushed passage of the state secrets act and his ties with Kōmeitō were frayed. Visiting the shrine risked making the situation worse. Even members of his own party grumbled about his judgment. He had scored his points and asserted his independence in the face of US pressure. But now his foreign policy team would have to mend fences with a US president who still had three years remaining.

Members of both Obama's and Abe's foreign policy teams—Yachi, Ambassador Caroline Kennedy in Tokyo and Ambassador Sasae Kenichi in Washington, Biden and his adviser Jake Sullivan, and Abe confidante Kawai Katsuyuki—worked to repair the damage.[46] Abe was simply too useful a partner to sideline. As Ben Rhodes, Obama's deputy national security adviser, observed of the president's relationship with Abe, "They didn't have a warm personal relationship, but they developed a very productive relationship. Abe's agenda had a lot of connective tissue to our Asian strategy."[47]

Ultimately, strategic imperatives would bring Abe back into Washington's good graces. For the rebalance to work, Obama needed Japan on side—and in Abe, the US finally had a Japanese prime minister willing to take domestic political risks to strengthen bilateral cooperation. He brought Japan into TPP over the objections of his own party. He had rushed the state secrecy bill through the Diet. And he wanted to do more.

In fact, even as Obama and Abe sparred over Yasukuni, Abe's government released Japan's inaugural national security strategy. The document articulated a vision of Japan's national interests, identified major threats, and detailed what the Abe government must do to defend Japan. It was a conscious effort to outline how to achieve Abe's fundamental mission, thrusting Japan back into power politics.

The national security strategy was not a dramatic break with prevailing thought on either the ends or means of foreign and defense policies. The Abe government would strive to preserve Japan's independence, sovereignty, and territorial integrity, defend the lives, liberty, and property of its people, and preserve national prosperity.

But the document hinted at a more global conception of Japan's national interests. The strategy identified Japan's need to strengthen regional and global free trade regimes and maintain an international order based on "rules and universal values" as necessary for defending Japan's most fundamental interests. It also identified some of the major threats to Japan's security as global, including WMD proliferation, climate change, international terrorism, conflict over global commons (including cyberspace), and the risks of economic and financial contagion in a global economy.

Meanwhile, China's burgeoning military power and the threat that China might "change the status quo by coercion" led the Abe government to identify China explicitly as a regional threat to national security, alongside North Korea and its ballistic missile and WMD arsenals. The strategy did not necessarily aim at containing China: Japan would continue to seek a "mutually beneficial relationship" with its neighbor in the hopes of encouraging it to act as a responsible supporter of regional peace and stability and upholder of international norms.

To face these challenges, the Abe government's strategy saw Japan as becoming a "proactive contributor to peace" by upgrading its own diplomatic and defense capabilities, strengthening the US–Japan relationship, and deepening partnerships with key partners in the region, including South Korea, Australia, India, and the ASEAN countries, and outside the region, including the EU, the leading members of the G20, and in the Middle East.

There were precedents for much of the strategy. But, with Abe determined to use the power that had accumulated in his office and facing few domestic obstacles, it augured a shift in Japan's place in the world. Abe's vision was of a Japan that could act decisively to defend itself and uphold the international order as a partner of the US and other liberal democracies.

The strategy, while intended to anchor Japan more firmly in US-led regional and global orders, may have also been a thinly veiled hedging strategy. Building up Japan's defense capabilities and forging closer relationships with other regional powers (including China) could help Japan brace for an isolationist turn by America. However, it was a hedge that dare not speak its name. Instead, the strategy reflected Abe's determination to make Japan a full-fledged partner of the US in preserving a regional order that had enabled Japan to prosper and which was increasingly threatened. Japan needed the US engaged, and it would do what it could to help. This approach to the world was distinct enough from the Yoshida Doctrine's vision of Japan's place in the world to merit a new name—the Abe Doctrine.[48]

The value of the Abe Doctrine to an Obama administration trying to reinforce the US-led order in Asia in an age of budgetary constraints and gridlocked politics was obvious, and explains how Abe and Obama were able to put the history wars behind them. Japan needed the US to help deter threats from China and North Korea and to contribute to forging alternate political and economic institutions in the face of the robust Chinese challenge to the status quo. For the US, a more decisive, confident, and unconstrained Japan would be a force multiplier for the rebalance, not just strengthening deterrence in Japan's immediate vicinity but also providing a strong voice in advancing the liberal principles the US sought to uphold while strengthening links among the countries along China's maritime frontiers. Abe's value as a partner became more apparent as China pressed its claims in the South China Sea and began rolling out the Asian Infrastructure Investment Bank and

BRI, major steps for Beijing in the competition to shape the region's political and economic integration.

By the end of 2013, Abe had brought Japan into TPP, articulated an approach for deepening Japan's ties with strategically important countries in Southeast and South Asia, and made major institutional changes as part of the construction of a Japanese national security state. As his tenure lengthened, he became increasingly focused on realizing the Abe Doctrine and willing to set aside new conservatism-fueled battles for "correct" historical interpretation. The ethic of responsibility would win out, as Abe sought the most effective means of strengthening Japan's security, maximizing its independence, and ensuring its continuing prosperity, without squandering the political power that he had amassed. Abe did not face a choice between pursuing the new conservatism's ambitions of building a strong state and a proud nation and pursuing Abenomics. Rather, he was moving forward on all three fronts, pursuing policies that would revitalize Japan's economy, bolster its alliances and defensive capabilities, and foster pride among the Japanese people.

But governing would only get harder. He would consolidate power and strengthen his grip over his party and the bureaucracy but translating his political might into enduring change would prove increasingly challenging.

14

THE SLOW BORING OF HARD BOARDS

"Two years ago today was the very eve of the change of government," Abe said. "Two years have passed since then, and the dark and heavy atmosphere that covered Japan has completely changed."

It was 15 December 2014, the day after he led his coalition to another general election victory.

The Liberal Democratic Party (LDP) had lost only three seats and the coalition retained a supermajority in the lower house. Much like Koizumi in 2005, Abe had called a snap election to strengthen his hand against critics in the LDP who were frustrating his agenda. By returning with a virtually identical majority—while preventing the Democratic Party of Japan (DPJ) from reaching their 100-seat target and depriving its leader Kaieda Banri of his seat—he had overawed his rivals within the LDP and accelerated the DPJ's decline.

But despite his triumph, Abe was not exuberant. "However, even now the sense of crisis and the sense of mission in me at that time are completely unchanged," he continued. "Difficult issues are heaped before us. Without forgetting my original intentions of two years ago, with all my heart and soul I am determined to fulfill my responsibilities for the state and the nation."[1]

He had accumulated ever-greater power, but converting his advantages into durable change was a slow, frustrating process that had to overcome resistance on all sides, leading to compromises that would undermine Abe's claims to be offering a radical new beginning for Japan.

The general election was a surprising denouement to a year that saw Abe's ambitions frustrated, while Abenomics struggled to find traction amidst a worsening global economy. Abe battled with ruling coalition lawmakers, interest groups, and public opinion as he tried to advance his vision for a new Japan—and had to settle for partial victories at best. It was government as trench warfare.

* * *

Even before the tax hike was finalized, Abe was ramping up his government's efforts to alter Japan's competitiveness and growth potential fundamentally. His government used an array of policy tools to encourage employers, farmers, and workers to change their behavior in dramatic ways.

But delivering on the promises of the third arrow was not easy. Even incremental gains at the expense of corporate Japan and the agriculture lobby—Abe's two main adversaries in his second year—took major efforts. It was another year and another general election before he was strong enough to cement real progress on these fronts.

Abe's first major confrontation was with Japan Inc. Even as Abenomics boosted corporate profits through fiscal and monetary easing, Japan's corporate bosses loomed as an obstacle to economic revitalization. Japan Inc. was too risk averse, too reluctant to gamble on innovation that could bolster national competitiveness in a cutthroat global economy, and its executives needed to be shaken out of their complacency. They were too content to accumulate cash, too tolerant of low returns on shareholders' capital, and too insulated from shareholders by the traditional institutions of postwar corporate governance that included close relationships with firms, unions, suppliers and subcontractors, and corporate boards stuffed with retired managers. Within this system, managers had little to fear from activist investors, hostile takeovers, or foreign buyers.[2]

The traditional model of corporate governance had begun to break down after the bubble burst, particularly as leading manufacturers became increasingly global, but it was still all too common, particularly in less efficient sectors of the economy.[3] Abe wanted to loosen the institutions that protected managers from shareholders, competitors, and potential buyers. Abe was not trying to enlist Japan in the "shareholder value" revolution that swept through corporate America in the last quarter of the twenty-first century.[4] But the complacency of Japan's corporate managers was an obstacle to shifting its productive resources to the high-value sectors of the future.

* * *

Abe's first target was wage setting. Customarily, wages for the core workers at Japan's largest manufacturers—who are represented by company unions that are part of national labor federations—have been set through an annual bargaining process known as the *shuntō*, the spring offensive. By the start of a new fiscal year in April, employers and labor representatives will have reached an agreement on pay increases. However, due to deflation and the global financial crisis, base pay increases—more likely to contribute to higher household spending—were stagnant. The growing use of temporary and other non-regular workers by manufacturers to reduce their labor costs also depressed incomes and contributed to widening inequality, as more young Japanese were left out of the social compact enjoyed by core workers.

The Abe administration rightly identified that increasing the money supply and weakening the yen would not lead to "good" inflation based on rising incomes and growing household demand unless the record profits enjoyed by corporate Japan were shared with workers. The administration hoped faster growth would lead to lower unemployment and tighter job markets and put upward pressure on wages. But Abe and his advisers believed that—due to the structure of wage setting—they could not simply rely on market forces to deliver pay increases. The government would have to step in.

Under Abe's leadership, the government would intervene in negotiations between employers and unions, implement multiple minimum wage increases, pass legislation aimed at reducing the pay gap between permanent and temporary or part-time workers and encouraging productivity improvements that would result in higher pay for workers.

The boldest stroke began in September 2013. After months of exhorting corporate Japan to raise wages, Abe convened a series of meetings with the heads of Keidanren, Japan's leading business federation, and Rengo, its leading labor federation, to pressure employers to raise pay by enough to outpace inflation. Abe was not trying to coerce employers into raising wages—in fact, his government proposed tax incentives to reward wage-raising firms with lower rates—but he was trying to leverage his political power to shame Japan Inc. into sharing its wealth. It was statism with a softer touch: Abe wanted the private sector to help his government achieve a fundamental national goal.

The Abe government thereafter convened a tripartite government-business-labor council to "realize an economic virtuous cycle." By December 2013, the council's members, which included Abe and his principal cabinet ministers for economic policy, the chairmen of Keidanren and other business associations, and the chairmen of Rengo and other organized labor federations, reached an understanding whereby employers would strive to raise wages for their core workers while also improving conditions for part-timers and small subcontractors. In exchange, Abe would accelerate the end of a corporate tax surcharge that had been levied to fund the reconstruction of Tohoku.[5] The tripartite pact was not necessarily celebrated. "While wage increases are certainly an issue for overcoming deflation," the *Nikkei Shimbun* wrote in an editorial, "the government should not intervene in private wage decisions. State interference can distort the market mechanism."[6]

Nevertheless, in January 2014, Keidanren recommended base pay increases to its members for the first time in six years, while Rengo instructed its member unions to seek increases of three percent, including an increase of one percent in base pay. Abe's intervention likely made it more difficult for employers to withhold increases. Keidanren found that more than a third of its members raised base pay in some form. The average pay increase was more than two percent for the first time in fifteen years.[7]

But it was not enough to keep pace with inflation or the consumption tax hike that kicked in the same day that the raises did. Despite Abe's extraordinary involvement, the results fell short of what was needed to boost real household incomes. And base pay increases were clearly not enough. The core workers covered by the spring offensive were a small minority of the workforce. A truly effective incomes

1. **The birth of a dynasty**. Kishi Nobusuke (second from right)—Abe Shinzō's maternal grandfather—was the fifth of ten children born to a minor prefectural official and sake brewer Satō Hidesuke and his wife Moyo. His six-decade career in government and politics would span Japan's tumultuous Shōwa period. His brother, Satō Eisaku (right), would become Japan's longest-serving postwar prime minister (1964–1972), a record that stood until his great-nephew surpassed him in 2019. (Photo credit: Wikimedia Commons)

2. **"The ghost of Shōwa."** Kishi (far right) was named minister of commerce and industry under Prime Minister Tōjō Hideki in October 1941. Imprisoned as an accused war criminal after the Second World War, he would reemerge as the leading proponent of Japan as a full-fledged great power—now allied to the US—and serve three tumultuous years as prime minister (1957–1960). (Photo credit: Wikimedia Commons)

3. **The anti-militarist Abe**. Abe's paternal grandfather Abe Kan (right) is pictured with his wife Shizuko from whom he would be divorced shortly after Abe's father was born in 1924. Kan's politics were dramatically different from Kishi's: Kan was an anti-militarist who was one of only eighty-five independent candidates to win a Diet seat in the 1942 general election. He died in 1946, before the first postwar general election. (Photo credit: Wikimedia Commons)

4. **The Abe-Kishi line**. After the war, Kishi was introduced to a journalist, Abe Kan's son Shintarō (second from right), who would soon court and marry his daughter Yōko (left) in 1951. Their first son Hironobu (in Shintarō's lap) was born in 1952; Shinzō (in Yōko's lap) in 1954. Around the time of this photo, Shintarō began working as Kishi's private secretary before entering the Diet in 1958. He would gradually climb the ranks of the LDP but passed away in 1991, his dream of winning the premiership unrealized. (Photo credit: Wikimedia Commons)

5. **An LDP prince**. After inheriting his father's seat in 1993, Abe rose rapidly in the LDP's ranks, helped by his late father's colleagues. Two patrons in particular—prime ministers Mori Yoshirō and Koizumi Junichirō—would elevate him to high office and propel him to the premiership at breakneck speed. As deputy chief cabinet secretary under both prime ministers Abe was a regular presence at their sides, including when Koizumi visited New York City days after the 9/11 terrorist attacks. (Photo credit: Government Public Relations Office, Japan)

6. **Japan's youngest postwar prime minister**. On 26 September 2006, five days after his fifty-second birthday, the Diet selected Abe as Japan's prime minister, its youngest postwar prime minister and its first born after 1945. Despite starting with sky-high approval ratings, he soon found himself beset by scandals and crises. On 12 September 2007, he announced that he would resign the premiership, his political career seemingly over. "I looked into hell," he later said. (Photo credit: Government Public Relations Office, Japan)

7. **The comeback**. Abe's time in the political wilderness was short. Although his family and some of his allies counseled against a bid for the LDP's leadership in September 2012, Abe defied them and entered a crowded field, as seen at this campaign event in Nagano prefecture. But the field winnowed, becoming a two-man race between Abe and former defense minister Ishiba Shigeru (fourth from left). Ishiba won the first round but Abe won a come-from-behind victory in a lawmakers-only runoff. By 26 December he was prime minister again. (Photo credit: Wikimedia Commons)

8. **"Alliance of hope."** Every prime minister is judged by his stewardship of the US-Japan alliance. Abe and Obama were not natural partners, but despite initial friction, their administrations worked effectively together and by 2016, they had strengthened the alliance, concluded the Trans-Pacific Partnership, and delivered dramatic moments of historical reconciliation in Hiroshima and Pearl Harbor. Here, the two leaders meet on 27 December 2016 with survivors of the Japanese attack on Pearl Harbor. (Photo credit: Government Public Relations Office, Japan)

9. **Donald and Shinzō**. Donald Trump's history of accusing Japan of taking advantage of the US raised fears of what he would mean for the US-Japan alliance. But Abe gambled that Trump might be amenable to personal diplomacy, and quickly visited the president-elect, bearing a golden golf club as a gift. They became "golf buddies"—but Abe struggled to change Trump's views. Here, Abe, Trump, and first ladies Abe Akie (far left) and Melania Trump (second from left) dine together during Trump's first presidential visit to Japan in November 2017. (Photo credit: Government Public Relations Office, Japan)

10. **Onsen diplomacy**. Abe sought a new relationship with Russia as part of his vision of Japan as a great power. Russia's annexation of the Crimea would derail early efforts, but by 2016 Abe had resumed his pursuit of a partnership with Russian President Vladimir Putin. In December 2016, he hosted Putin at a traditional hot spring resort that he hoped would catalyze a new era in Japan-Russia relations. Abe would receive little for his efforts. (Photo credit: Government Public Relations Office, Japan)

11. **"India's Abe."** Abe's close partnership with Indian Prime Minister Narendra Modi helped cement closer political, economic, and security ties between the two governments. The two would exchange greetings on social media and lengthy visits in each other's countries, while concluding deals with significant implications for Asia's future. Here, they prepare to board Japan's shinkansen in November 2016, part of a celebration of a pact for Japanese companies to build a high-speed rail line between Mumbai and Ahmedabad. (Photo credit: Prime Minister's Office, Government of India)

12. **Asia's giants**. Abe and Chinese President Xi Jinping took power at roughly the same time, but their first two years were marred by tensions in the East China Sea and disputes over historical memory. By 2017, they began to see the value in closer economic ties, leading to Abe's first visit to China for a bilateral meeting with Xi in October 2018 (pictured here). However, the detente was fragile and was severely disrupted by the Covid-19 pandemic and its aftermath. (Photo credit: Government Public Relations Office, Japan)

13. **"Defeatism is defeated."** After 2016, Abe walked a tightrope between Trump's America and Xi's China, trying to safeguard a global trading system under threat from mounting friction between the world's two largest economies. By the time Abe addressed the World Economic Forum in Davos, Switzerland in January 2019, he could celebrate having revived TPP after the US withdrew and having concluded a landmark trade agreement with the European Union. "Defeatism about Japan is now defeated," he declared. (Government Public Relations Office, Japan)

policy would have to extend to the non-regular workers trapped in part-time or temporary positions. It would also have to reach small firms and their employees, not covered by the spring offensive. Abe continued to convene these meetings annually, with much grumbling from employers and unions about the "government-manufactured" *shuntō*—and their effectiveness diminished over time.[8]

Nevertheless, the Abe government's involvement had established a precedent. It also hinted at a tacit alliance between Abe and organized labor. In 2014, he became the first LDP prime minister in thirteen years to attend Rengo's May Day celebrations, where he touted his efforts to pressure employers to raise wages and ensure that all shared in the benefits of faster growth.[9]

And Abe's intervention in wage negotiations was just the first salvo in his bid to change corporate behavior. His administration was also preparing to confront corporate managers on their own turf by taking on corporate governance reform.

The Abe government's approach to corporate governance was two-pronged. First, it would mobilize pension funds to pressure managers to seek better returns and pay out more to shareholders and workers. Second, it would spearhead a top-down effort to modify the institutional framework for corporate governance.

The centerpiece of the former effort was reforming the government pension investment fund (GPIF). The GPIF, one of the world's largest pension funds, has been responsible for managing the retirement savings of millions of Japanese, with more than $1 trillion in assets under management at the start of Abe's second government. Although nominally an independent agency, it was effectively controlled by the ministry of health, labor, and welfare (MHLW), which managed the fund conservatively, parking most of its holdings in safe but low-yielding Japanese government bonds.

The fund's portfolio was doubly problematic for Abe. If the Bank of Japan (BOJ) raised inflation, the fund's holdings would erode in value, with dire implications for the government's balance sheet and pensioners. At the same time, however, if the fund did not diversify, it would imply it did not expect inflation and could dampen inflation expectations among investors more broadly. The Abe government therefore had to wrest control of the fund away from the MHLW and then encourage the fund's new managers to shift the GPIF's portfolio to riskier domestic and foreign equities (which would also keep the stock market booming). With the nation's retirement savings increasingly invested in stocks, the fund could then use its clout as a shareholder to press corporate managers to deliver higher returns.

In 2013, the Abe government convened an advisory group chaired by economist Itō Takatoshi to draft recommendations for GPIF reform. Itō's group issued its final report in November, recommending sharp cuts in Japanese government bond (JGB) holdings and reforms that would give the fund's managers greater independence from administrative authorities. But translating Itō's proposals into reality proved significantly more complicated than Abe had hoped.

The following spring, the MHLW issued a counterproposal that recommended keeping the fund under its authority and pursuing portfolio rebalancing more gradually. The minister, Tamura Norihisa, sided with his ministry over Abe, joining forces with GPIF director Mitani Takahiro, who simultaneously sought to undertake a modest shift in the fund's holdings while resisting proposals that would fundamentally change the GPIF's management structure.

The Abe administration won an important victory in April, when turnover at the GPIF's investment committee led to an influx of new members, several of whom had been on Itō's panel. But the new committee would pursue Mitani's more gradual rebalancing rather than Itō's preferred "big bang" approach, and the desire of reformers for the fund to act as an activist shareholder remained unfulfilled.

Nevertheless, even a partially reformed GPIF was an important ally. In 2014, for example, an advisory group at the financial services agency (FSA) promulgated a stewardship code for institutional investors that would encourage funds like the GPIF to seek greater transparency from businesses.[10] The GPIF quickly embraced the new code, inspiring other funds to follow.

But the Abe government's work on corporate governance was unfinished. Abe could not simply browbeat Japan Inc. into satisfying his demands. He had to offer a mix of carrots and sticks. The sticks were relatively gentle, and the carrots, mainly corporate tax hikes and other tax incentives to reward good behavior, were generous. He declined to use what might have been one of its most potent weapons aimed at corporate Japan, a tax on accumulated cash holdings. It took another year, a climactic battle with the ministry of finance (MOF) and the LDP's fiscal hawks over corporate taxes, and another general election before Abe could achieve a more complete victory.

* * *

As challenging as Abe's battles with Japan Inc. were, there was no greater political challenge than agriculture reform. The agricultural sector continued to wield outsized political power in the LDP. Abe might not have shared his mentor Koizumi's zeal for attacking the LDP's rural machine, but he—and Suga, whose father had been a strawberry farmer—recognized that Japanese agriculture was in dire need of reform, as the rural population aged and investment in agricultural production stalled.[11]

The goal was to realize "agriculture on the offensive," shifting agricultural policies from being predominantly about protecting farmers and preserving their way of life to an "industrial policy" for agriculture. Abe wanted agricultural producers to compete in foreign markets. Farmers would have to grow more valuable produce, invest in advanced technologies to improve yields, and utilize resources more productively, including by reclaiming and consolidating abandoned farmland.[12] He would also tackle an inefficient rice set-aside system (known as the *gentan*), whereby the government paid farmers to limit rice production acreage, artificially limiting supplies and increasing prices for consumers. This system was part of a vast suite of policies—including tariffs and import quotas—intended to subsidize rice farmers, many of whom farmed part-time and had little interest in competing overseas. The first growth strategy included a target of more than doubling Japan's agriculture exports from less than ¥500 billion to at least ¥1 trillion. Japan's participation in TPP would open new markets to Japan's exports and expose farmers to more intense competition.

But it was easier to outline an agenda than to realize it. The sluggish performance of farmers made them a ripe target for an administration determined to find new sources of growth. But Abe was indebted to rural voters. As in other sectors, revitalizing the agricultural sector would first require significant and unprecedented political reform.

Throughout the postwar era—with antecedents in the wartime command economy—agriculture had been organized around agricultural cooperatives, which had a virtual monopoly in the sale of equipment and other inputs, the transport and marketing of goods, and the provision of banking and insurance services to farmers.[13] The local co-ops were grouped into prefectural federations, which formed the national federations of the Japan Agriculture Group (JA, abbreviated as Nōkyō in Japanese). At the peak was the Central Union of Agricultural Co-operatives, JA-Zenchū, which functioned as a super-empowered interest group and lobbying outfit that worked closely with the LDP and the bureaucracy to craft agricultural policy. Referring to JA-Zenchū as the agricultural lobby understates its influence, particularly within the LDP, since the group and its prefectural branches not only mobilized rural constituents but had a formal consultative role in policymaking. Despite the long-term decline in its membership—increasingly part-time farmers—and growing dependence on financial services, the group was a formidable opponent to any change in agricultural policy.

Abe launched an initial skirmish against JA in December 2013. During its autumn session, the Diet passed a bill reversing restrictions on agricultural landholding dating back to occupation-era land reforms.[14] Then, Abe announced that his cabinet would phase out the *gentan* system by 2018. "Many have believed that abolishing the gentan system is something that the LDP could not possibly do," Abe said. "However, with the kind assistance of Mr. Kanemaru [Yasufumi] and Mr. Niinami [Takeshi] [two corporate members of the Industrial Competitiveness Council], we succeeded in conducting a major transformation of agricultural policy."[15]

Neither policy convinced doubters that Abe could break JA. Companies may have just preferred to lease small farm plots—and farmers may not have wanted to sell. Meanwhile, as Yamashita Kazuhito, a retired bureaucrat and leading advocate of agricultural reform argued, the *gentan* phase-out was oversold. The government would simply shift to encouraging rice production for animal feed.[16] The over-hyped announcement seemed to be a red flag, warning that Abe would not have the clout to deliver meaningful reform, but would try to convince the public and investors that the third arrow was working.

In 2014, however, the debate shifted in Abe's favor. Agricultural reform was a major pillar of that year's growth strategy and MAFF—

with considerable input from Suga and the cabinet secretariat—began outlining "agriculture on the offensive," programs that would, in partnership with big business, increase agricultural productivity, achieve greater economies of scale, and introduce more sophisticated marketing and technical knowhow to the agricultural sector.[17]

But the most significant proposal came from the prime minister's regulatory reform council, which spent months on how to reform the cooperative system. The implication was that while JA-Zenchū and the JA Group were untouched by reform, it would be impossible to move ahead with wider-reaching changes. Accordingly, the council proposed the new growth strategy should call for breaking up the group, spinning off its wholesale and marketing arm into a purely private company, restricting co-op membership for part-time farmers, and, most importantly, separating local co-ops and agricultural committees from JA-Zenchū. The latter would deprive the national organization of influence and funds, while enabling new players to enter the market and farmers to experiment with new methods.[18]

The national federation and its prefectural branches mobilized, pressuring LDP representatives to oppose the proposal. At the last moment, LDP backbenchers floated a plan to shelve the government's plans and give JA-Zenchū a chance to develop a plan for reforming itself. It worked: the proposal to dismantle JA-Zenchū was excluded from the strategy.

By mid-year, when the government issued its revised growth strategy and prepared for the budget cycle, Abe's record in finding new drivers of economic growth was disappointing. He had also failed to deliver the resumption of nuclear power generation, which Abe felt was important for economic recovery. The nation's fifty-strong fleet of reactors was still offline after the post-3/11 shutdown as the newly created nuclear regulation authority (NRA) inspected their vulnerabilities and disaster preparedness. Behind the NRA stood skeptics in the ruling coalition—who pushed back against the government's basic energy plan, which included plans for nuclear to remain a base load source of power—and Abe's onetime mentor Koizumi, who reentered political life to mobilize public opinion in favor of the rapid phase-out of nuclear power from Japan's energy mix.[19] Although in July the NRA approved two reactors for the first time under the new regulations, it would be more than a year before any reactor resumed operation, another sign that decisive change continued to elude Abe.

* * *

Despite these frustrations, Abe enjoyed more success in his pursuit of the Abe Doctrine abroad. The Yasukuni visit and the war of words between Japanese and Chinese officials did little to deter Abe from strengthening Japan's defense capabilities, bolstering the alliance with the US, and forging new relationships across Asia.

The national security strategy immediately impacted administration policies, since the strategy heavily influenced two key defense policy documents—the national defense program guidelines and the mid-term defense plan, which dictate defense budgetary priorities for five years—that would put the strategy into action. The government would spend bigger defense budgets on new destroyers and fighter aircraft to bolster defenses in its southwest and transform the Ground Self-Defense Forces into "rapid deployment" brigades that could respond to a crisis at short notice.[20] These plans would require defense spending to increase by roughly two percent in FY2014.[21]

* * *

In April 2014, the Abe government replaced the Three Principles on Arms Exports, introduced in 1967, which had placed stringent restrictions on arms exports and limited the growth of a defense industry. Under the new principles, Japanese companies were still prohibited from exporting arms in violation of international law but could transfer defense technology when doing so "contributes to the active promotion of peace contribution" and Japan's national security.[22] The new principles would strengthen Japan's defense industrial base and marked another way in which Abe was building a national security establishment—although Japanese firms would struggle to win defense contracts overseas.[23]

Abe continued his frenetic travel, visiting thirty-one countries in 2014. These foreign trips were important tools for Abe to advance his strategic priorities. In February, for example, he attended the Sochi Olympics, where he signaled to Russian President Vladimir Putin that a strong personal relationship could help resolve the long-standing territorial dispute between Japan and Russia, a determination that was knocked off course by the worsening Ukraine crisis and Russia's annexation of the Crimea. Abe's attendance at the nuclear security summit in The Hague in March, meanwhile, led to his first meeting with Park as part of a trilateral summit with Obama, a diplomatic opening for the two US allies as North Korea expanded its arsenal of weapons of mass destruction and ballistic missiles (several of which it launched into the Sea of Japan while the leaders met).[24]

Finally, at APEC in Beijing in November Abe met Xi, thanks in part to shuttle diplomacy by Fukuda—although the meeting was memorable mostly for a photograph in which the two leaders shake hands limply and glower.[25] Abe even reopened talks with North Korea on the fate of Japan's abductees, in which Pyongyang agreed to review possible abductee cases and Tokyo lifted some sanctions, including a ban on the entry of North Korean citizens into Japan. This process was, however, short-lived, as Tokyo reintroduced sanctions after Pyongyang stonewalled and ramped up its nuclear and missile testing.

* * *

Abe's greatest diplomatic triumphs came in rebuilding his relationship with Obama and building strong partnerships with India and Australia. The relationship between the four "maritime democracies"—a grouping Abe initially called the "democratic security diamond" and which would later be more commonly known as the "quad"—was advanced in 2014, as Abe conducted personal diplomacy with his US, Australian, and Indian counterparts.[26]

Abe had long seen India as a strategic linchpin for Japan. "India's population is currently one billion people, but it is said that it will increase further in the future to reach 1.6 billion people. There are many hard-working and excellent people in India, and it is one of the most advanced countries in Asia in the IT sector," Abe wrote in 2006. "Further strengthening the relationship with India is extremely important for Japan's national interest."[27] Japan's relationship with India was part of Abe's political inheritance. An Indian judge, Radhabinod Pal, had dissented in the Tokyo tribunals—arguing against the tribunal's "victors' justice"—and in 1957, Kishi became the first prime minister to visit India.[28] But Abe was hardly the first Japanese leader to look to

India, a nuclear-armed democracy with a young, burgeoning population that would surpass China's, as the great hope for preventing Chinese hegemony in Asia.[29]

While Washington's hopes for India as a democratic counterweight to China have often outpaced reality, Japan, as a fellow Asian democracy without Washington's history of Cold War machinations in South Asia and as a generous source of aid, has been viewed more favorably in Delhi. "I am convinced that the bilateral relationship between Japan and India is blessed with the largest potential for development of any bilateral relationship anywhere in the world," Abe said when he traveled to Republic Day celebrations in January 2014. That trip produced a lengthy joint statement between Abe and Prime Minister Manmohan Singh that celebrated progress in strengthening bilateral defense ties as part of a "strategic and global partnership."[30]

After India's general election that spring, in which the right-wing Bharatiya Janata Party's (BJP) coalition won a majority and made Hindu nationalist Narendra Modi prime minister, the relationship deepened. There were strong affinities between Abe and Modi, who was described as "India's Abe."[31] They quickly developed a strong rapport, perhaps the closest personal relationship Abe enjoyed with another world leader. Even before Modi was sworn in, Abe invited him to visit Japan. Modi finally went in late August, staying for five days. Their joint statement referred to a "special" strategic and global partnership, and included new agreements on defense cooperation and, more importantly, the creation of a new partnership to promote Japanese investment in India, particularly to build high-speed rail and other infrastructure. Meanwhile, Modi flattered his host's sensibilities by reportedly praising Judge Pal at one of several private dinners during his visit.[32] Abe's bid for a special relationship with Modi and India received a boost when a Chinese incursion into disputed territory overshadowed Xi Jinping's visit to India weeks after Modi's visit to Japan—and when Modi struck up a surprisingly strong rapport with Obama, which led to his becoming the first US president to attend Republic Day celebrations the following January.[33]

Abe's outreach to Australia was less passionate than his courtship of India and its new prime minister, but still a critical piece of the Abe Doctrine. In July, Abe became the first Japanese prime minister to visit Australia for a bilateral summit since Koizumi in 2002. In Canberra,

Abe hailed the creation of a "special relationship" with Prime Minister Tony Abbott, another conservative. The two governments inked a landmark defense technology agreement—a direct result of the new arms export principles—and signed a free trade agreement, a subtle tool for pressuring the US to come to terms in TPP since the US and Australia have competed fiercely in sales of beef to Japan. The signature moment was an address to the Australian Parliament, in which Abe sought to soften his image on history issues—expressing condolences for Australians killed and wounded in the Second World War and vowing to "stay humble against the evils and horrors of history"—while hailing the prospects of a special relationship grounded on shared interests and common values.[34]

The prospect of being Japan's partner in a league of maritime democracies that was implicitly aimed at countering China was not universally welcomed in Australia. For example, Hugh White, a prominent skeptic of efforts to contain China's rise, argued, "Abe wants Australia to become Japan's ally against China" and questioned whether an increasingly formal alliance between Japan and Australia was in Australia's interest.[35] Nevertheless, Abe and Abbott had established a blueprint for the Japan–Australia relationship that outlasted Abbott, who in 2015 was replaced by Malcolm Turnbull, who kept the 2014 relationship intact.[36]

* * *

But rebuilding ties with Obama was Abe's top priority. The Obama administration's realists won out. Both governments were determined to put the Yasukuni incident behind them and press on with deepening their relationship as part of the broader rebalance strategy. Despite the discomfort of some members of the administration about Abe's historical views, China's burgeoning military might and the ongoing threat of North Korea's arsenal made it imperative that the US and Japan kept their relationship on track—and that Japan and South Korea worked together for the sake of regional security. Within weeks of the Yasukuni visit, Washington indicated that Obama would visit Japan as part of a swing through Asia in the spring.

Obama's 23–25 April state visit, which included an audience with the emperor and empress and a visit to Sukibayashi Jiro, the sushi restaurant featured in the documentary *Jiro Dreams of Sushi*, helped patch up the relationship. Although negotiators could not achieve the breakthrough in TPP negotiations they had hoped for ahead of the summit, Obama's visit signaled that the two leaders were in agreement on the most fundamental issues facing the region. Obama viewed Abe's Japan as an indispensable partner in bolstering the US in the region and a valuable member of the TPP. Most importantly, in their joint press conference, Obama gave Abe a hugely important commitment. "Let me reiterate that our treaty commitment to Japan's security is absolute," Obama said, "and Article 5 covers all territories under Japan's administration, including the Senkaku Islands."[37] While other senior US officials had reassured Tokyo of this understanding, Obama's unambiguous public statement sent a clear signal to Japan and China, arguably reinforcing deterrence in the East China Sea.

The Obama administration continued to press Abe quietly on history issues and use its resources to bring Park and Abe closer together, but Obama had made clear that his administration needed Abe. Soon after the state visit, Abe showed just how much he was willing to gamble on behalf of Japan's alliance with the US.

* * *

The creation of the Self-Defense Forces (SDF) despite Article 9's prohibition of "war potential" meant that debates about national defense turned on elaborate legal gymnastics. In the 1950s, the Cabinet Legislation Bureau (CLB), an elite legal advisory body responsible for assessing the constitutionality of the government's proposed legislation, issued a series of interpretations that established boundaries on what defense capabilities were permissible. Article 9, the bureau maintained, recognized that Japan had an inherent right of self-defense and could therefore maintain "war potential," provided it was "not exceeding the minimum necessary level for self-defense."[38] Subsequent interpretations indicated, for example, that Japan could possess nuclear weapons but that collective self-defense—deploying the SDF to defend an ally—exceeded the "necessary level" threshold. Japan possessed the right to engage in collective self-defense, but CLB's interpretation prohibited it, an understanding reinforced by Japan's Supreme Court in a landmark 1959 decision.[39] Over time, this interpretation was refined. By the

1970s, the prevailing interpretation became that Japan's exercise of self-defense was limited to cases in which it faced imminent threat of armed attack by another state in which the rights to life, liberty, and the pursuit of happiness were at risk and the use of force was unavoidable—but it could still not exceed the "minimum necessary level."[40]

Defense hawks had chafed against this interpretation. For Kishi, Japan's inability to come to the aid of the US in a conflict was an enduring symbol of Japan's status as the junior partner and constrained independence. As a young lawmaker, Abe called for reinterpretation of the constitution to let Japan engage in collective self-defense, arguing that it was necessary to make the alliance truly equal and Japan a full-fledged member of the international community.[41] During his first premiership, Abe had convened an advisory council on the "Reconstruction for the Legal Basis of Security," which would likely have recommended constitutional reinterpretation. The council reconvened in February 2013, under the leadership of Yanai Shunji, a former top diplomat and judge on the International Tribunal for the Law of the Sea, and Okazaki Hisahiko, Abe's foreign policy guru.[42]

The council was tasked with assessing Japan's security environment and determining whether the prevailing legal framework was adequate, given new challenges facing the country in the twenty-first century. The council's May 2014 report, citing the threats posed by new technologies, globalization, and a rapidly shifting balance of power in East Asia as well as the reality that Japan needed a strong alliance with the US, recommended changes to the prevailing interpretation and domestic law to enable the SDF to participate in collective self-defense.[43]

The challenge for Abe was translating these recommendations into policy. In 2013, he had prepared the groundwork for reinterpretation by asserting that his constitutionally ordained appointment power gave him the power to appoint the head of the CLB, implying that the bureau was ultimately responsible to him.[44] "The chief executive is me!" exclaimed Abe in a parliamentary debate in February 2014. "It is also I who hold the responsibility for government replies [to submitted questions], having received the [public's] judgment by election. It is not the director-general of the legislation bureau who received the judgment. It is I."[45]

* * *

But despite Abe's broad interpretation of his powers, political calculations prevailed. Abe had to reckon with the fact that a solid majority of the public opposed reinterpretation, which made it easier for members of the ruling coalition to speak out against him.

Kōmeitō was also reluctant to support reinterpretation when doing so risked alienating the party's supporters. As the panel's deliberations continued into 2014, Yamaguchi Natsuo, Kōmeitō's leader, cautioned Abe against reinterpretation and urged him to prioritize the economy. More surprisingly, Abe also faced vocal opposition within the LDP as the panel concluded its deliberations. LDP and Kōmeitō lawmakers objected to both the process of reinterpretation and the substance. They feared that moving ahead with reinterpretation simply as an act of cabinet—without formal deliberations between the ruling parties or in the Diet—would generate a public backlash.

Abe permitted the ruling parties to give their assent before the cabinet would proceed but he also played hardball with Kōmeitō, hinting, for example, at his desire to form a new coalition with one of the smaller conservative opposition parties that would be more amenable to reinterpretation.[46] Even after Abe accepted that the government would introduce only "limited reinterpretation," Kōmeitō leaders pressed Abe for more clarity in how those limits would be phrased, seeking to avoid the potential for open-ended involvement in overseas conflicts.

Nevertheless, by late June, coalition negotiations produced a compromise. The prevailing conditions governing the right to self-defense were refined and broadened to allow Japan to exercise its right of collective self-defense. Now, in the event of an attack on a foreign country "in a close relationship" with Japan that both "threatens Japan's survival" and "poses a clear danger to fundamentally overturn" the rights of the Japanese people, the government could use the SDF to aid its ally, provided there were no other means of repelling the attack and that the use of force would not be disproportionate.[47] On 1 July, the cabinet formally approved this interpretation.[48]

Both Abe and Kōmeitō downplayed the significance of what had been decided. "The course Japan has taken as a peace-loving nation will remain unchanged," said Abe in a press conference announcing the decision. "Rather, Japan will continue these steps to further consolidate that position. It is precisely our determination towards that end that permeates today's Cabinet Decision."[49] Kōmeitō's Yamaguchi added, "Most important was the fact that the principle of pacifism that is at the heart of the Constitution has been firmly maintained and the limits of defensive measures permitted under Article 9 of the Constitution have been clarified."[50] Once again, Abe had bowed to political constraints and accepted a less-than-total victory. His approval ratings suffered, falling to the low forties, their lowest level since his return. But he had patiently ground out victory on a major priority.

There was still more work to do, since, having changed what would be possible for the SDF to do in Japan's defense, the government had now to write the new interpretation into law. But, in the meantime, he had to save Abenomics.

* * *

The economy was not faring well after the tax increase. In the first quarter following the hike, GDP fell more than seven percent, an unexpectedly large drop. The economy's sluggish performance continued into the summer. After rising steadily in 2013, price increases slowed, not least because of a steep fall in global energy prices. Global growth was slowing, too. Despite the government's steps to soften the impact, the tax hike had inflicted a significant blow, particularly to private consumption, which fell by roughly 1.5 percentage points of GDP and remained sluggish for several years thereafter.[51]

This unexpectedly large impact fundamentally altered the debate regarding the second tax hike, mandated for October 2015. This time, Abe would not be constrained by the LDP's fiscal hawks or the business establishment.

As early as September, when second-quarter GDP figures were worse than expected, Abe was determined to shelve the hike and call a snap election. He was already engaged in a protracted struggle with MOF and LDP backbenchers over corporate taxes. As part of the bargaining with corporate Japan over wages and investment, Abe had pledged to cut corporate rates to bring them in line with Japan's developed-country peers. A panel recommended Japan's average corporate tax rate should be reduced by roughly ten percentage points from thirty-five percent starting in 2015, while taking other measures to limit the blow to revenues. Naturally, Abe and his growth-focused advisers emphasized the tax cut; Asō, Kuroda, and other fiscal hawks were focused on revenue neutrality. The LDP's tax commission—nicknamed the LDP's "greatest sanctuary" for its ability to resist interference from prime ministers—preferred narrow tax incentives targeted at encouraging investment and R&D spending to a broad tax cut.[52] Naturally, the fiscal hawks assumed that a corporate tax cut would have to be accompanied by the second consumption tax hike to limit the hit to government finances—which would mean Abe was pushing for a big tax cut for corporations at the same time he would impose a hike on households.

The impasse continued into October, when MOF and its allies began a public campaign to pressure the prime minister to implement the next consumption tax hike.[53] Kuroda also did his part, not only warning against the risks of a delay but also—on 31 October—shocking markets by announcing another round of stimulus that increased the BOJ's annual pace of government bond purchases to ¥80 trillion and tripled its purchases of ETFs and REITs, an announcement that quickly became known as Kuroda's "second bazooka." While the slowing economy and the onset of disinflation gave the bank ample reason to expand the QQE program, Kuroda's open advocacy for the tax hike fueled speculation that he was trying to forestall a delay.[54] Either way, Kuroda's second round of easing—which was approved by a razor-thin 5–4 margin compared to the 9–0 margin in favor of QQE in April 2013—signaled that all was not well with the economy. Abe, facing pressure from fiscal hawks but also growing signs of a slowdown, kept his cards close, but hinted that he was open to a delay, telling the *Financial Times* that it would be "meaningless" if the tax hike simply triggered a recession.[55]

When third-quarter GDP data was released on 17 November, it gave Abe all the justification he needed to delay the tax hike and call a snap election. Japan was in a recession, as real growth fell by 1.6 percent, substantially worse than the consensus view that growth would return.[56] The following day Abe announced that he would delay the tax hike to April 2017 and, furthermore, that he would dissolve the lower house and call a general election for 14 December. He would, he said, seek a new mandate for Abenomics.

"Now, there is criticism that Abenomics has failed, that it has not turned out well. However, what should be done? I'm afraid to say that not once have I heard a concrete idea. There is no room in Japan today for the repetition of criticism for criticism's sake. Are our economic policies wrong or right? Is there truly any alternative?"[57]

The LDP's slogan would encapsulate this view: "For economic recovery, this is the only way."

When the vote was called, the public was puzzled. There seemed to be little reason for a snap election. The confusion was largely because Abe called the election not because he was losing the confidence of the people, but because a snap election is a good way for a prime minister to impose discipline on his party. MOF and its LDP allies were trying to force Abe to accept that fiscal consolidation should take precedence over growth, but the critics Abe was calling out via the snap election were not all on the opposition benches. In fact, the weakness of the DPJ made it possible for Abe to play the snap election card. There was little chance that he would lose his majority to the DPJ, which languished in the single digits.

His gamble paid off. The snap election marked a sharp turn in favor of fiscal stimulus. Thereafter, MOF and its allies were repeatedly bested by Abe and Suga.[58] In 2015, Abe even forced out Noda Takeshi, a former MOF official and head of the LDP's tax commission, reducing its independence.[59] While Abe has been accused of conducting a "bait-and-switch" campaign in 2014, calling an election on Abenomics but then claiming a mandate for a broadly conservative agenda, this criticism ignores the real consequences the election had for Abe's power.[60]

For Abe the 2014 election was vindication that his approach could work. He could wield power by grinding away at problems, patiently deploying his assets, strategically distributing posts and co-opting rivals, knowing when to forge ahead despite opposition and when to back down, and always being willing to compromise. He would win by being inexorable. It might be less glamorous than Koizumi's made-for-TV showdowns with the "resistance forces," but the virtues of this approach would be readily apparent soon after the general election.

15

ALLIANCE OF HOPE

On the morning of Wednesday, 29 April 2015, the chamber of the House of Representatives in the US Capitol was packed. Senators and representatives congregated on the floor. Speaker of the House John Boehner and Vice President Joe Biden waited at the rostrum. Staffers squeezed into the back. In the galleries, no seat was vacant.

At 11:15am, the sergeant of arms announced, "Mr. Speaker, the Prime Minister of Japan." Abe entered to a standing ovation, followed by Republican and Democratic congressional leaders. He was the first Japanese prime minister to address a joint session of Congress.[1]

Abe spoke deliberately, in English, reading from his prepared text. After opening with a tribute to his grandfather and to former members of Congress who served as ambassadors to Japan—as well as to the incumbent ambassador, Caroline Kennedy, seated with his wife Akie in the gallery—he spoke for forty-five minutes about what he called the "alliance of hope" between Japan and the US. He recalled his youthful sojourn in the US. He talked about bitter memories of the war and acknowledged the suffering Japan inflicted on Asian peoples.

But he also explained how the former adversaries reconciled and became allies, expressing his gratitude for how the US helped Japan rebuild. And then he laid out a vision for future cooperation. He called upon members of Congress—many of whom were skeptical—to back TPP, touting its ability to deliver peace and prosperity to the region.

He explained how Abenomics was changing Japan, highlighting his accomplishments in corporate governance and agricultural reform. And he demonstrated how Japan would support the US rebalance to Asia, both by strengthening ties with key partners and by deepening alliance cooperation with the US.

He received robust ovations. Fewer than eighteen months after the vice president had warned him not to visit Yasukuni and the US ambassador had reprimanded him for going, Abe was accorded one of the greatest honors a foreign leader could receive.

It was the capstone on one of the most successful periods in the history of the US–Japan alliance. Thanks to Abe, Japan could argue that it was the most important US ally in the region. It helped that during this period Abe put the early stumbles of Abenomics behind him, as he redoubled his efforts to boost Japan's economy. And, as he showed in Washington, he would make meaningful strides in trying to heal the divisions caused by historical memory.

* * *

By April 2015, Japan and the US faced a strategic environment that had changed dramatically since 2013. Xi had aggressively consolidated power, waging a wide-reaching campaign against corruption in the CCP and reforming the Chinese state to strengthen his domination of decision-making. He wished to convert China's wealth into power and influence beyond its shores. "What sets Xi's foreign policy apart the most," wrote Kurt Campbell and Robert Blackwill, veteran American Asia hands, "is his willingness to use every instrument of statecraft, from military assets to geoeconomic intimidation, as well as explicit economic rewards, to pursue his various geopolitical objectives."[2] Under Xi, it seemed China might finally become the aspiring regional if not global hegemon that many in the US and Japan had warned about for years.

For Japan, China's military power was increasingly a direct threat. Its navy and air force were both more sophisticated and more active in both the East and South China Seas, the latter a particularly important conduit for hydrocarbon imports upon which Japan had become even more dependent since 3/11 shuttered its nuclear reactors.[3]

There had been an uptick in China's clashes with other countries bordering the South China Sea—most of which China claims on the basis of a pre-1949 map that showed a nine-dashed line extending from mainland China south, like a tongue—since the start of the decade, but its assertiveness in the sea had grown. In recent years, China had clashed with both Vietnam and the Philippines over disputed islands.[4] At the same time, China intensified work on what Admiral Harry Harris, commander of the US Pacific fleet, would call China's "Great Wall of Sand," a string of filled-in reefs and artificial islands that allowed Beijing to deploy assets to strengthen its grip on the South China Sea.[5]

In Tokyo and Washington, these activities, together with China's behavior around the disputed Senkakus, its navy's passages through the Japanese archipelago into the Western Pacific, its growing defense budgets, and its modernization of the PLA presented a serious local challenge to the US and its allies. Beijing's approach to a potential conflict with the US emphasized new capabilities that could hinder the ability of enemy forces to enter a combat theater and maneuver within it, allowing China to win a short war, say, with Taiwan or with Japan for control of the Senkakus.[6] Both the US and Japanese governments feared that in a conflict China could push the US out of Asia and isolate it from its allies.[7] The allies also had to fear "hybrid warfare," the use of proxy militias backed by cyber warfare, political and psychological warfare, and other "non-physical" means to achieve victory in "gray zones," conflict areas that fell somewhere between war and peace.[8]

For both Abe and Obama, however, the challenge posed by China was not just about its military might. They were in a struggle to shape the political and economic future of the region that would be the main driver for global growth in the twenty-first century.[9] While it seemed the Pentagon was dominating the rebalance to Asia, the administration's vision was more comprehensive: the US had to be present in the region so as to be involved in building institutions and writing rules that would draw the region closer together in a manner that included the US and reflected US interests and values, while complicating a Chinese bid for hegemony.[10]

The scale of the competition became clearer in 2013, when Xi unveiled a grandiose plan to strengthen commercial links with partners in all directions across Eurasia that became known as the Belt and Road Initiative (BRI). Chinese companies, financed by Chinese capital and often employing Chinese laborers, would, along a series of land and maritime economic corridors extending from China, build the ports, highways, railroads, power grids, and fiber-optic cables that Eurasian countries needed for growth.

While sometimes referred to by Chinese thinkers as a trillion-dollar "Marshall Plan," the BRI had a broader political purpose. China would use economic largesse to reshape the global order, turning trading partners into allies, fostering new institutions, and transforming old ones.[11] The initiative's importance for Xi became apparent in 2017, when the CCP incorporated it into its constitution.

The BRI touched every part of Xi's national strategy. It would strengthen under-developed regions within China. It would shore up state-owned enterprises, which would find new opportunities for growth. It would also help China achieve the goals of the "Made in China 2025" industrial policy program—a strategy unveiled in 2015 that called for upgrading China's competitiveness in ten high-tech industries—by fostering new export markets for burgeoning national champions. And it would justify the creation of Chinese-led international institutions, most notably the Asian Infrastructure Investment Bank, a Beijing-based development lender that would divide the US and many of its allies before it even opened for business.[12] Japan, alone among major US allies, stayed out of the AIIB.

Open-ended competition with a rival great power like China would be a complicated—and subtle—challenge. The US and its allies were battling for influence across the region with a rising power that boasted a successful development model, had a huge domestic market that could influence the behavior even of staunch US allies, and was investing its wealth in helping its middle-income neighbors move up the ladder. The US and its allies needed to provide an attractive alternative to Chinese money and institutions for China's neighbors.

In 2015, the Abe Doctrine began to leave its mark in this contest. The US and Japan updated their defense guidelines for the first time since 1997. Abe's government navigated landmark legal changes that enshrined the 2014 constitutional reinterpretation through the Diet. And the twelve TPP countries concluded negotiations. Abe also visited India again, where he cemented his relationship with Modi by concluding agreements on nuclear cooperation and Japanese investment. Abe also began pursuing a more pragmatic approach to Japan's historical disputes with its neighbors, including a surprisingly mild statement marking the seventieth anniversary of the end of the war and an agreement with Seoul that appeared to mark the end of their dispute over restitution for South Korea's surviving comfort women.

* * *

The most immediate challenge lay in updating national security laws. While Abe's decision to change the prevailing constitutional interpretation hurt his approval ratings, the drama had played out behind closed doors as ruling parties negotiated the terms of the new interpretation. To pass the national security bills, Abe would have to win the support of the ruling coalition for specific legislative changes, and then navigate them through the Diet.

The government and ruling parties agreed to changes to ten laws governing the Self-Defense Forces (SDF) and the ministry of defense (MOD), and two laws pertaining to peacekeeping operations (PKO). Most importantly, the SDF would be able to coordinate and support allied forces in situations when an armed attack had occurred or was expected (assuming it met the threshold dictated by the constitutional reinterpretation).

But Japan's armed forces could now provide rear-area support anywhere in the world for US operations, ostensibly on behalf of Japan's national security. The government would no longer need a special enabling law as had been the case for contributions to allied operations in Afghanistan and Iraq. At Kōmeitō's insistence, overseas deployments had to be consistent with international law, subject to democratic oversight and public understanding, and include measures ensuring the safety of SDF personnel.[13] The Diet would have the right to approve deployments in advance, but the process could be streamlined in case of emergency. The logistical support Japan could provide might now include munitions and fuel for aircraft heading out on combat missions, as well as support for rescue operations for Japanese nationals in a conflict zone.

Japan's PKO law, meanwhile, would be amended to expand the situations in which SDF personnel deployed as part of a PKO could use weapons to include area security and rescue operations to aid personnel from other countries.

Ruling coalition negotiations on the bills were contentious, and the parliamentary debate did not begin until 25 May 2015, well into the session. The ruling parties had little choice but to extend the session to 27 September, setting the stage for a lengthy parliamentary battle that would stretch through the summer and prompt the largest protests Japan had seen in decades.

The ensuing debate was not Japanese democracy's finest hour. For four months, the government and opposition parties shouted past each other. Abe repeatedly insisted that "the government will explain thoroughly, clearly and carefully that the development of the legislation is necessary [for the government to fulfill its duties to the Japanese people]."[14] But Abe, Defense Minister Nakatani Gen, and other officials repeatedly struggled to explain what the legislation would change when questioned, and often fell back on the argument that Japan's security environment had worsened and therefore these legislative changes were necessary. They downplayed the likelihood that Japanese forces would be sent into harm's way or even that the legislation could be a particularly important milestone for the evolution of Japan's security policy.

The opposition, led by the Democrats but including the Communists on the left and the Japan Restoration Party (JRP) on the right, was little better. Left-wing opposition lawmakers dubbed the legislation "war bills"—arguing they greatly increased the likelihood Japan would be drawn into US-led wars—and sought to highlight inconsistencies in the government's arguments. A constitutional law scholar called as a witness by the LDP gifted the opposition a talking point at the outset of the debate when he agreed that the government's reinterpretation the previous year was "unconstitutional."[15]

It was a particularly challenging summer for Abe. On the one hand, he led in the way that worked best for him. He had allowed Kōmeitō and more reluctant LDP members to shape the legislation and introduce provisions that would limit the government's ability to deploy the SDF. He was willing to tolerate months of frustrating and almost futile debate to satisfy ruling party lawmakers and to give opposition lawmakers ample time to question the bills. But his frustration—and his longstanding impatience with parliamentary deliberations—repeatedly got the better of him.

* * *

Abe had always relished fighting for his convictions and hitting back at critics, especially those in the center-left media. In his second administration, he used Facebook to attack, among other critics, his old adversary Tanaka Hitoshi and an anonymous college student who set up a website to criticize his policies; snapped at newscasters for asking overly critical questions; and heckled questioners in parliamentary proceedings.[16] He explicitly attacked the *Asahi Shimbun* on the floor of the Diet for impugning Japan's honor by publishing a later-discredited account by a former Japanese soldier of his role in recruiting comfort women.[17] The threat in the state secrets law to punish journalists who publish designated secrets also cast Abe as an enemy of press freedom in the eyes of his critics. In one commonly cited metric, Japan fell from fifty-three to seventy-two on the Reporters Without Borders (RWB) annual press freedom index, although it recovered slightly in the later years of his government, in part because other governments were worse.

There had never been much love between Abe and the media establishment. From early in his career, he saw it as an adversary, part of the "postwar regime" that had advanced the "masochistic" view of Japan's past that had kept the country in fetters. His 2007 resignation, which he blamed partly on a biased press, only strengthened his conviction that the media could not be trusted. He returned to power determined to wield more control over the story told about his government. He scrapped Koizumi's practice of holding daily on-camera sessions with the media, opting for more structured sessions and one-on-one interviews with favored domestic reporters and foreign correspondents.[18]

Abe's reputation as an enemy of the press, however, can be overstated. The RWB index, for example, has methodological flaws that undermine its value.[19] His relationship with the press was more nuanced than Donald Trump's attacks on the "fake news" media. He used the Japanese media establishment's coziness with power to reward favored outlets and reporters with access. Early in his tenure, journalists suggested that the government's "carrots-and-sticks" approach was leading reporters to practice self-censorship, but Abe was still unable to prevent all media outlets from pursuing serious allegations of corruption against the prime minister and the first lady. As Martin Fackler, a former *New York Times* correspondent in Japan, argues, the Japanese media establishment failed to keep pace with a Japanese government that had grown more sophisticated in controlling access to reward and punish news organizations.[20] And despite a boast to Trump that he had "tamed" *Asahi*, the paper and other outlets held Abe's feet to the fire later in his tenure when he was accused of influence peddling.[21]

Nevertheless, the mutual suspicion between Abe and the media establishment complicated Abe's determination to explain his government's bills to the public. Abe's critics in the media would gleefully amplify moments when he lost his cool or contradicted himself or one of his ministers.[22] Opposition attacks on the government's bills had a relatively uncritical airing. It may not have been fair, but it was the reality Abe faced as he tried to move controversial legislation through the Diet.

* * *

What resulted were testy debates inside and growing protests outside the Diet and across the country. Abe had the votes in both houses—and a supermajority in the lower house that could override the upper house if necessary. But the opposition had the public behind it: polls consistently showed that a majority opposed the government's bills and an even larger majority believed that the prime minister's explanations were inadequate.

Inside the Diet, the opposition parties demanded more time for debate and warned the government against "steamrolling" the legislation. Opposition lawmakers were hoping to delay a vote until late July. If they could delay a vote until fewer than sixty days before the extended session would end in late September, it would force Abe either to extend the session again—to give the lower house time to overrule the upper house—or admit defeat. Delaying passage would raise the stakes in the upper house, where the government's majority was smaller. The lower house's special committee established to consider the legislation deliberated for 116 hours, as lawmakers sought to poke holes in the government's arguments and quiz Abe for details on how the SDF's new powers would apply in various hypothetical situations. The bills finally passed the committee on 15 July and, with opposition lawmakers vacating their seats, the whole house on 16 July.

With more than sixty days remaining, the lower house would have a chance to vote again if the upper house was deadlocked. But Abe had paid a heavy price. A poll conducted in late July by the *Yomiuri Shimbun* found that not only had the cabinet's disapproval rating surpassed its approval rating for the first time, but the public was overwhelmingly opposed to Abe's handling of the legislation. Sixty-four percent of respondents opposed ratification during the current session. Eighty-two percent said the government's explanation of the bills was insufficient. Sixty-one percent opposed the ruling coalition's decision to hold a vote without the opposition parties.[23] In other polls, Abe's approval fell below forty percent. In late summer, Abe took to the airwaves to convince the public of the necessity of his bills.

But he faced a growing challenge in the streets. By the eve of the legislation's passage by the lower house, more than 20,000 marched to the Diet in opposition. Nagatachō rang with calls of *Abe Yamero!*—Abe quit! Abe, the protestors said, was "running wild." Galvanized by a student movement called the Students Emergency Action for Liberal Democracy (SEALD) but bringing together Japanese of all ages, the protests continued to grow.[24] On the final Sunday in August, more than 300 protests were held across the country. Central Tokyo was overwhelmed by a protest that organizers claimed drew 120,000 people (although police estimated just 30,000 attended).

Abe refused to yield. Despite the protests, the falling approval ratings, and an upper house debate that at times seemed completely stalled, he forged ahead—and his party remained united behind him. On 8 September, the LDP granted him a second term as party leader by unanimous consent after no candidate filed to run against him. His reelection was less unanimous than it appeared—party bosses pressured backbenchers not to endorse Noda Seiko, a moderate lawmaker who was one of the LDP's most promising female politicians, depriving her of the nominations needed to run.[25] However unnerved party leaders were by the backlash to the security bills, there was no alternative to Abe.

Tensions mounted as the end of the session approached. Finally, on 17 September, the upper house's special committee approved the legislation despite attempts by opposition lawmakers to physically prevent a vote from being held, resulting in altercations between LDP and opposition members in the committee room. That evening, the legislation was rushed to the whole house. The following day, opposition parties tried to short circuit the debate by submitting a no-confidence motion in the lower house and a censure motion in the upper house, both of which were defeated. Finally, in the early hours of 19 September, the legislation passed.

It was the single greatest victory of Abe's career. He had weathered the protests and the falling approval ratings—after bottoming out in the low thirties, his support began to recover in October—and secured a landmark shift in security policy. It was not just a victory for Abe's vision of a Japan that could join the competition among the great powers. It was also a victory for his vision of majoritarian democracy. Centrists in Kōmeitō might wheedle concessions and opposition lawmakers and demonstrators could protest the government's actions and occasionally hold up the legislative process, but a determined prime minister wielding majorities in both houses could move a legislative agenda while paying little heed to opposition parties, opinion polls, or protestors.

* * *

As with many of Abe's legislative victories, it was ambiguous. The intensity of public opposition made it less likely that Abe would rush to deploy Japanese forces overseas. The SDF deployed under the new rules of engagement in 2016 as part of the UN peacekeeping mission in South Sudan, but the deployment was a fiasco, as the security situation deteriorated to such an extent that the SDF's presence was not permitted even under the revised peacekeeping law. When it emerged in 2017 that the SDF had concealed evidence of the worsening situation, Defense Minister Inada Tomomi, a conservative protégé of Abe's and widely seen as a contender to succeed him, was forced to resign, spoiling her political prospects. Later, SDF warships escorted US naval vessels—a symbolic exercise of collective self-defense—although they were not in harm's way.[26]

While the national security bills commanded the bulk of the public's attention, the most consequential changes to Japan's security policy may have happened before the legislation was even submitted to the Diet, when the Japanese and US governments signed the new guidelines for defense cooperation in April.[27]

The new guidelines were the most tangible sign that for Abe there was no alternative to keeping the US committed to Japan's security and the security of East Asia. The allies agreed to strengthen coordination in both peacetime and crises, and all situations in between, including the "gray zone" scenarios that alarmed Japan's leaders; broaden alliance cooperation to include space and cyberspace; and use Abe's relaxation of arms export rules to expand defense technology cooperation. In the interest of strengthening deterrence for defending Japan, the two militaries would strengthen coordination against countering threats on land, at sea, and in the air, as well as from ballistic missiles through their joint deployment of ballistic missile defenses.[28] The allies also agreed to expand their cooperation regionally and globally, including partner capacity building, an oblique reference to measures to strengthen the defenses of, for example, Southeast Asian countries battling with China in the South China Sea. The two governments also sought to reinforce the US military's presence in Japan, with the Obama administration committing to deploy the most advanced hardware to Japan, while the Abe government reaffirmed its commitment to facilitate the realignment of US forces in Japan, which included a plan to shutter the controversial Futenma marine air station in Okinawa and build a new air station on an infilled bay at more remote Henoko.

But as important as the defense guidelines and Abe's security legislation were for upgrading the US–Japan partnership for a new era, in 2015 the most important development for the long-term future of the US in Asia was playing out not in Tokyo, but in the US Congress.

* * *

In the two years since Japan entered TPP negotiations, US and Japanese negotiators had met dozens of times. They were in accord on the most innovative chapters in the agreement—rules to govern digital trade, state-owned enterprises, investment, intellectual property rights, and labor and environmental standards—but struggled to finalize what would effectively be a bilateral FTA within the multilateral accord.

The Obama administration faced heavy pressure from farmers to force Japan to liberalize its markets for most agricultural commodities, while the US automobile industry and the United Auto Workers wanted TPP to tackle what it saw as Japan's "currency manipulation" and non-tariff barriers they believed kept them from selling more cars in Japan. The path to a bilateral agreement was narrow, having to satisfy Japan's farmers—who demanded significant carve-outs for the five "sacred" commodities: rice, wheat, beef and pork, dairy, and sugar—and US business interests, who at times called for Japan to be left behind if it was unwilling to compromise.

But there was a path forward. Japan had offered a key concession, accepting that US tariffs on automobiles and light trucks would be phased out over an extensive time frame. Abe and Amari were also willing to push back against the agriculture lobby as they searched for ways to satisfy US demands for a market access agreement that met the WTO standard for tariff elimination on more than ninety percent of products, while also protecting the sacred commodities. It helped that both governments saw the strategic value of an agreement. As Defense Secretary Ashton Carter said, "You may not expect to hear this from a Secretary of Defense, but in terms of our rebalance in the broadest sense, passing TPP is as important to me as another aircraft carrier."[29] Obama, meanwhile, emphasized that the US was in a competition with China for influence over Asia's economic future.[30]

But the fact was that in 2015, the US was the biggest obstacle to TPP. Obama needed Congress to grant him "fast track" trade promotion authority (TPA), which would reassure negotiating partners that Congress would be unable to amend an agreement and would be limited to a simple up-or-down vote on ratification. Without fast track, TPP would be dead. No negotiating partner would make significant concessions or commit to an agreement that could be amended to death by the US Congress.

Obama, entering his final two years in office, had lost control of the Senate to the Republican Party in November 2014 and looked increasingly like a lame duck. Both parties were looking ahead to the 2016 elections. Obama was eager to pursue a major trade deal that would seal his legacy as a "Pacific president," but few Democrats wanted to vote for an agreement that would drive a wedge between their competing constituencies. Republicans, particularly in the Tea Party wing, were reluctant to give the president a victory on his way out. The Republican-controlled Senate might have been more inclined to cooperate than the outgoing Democratic Senate.[31] But Republican leaders in both houses were reluctant to move without signs that Obama could convince Democrats to back it. It had to be a bipartisan initiative, or it would not happen.

When TPA was submitted to the Senate in April, it received enough support from Democrats on the Finance Committee to suggest that it could get a filibuster-proof majority of sixty votes in the full Senate. However, after leaving the committee, it was held up by Democrats seeking a broader package of trade legislation that would include assistance for workers displaced by trade. But these concessions were unacceptable to House Republicans. Finessing these dynamics took most of June, and TPP negotiations were on hold while the bloc waited to see whether Obama could win fast track. In the end, the House passed the TPA package on 18 June, with only twenty-eight of 188 Democrats supporting it. Fifty Republicans—mainly from the populist Tea Party wing—also voted against it.

TPP negotiators could race to the finish. In early July, US and Japanese negotiators suggested that they were close enough to an agreement that it was conceivable that TPP itself could be concluded at the next ministerial meeting, at the end of July. It took a bit longer, but on 5 October 2015, after a marathon five-day ministerial meeting, an agreement in principle was announced.

For the moment, it seemed a genuine victory for Obama and his Asia rebalance. After watching Xi roll out the BRI, the US and its regional partners showed that they too were able to advance a constructive vision for Asia's future. "We take high pride in the fact that we have been the member to construct the original treaty," said Amari in the joint press conference announcing the agreement. "And by spreading the rules we can make the world more affluent and strengthen the relationship of mutual interdependence. So it will mean the economic security, but at the same time in an indirect sense, it will enhance the security in the region and to promote the solidarity in the region."[32]

Within days, Abe reshuffled his cabinet, bringing on a major ally of the farm lobby as agriculture minister to smooth the treaty's ratification. He established a headquarters at the prime minister's office that would manage the ratification process, which would require convincing the public that—although Japan agreed to tariff cuts on some of the nearly 600 tariff lines that made up the "sacred" commodities—Abe had kept his promise to defend politically sensitive products in negotiations.[33]

But he still recognized that Japan's inclusion in the bloc was the start of a new era, in which all Japanese would look abroad for opportunities to prosper. "The TPP is truly a grand plan for the long-term future of our nation," he said in his policy speech in January.[34] He pledged to follow TPP by concluding an agreement with the EU as well as the Regional Comprehensive Economic Partnership (RCEP), which included the ten countries of ASEAN, Japan, South Korea, China, India, Australia, and New Zealand.

But even as Abe was stepping into a new role as a full-throated advocate for globalization, it looked as if the US would yield leadership of the liberal global trading regime. Ominously, two days after the agreement was announced, Hillary Clinton, the presumptive Democratic Party nominee for president, came out against TPP, despite having described the pact as the "gold standard" and promoted it as part of the "pivot to Asia" when she served as Obama's secretary of state.[35] Donald Trump, the New York businessman and reality TV star who was the Republican frontrunner, also opposed the deal. "TPP is a terrible deal," he tweeted on 5 October. He had urged Republicans to vote against fast track.[36] After the agreement was signed in February, and as he completed his march to the Republican Party's presidential nomination, Trump stepped up his attacks on TPP. "It's a rape of our country," he said in June 2016.[37]

Obama unsuccessfully tried to convince the Republican congressional leaders to take up the treaty. The US and Japan appeared to be trading places. Japan, which had resisted pressure to open its markets in the interests of protecting farmers and other inefficient producers, had become a full-throated supporter of a new trade regime, thanks to a prime minister who saw the strategic value and enjoyed the backing of the general public and corporate Japan. The US, meanwhile, after forty years of pushing free trade agreements for strategic reasons and for the benefit of consumers and big business at the expense of manufacturing firms and their workers, was increasingly divided about the trading order past leaders had built.[38]

* * *

For Abe, TPP was a victory at a moment when Abenomics's fortunes were sagging.

Fresh from his electoral victory in December 2014, Abe leveraged his new mandate to complete some of the unfinished work from the first phase of Abenomics. By February 2015, Abe could use the possibility of a breakthrough in TPP negotiations to complete agricultural reform. Having wearied of JA-Zenchū's attempt at "self-reform," the government forced the organization to accept a plan that would strip it of much of its power over local cooperatives, enabling the latter to pursue "agriculture on the offensive."

It was not a total victory over the organization—prefectural associations would still maintain some control over local cooperatives and collect fees from them, which could be turned over to the national organization—but the government's reforms reduced the organization from a quasi-monopoly intimately involved in the production and distribution of agricultural products to a more conventional interest group. This reform simultaneously created more room for experimentation with new forms of production and signaled that the group's dominance of agriculture policymaking was over. "Cracks have appeared in the strong and solid ties binding MAFF, the JA, and the legislators," wrote former bureaucrat Yamashita Kazuhito. "The reform package may not have quite lived up to expectations, but it is highly significant that it has caused these cracks to emerge."[39]

Simultaneously, Abe was pressing ahead with corporate governance reform. He was again directly involved in discussions between employers and unions ahead of the annual wage negotiations, resulting in some of the largest pay increases in twenty years. A corporate tax cut and tax incentives that would further reduce the tax bill for firms that raised wages may have helped.[40]

Meanwhile, on 22 February, the Tokyo stock exchange (TSE) and the financial services agency (FSA, the leading financial regulator) released a new corporate governance code. LDP backbenchers, led by Shiozaki Yasuhisa, who would join the government in September 2014 as the health, labor, and welfare minister, played an instrumental role in pushing the administration to prioritize a corporate governance code, with the help of Nicholas Benes, an American and long-time advocate for corporate governance reform in Japan.[41]

The code, which built on a 2014 revision to the Companies Act, was not a radical departure from the prevailing model of corporate governance. These changes mainly sought to pressure corporate managers to include more outside directors on corporate boards or explain why they refused (a "comply or explain" model), with the updated law stipulating that firms need only appoint one outside director to avoid having to explain their failure to comply. (The governance code required TSE-listed companies to appoint two outside directors or explain their non-compliance.)

The corporate governance code urged managers to engage in "constructive dialogue" with shareholders and provide more information about long-range planning, compensation, activist and takeover defenses, and other practices, but did not enshrine shareholder value as the overriding goal for Japanese companies. Nevertheless, the code was, like agricultural reform, an important step to expose economic actors insulated from competition to external pressure that could force them to adapt. To the extent Abe was trying to attract more FDI—and that the code could render corporate Japan more vulnerable to takeover bids—it was another piece of Abe's bid to raise global competitiveness, particularly as TPP neared completion.

Corporate governance reform, however, would in time prove disappointing. Japanese companies brought in more independent directors, but corporate bosses continued to resist external pressure to use their assets more productively or pay their workers more (although they would dramatically increase share buybacks and divided payouts).[42] Inbound mergers and acquisitions were dwarfed by Japan Inc.'s overseas purchases, FDI remained below that of its developed-country peers, and by September 2019, corporate Japan was sitting on more than ¥500 trillion in cash, more than three times as much as at the start of Abe's second tenure.[43] High-profile cases of corporate malfeasance, meanwhile, illustrated how managers at Japan's most prestigious firms were shielded from accountability to shareholders and other stakeholders. As legal scholar Curtis Milhaupt argues, it may be corporate governance is a "*reflection* of a nation's variety of capitalism" and therefore it is unreasonable to expect corporate governance reform to deliver the transformational change hoped for by the Abe government.[44]

* * *

By late 2015, Abe's economic priorities began to shift. He had previously downplayed the significance of Japan's demographic outlook as a constraint on Japan's long-term growth.[45] But now, demographics would increasingly be the central focus of Abenomics. Immediately after his reelection as LDP leader in September, he announced that his government would launch the "new three arrows"—Abenomics 2.0. Everything that had been included under the first "three arrows" became the first arrow of Abenomics 2.0, "a strong economy." The government wanted to increase the size of Japan's economy to ¥600 trillion by 2020, a sizable increase relative to Japan's nominal GDP of roughly ¥530 trillion when the new arrows were announced and significantly more than the roughly ¥500 trillion economy that Abe inherited in late 2012.

The new second arrow, however, was the heart of Abenomics 2.0. The government would explicitly target a higher birth rate, aiming to raise Japan's total fertility rate from 1.4 children per woman to 1.8, which would still be below the replacement rate of 2.1 but would help to stabilize the population at 100 million people. A new third arrow was aimed at eliminating the need for workers to exit the labor force to provide care for elderly parents, a recognition that Japan could not afford to lose productive workers.

Abe had not belatedly realized the severity of Japan's demographic crisis. He devoted an entire chapter of his 2006 book to Japan's shrinking, aging population and the need to both upgrade the social safety net and boost productivity to compensate for the smaller workforce.[46] Rather, the new three arrows was an admission that the reflationists had failed. Japan would not be saved by flooding its economy with cash. In fact, flooding the economy with cash had barely delivered inflation.[47] The BOJ was struggling just to keep prices rising. Fighting deflation would still be important, but the Abe government had to address what Shirakawa had warned about: the graying of Japan was a constraint on growth in the present, not just in the future. As Martin Wolf put it, "You can't print babies."[48]

* * *

Japan's population was estimated to have peaked at 127 million in 2015 and, according to projections based on that year's census, in the best-case scenario could still fall below 100 million by 2059 and continue to drop. The worst-case scenario, meanwhile, anticipated that Japan's population could fall to 82 million by 2065. The graying would be more severe. Japan's working-age (aged 15–64) population had peaked in the late 1990s and the losses accelerated as baby boomers retired. During Abe's first six years in office, the working-age population shrank by 4.5 million people. Fewer workers meant fewer taxpayers and pension contributors supporting a swelling population of retirees. The elderly, already more than a quarter of the population by 2015, would be more than a third by the 2030s.[49]

"We will bring a halt to the dwindling birthrate and aging population and maintain a population of 100 million people even 50 years from now," Abe said when announcing his new cabinet in October 2015, in which Kato Katsunobu was given responsibility for coordinating the government's response across ministerial lines.[50] Demographics had always been part of Abenomics—the "Womenomics" agenda, included as part of the third arrow in 2013, was in part a demographic policy, since drawing women into the workforce and giving them more opportunities for advancement could slow the shrinking of the workforce and, if done properly, make it easier for working women to start families, in part by making it easier for men to be more involved in family life.[51] But now it would be the central focus of the program.

The Abe government might set a fertility rate "target" but Japan's birth rate was not something that could be changed by decree.[52] Instead, the Abe administration spent the next nine months drafting a plan to achieve a demographic virtuous cycle. Near-term growth would enable social policy changes to support family formation and support the employment of older Japanese past retirement—which would in turn boost consumer demand and investment. This plan, which would encompass changes to how Japanese work, raise their children, and retire would become the blueprint for much of the Abe government's economic program for the remainder of Abe's tenure.[53] It would also spur a broader discussion of how foreign workers could slow Japan's demographic crunch.

* * *

But a plan to save Japan from demographic oblivion would be futile if Abe's government could not generate the short-term growth that would boost the confidence and bank accounts of ordinary Japanese.

And in 2015, nearly a year after the consumption tax hike, the Japanese economy was sputtering. Price increases had receded, and Japan seemed on the brink of a return to deflation. There were loud grumbles, even from within the LDP, about the wisdom of carrying on with the BOJ's QQE program. There were even signs that Abe and Kuroda were at odds over the direction of Abenomics—and Abe was also fighting with Asō, the finance ministry, and LDP backbenchers again over fiscal policy, as his government sought to update its medium-term fiscal plan after Abe's decision to postpone the tax hike. The Nikkei 225 fell sharply, as the economy dropped into a technical recession again in the second half of 2015. Nearly three years into Abe's tenure, it appeared the macroeconomic benefits of Abenomics were modest at best.[54]

Despite his personal commitment to reflationism, Abe and his advisers seemed unperturbed by the return of deflation. "We have successfully created a situation that is not deflationary anymore," Abe said in October 2015. Reaching the BOJ's two-percent inflation target was "not an essential condition" for declaring deflation defeated, added Amari in December 2015.

The new three arrows, however, would provide the backdrop for a new surge of fiscal and monetary stimulus in 2016, particularly as Abe sought to recover from the battle over the national security bills and looked ahead to upper house elections in July 2016.

Kuroda shocked markets in January by announcing that the BOJ would follow some European central banks in introducing negative interest rates, using a limited negative interest rate policy (NIRP)—the negative 0.1 percent interest rate would apply only to reserves deposited by banks with the central bank, and even then, only new deposits and not the nearly ¥2 trillion already deposited.

The immediate market reaction was negative. The Nikkei plunged, the yen rallied, and interest rates on government bonds fell below zero, reflecting higher demand for safe government debt compared with other assets. It was inferred that the NIRP indicated Abe and Kuroda were running out of options, particularly since the global economy continued to grapple with sluggish growth in the US, Europe, and China.

Abe therefore began laying the groundwork for once again delaying the consumption tax hike—now a little over a year away in April 2017.

In the spring of 2016, before public debate of the tax hike began in earnest, Abe brought in foreign economists—including Nobelists Paul Krugman and Joseph Stiglitz—most of whom opposed the tax hike and whose expertise and reputations could gird the prime minister for battle with the fiscal hawks.[55] Abe claimed that he would only delay the tax in the event of a natural disaster or a "Lehman-style" financial shock, but this justification appeared increasingly threadbare.

By the start of April, he was already considering new fiscal stimulus, which, combined with a delay to the tax hike, could jolt the economy. Conveniently, Abe would also host world leaders in late May as the chair of the G7. He could use his G7 presidency to push for global macroeconomic policy coordination and at the summit would unveil a new stimulus package, delay the consumption tax hike, and call a snap election that would be held along with upper house elections in July. The snap election was shelved—and Abe's G7 peers reacted frostily to an attempt to argue that the world was on the brink of another Lehman shock—but the summit endorsed the need for "mutually reinforcing fiscal, monetary, and structural policies" and on 1 June Abe announced that the tax hike would be postponed again.[56]

Naturally, electoral politics figured in Abe's decision-making, and he was rewarded, when the LDP and Kōmeitō increased their majority in the upper house. Parties in favor of constitutional revision won enough seats to wield a supermajority, clearing an important hurdle. But revision would have to wait. In the immediate term, Abe used the election to complete the development of Abenomics 2.0. As he acknowledged on the campaign trail, the work of Abenomics was "only halfway done."

Following the election, Abe would unveil a nominal ¥28 trillion fiscal stimulus package (although only ¥6 trillion was new government spending, with the remainder being loans from public financial institutions).[57] Meanwhile, as the Abe government prepared new fiscal stimulus, Kuroda's BOJ conducted a policy review that would deliver another monetary policy shock in September—the birth of what the BOJ called "yield curve control" (YCC). This new framework was structured around interest rate targets: the bank adjusted its bond purchases to shape the schedule of interest rates, from –0.10 percent on short-term bonds to interest rates around zero on long-term (ten-year bonds) to more freely floating rates on bonds with longer maturities. The BOJ would leave other components of its program unchanged, but YCC became its dominant tool, enabling the bank to adjust its bond purchases in response to market conditions, buying more if market interest rates rose and fewer if they fell.[58] Over the next three years, the BOJ scaled back its bond purchases—although it was still nominally committed to buying ¥80 trillion annually—to the extent that analysts referred to a "stealth taper." But its commitment to fighting deflation did not flag. The BOJ still dominated the market for JGBs, holding roughly fifty percent in the later years of Abe's tenure, and it also became, alongside the GPIF, a top shareholder through its ETF purchases.[59]

Thus, by late 2016, Abenomics had been relaunched, with new fiscal and monetary policies and a new demographics and structural plan in the process of being translated into legislation. With the global economy recovering and Japan's economy improving—after 2016, unemployment plunged to just above two percent and remained there, while the jobs-to-applicants ratio reached record highs, as employers in higher-performing sectors struggled to find workers—Abe would have another chance to save Japan's economy.

* * *

On 27 May 2016, after the G7 summit, Barack Obama visited Hiroshima. Ambassador Kennedy had cajoled him to visit before his term ended, making him the first sitting president to visit

In a speech in the city's Peace Park, Obama did not apologize for the atomic bombings of Hiroshima and Nagasaki—most Americans still approved of them. Instead, he confronted the suffering of innocents in the Second World War and all wars and called for a "moral awakening" that would prevent the suffering from being repeated at other times and in other places.[60] It was a moment for the outgoing president to reflect on, as his speechwriter Ben Rhodes noted, "his own constant struggle to constrain our own warmaking."[61]

But it was also recognition that Obama and Abe had put their pasts behind them. After the bitterness surrounding Abe's Yasukuni visit, the two leaders reached an understanding. Abe had backed down from his more provocative revisionist stances, at least in public. His government upheld the Kōno statement on the comfort women. Abe's

August 2015 statement on the seventieth anniversary of the end of the war retained key phrases from earlier apologies and expressions of remorse at the "immeasurable damage and suffering" Japan had inflicted upon innocent people across Asia.[62] And in December 2015, with the tireless involvement of Obama administration officials, including ambassadors in Tokyo and Seoul, Abe and South Korean President Park concluded an "agreement" on the comfort women in which Abe expressed his "most sincere apologies" and the Japanese government agreed to contribute to a Korean-established fund to support surviving comfort women, in exchange for Seoul's agreement that the issue was "resolved finally and irreversibly."[63]

Through these actions, Abe put the national interest first—and by November 2016, he had a landmark trade agreement with the US and ten other countries in Asia-Pacific and new defense cooperation guidelines that promised to integrate the US and Japanese armed forces more than ever before. Japan's economy also appeared to be back on track. There were still looming challenges. Relations with China remained frigid. North Korea was still refining its arsenal. The agreement with South Korea had almost immediately encountered difficulties and looked endangered as Park's administration tottered. But with Hillary Clinton on track to the win the US presidency, it seemed Abe could count on a new president committed to the rebalance and whose administration would undoubtedly be staffed with familiar faces from the previous administration.

History had other ideas.

16

THE GAMBLE

On 26 December 2016, three years to the day after his visit to Yasukuni, Abe arrived in Hawaii for his final meeting with Obama. The following day they visited Pearl Harbor for the final act of what had become a joint effort to grapple with the Asia-Pacific's bloody past.

The spirit of Abe's remarks at the USS Arizona Memorial echoed that of his speech before Congress and, to a point, Obama's speech in Hiroshima. Abe offered no apology but lamented the suffering caused and vowed that Japan, with the US, would work towards a world filled with tolerance and reconciliation. "The world needs the spirit of tolerance and the power of reconciliation now—and especially now," Abe said.[1]

"It is here that we remember that even when hatred burns hottest," Obama said, "even when the tug of tribalism is at its most primal, we must resist the urge to turn inward. We must resist the urge to demonize those who are different."[2]

These were words for an uncertain future. One month to the day later, Donald Trump issued Executive Order 13769, a sweeping ban on the admission of all refugees for 120 days and a prohibition on the entry of all citizens from a handful of Muslim-majority countries, triggering massive protests at American airports and around the world.

In 2017, Abe would be tested as never before. Even as he faced the most serious allegations of corruption he had ever faced, he would have to weather the arrival of a new US president whose approach to the world not only threatened his efforts to bind Japan and the US closely together in the name of upholding a liberal world order, but would hasten the transition to an increasingly multipolar world. And yet by the year's end, he would be stronger than ever. Not only would he win a new parliamentary mandate, he would increasingly appear to be the world's leading champion of globalization at a time of rising protectionism. But it would be a tenuous position, as Abe tried to balance his new role as a defender of a liberal order with his relationship with a president who was fundamentally opposed to its core tenets.

* * *

At three o'clock in the afternoon in Tokyo on Wednesday, 9 November 2016, it became clear that Donald Trump, the real estate tycoon-turned-reality television star, would defeat Hillary Clinton to become the next president of the United States.

As swing state after swing state went for Trump, the Nikkei 225 plummeted, falling more than 900 points, the largest single-day drop save for the day the UK voted to leave the EU. The yen rallied, creeping up to ¥100 to the dollar. At 6:30 that evening, Abe addressed Trump's election. He briefly congratulated the president-elect and noted, "The US–Japan alliance is an unwavering alliance bound by universal values. I want to make those bonds even stronger."[3] The following morning, Abe spoke directly with Trump, who assured Abe that he wanted to strengthen the "special relationship" between their countries.

Abe was not entirely shocked by Trump's victory, although his government did not necessarily desire it. But Abe's government had not assumed it was impossible—and could not afford to be caught off guard.

While the LDP has generally viewed Republicans as friendlier to Japan, some of Abe's closest friends in Republican circles had vocally opposed Trump. Richard Armitage had explicitly endorsed Clinton.[4] Abe, meanwhile, had met with Clinton briefly during the campaign. He, like most observers around the world and even Trump himself, had little reason to believe that he could pull off an upset.

But he nevertheless quietly prepared for the chance that Trump could win. He did not meet with Trump during the campaign, but on the day he met Clinton, he privately conferred with Wilbur Ross, a private equity magnate who was an old friend of Trump's. Meanwhile, Sasae Kenichi, Japan's ambassador to the US since 2012, had opened a channel to Jeff Sessions, the first sitting Republican senator to endorse Trump, as well as to members of the Trump family, including daughter Ivanka and son-in-law Jared Kushner.[5] Michael Flynn, who would become Trump's first national security adviser, was an important link, visiting Japan a month before the election to urge Tokyo not to panic about Trump and to reassure the Abe government that despite Trump's more outlandish remarks—musing in a campaign town hall that it might be better for Japan and South Korea to acquire nuclear weapons, for example—if elected, he would see Japan's value as a partner in dealing with China's rise and North Korea's provocations.[6]

But Japanese officials had reason to worry. Trump had never held elected office, but he had dabbled in politics since the 1980s. The worldview he articulated was that other countries had taken advantage of the US, using America's security guarantees and open markets to drive American firms out of business. The list of adversaries taking advantage of the US would change, but there would be one country that never ceded its place on Trump's list: Japan.[7] "Make Japan, Saudi Arabia, and others pay for the protection we extend as allies," he wrote in an open letter on American foreign policy that ran as a full-page ad in the *New York Times*, *Washington Post*, and *Boston Globe* in September 1987.[8]

He delivered the same message on the campaign trail. He railed against Japan as "killing us on trade," "taking our jobs," and "devaluing their yen." Japan, he said, "they send the cars by the millions, 70 billion a year." "If we get attacked, Japan doesn't have to do anything," he said in September 2015. "If Japan gets attacked we have to go fight for them." He even shared his opinion of Japan's prime minister. "Japan now has a great leader, Shinzo Abe," he said at a campaign stop in New Hampshire. "He's a killer." His views of Japan partly reflected his age. As part of the generation born just after the war, Trump repeatedly mentioned Pearl Harbor and Japan's "samurai past" in meetings with Abe.[9]

But ultimately for Trump, Japan was an ungrateful ally. His hostility to the US alliance with Japan was part of a broader hostility to the postwar US-led international order, the network of alliances, multilateral institutions, and trade agreements that, while deterring the Soviet Union, had entrenched democracy, promoted trade and investment, and preserved peace and stability throughout much of the world.

As Trump intuited, this regime had allowed Japan to rebuild after the war and enjoy rapid growth, while limiting its defense expenditures and relying on the US to defend it. Every US president since Eisenhower had wanted Japan to contribute more to the alliance, but for many US strategists the US–Japan relationship was a bargain. The US military received strategically valuable bases for which Japan footed much of the bill and, by guaranteeing Japan's security, Washington and Tokyo could reassure Asia that Japan would not return to militarism. As Japan grew wealthy, US negotiators struggled to restore balance to their economic relationship, but alliance managers were largely untroubled by Japan's exporting prodigious amounts of cars and electronics and buying comparatively little in return.[10] In fact, Trump's ire was directed as much at past US administrations as at foreign governments. The "globalists" had allowed Japan and other countries to get away with exploiting the US. That time was over.

In short, Trump threatened a world order that had proven beneficial for Japan. But it was not just that his most long-held opinion as a public figure was that Japan and several other countries were taking advantage of the US. Rather, it was that he was impulsive, unpredictable, and tended to view all transactions as zero sum. "He'd like people when they were helpful, and turn on them when they weren't. It wasn't personal. He's a transactional man—it was all about what you could do for him," said Tony Schwartz, Trump's ghostwriter.[11] He would also retaliate if he felt he was crossed. "When someone attacks me, I always attack back...except 100x more. This has nothing to do with a tirade but rather, a way of life!" he once tweeted.[12]

Trump kept allies and adversaries guessing: "We have to be unpredictable. And we have to be unpredictable starting now."[13] While unpredictability may be useful to keep adversaries off balance, it was a chilling prospect for an ally in need of help to deter China and North Korea.

But it was not all gloom. Candidate Trump also wanted to get tough on China—including in the South China Sea—which would be hard without allies like Japan.[14] Maybe, some Japanese officials hoped, the new president would be a useful corrective to what they saw as Obama's dovish inclinations on China.

Abe would have to adjust. He would have to work harder to keep the US committed to Japan, while seeking insurance against a worst-case scenario in which Trump abandoned Japan militarily and punished it economically. Abe had inherited from Kishi a belief in the importance of national independence, but knew Japan had no alternative but to preserve its alliance with the US. He would have to do whatever it took to keep Trump satisfied, the alliance intact, and Japan's access to US markets unimpeded. The ethic of responsibility would win out, and the Abe Doctrine—which originally served to strengthen ties with a president who wanted the US to be more firmly embedded in Asia—would now have to draw a reluctant president into the region.

* * *

Unlike Obama, Trump, it seemed, might be more receptive to the personal touch.

Abe therefore maneuvered to arrange a meeting with the president-elect immediately after the election. It was a delicate issue. As Obama warned that week, "There is only one president at a time."[15] Customarily, a foreign leader would not travel to the US to meet with the president-elect, certainly not without seeing the president.[16]

The following week, Abe would be traveling to Peru for APEC and would need to stop in the US to refuel. Could they meet in New York on 17 November, Abe asked Trump. "That would be awesome," Trump reportedly replied.[17] His goal, Abe told lawmakers, was to have a "candid exchange of opinions" and "build a relationship of trust."[18] Trump would later say that his staff advised him not to meet Abe before his inauguration. "I think it's absolutely fine, but I didn't really mean now. I meant some time in February, March, or April. Meaning, you have a very aggressive—very, very aggressive, strong, tough Prime Minister," he said.[19]

Abe was making the single greatest gamble of his premiership. He bet on a personal relationship with Trump, despite uncertainty about how he would manage the US–Japan relationship and his unpopularity both at home and in Japan.[20] Abe, visiting the president-elect at Trump Tower, had to mollify an incoming president who had little interest in maintaining the status quo.[21] He used flattery, diversionary tactics, repetitive and simple talking points, hyperbole, and, he is even alleged to have nominated Trump for the Nobel Peace Prize.[22] He arranged for Trump to be the first state guest when Naruhito was enthroned in May 2019—when Trump also presented a prize to a champion sumo wrestler. And Abe also used golf to forge a unique relationship with the incoming president. Abe brought the president-elect a gold-colored driver to their meeting as a gift, and the two discussed playing subsequently.[23] They played several times, often joined by a famous pro.

Abe was cagey about discussing their private conversations. In a press conference after the Trump Tower meeting, Abe said only, "I am convinced Mr. Trump is a leader in whom I can have great confidence."[24] In his public utterances, he has only ever expressed feelings of friendship and admiration, and even in private his advisers claim that Abe and Trump genuinely enjoy their encounters.

Nevertheless, Abe was attacked for his decision to bet on a personal relationship with Trump. Shortly after his trip, he had a testy exchange with Renhō, at the time the leader of the opposition Democrats. Why, she asked Abe, did he feel like he could trust Trump after so many "reckless remarks" during the campaign? Abe struggled to be heard over heckling from opposition lawmakers and gave repetitive, long-winded responses about the importance of personal relations between the US president and Japanese prime minister, so long winded in fact that Abe was told by the committee chairman to answer concisely. He again refused to divulge the substance of their meeting—even regarding TPP, which the Diet would ratify in December even as Trump reiterated his pledge to withdraw—stating that to do so would betray Trump's confidence.[25]

But Abe was undaunted by the criticism, and persisted in his efforts to become friends with Trump after his inauguration.

* * *

"Hitherto, at the present time, and henceforth, the Japan–US alliance has been the cornerstone of our country's foreign and security policies," he said in his speech to open the ordinary Diet session on 20 January, hours before Trump's inauguration. "This is an unchanging principle. I intend to visit the United States as quickly as possible to further strengthen bonds with the new president Trump and the alliance."[26]

Abe would arrive in the US for meetings with Trump in February. He would not be Trump's first foreign visitor, but he would be accorded a unique honor. After initial meetings in Washington, they would travel to Florida for further discussions and golf at Trump's Mar-a-Lago resort.

On 10 February, Trump welcomed Abe to the White House with a hug—"I shook hands, but I grabbed him and hugged him because that's the way we feel," he said—but more importantly for Abe, he issued a statement in which he affirmed his commitment to basic principles of the US–Japan relationship.

Abe, meanwhile, established what would become the blueprint for his subsequent engagements with the president. He flattered Trump, praising him for his victory and saying that his golf game was "not up to the level of Donald at all."[27] He highlighted Japanese investments in America and hinted at more to come. To deflect pressure, he convinced Trump to accept a new dialogue between Vice President Mike Pence and Asō that would focus on issues in the bilateral economic relationship. The two leaders sought to downplay any indication of friction, notwithstanding Trump's announcement on 23 January that the US would withdraw from TPP.[28]

In Florida Abe's visit took a strange turn that highlighted the through-the-looking-glass quality of the new era. They traveled together on Air Force One to Florida and dined at his club that evening. The following morning, they golfed at Trump National with Ernie Els, where Trump was photographed using the golden driver Abe had given him. After their round, they played an additional nine holes at another Trump course. It was unclear what they discussed during their hours on the links. Some critics fretted that Abe would make secret verbal commitments and lamented that they were spending time together golfing when Trump was facing global criticism for the "Muslim ban."[29] But it seemed that Trump just wanted to talk about golf. "Japan is very well represented!" Trump tweeted after their outing.

The strangest moment would come that evening.

North Korea had for several weeks been preparing for a possible intercontinental ballistic missile launch, its first since Trump's inauguration and a continuation of an intense period of testing that had seen

Pyongyang conduct two nuclear tests and nearly a dozen medium- and intermediate-range ballistic missile tests in 2016. Obama had impressed upon Trump that North Korea's arsenal would be perhaps the single greatest challenge he would face, and it seemed only a matter of time before North Korea would test the new president's commitment to defending US allies in Northeast Asia.

Before the two leaders repaired to dinner, North Korea launched an intermediate-range ballistic missile into the Sea of Japan. As intelligence about North Korea's launch came in, Abe and Trump, dining at an outdoor patio at Mar-a-Lago, hashed out a response in full view of club members. At least one member posted photos of the leaders and their teams reading documents using cell phone flashlights.[30]

The patio strategy session was followed by a late-night press conference that lasted no longer than two minutes. Abe, unusually, spoke first. "We absolutely cannot approve of North Korea's latest missile launch. North Korea must completely comply with UN resolutions," he said.[31] Trump then took the lectern and delivered a one-sentence statement: "I just want everybody to understand and fully know that the United States of America stands behind Japan, its great ally, 100 percent."[32]

For the moment, it appeared that the balance of power between the two governments had shifted. Abe looked like a seasoned pro. Trump, less than a month into his presidency, looked unprepared to deliver an effective message to Pyongyang, allies in Tokyo and Seoul, or the international community. In fact, Michael Flynn, Trump's first national security adviser, resigned two days later and it was not until 20 February that H.R. McMaster succeeded him and promptly launched a comprehensive North Korea policy review.[33]

Abe nevertheless had a successful weekend. Trump had said the right things about the alliance. He and Trump had spent over eleven hours together, mostly on the golf course. The two governments had agreed to shift fraught economic issues to a more anodyne setting. While opposition lawmakers would criticize Abe, opinion polls showed that the Japanese public largely approved.

* * *

But it was still unclear what the Trump administration would do in Asia. Beijing assiduously courted the new president, with Ambassador

Cui Tiankai launching a charm offensive aimed at Jared and Ivanka. While the new administration was filled with China hawks—chief strategist Steve Bannon warned early in the administration of the risk of war over the South China Sea and after leaving the administration would start a lobbying group advocating a hardline approach to China, while trade adviser Peter Navarro had attracted Trump's attention peddling anti-China books and documentaries—they were balanced by Wall Street-oriented free traders who wanted to preserve the broad contours of the US–China relationship.[34] While Trump had lambasted China for its trade and industrial policies, Tokyo feared he might nevertheless see the opportunity for a grand bargain with Xi. Trump's hosting Xi for a summit at Mar-a-Lago in early April only reinforced these concerns, particularly after the summit launched to a new round of trade negotiations and Trump looked to Xi for help with North Korea.

These initiatives went nowhere, and Trump veered between attempts to coax China to cooperate and threats about China's trade practices. With the US focused on renegotiating the North American Free Trade Agreement (NAFTA) and its free trade agreement with South Korea, Japan receded to the background, the issue of its trade surplus with the United States left for Asō and Pence to discuss in a bilateral dialogue that met only twice in 2017. For most of 2017, it appeared that Abe's gamble was paying off.

Meanwhile, Trump's embrace of a "maximum pressure" approach to North Korea put US muscle behind his commitment to stand behind Japan. The president engaged in ever more dramatic shows of force around North Korea to reestablish deterrence, administration officials argued, and signal the new administration's resolve to defend its allies from any attack. As North Korea conducted a series of missile tests in the spring and summer that appeared to show it was close to perfecting an intercontinental ballistic missile that could strike Guam and Hawaii and perhaps even the US mainland, the Trump administration signaled to Pyongyang that it was willing to wage preemptive or even preventive war. "All options are on the table," McMaster said in April. Trump would repeatedly and more explicitly allude to the possibility of war—"North Korea best not make any more threats to the United States—They will be met with fire and fury like the world has never seen," he said in August—while his administration applied sanctions pressure that left Kim with little choice but to respond with his own provocations to signal his unwillingness to submit.

While Trump's war of words with "Little Rocket Man" would resemble an unusually high-stakes professional wrestling bout, the situation was increasingly grave. North Korea tested a hydrogen bomb in early September and then in late November tested a road-launched ICBM that led the DPRK to declare that it had "[completed] the state nuclear force." By December, it appeared that the Trump administration was willing to risk escalation. Anonymous administration sources were quoted speculating about the appeal of a "bloody nose" strike on a limited number of targets that would degrade North Korea's nuclear capabilities. There were reports that the administration was considering the evacuation of American civilians from South Korea. In this atmosphere, the chances of war—even accidental war—grew considerably, since Kim, fearing an attack that would deprive him of his nuclear deterrent and overthrow him, could be encouraged to launch a first strike at the first sign of a potential attack.[35]

Abe was in the uncomfortable position of backing Trump's hardline approach even as Japan was at greater risk of being drawn into a conflict that could mean the deaths of hundreds of thousands if not millions of Japanese. He had become, the *Wall Street Journal* noted, "Trump's loyal sidekick on North Korea."[36] Abe, who had long championed a "pressure and dialogue" approach to North Korea, could hardly break ranks with Trump. The missile tests not only put Japan directly in harm's way—on 29 August and 15 September North Korea fired its intermediate-range Hwasong-12 ballistic missile over Japan into the Western Pacific—but if North Korea's arsenal could strike the US directly, it could pose an existential threat to Japan by forcing US leaders to decide whether it was worth "trading" Los Angeles for Tokyo. Decoupling, an old fear from the Cold War, was back.[37]

The crisis with North Korea laid bare the risks Abe was running by gambling on Trump. Japan needed the US more than ever. "Tensions are increasing in the region, from the Sea of Japan to the East China Sea and the South China Sea," Abe said in his policy speech to the Diet in January 2017. "And the security environment surrounding our country is becoming increasingly severe."[38] Thus, as Washington and

Pyongyang rattled their sabers, Abe was unstinting in his support for "maximum pressure." In 2017, Abe and Trump met four more times and spoke over the phone sixteen times, more than twice as many phone calls as between Abe and Obama. Whether initiated by Trump or by Abe, these calls allowed Abe to regularly show the Japanese people that he was always working to maintain his relationship with the president. He also used his conversations with Trump to enlist him as an ally in the recovery of Japan's abductees in North Korea, an effort that had gone nowhere since talks with Pyongyang had broken down earlier in Abe's administration. This effort paid off when, in his speech to the UN General Assembly in September, Trump alluded to the abduction of Yokota Megumi as part of a broadside against North Korea: "We know it kidnapped a sweet 13-year-old Japanese girl from a beach in her own country to enslave her as a language tutor for North Korea's spies."[39] Trump met with the families of the abductees when he visited Tokyo in November.[40]

Trump's first presidential visit to Japan came on 5–6 November. Trump and Abe golfed for the first time since February, joined by pro Matsuyama Hideki. The president and the first lady had an audience with the emperor and empress. The two allies celebrated their coordination in the maximum pressure campaign against North Korea. And they embraced a new concept—the "Free and Open Indo-Pacific"—as an organizing principle for deeper cooperation not just between the US and Japan but also with other "maritime democracies."[41] Japanese officials would take heart the following month when the Trump administration's National Security Strategy identified China as a "revisionist power" determined to use political, economic, and military tools to push the US out of the Indo-Pacific and specified cooperation with Japan, Australia, and India as part of its strategy for maintaining order in the Indo-Pacific region. "We welcome and support the strong leadership role of our critical ally, Japan," the report noted.[42]

But during his visit it became increasingly apparent that Trump remained dissatisfied with the economic relationship. "We want fair and open trade. But right now, our trade with Japan is not fair and it's not open, but I know it will be, soon," he said at a meeting with business leaders.[43] He appeared to be losing patience with the Asō–Pence dialogue and wanted formal negotiations for an FTA. It was an omen. In his second year, Trump would lean hard on allies and adversaries to achieve his vision for "free, fair, and reciprocal" trade.

As the so-called "axis of adults" left the administration and were replaced by others more committed to Trump personally, it became apparent that the Trump administration's approach to the world would never just be a more idiosyncratic variation of the bipartisan foreign policy consensus that prevailed before his election.[44] No amount of personal diplomacy by Abe could change that.

* * *

Despite his investment in a personal relationship with Trump, Abe had not lost sight of his strategic vision. "Building on the over 500 summit meetings conducted so far," Abe said on 20 January 2017, "Japan will engage in dynamic peaceful diplomacy and economic diplomacy, and fulfill its responsibilities at the center of the world stage, while taking a panoramic perspective of the world map."[45]

His greatest accomplishment after 2016 was his ability, even as he courted Trump, to pursue a more independent global leadership role for Japan that went beyond anything his predecessors had been able to achieve. Japan could not afford to turn inward. It needed a global order that would encourage more flows of goods, capital, people, and data to ensure its prosperity.

Japan's leaders have long seen their country as small, resource poor, and isolated, surrounded by continental giants that could overwhelm Japan. It was this sense of isolation amidst looming giants that Japan's wartime planners claimed necessitated Japan's imperialism on the Asian continent as it sought to build its own continental bloc, to break out of isolation.[46]

In the early twenty-first century, Japan's leaders once again found themselves surrounded by looming continental powers—and once again saw protectionist walls going up, threatening Japan with isolation. Abe had absorbed an important historical lesson. A protectionist world order would leave Japan less prosperous and more isolated, consigned to demographic oblivion and irrelevance. Despite former Trump adviser Steve Bannon's attempt to enlist Abe in his global nationalist movement—"Prime Minister Abe was Trump before Trump," he told a gathering of LDP lawmakers in March 2019—Abe saw that "globalism" was in Japan's national interest, and he was even willing to break ranks with his conservative allies in pursuit of a more global Japan.[47]

In the early days of Trump's presidency, it was Xi, not Abe, who made a bid for global economic leadership. Xi, speaking in Davos days before Trump's inauguration, highlighted the ways in which China had benefited from globalization, warning, "No one will emerge as the winner in a trade war."[48] But Xi was an unconvincing champion. Many governments were concerned with how China violated the letter and spirit of international trading rules. Europe, meanwhile, was too divided, its leaders too focused on their domestic problems to lead the way on globalization.[49] There was a global leadership vacuum to be filled.

Abe was not the most likely leader to fill it. Not only was Abe preoccupied with preserving Japan's relationship with the US, but Japan had a history of "passive trade strategy."[50] It had benefited from the open trading system but had always fought hard to protect its farmers and other inefficient producers. Japan had been late to the race to conclude bilateral and regional trade agreements when global liberalization faltered, and its agreements were not ambitious. Only four years earlier, Abe had to overcome significant domestic resistance to join TPP.

But TPP gave Abe an opening. The agreement, after all, was finished and some members—including Japan—had ratified it. Saving a trade pact that appeared to be all but dead, particularly after the US withdrew, would be a relatively easy way to strike a blow on behalf of the global economic order—at least, easier than forging a new agreement from scratch.

However, when Trump announced that he would withdraw, Abe did not immediately try to revive it. "The TPP is meaningless without the participation of the United States," he said in a press conference at APEC in November 2016.[51] Abe's first priority after the US presidential transition was fending off demands for a bilateral FTA and trying to persuade Trump to reverse course.[52]

But even without the US, Japan could benefit. The agreement still represented a significant upgrading of global trade and investment rules. It drew Japan closer together with some of Asia's other middle powers, countries economically dependent on China but keen to keep the US engaged politically, militarily, and economically. Other Asia-Pacific economies could still aspire to join. And, if Japan could preserve the agreement, it might also enhance its leverage in trade talks with the US.

When it became apparent that Trump would not change his mind—and that the US would not impede Japanese efforts to preserve TPP—Abe could change course. Others had expressed interest in saving it. Chile hosted a TPP ministerial in early March to discuss a path forward that also included China and South Korea. But Abe's decision in April to recommit was a turning point. Abe was not just committed to TPP—he was committed to globalization. "Let us move forward in order to advance free and fair trade," he said in an address in June 2017. "Together with all of you here who share this ambition, I intend to hold this flag high going forward."[53]

Japan's leadership was vital as the remaining members tried to determine what the agreement would look like without the US. Would all eleven be willing to stay in the bloc? Developing-country members like Malaysia and Vietnam had been drawn to TPP because, in exchange for undertaking domestic reforms to comply with chapters on investment, state-owned enterprises, and labor and environmental standards, they would receive substantially greater access to the US. Without the US, the benefits of TPP were markedly smaller. Meanwhile, Canada and Mexico were preoccupied as they faced Trump's demands to renegotiate NAFTA.

Meanwhile, even if the bloc could be held together, some members wanted to make changes to the agreement signed in 2016. Should the remaining members roll back provisions in areas like intellectual property rights, or preserve as much of the agreement as possible to keep the door open for Washington?

Abe, as the informal leader of the bloc, had to overcome these challenges as the TPP-11 announced on 3 May that they wanted an updated agreement by November. They missed the November target but by January 2018, an agreement was ready to sign.

Japan had resisted demands for substantial changes and convinced its partners that they should "freeze" (i.e. suspend implementation) of a select number of provisions that had been favored by the US unless the US returned to the group. Meanwhile, all eleven members remained.

Japan even accepted a demand from Canada to replace the increasingly toxic TPP name with the more cumbersome Comprehensive and Progressive Agreement for the Trans-Pacific Partnership (CPTPP), a change that might help some members sell it domestically.

CPTPP was signed on 8 March and would enter into force as soon as six members ratified it. Four months later, Japan became the second to ratify, and by the end of October five more had followed. The agreement came into force at the start of 2019. Almost immediately, other governments in the region—as well as the UK, thinking about its post-Brexit trade policy—expressed interest in joining.

It was a significant moment. Other countries were prepared to deepen global economic integration even as the US turned to protectionism. And it was a personal victory for Abe, who in fewer than six years had transformed his country from a reluctant participant that US officials feared might spoil negotiations to the savior of the ambitious regional trade pact.

* * *

Abe also prioritized the conclusion of negotiations for an economic partnership agreement with the EU. Brussels and Tokyo had launched negotiations in 2013, but they had lagged behind TPP. But in late 2016, both Japan and the EU recognized that a bilateral agreement could give them more leverage in confrontations with Trump. As Abe said at a summit with EU leaders in Brussels in March 2017, when they reaffirmed their commitment to conclude negotiations swiftly, "It is extremely important to send a strong message to the world."[54]

Not unlike the bilateral negotiations between the US and Japan in TPP, the Japan–EU talks became stuck on agriculture and autos, the most politically palatable concessions on market access for Japan's cars (and electronics) and European agricultural products. Abe and his counterparts finally reached a deal on 6 July 2017, enabling them to announce an agreement in principle that was the first sign that the world's major economies would not simply react defensively to the Trump administration.

European producers would enjoy TPP-like levels of market access for key agricultural commodities, giving them an advantage over their American competitors. The agreement not only lowered trade barriers but also updated rules governing bilateral commerce, including trade in services.[55] The agreement was eventually signed in July 2018, and took effect on 1 February 2019. Japan and the EU simultaneously concluded a strategic partnership agreement, which called for the partners to deepen coordination across a wide array of economic, security, and cultural issues and to manage global challenges like climate change. It also signaled a greater role for Europe in Asia's security competition, with the EU functioning as a supporting partner of the evolving Free and Open Indo-Pacific strategy.

They were not drawing together strictly to hedge against the US; they were not even opposed to working with the Trump administration. Japan, the EU, and the US would, for example, convene trilateral consultations on WTO reforms to deal with China's trade and industrial policies. But Japan and the EU would not wait for the US to strengthen coordination regarding the global economic order or, for that matter, countering China's effort to build its own Eurasian order.[56] They hoped for US leadership to be reborn, but they would not stand still in the meantime.[57]

* * *

At its national convention in March 2017, the LDP granted Abe a gift. It would change party rules so that Abe, his second term as LDP president and therefore his tenure as prime minister scheduled to end in September 2018, could seek a third term. A third term would enable him not only to surpass his great-uncle Satō Eisaku's record as the longest-serving postwar prime minister but also to become the longest-serving prime minister since the start of constitutional government in 1889. He would also be able to open the 2020 Olympics.

The timing of the LDP's change was inauspicious. Abe would soon be fighting for his political survival.

On 9 February, the *Asahi Shimbun* reported a suspicious public land sale in Osaka to Moritomo Gakuen, a private school operator headed by an acquaintance of the prime minister's named Kagoike Yasunori. Kagoike, a right winger involved with his local Nippon Kaigi chapter, planned to open what he called Japan's first Shinto elementary school. First Lady Abe Akie would be an honorary principal, and Kagoike reportedly raised funds for the school suggesting it would be named after Abe. Kagoike even claimed that Akie had given him a donation that she claimed was from Abe himself. *Asahi* found that MOF had sold public land to Moritomo for a tenth of what it had sold a similar plot of land for recently—and had concealed information regarding the sale. The official story was that Moritomo, which had leased the land, had discovered industrial waste on site and was able to purchase the land so cheaply because MOF deducted cleanup costs from the sale price.

Moritomo Gakuen soon became the biggest scandal that Abe had faced. It had everything: influence peddling; a shady right-wing crony; the involvement of the first lady; and administrative malfeasance. The scandal soon overwhelmed Diet business as opposition lawmakers pressed Kagoike and other witnesses for answers. Abe said he would resign if evidence showed his direct involvement in the sale, but none was forthcoming. The scandal produced a lot of smoke, but the only fire it uncovered was that Kagoike appeared to have defrauded both the national government and the Osaka prefectural government in paperwork regarding the site cleanup and purchase—which made it easier for the Abes to distance themselves from him. Kagoike and his wife were later charged with fraud.

The scandal reintroduced a word to Japan's political vernacular: *sontaku*, which is used to describe how bureaucrats surmised the intentions of their political masters and acted accordingly. This concept enabled Abe and his allies to shift the blame to MOF officials, arguing that they had acted independently to assist a project with which the first lady had been involved.

Without concrete evidence of wrongdoing on Abe's part, the Moritomo scandal faded, but just as it did, another influence peddling scandal emerged in May, again involving a private school operator, Kake Gakuen. The Kake Gakuen scandal hit closer to Abe, since the company's head, Kake Kōtarō was a friend dating back to his time in the US and a regular golfing companion. Kake had applied for a license to open a new veterinary school in one of the national strategic special economic zones that were a signature piece of the third arrow of Abenomics.

Once again, the *Asahi Shimbun* broke the story. Leaked documents from the education ministry showed communication between the ministry and the cabinet office suggesting it was the "prime minister's intention" for Kake's application to be approved quickly. The scandal again turned on a key witness whose credibility could be questioned by Abe's allies: Maekawa Kihei, who had been forced out as the education ministry's top bureaucrat in January for his suspected role in illegally helping former bureaucrats land post-retirement jobs and was suspected of leaking the Kake documents in retaliation.

The Abe government first claimed the documents were fake and rejected calls for Maekawa to testify, but this position was untenable. Democratic lawmakers produced evidence that confirmed their veracity. One document described conversations between Hagiuda Kōichi, a deputy chief cabinet secretary and ministry officials about Kake's application.

Abe paid a significant price for these scandals. His approval ratings plummeted in June, as voters overwhelmingly believed that the government's explanation for the scandal was inadequate.[58] At the end of the Diet session, Abe apologized for his government's handling of the allegations and acknowledged that its response had "invited mistrust for the government from all people."[59] The public's loss of trust in Abe extended to the LDP, which in July suffered a defeat in the Tokyo legislative elections after Kōmeitō's local branch formed a coalition with Tokyo Governor Koike Yuriko's Tokyoites First party. Koike, a onetime LDP member and Abe ally, had defied the LDP to launch a successful independent campaign for Tokyo's governorship in 2016, and her victory confirmed that she could be a threat to Abe's leadership.

The summer gave Abe a strategic pause. He reshuffled his cabinet in early August, appointing popular maverick Kōno Tarō as foreign minister, bringing back respected experts Onodera Itsunori and Hayashi Yoshimasa to lead the troubled defense and education ministries, and drawing on economic policy expert Motegi Toshimitsu to serve as economic revitalization minister and chief trade negotiator. He also brought in Noda Seiko, one of his most vocal critics in the LDP, to serve as internal affairs minister. It was a sober, serious cabinet and it helped arrest Abe's slumping approval ratings.

Meanwhile, in August and September, North Korea fired ballistic missiles over Japan and tested a thermonuclear bomb. The government's handling of a couple of minor school contracts suddenly seemed less important. And the opposition Democratic Party, far from gaining support for its dogged pursuit of Abe's scandals, was shedding members rapidly. The narrative had changed. Abe was once more the leader who would keep Japan safe in a dangerous neighborhood. His approval ratings recovered, and Abe decided to gamble again. On 25 September, he announced that he would dissolve the Diet and call a snap election.

* * *

On Saturday evening, 21 October 2017, the LDP held a large rally in a plaza outside Tokyo's Akihabara station. It was the last day of the general election campaign.

Abe, heralded by a swell of brassy music, climbed atop a campaign truck just before eight o'clock. Tokyo had been blanketed in cold rain for days, the rain reaching a crescendo as election day approached. Despite the rain, however, the plaza was full of LDP supporters, who fervently waved Japanese flags and roared their approval for the prime minister.

Abe was also undaunted by the rain. Neatly coiffed and dressed in a navy suit, he hardly looked like a man who had spent the previous eleven days stumping for candidates from Hokkaido to Nagasaki. He looked calm and self-possessed, confident that voters would return him to power the following day.

Victory was not inevitable. When he called a snap election, the decision was roundly criticized as nakedly opportunistic, timed to exploit an uptick in his approval ratings after months of weak polling. Within hours, it seemed Abe may have grossly miscalculated: Koike promptly announced that she would form a new party—the Party of Hope—aimed at ousting Abe in the election.

Koike's announcement followed months of speculation that she would use her national popularity to take on the suddenly vulnerable prime minister. Soon thereafter, opposition leader Maehara Seiji, who headed the Democratic Party, the product of a merger between the DPJ and some members of the Japan Restoration Party, announced that he and his party would join forces with Koike. It seemed Koike might be able to catch a wave of popular enthusiasm, bring the elusive "floating voters" to the polls, and win enough seats to drive Abe from power.

But after a series of tactical misfires and crippling indecision over whether Koike would abandon Tokyo's governorship to head her party's parliamentary ticket, enthusiasm for the Party of Hope collapsed. Koike's and Maehara's gambit did little more than ensure that the opposition vote would be divided between candidates from various DPJ splinter parties and the Communists, easing the path to victory for many LDP candidates.

Abe therefore had every reason to feel confident. He had faced down Koike's threat. He had overcome two scandals. He had deftly managed new international challenges. Assuming he could preserve his government's supermajority in the lower house, he also appeared to be on track to achieve his—and his family's—longtime political dream, the revision of Japan's postwar constitution, which Abe had said in May that he wanted to accomplish by 2020.

And yet, the speech Abe gave in Akihabara—indeed, the entire campaign—betrayed deeper anxieties about the state of his country and his legacy. After all, Abe himself, in his press conference announcing the snap election, said he was calling it to secure a new mandate for "surmounting national crises," referring to the immediate threat of North Korea's nuclear and ballistic missile programs and the long-term challenge of demographic decline.

The following day, Abe was returned to power with a bolstered majority, his party winning the exact number of seats—284—that it held before the election, in a chamber ten seats smaller. The newly formed Constitutional Democratic Party, a left-wing splinter from the old Democrats, became the largest opposition party. Together with Kōmeitō, Abe's government continued to command a supermajority. Whatever misgivings the public had about Abe's trustworthiness as a leader, for many voters there was no alternative—other than staying home.[60]

Despite his domestic challenges, Abe had spent the year navigating an increasingly volatile world, building a relationship with Trump, pursuing rapprochement with China and Russia, sealing a trade agreement with the EU, and reviving TPP after the US withdrawal. No one had better ideas for how to manage Trump, Kim, or Xi. Abe was dominant at home and, having led his party to another victory, likely to win a third term as leader. But Japan still faced an uncertain future. With a new mandate in hand, Abe's attention turned to his legacy, where it had become all too apparent that he would leave unfinished business for his successors.

17

IN SEARCH OF A LEGACY

"We surely stand at a historical turning point. The future of Japan is opening," Abe said on 20 September 2018. "I am determined to lead."[1]

He had just been reelected to a third term as the LDP's leader, defeating his old rival Ishiba. He had won despite having to overcome more allegations of influence peddling: new evidence surfaced in both the Moritomo and Kake Gakuen scandals in the spring that hinted at an attempt to conceal documents and seemed to implicate senior advisers, if not the prime minister himself. Abe's approval ratings dipped but quickly recovered as his domestic headaches were overshadowed by summit diplomacy on the Korean Peninsula.[2] And while independents may have wavered, the LDP continued to stand by its leader.

His victory was a foregone conclusion by the time the LDP voted. His lieutenant Nikai Toshihiro had, since becoming LDP secretary-general in August 2016, cemented Abe's dominance of the party and engineered the rule change that allowed him to run again.[3] LDP lawmakers overwhelmingly supported Abe's reelection. Ishiba entered the race more to deprive the prime minister of a unanimous victory than out of a sincere belief that he could win. Ishiba had been outmaneuvered by Abe and locked out of power. He had been a vocal critic of Abenomics, had questioned Abe's handling of the scandals, and during the campaign even criticized Abe's "flattery diplomacy" with Trump. These critiques did little to endear Ishiba to his LDP colleagues, and while he performed better than expected in grassroots voting, all but seventy-six of the LDP's 405 parliamentarians backed Abe. It was still Abe's party.

With another three years to govern, Abe would have a chance to become Japan's longest-serving prime minister; to usher Japan into a new age when Akihito abdicated in 2019; lead the G20 in 2019; and host the 2019 Rugby World Cup and 2020 Olympics. But there was no guarantee that he could cement a legacy that would outlast him. He may have dominated the political system and freed the Japanese state of many of the constraints that had limited Japan's role in geopolitical competition, but translating his domestic clout in durable changes in Japan's international position was repeatedly frustrated.

* * *

Trump's visit to Tokyo in November 2017—when the US president embraced Abe's "Free and Open Indo-Pacific" vision—may have been the high point of Abe's relationship with him. Thereafter, despite his investment in a personal relationship with Trump, Abe had not been able to change his beliefs about Japan. Trump still believed that allies were taking advantage of America. He still wanted to use US power in bilateral negotiations to end "unfair" trade—and, whatever friendship existed between them, Japan was not exempt from his determination to put America first.

Whatever illusions Tokyo had about Abe's influence over Trump were shattered in the early months of 2018. The year began with Kim Jong Un's declaration in his New Year message that, having completed "the great, historic cause of perfecting the national nuclear forces," the time was right for "[improving] the frozen inter-Korean relations" and building a peaceful environment on the Korean Peninsula. It was a timely gesture.

South Korea, after impeaching and jailing Park Geun-hye, had elected Moon Jae-in as president in May 2017. Moon was a veteran left-wing politician who believed deeply in the possibility of reunification. The Trump administration was still agitating for conflict with Pyongyang. In February, South Korea would host the Winter Olympics; Moon wanted them to be an "Olympics of Peace," with North Korea participating in the games.[4] Perhaps Olympic diplomacy could walk the US and North Korea back from the brink of war.

Moon welcomed Kim's message and soon North Korea announced that it would in fact participate. North Korea sent a high-level delegation to the games, including Kim's sister Kim Yo Jong, who invited Moon to visit Pyongyang. Moon then launched a campaign of shuttle diplomacy to turn truce into a lasting peace. North–South talks yielded an agreement to convene the third-ever inter-Korean summit in April, a pledge to refrain from missile testing while talks were ongoing, and a proposal—delivered by Moon's advisers to Trump—for a direct meeting between Trump and Kim, which would be the first-ever summit between sitting US and North Korean leaders. On 8 March, Trump agreed to meet Kim without preconditions.

Trump gave no prior notification to Abe, who scrambled to keep up. Abe risked isolation as Kim suddenly had meetings with Moon, Trump, and—in late March—Xi, when Kim traveled to China for his first foreign trip since taking power.

Abe traveled to Washington in April to confer on North Korea. He suggested that North Korea's shift was the result of "maximum pressure" on Pyongyang and said he would remind Trump about the plight of the abductees.[5] Abe and Trump again went to Mar-a-Lago and golfed, but the mood had changed. Now, Abe came to beseech Trump not to be tricked by North Korea and not to forget Japan's interests, even as Trump appeared eager to play peacemaker.

Between 8 March and 12 June, when Trump and Kim met in Singapore, Abe met with Trump in April and again in early June and talked with him five times on the phone. Abe could take some comfort that there were still players in the Trump administration who would help make its case in internal deliberations, including Pence and the new national security adviser, John Bolton. But Trump would be in the room with Kim—and Abe would have to trust him not to forget Japan. Trump said the right things when they talked, but there was no guarantee that he would follow through in negotiations, not least because, as Trump said at a press conference with Abe in June, "I don't think I have to prepare very much. It's about attitude. It's about willingness to get things done."[6]

When Trump and Kim finally met, the outcome was anticlimactic. The two leaders agreed to start a diplomatic process aimed at the "denuclearization of the Korean peninsula" and the creation of a "peace regime" on the peninsula—but there was no grand bargain. There were tangible consequences, however. Trump surprised both his own military and South Korea by agreeing to suspend joint exercises between the US and South Korean militaries while talks were ongoing, "war games" that he repeatedly described as "very expensive." With North Korea having suspended its tests, Trump had effectively endorsed a China–Russia "freeze-for-freeze" proposal that his administration rejected the previous year.[7] But perhaps most troubling was the effusive praise that Trump heaped on Kim. "He is very talented," Trump said. "Anybody that takes over a situation like he did, at 26 years of age, and is able to run it, and run it tough—I don't say he was nice or I don't say anything about it—he ran it." ("We fell in love," he gushed at a rally later that year.)[8]

Despite the spectacle, Trump would not abandon sanctions, to Kim's frustration. Working-level talks went nowhere, and by late 2019 Pyongyang warned that without sanctions relief it could break off all negotiations. The two sides could not agree on what denuclearization should entail and whether the US would offer political and economic concessions incrementally or after significant and ideally irreversible steps by North Korea. North Korea continued to refine its arsenal, while nominally abiding by the testing freeze.

In other words, although Trump returned from Singapore declaring that "there is no longer a nuclear threat from North Korea," as far as Japan was concerned, North Korea was as capable as ever. It had driven a wedge between Japan and the US, and was determined to isolate Japan further, having repeatedly refused Abe's requests for a summit to resolve the abductee issue once and for all. Abe was not without friends in the Trump administration but Trump's interest in personal diplomacy with Kim meant that it was impossible to rule out the possibility of a strategic surprise between the two leaders.

In the meantime, it would be Japan's turn to feel the brunt of US economic pressure.

* * *

"When a country (USA) is losing many billions of dollars on trade with virtually every country it does business with, trade wars are good, and easy to win," Trump tweeted on 2 March 2018.

The previous day Trump had announced that, based on defending US national security per Section 232 of the Trade Expansion Act of 1962, he would impose tariffs of twenty-five percent on steel and ten percent on aluminum. There was significant opposition to this decision within the administration. Jim Mattis, the secretary of defense, argued that US production was more than adequate for defense needs. Treasury secretary Steve Mnuchin, National Economic Council director Gary Cohn, and White House staff secretary Rob Porter had all sparred with protectionists like US trade representative Robert Lighthizer, commerce secretary Wilbur Ross, and economic adviser Peter Navarro, as well as with the president himself as part of the struggle to uphold the US commitment to the global rules-based trading system. In Trump's first year they had won some important victories.[9] But by March, Porter and Cohn had left, and Trump was feeling more confident.

The country's allies, who were among the largest exporters of steel to the US, were not exempt. That included Japan, which did not even get the temporary exemption granted to the EU, Canada, Mexico, South Korea, and Australia. When Abe took his second trip to Mar-a-Lago the following month, he not only failed to secure an exemption but was forced to accept a new set of talks between Lighthizer—a veteran of trade friction with Japan in the 1980s—and Motegi, minister of economic revitalization. These talks would be more focused on trade imbalances than the Asō–Pence dialogue and could set the stage for formal free trade agreement (FTA) negotiations.

The metals tariffs were not catastrophic for Japan, a relatively modest steel exporter that mostly exported specialized products for which there were few substitutes.[10] But the tariffs were a reminder that Trump had not abandoned his longstanding beliefs about Japan. "I'll talk to Prime Minister Abe of Japan and others—great guy, friend of mine—and there will be a little smile on their face," Trump said in late March as he announced what turned out to be the first stage of the increasingly open-ended trade war with China. "And the smile is, 'I can't believe we've been able to take advantage of the United States for so long.' So those days are over."[11]

Abe had hoped to avoid bilateral negotiations with Trump. There seemed little for Japan to gain and much to lose, given both the history of friction in US–Japan trade negotiations and Trump's sharp-elbowed approach to negotiations. But in May, Trump scrambled Abe's calculations when he launched a national security investigation into imports of automobiles and auto parts, which could result in new tariffs as high as twenty-five percent.

Abe could not ignore this threat. Nearly forty percent of Japan's $125 billion in exports to the US were automobiles or auto parts. Beyond the economic impact, it would be a devastating blow to national pride and to Abe's political standing at home if Trump followed through—and Abe might find himself trapped between his desire for friendship with the US president and calls for retaliation from an outraged public. It would be months before Trump would have to decide on automobile tariffs—Section 232 stipulates that the Commerce Department has 270 days to investigate before referring the matter to the president—and difficult for Abe to resist demands for an FTA in the hope that Trump was bluffing.[12]

Therefore, in September 2018, Abe and Trump announced that the US and Japan would launch FTA negotiations. Abe took pains to stress that he had not broken a pledge not to enter into FTA negotiations with the US: these negotiations would be, the joint statement indicated, for a "Trade Agreement on Goods" (TAG), not an FTA. The joint statement, setting out the framework for the talks, did suggest that negotiations would be limited. The US, for example, agreed to respect Japan's desire that concessions on market access for agricultural products should not exceed what it had offered in previous agreements. The two governments essentially agreed to talks for a bilateral agreement that would be limited in scope and limited in time, since Trump wanted a trade win that he could use to bolster his reelection prospects, particularly as American farmers suffered from Chinese trade sanctions and the impact of Japan's trade agreements with their competitors.

It was nearly seven months before negotiations began in earnest—in part because the Trump administration had to comply with "fast track" rules, which mandated time for consultations with Congress before entering talks.[13] But Abe faced upper house elections in July 2019 and did not want to appear to be caving to US pressure before going to voters. Therefore, despite a series of summits between Abe and Trump—Abe went to Washington in April, and then Trump visited Japan to become the first foreign leader to receive an audience with the newly enthroned Naruhito in May, and again in June for the G20 summit in Osaka—Trump agreed that a deal could wait until after Japan's elections.

Once the elections were over, it took just two months for an agreement to be announced. It was limited in scope. Japan would cut or eliminate a range of tariffs on agricultural commodities, most notably beef and pork, much as in TPP—although rice was excluded—while the US would offer some modest industrial and agricultural tariff cuts. The US would not explicitly promise not to raise auto tariffs, but Japanese officials trusted assurances from Lighthizer that if Japan adhered to the agreement, they would not need to worry about auto tariffs. A separate agreement would liberalize data flows in a manner consistent with the "data free flow with trust" approach that Abe had promoted via Japan's leadership of the G20.

It was, in a sense, another admission by Abe that he could not convert his personal relationship with Trump into favorable treatment. Opposition lawmakers picked holes in the agreement when it went to the Diet. But it is impossible to know the counterfactual—and it is hard to argue that Abe would have enjoyed better treatment if he had taken a more confrontational approach. He held out for nearly three years and only conceded in the face of an extraordinary threat.[14] As was the case with North Korea, Trump's bark may have been worse than his bite. Trump may not have changed his deeply held views about Japan, but Abe managed to deflect potentially harmful actions.

* * *

While Abe struggled to leverage his friendship with Trump, their administrations nevertheless worked as closely as ever, at least on defense. There was a great degree of continuity in military affairs from the Obama administration to the Trump administration. It helped that the Trump administration came into office prepared to take a significantly harder line towards China. It articulated a comprehensive approach to China's military modernization, trade practices, and intelligence and surveillance activities—best illustrated in a speech by Pence at the conservative Hudson Institute in October 2018—that triggered speculation about the dawn of a new Cold War in Asia.[15] The

Abe administration viewed favorably the Trump administration's defense spending increases and its programs to modernize the US nuclear arsenal, upgrade missile defenses, and develop greater space and cyber capabilities.

It was difficult for Tokyo to entirely trust that Trump would not abandon Japan—in June 2019, shortly before he was due to travel to Japan for the G20, reports suggested Trump had mused about ending the security treaty—but the administration as a whole continued to see Japan as an important partner in the Indo-Pacific. There was no better example of just how well the two governments worked together than in the Trump administration's embrace of the "Free and Open Indo-Pacific" concept, which articulated a vision of the region based on respect for sovereignty, the peaceful settlement of disputes, "free, fair, and reciprocal" commerce, and respect for international rules and norms. These principles were in most cases thinly veiled criticisms of China, and for the US government it became an organizing principle for a Manichean struggle against China—perhaps even more than Abe had intended when he first articulated the concept.

Nevertheless, it was the Abe Doctrine in action. Abe had furnished the language that would undergird the Trump administration's approach to the region and its efforts to strengthen ties with Australia, India, ASEAN countries, and other partners.[16] While it would have its economic components—development finance institutions from the US, Australia, and Japan would sign an agreement in November 2018 to cooperate on infrastructure investment in accordance with the "Quality Infrastructure" principles the Abe administration had articulated several years prior—it was predominantly a military initiative. Notwithstanding Trump's skepticism of longstanding US alliances, his administration's approach to the Indo-Pacific depended heavily on strengthening defense ties with traditional treaty allies, upgrading ties with new partners like India, and even coordinating with European allies like the UK and France to increase their involvement in regional security.

The Abe administration's second National Defenses Program Guidelines (NDPG) and mid-term defense plan, published in December 2018, reflected Japan's commitment to allied cooperation. While Japan would continue to strengthen its ability to defend its outlying islands and enhance its capabilities in new domains like space and cyber, the latest defense plans showed that it continued to depend on the US. The Abe administration not only prioritized closer coordination with the US military to bolster deterrence in peacetime and plan for possible crises in East Asia, Japan would also become a more significant consumer of US military equipment. The mid-term defense plan was the largest ever, envisioning nearly $250 billion in defense acquisitions over the subsequent five years, including a significant increase in Japan's purchases of F-35 fighter jets from the US.

Abe sought closer defense partnerships with other countries but these activities were a complement to, not a substitute for, the alliance with the United States. They were also part of a broader trend of US allies and partners seeking to strengthen defense ties amongst themselves, without the direct involvement of the United States. In this sense, Japan's activities could be part of a transition away from the US-led "hub-and-spokes" alliance system to a more networked approach to regional security—particularly among China's neighbors—as the region's middle powers, anxious about China and also worried about the potential for US retrenchment, bolster their defense ties to make it harder for a stronger China to coerce any single country.[17]

* * *

Trump and his China hawk advisers had warned of the threat posed by Chinese state capitalism since before Xi came to power.[18] Trump himself had come to see China as one of the greatest threats to the US economy and, as a candidate, threaten to pursue cases against China at the WTO and to impose unilateral sanctions to combat China's "illegal activities." "I will use every lawful presidential power to remedy trade disputes," he said in June 2016.[19]

In 2018, as China hawks gained influence in the administration, it unveiled its new approach, launching an increasingly sprawling "trade war" that was a frontal assault on the prevailing terms of the US–China economic relationship that may even have been intended to "decouple" the world's two largest economies by making it harder for US companies to relocate production to China. The administration did not necessarily have a clearly articulated goal—Trump often seemed mainly concerned about the bilateral trade deficit with China, Lighthizer seemed mainly interested in encouraging China to reform if possible, and Navarro, skeptical of China's willingness to compromise, seemed mainly interested in decoupling. But its new approach seemed designed to convince China either to reform its state-led development model in fundamental ways or to see its access to the global economy sharply curtailed.

To deliver this message, the Trump administration ratcheted up tariffs on an ever-greater share of imports from China; tightened restrictions on Chinese investment;[20] introduced measures to combat the global market power of Chinese telecommunications giant Huawei; and even considered preventing Chinese citizens from studying in the US. The Trump administration also tried to enlist the support of allies and partners in challenging China's policies. It pressured its allies to not purchase 5G network technology from Huawei due to purported security risks and included a provision in the US–Mexico–Canada agreement (USMCA) that appeared to give Washington a veto over Mexico's and Canada's relationships with China.[21] It warned Asian countries about China's "debt-trap diplomacy," and it bashed the WTO while working with Japan and the EU on reforms that would strengthen the organization's ability to punish Chinese policies that appeared to violate the spirit of the rules-based trading system.[22]

But even before the Trump administration began ramping up its trade war, Abe launched a diplomatic initiative seeking rapprochement with Beijing. Abe shared many of the Trump administration's concerns about China's industrial policies—particularly the "Made in China 2025" plan, targeting innovation in high-technology sectors in which Japan also had or sought significant market share—and remained alarmed by China's growing military might.[23] He nevertheless recognized that China and Japan had a shared interest in the preservation of a global rules-based trading system.[24] Thus, as Abe weighed his options after the US withdrawal from TPP, his government reached out to Beijing.

In February 2017, Suga and Nikai dined together ahead of Abe's trip to the United States. Nikai was the LDP's leading China hand, with thick connections to the CCP.[25] "The prime minister's feelings towards China are deepening," Suga said. "We want to raise the level of our relations with China, so we would absolutely appreciate your help."[26]

This meeting set in motion a top-level effort by the Abe administration to move beyond friction between Abe and Xi. It would be inextricably linked with Abe's campaign to preserve an open international economic order. Both governments were willing to compartmentalize their military competition—and even work to establish a crisis management mechanism—and downgrade their dispute over historical issues.

This approach was not universally supported within the Abe government. National Security Adviser Yachi and MOFA worried that it could be risky to ramp up Japan–China economic engagement just as a new US administration was contemplating a hardline approach. However, the ministry of economy, trade, and industry (METI)—including its current and former officials at the Kantei, notably Imai—fretted that growing protectionism from the US could harm Japan, and looked to China as an ally in defending globalization. In late March, METI's administrative vice minister held the first meeting with his Chinese counterpart in five years, where they agreed that rising protectionism posed a danger to both countries.[27] By May, they had agreed that the foreign and finance ministers would again convene regular ministerial dialogues.

Sino–Japanese rapprochement would ultimately center on the BRI. China had been seeking international partners and convened the first Belt and Road Forum in May 2017 to celebrate the initiative. Japan was an attractive partner. Japan's companies competed for infrastructure projects and Japan had been quietly challenging the BRI by promoting a vision of "quality" infrastructure that met high standards for social, financial, and environmental sustainability. Tokyo's support might quiet growing criticism that the BRI was little more than Chinese economic imperialism.

In late April, Nikai announced that he would attend the Belt and Road Forum, leading a delegation that would include the chairman of Keidanren. Imai would go too, signaling Abe's personal investment in a new relationship. Nikai hand-delivered a letter from Abe to Xi—a letter Imai had modified to include language more optimistic about the possibility for bilateral cooperation as part of the BRI than that originally included. Yachi was infuriated by Imai's change when he found out and, far from conceding the issue, continued to battle within the administration for a tougher approach to Beijing.[28] Abe sought a middle path between his advisers, embracing the overall campaign to put relations with China on a sounder footing while discouraging the more ambitious goals of the China hands.

When Abe met Xi on the sidelines of the G20 in July, their joint statement included a mention of the BRI for the first time.[29] By November, when Abe met Xi and Li at APEC, the language had been upgraded: the joint statement now said, "The two sides shared the view that they will together discuss how Japan and China will contribute to the stability and prosperity of the region and the world, including the 'the Belt and Road' Initiatives."[30]

Even then, Abe was still determined to set the terms of Japan's engagement. At a Keidanren-hosted Japan–China CEO Summit in December, Abe noted that Sino–Japanese cooperation on infrastructure could "contribute greatly to the prosperity of Asian peoples" and suggested the possibility of cooperation as part of the BRI, but also said such cooperation would be under Japan's "Free and Open Indo-Pacific Strategy" framework.[31] Japan would only provide financial support for firms participating in BRI projects if the projects satisfied Abe's "Quality Infrastructure" principles, meaning cooperation would be on a case-by-case basis.

It was the better part of a year before the two governments could announce the start of a more formal initiative—during which time Japan's leverage only grew as the US embarked on its trade war with China and stepped up its own efforts to promote infrastructure investment in developing economies, particularly in cooperation with the Quad countries. By the time Abe arrived in Beijing in October 2018 for the first visit by a Japanese prime minister for a bilateral meeting since 2011, a public-private committee on joint investment in "third countries" had concluded an agreement on limited cooperation on infrastructure development. References to the BRI had been dropped.

Nevertheless, Abe's visit confirmed that both leaders were determined to keep their territorial dispute and military tensions—and Washington's appetite for a new Cold War—from dominating their relationship and explore new forms of political, economic, and financial cooperation, including a shared desire to finalize negotiations for the Regional Comprehensive Economic Partnership (RCEP). There were also plans for Xi Jinping to undertake a state visit to Japan.

It would be difficult to describe Abe's rapprochement with Xi as a hedge, with Japan's defense establishment primed to counter China's burgeoning military might and the Japanese public overwhelmingly skeptical of their giant neighbor.[32] Japan was not entering China's orbit yet—Abe would send a potent signal of his strategic priorities when he hosted Narendra Modi at his private countryside villa immediately after his visit to Beijing—but it was emphatically not decoupling from Asia's largest economy, either. For Japan, opening to the world has meant opening to China.

Although the fallout from the flare up in the East China Sea at the start of the decade led Japanese firms to diversify their operations in Asia—the so-called "China-plus-one" strategy—China remained one of the largest recipients of Japanese investment, well integrated into Japanese supply chains. The countries were each other's largest market for exports. Chinese tourists surged into Japan. In 2012, fewer than 1.5 million Chinese tourists visited Japan, the third-most after South Korean and Taiwanese. By 2018 that number had swelled to nearly 8.5 million, surpassing South Korea to become the single largest country of origin, and amounting to nearly twenty-seven percent of tourists to Japan.[33] China was also the single largest source of foreign students and, as Japan's population of foreign nationals reached record highs, more than one in four foreign residents was Chinese in 2017.[34] The story of Japan's internationalization is the story of integration with a wealthier China and its burgeoning middle class. Abe's pursuit of a global Japan necessarily meant breaking ranks with the US to work with Beijing on economic integration.

* * *

For Abe, forging a new relationship with Beijing was intended to preserve strong commercial ties while also reducing a source of anxiety at a tense moment for relations with the US, whether or not that amounted to a full hedge against abandonment by Washington.

Abe's desire for strategic independence also led him to Vladimir Putin. The commercial logic was weaker—although Russia was an important energy supplier as Japan's fourth-largest and fifth-largest supplier of crude oil and natural gas, it was otherwise not an important trading partner—but a new relationship with Russia could give Japan another friend in Northeast Asia and complicate China's most important relationship in the region.

Immediately upon taking office, Abe and his advisers saw the value in pursuing a rapprochement with Russia, at least in part to disrupt Moscow and Beijing from drawing nearer. As the 2013 National Security Strategy stated, "As the security environment in East Asia becomes more severe, promoting cooperation with Russia in starting with security and energy but including all areas and enhancing the Japan–Russia relationship as a whole is extremely important for ensuring our country's national security."

Abe made resolution of the territorial dispute and a peace treaty with Russia a top priority for his government—part of what he would in 2018 refer to as "settling the accounts of postwar Japanese diplomacy."[35] He had a personal stake in building a new relationship with Russia—his father had tried to achieve a breakthrough with Mikhail Gorbachev during the final years of his life—but his family's history should not obscure the more fundamental reasons for Abe's dogged pursuit of an entente with Putin. If Asia was indeed becoming more multipolar, Japan could ill afford to be at odds with Russia, an energy-rich nuclear and conventional military power determined to conduct its own "pivot to Asia" through its "Look East" policy. But to achieve this realignment, Abe had to overcome the legacy of the Second World War, which three generations of leaders had been unable to accomplish.

In the weeks following Japan's surrender in August 1945, Soviet forces seized the Kuril Islands, an archipelago separating the Sea of Okhotsk from the Pacific, and expelled more than 15,000 Japanese civilians living there, including the four southern islands of Etorofu, Kunashiri, Shikotan, and Habomai, which had never been Russian. While Japan and the Soviet Union reestablished ties in 1956, Japan's claim to sovereignty over the four contested islands—which became known as the "Northern Territories"—remained a sticking point, precluding the conclusion of a formal peace treaty.[36]

To achieve a strategic realignment, Abe had to solve the territorial dispute and conclude a peace treaty. That would require the leaders of both countries to overcome domestic opposition to any compromise that divided the disputed islands.

With Putin too, Abe tried personal diplomacy. In 2013, Abe visited Russia for a summit in April and convened a "2+2" meeting of foreign and defense ministers for the first time in December. He then attended the Winter Olympics in Sochi in February 2014. The expectation was that Putin would visit Japan later in the year for their next meeting, but the Ukraine crisis intervened. With Russia sanctioned and expelled from the G8, Abe could hardly conduct a vigorous charm offensive.

But by 2016, Abe began to seek an opening. He might be able to resume his personal outreach to Putin without alienating other partners. To convince the Russian president that engagement was worthwhile, Abe planned a new offer. He would soften longstanding Japanese demands for the immediate return of all four islands and perhaps be willing to accept an arrangement whereby Russia recognized Japan's sovereignty over the four, but would only commit to returning the two smallest in the immediate term. In the meantime, Japan would also offer a significant increase in economic cooperation, particularly in the development of the Russian Far East. Abe's willingness to consider the latter—which his predecessors had been reluctant to do before the territorial dispute was settled—was intended as a gesture of good faith, showing Japan's willingness to help Putin address what his government had identified as a key strategic priority.

At the Eastern Economic Forum in Vladivostok in September 2016, the two governments announced that they would cooperate on more than $1 billion in joint projects in the Russian Far East, with the expectation of more to come. Meanwhile, Putin would take his long-delayed visit to Japan in December, when Abe would host the Russian president for an "onsen summit" at a hot spring resort in his home prefecture. The hoped-for breakthrough did not occur when the two leaders soaked together—nor in the nine bilateral summits or numerous ministerial and sub-ministerial meetings that were held in the following years. Abe beseeched his Russian counterpart to compromise—and even dropped some of the more assertive language about Japan's claims to the islands, inviting severe criticism in the Diet—but had no success.

Whereas Japan and China had reasons to compartmentalize their territorial dispute and the broader clash of security interests, Putin had little reason to do so. He had no reason to cede territory Russia controlled and could pocket whatever economic concessions Abe was willing to offer. Indeed, as James D.J. Brown, a leading specialist on Japan's relationship with Russia argues, Putin delights in spurning Abe.[37] Abe's diplomatic outreach to Putin, far from driving a wedge between Russia and China, instead enabled the Russian president to drive a wedge between Japan and the US. Putin has chided Japan for its strategic dependence on the US and pressed Abe for assurances that if Russia were to cede territory, US forces would not be deployed on the islands and that the US–Japan security treaty would not extend to the Northern Territories.[38] At the same time, Russia strengthened its military presence on the disputed islands and deepened both military and economic ties with Beijing, potentially turning what had long seemed like a marriage of convenience based on shared interests in defying the US into a more durable partnership.

Abe is unlikely to abandon his "new approach" to Russia. He has invested too much effort in courting Putin—and the prospect of being the leader who finally settles the dispute is too inviting as a legacy—for him to admit defeat easily. But he will leave office with little to show for his Russia diplomacy. Moreover, his exuberant pursuit of a closer relationship with a Russian strongman who has flagrantly violated international law and international norms, used "hybrid warfare" to seize territory from a neighbor, and sought to undermine liberal democracies from within sits awkwardly with Abe's emphasis on universal values of freedom, democracy, and the rule of law as part of his Free and Open Indo-Pacific vision. The same could be said for Abe's rapprochement with Xi in light of alarming reports of China's treatment of the Uighur population of Xinjiang, the crackdown on protests in Hong Kong, and China's exporting of its increasingly sophisticated "digital authoritarianism."[39]

But for Abe, a realist who has frequently been willing to bend his principles to further the national interest, the problem with his Russia diplomacy is not that he has risked looking hypocritical. It is that he has risked being accused of hypocrisy but has so little to show for it.

* * *

Abe similarly faced charges of hypocrisy for his handling of Japan's relationship with South Korea, which during his third term reached its lowest point since at least the establishment of diplomatic relations in 1965. To be sure, the deterioration of relations with Japan's fellow Northeast Asian democracy and US ally is not simply Abe's fault.

Moon's election—soon after Trump replaced Obama—fundamentally transformed the circumstances surrounding Japan's relationship with South Korea.

While Park initially refused to meet with Abe due to his handling of history issues, they did, thanks to Obama's involvement and the need to coordinate in response to North Korea's provocations, achieve a thaw in their relationship. They concluded their 2015 agreement that appeared to settle the "comfort women" dispute. After a long delay and in the face of significant domestic opposition, Park signed the General Security of Military Information Agreement (GSOMIA) in 2016, allowing Tokyo and Seoul to share intelligence and bolster their coordination against North Korea.

Park's rapprochement with the Japanese prime minister did not enjoy widespread domestic legitimacy—and indeed, South Korea's relationship with Japan was indelibly entangled with domestic political cleavages that resulted from decades of right-wing military rule and the popular movement for democracy. The 1965 basic treaty that established the bilateral relationship—which the Japanese government interpreted as marking the final settlement of any claims for compensation by South Korea, including individual claims against the Japanese government and Japanese companies—was made by Park Chung-hee's government, which put Japanese financial compensation towards industrialization instead of paying out to Korean victims of Japanese imperialism. After democratization, Korean conservatives remained more favorably disposed to Japan and appeared more tolerant of attempts by Japanese politicians—including Abe—to evade responsibility for the harsh treatment of Koreans during the colonial period. For the Korean left, now led by veterans of the pro-democracy movement in the 1980s, revising South Korea's relationship with Japan to accommodate demands for justice was part of the unfinished work of Korea's democratization. There would be no better example of this argument than revelations that Park had conspired with the chief justice of South Korea's Supreme Court to delay rulings on lawsuits filed by former Korean labor conscripts against Japanese companies, which resulted in the justice's arrest in 2019 on conspiracy charges.[40]

Moon had been arrested for his part in resisting the military dictatorship and was elected thanks to his ability to capture the desire for a better democracy that had animated the "candlelight protests" that ultimately forced Park from power. He was less willing to indulge Abe. It did not help that Moon was obsessed by a vision of a reunified Korea. North Korea, once a unifying factor that had helped Japanese and South Korean leaders overcome their differences on history issues, was now a wedge that forced them apart. Moon's government seemed willing to prioritize confidence-building measures and economic cooperation that would benefit South Korea but would leave intact the missiles and weapons of mass destruction that most concerned the Abe administration.

As president, Moon therefore pushed for a significant shift in the spirit of South Korea's relationship with Japan. He campaigned to reopen negotiations on how Japan should make amends to surviving comfort women, and his government investigated Park's negotiation of the agreement, criticizing the former president for negotiating in secret and without consulting the survivors themselves. While Moon would not formally abandon the 2015 agreement, he effectively gutted it by all but dismantling the foundation established to distribute funds contributed by the Japanese government to the women. The foundation would be formally dissolved in July 2019 as bilateral tensions mounted.

But for the Abe government, the real betrayal would be decisions by the Korean Supreme Court in the autumn of 2018 that ordered major Japanese companies, including Nippon Steel and Mitsubishi Heavy Industries, to pay reparations to former forced laborers and their descendants, decisions that were ultimately enforced by the expropriation of some of their South Korean assets when, with the Japanese government's backing, they refused to provide other forms of compensation. From Tokyo's perspective, Park's intervention in the judiciary to keep the court from rendering verdicts in the forced labor cases was consistent with the spirit of the 1965 agreement. But to expect the same from Moon—when doing so would rightly be viewed as a betrayal by protestors who had taken to the streets to oppose Park's corruption and then backed Moon as someone who would revitalize Korean democracy—was unreasonable.

Abe was increasingly stuck between his government's commitment to the 1965 treaty and a South Korean government and people that increasingly viewed the 1965 agreement as an outdated relic from a time when South Korea was too weak to demand a more just settlement.

Facing this impasse, Abe escalated the dispute. In July 2019, when talks with Seoul on the forced labor issue had gone nowhere, the Abe government announced that it would remove South Korea from its "white list" of friendly countries exempted from export controls for sensitive items, for three chemicals essential for the manufacture of semiconductors—chemicals for which Japanese companies were virtually irreplaceable suppliers.

It was a calculated risk for Abe. The decision jeopardized an important trading relationship for Japanese manufacturers, risked undercutting Japan's market share as Moon's government began immediately to build indigenous capacity, and triggered worldwide alarm about how Japan's export controls would ripple downstream and impact the global supply of smartphones and other devices when markets were already anxious about the US–China trade war.

It also appeared to undercut Abe's claim to leadership of the global rules-based trading system. Although the Abe government said the decision had nothing to do with the forced labor cases and was more about South Korea's failure to consult with Japan about compliance with conditions for staying on the white list, it was difficult to take these claims at face value. Abe, South Koreans argued, was just like Trump, using trade as a bludgeon to gain the upper hand in other disputes.[41] This comparison is overwrought—withdrawing privileges unilaterally granted is hardly the same as unilaterally imposing trade sanctions on dubious national security grounds—and despite fears that Japan had effectively imposed an embargo on the sensitive goods, they continued to flow regardless of South Korea's loss of "white list" status. It is also hard to argue that Abe's actions vis-à-vis South Korea outweighed his efforts to preserve global economic integration by reviving TPP or concluding the economic partnership agreement with the EU.[42]

Nevertheless, Abe's decision to de-list South Korea virtually guaranteed that relations would worsen. Moon could not cave to Japanese economic pressure; Abe could not back down without South Korea's making significant concessions. The "white list" decision was therefore followed by a series of increasingly dramatic steps by both countries. Japan removed South Korea from its "white list" entirely; South Korea did the same. South Koreans launched a widespread boycott of Japanese retail brands and tourism to Japan. The Moon administration filed suit against Japan at the WTO. And, in August, it announced it would back out of the GSOMIA, just as North Korea resumed testing short-range ballistic missiles.

While US pressure eventually forced Seoul to back down from its threat to quit the intelligence-sharing agreement six hours before the decision would take effect, without significant political change in South Korea, it is unlikely that the situation will improve before either leader leaves office. The gap between Abe and Moon—and their key constituencies—is too wide for either leader to back down. Nor is it obvious that a US president more willing to intervene in the dispute would be able to fix what has been broken.

The two countries may be in for a prolonged deep freeze—or may even be undergoing at least partial decoupling. Abe's "white list" decision may have precipitated an escalatory spiral, but his action was a symptom of a broader erosion of trust between the two countries, rather than the cause.

Abe's fundamental error with South Korea may be a failure of strategic imagination. Can a strategy that aims to rally Asia's democracies in favor of liberal principles be successful while excluding one of the region's most successful and prosperous democracies? In the name of Japan's strategic independence and rallying all Asian democracies behind the "Free and Open Indo-Pacific" vision, he should have been more willing to accommodate South Korean demands for new terms of the relationship, even if it meant conceding that the 1965 treaty was not entirely fair. But it may have been unrealistic to expect Abe to show strategic flexibility when his government felt that—after Moon backed away from the 2015 agreement—it could not trust South Korea to negotiate in good faith. And through the crisis, polls showed that Abe had the support of most of the Japanese public, including voters who otherwise opposed his premiership.

It is possible that an external shock could lead Abe and Moon to reconsider how they have allowed the bilateral relationship to fray, but unlikely. The dramatic deterioration of Japan's ties with South Korea will be part of Abe's legacy with which his successor will have to grapple.

* * *

On 20 January 2017, hours before Trump was sworn in as America's forty-fifth president and warned, "From this moment on, it's going to be America First," Abe opened that year's ordinary session of the Diet. Japan, Abe said, would "fulfill its responsibilities at the center of the world stage, while taking a panoramic perspective of the world map." As Japan stood on the precipice of a new, uncertain era, Abe was determined not only to keep his country safe but to carve out a leadership role in a world in which leadership was increasingly up for grabs.

The Abe Doctrine would weather the transition to a new US administration—and Abe would seize the opportunity to assume a new role as champion of globalization. But while Abe's Japan became less hesitant about pursuing a global leadership role, his legacy as a global statesman would be surprisingly tenuous.

It was not only that Abe's diplomatic initiatives yielded surprisingly little fruit. For all of Abe's regional and global activism, Japan remains insecure in its own neighborhood. China's military power continues to grow and is increasingly aligned with Russia. North Korea's nuclear deterrent has only grown more capable. Authoritarianism is on the march. The global economy may be drifting to competing economic blocs. And Japan remains no less dependent on the US for its defense than in the past. Under Abe, Japan has become more active—but still faces an increasingly insecure future. Difficult choices about securing Japan may yet await his successors.

18

A NEW JAPAN

On Wednesday, 20 November 2019 Abe marked his 2,887th day as prime minister, surpassing Meiji-era Prime Minister Katsura Tarō's record for longevity. For a politician who twelve years earlier appeared to have no future in politics, it was an extraordinary achievement. And as he looked back on his tenure, he could claim some significant accomplishments towards building, as he said in 2007, "a nation which can withstand the raging waves for the next 50 to 100 years to come."

But it was also clouded by knowledge that—after governing Japan for the better part of a decade—Abe still faced significant challenges that would shape his legacy as prime minister. "I still have nearly two years left in my term as president of the Liberal Democratic Party," he said. "Under the weight of my responsibility, I will make an all-out effort to tackle policy goals, remembering the time when I first started out feeling nervous as if walking on thin ice."[1]

By the end of 2019, Abe was dominant as no prime minister had been before—and no prime minister might be again. He won six consecutive national elections, cementing his party's dominance. He opened Japan to the world. He assumed a new role for Japan as a champion of globalization even while preserving Japan's alliance with an increasingly protectionist America. And he led Japan to its longest stretch of economic growth since 1945. But when he leaves office—presumably in September 2021—he will leave his successors a legacy of unfinished tasks and missed opportunities. Japan's next leaders will wield more power but will face greater problems as Japan's population shrinks and ages, as American leadership recedes, and as climate change begins to wreak havoc on world order.

* * *

There could be no better example of Abe's unfinished legacy than constitutional revision. The constitution was the great, untouched pillar of the postwar regime, Article 9 the final institutional barrier to Japan's becoming a full-fledged military power. As prime minister, it was never far from Abe's mind, even as he pursued economic revitalization and other priorities.

On 3 May 2017, the seventieth anniversary of the promulgation of Japan's constitution, Abe recorded a message for Nippon Kaigi's annual Constitution Day forum.

"2020 is becoming a major common milestone for Japanese," he said. "I fervently wish that it is the year when a newly reborn Japan firmly begins to stir, and for 2020 to be the year when a new constitution comes into force."[2]

After pro-revision forces won a supermajority in the House of Councillors the previous summer, Abe was finally ready to push ahead with revision of the constitution. He wanted nothing more in his political life than to change the constitution, the enduring symbol of Japan's defeat and its subordinate independence. For Japanese hands to write even a single character of the charter would symbolize Japan's reclamation of its independence—and revised once, the door would be open for further changes. But he had not forgotten his Weber. In his message, Abe signaled his willingness to make significant concessions to achieve revision before leaving office.

He dropped the LDP's 2012 controversial draft constitution and, instead floated two possible revisions, an addition to Article 9 that would explicitly state that the SDF is constitutional and an amendment that would guarantee universal free education. The former could entice Kōmeitō; the latter was of particular interest to the Japan Restoration Party, whose votes would be needed to pass revisions. By taking a realistic and flexible approach to revision, Abe also hoped to drive a wedge into the Democratic Party, which was split between a right wing that wanted to approach revision pragmatically and a left wing that was opposed to any compromise, at least as long as Abe was prime minister.

The process never really got started. His proposals put revision on the electoral agenda for 2017, forcing all parties to articulate their positions.[3] But, as the returns came in, he made no mention of the constitution.[4] The following year afforded little time for the constitution. The LDP's constitution revision headquarters did use the spring of 2018 to put Abe's proposals into writing, even as they were criticized from the right—including by Ishiba—for being too modest, particularly on Article 9.

Despite Abe's willingness to compromise on the substance of constitutional change, he was unable to convince Kōmeitō to join forces to draft amendments ahead of time. The junior coalition partner wanted any deliberation about revisions to be public, in the constitutional commissions of the two houses of the Diet. The left-wing opposition parties, meanwhile, were not interested in opening a debate on the LDP's proposals.

The ruling parties had enough votes to force the Diet to begin deliberations, but Abe was constrained by political convention and public opinion. An informal rule stipulated that the debate should proceed with the consent of the minority and give minority parties ample time to debate. The majority would be generous to minority perspectives while the opposition would approach the debate in good faith and not "politicize" the revision debate.[5] But the rule's impact was asymmetrical. The opposition could and did violate it, repeatedly using other issues to prevent debate. However, if Abe were to push for revision without the consent of the opposition, he would be punished by voters, who were divided about the need for constitutional revision, generally see it as a low priority, and have repeatedly voiced their disapproval of Abe for undermining consensual norms.

With supermajorities in both houses, Abe could move revisions through the Diet but by doing so over the objections of the opposition he would jeopardize the chances of securing majority support for revision in a national referendum.[6] Of course, after the 2019 upper house elections, in which the pro-revision parties fell short of the supermajority threshold, Abe had no choice but to seek the support of opposition parties.

To a certain extent, Abe was a victim of his own success. His zeal for constitutional revision, dating back to the start of his career, had paid off: the prime minister could now talk openly about revision and even offer his own proposals without facing any backlash. Constitutional change had become a legitimate subject of political discussion. At the same time, however, he paid a price for his iconoclasm. The public might be willing to consider revision in the abstract but was opposed to revision according to Abe's vision or timeline.

Abe may still find a way to move constitutional changes through the Diet without triggering a public backlash that results in a government-ending referendum defeat. But as he enters his lame-duck stage, it is less likely that he will be able to convince members of his own party, let alone Kōmeitō, to gamble on revision. The greatest irony of Abe's tenure may be that, despite being the longest-serving and most powerful prime minister of the postwar era, he will leave office having failed to achieve the one change he sought above all others, an ambition that he had absorbed from the time he was dandled on his grandfather's knee.

* * *

As a practical matter, Abe's failure to change the constitution may be more of a personal disappointment than a dramatic failure to change Japan. After all, he delivered significant constitutional reform when he reinterpreted the constitution and implemented changes to Japan's national security laws. His more enduring legacy will be as the godfather of a global Japan.

Abe did not merely pursue globalization in the form of high-profile "mega" trade deals. While the US and other countries were putting up trade barriers, building walls, and seeking to curb foreign influences, the Abe government opened Japan to more foreign visitors and foreign residents than ever before. The Abe government did not embrace globalization out of altruism or cosmopolitanism. Abe was the man who had, after all, talked in his memoirs about the absurdity of a person calling oneself a "citizen of the world."[7]

But Abe used a variety of policy tools to open Japan to foreign goods, foreign capital, foreign workers, foreign visitors, and foreign influences. These policies were not all unqualified successes. But together they demonstrated that for Abe, globalization was a strategic necessity. "In order to attract the world's talent, capital, and technology, which are bound to Japan's growth, we must advance the complete globalization of Japan at home," he said in 2014.[8]

Perhaps the most visible piece of the Abe's globalization agenda was his pursuit of tourism as a growth industry. Although his predecessors targeted tourism before 2012, Japan still lagged well behind not only developed-country peers like France and Italy and continental giants like the US and China, but also its neighbor South Korea in terms of international arrivals. Tourists, particularly from the burgeoning middle classes of developing Asia, would be a vital source of demand. Visitors to Japan spent roughly ¥4.5 trillion in 2018, four times more than in 2012 (although per capita spending had stagnated).[9]

The 2013 growth strategy established a target of 20 million international visits by 2020, roughly double the number of visits in 2013. Japan would relax entry requirements, particularly for visitors from China and Southeast Asia; upgrade its travel infrastructure, with a particular focus on expanding the number of international arrivals at Tokyo's Haneda airport; and improve the country's capacity for hosting international visitors, which included changes as mundane as providing signs and announcements in multiple foreign languages. The 2020 Olympics forced the government to accelerate these efforts.

Thanks to a weaker yen and the global appeal of Japanese culture, the government blew past its targets, prompting the government to double its target for 2020 to 40 million visitors. By 2018, more than 31 million tourists visited. This caused problems as localities struggled to deal with the rapid surge of visitors, and some international friction, particularly but not only with Chinese visitors, who by 2019 had become the single largest nationality among international visitors.[10] Accommodating this upsurge has forced Japanese to adapt in large ways and small, and tourists, particularly from the Asian continent, will remain a fixture even after the Olympics, especially after Japan's much-anticipated casinos open for business in the 2020s.

While the tourism boom has remade Japan in visible ways, Japan's embrace of foreign labor has been no less important. Reformers have long argued that Japan needs to attract millions of immigrants to stabilize its population. Nakagawa Hidenao, for example, proposed in 2008 that Japan should aim for ten million immigrants and strive to become a "multi-ethnic nation" by mid-century.[11] It was precisely the kind of issue that divided Koizumi's neo-liberals from the new conservatives, who, beyond worrying about the threats to public order from a larger foreign population, also fretted that a multi-ethnic Japan would simply mean a Japan with a large Chinese minority.[12] It seemed, therefore, that Abe would resist including immigration as part of Abenomics, even after the post-2015 shift to a focus on Japan's demographic future.

But Abe surprised his critics and his admirers with his willingness to open Japan to foreign residents. Abe was not a convert to his onetime adviser Nakagawa's dream of a multicultural Japan, but he accepted that labor shortages in the immediate term and the long-term decline of the working-age population meant something had to change.

The changes were initially gradual as his government focused its efforts on reforming Japan's "technical intern training program." This program, described by the US State Department as "having effectively become a guest-worker program," allows foreign "trainees" to work in designated sectors and ostensibly receive on-the-job training that would benefit their home countries. The program was rife with abuse, exploitation, and forced labor—and in many cases the "training" was nominal—but Abe hoped to crack down on abuses while simultaneously expanding the program to new sectors and enabling trainees to stay for longer. But if Japan wanted to host more foreign workers to do the less-skilled jobs that it was becoming difficult to find Japanese citizens to do, a de facto guest worker program was inadequate. Abe was surprised to learn, for example, that sixty-nine trainees, most of them in their twenties, had died between 2015 and 2017 alone.[13]

As a result, in 2018 Abe decided to establish a more formal guest worker program. In practice, he deferred to Suga, who was absolutely convinced of the need for foreign workers. "The Japanese economy is coming to the point where it cannot function without the work of foreign talent," he said in an interview in August 2018.[14] Suga had to convince Abe that it would not be an immigration program, reflecting Abe's discomfort with the issue.[15] The Abe government's economic policy plan for 2019, released in June 2018, indicated that the government would introduce reforms to the visa system, but left the chief cabinet secretary to fill in the details.

The reform bill passed in the autumn of 2018 created new categories of work visa to allow foreigners who demonstrated a certain degree of technical skill and Japanese language ability to work in Japan for up to five years. Technical interns could switch to the new visa, if they qualified. Workers admitted on this visa would not have the option of bringing spouses or other family members; a separate visa would be created for highly skilled workers, who could bring families and would qualify for permanent residence after ten years. Japan had already introduced a point system for highly skilled migrants in 2012, and the Abe government introduced a fast-track system in 2017 that would award them permanent residence after only one year.

At least initially, the new visas would only be available to workers in a few industries facing acute shortages of workers; for example, agriculture, construction, and nursing care. The bill mandated that foreign workers should receive similar pay and similar working conditions as citizens, and a new agency would be created to monitor for abuse and ensure that foreign workers were abiding by the terms of their visas. The government would also invest in language training and other programs to help foreign workers acculturate. These changes would take effect on 1 April 2019. "If the Abe administration cannot do this, the next administration will not be able to do this," an anonymous official told *Nikkei*. "It's the last chance."[16]

As the Diet deliberated, Abe fended off accusations that it was not an immigration program, as opposition parties tried to tangle up the prime minister. They opposed the bills mostly on procedural grounds, arguing that the abuses in the technical intern program showed that the Abe administration was not up to administering the new program. Predictably, the right wing was also unhappy. Abe and Suga faced strenuous opposition from backbenchers within the LDP, who demanded assurances that the government would protect public order and received a concession that the government would conduct a review of the new visa program after three years. Nevertheless, there were murmurs on the right that Abe was making the same mistake that German Chancellor Angela Merkel had made, crippling his mandate in the name of opening his nation's doors.[17]

Despite angst from Abe's right-wing allies and public anxiety, the legislation passed. Japan could begin to take in as many as 345,000 guest workers annually from the following fiscal year. Abe was right: it was not an immigration policy, but would, his government hoped, allow foreign workers to contribute safely and productively, with greater protection of law. It would not reverse Japan's shrinking population; it was not even clear whether Japan would be able to attract enough migrants to claim all of the available visas. By December 2019, only 1621 had arrived on the new visa category, reflecting the fact that it was rushed into law without adequate preparation.[18]

But Abe's right-wing critics were also right. The guest worker program could have a profound impact on Japanese society. Japan's foreign population was already the largest it had ever been.[19] The influx of new waves of foreign workers from across Asia will undoubtedly leave their mark on Japan. Whatever his reservations, Abe used his power to defy his conservative allies and open Japan to the world. Abe's willingness to support Suga's migrant worker bill over the opposition of his right-wing allies was the ultimate symbol of his realism.[20]

* * *

As Abe began to consider his legacy, Abenomics faded into the background. The shift that began when he announced the "three new arrows" in 2015 continued. When Abe called a snap election in October 2017, he cited Japan's aging, shrinking population as one of the two national crises that he needed a new mandate to address. But Abenomics repeatedly took the back seat to foreign policy or to Abe's political machinations.

Earlier in 2017, the administration had unveiled a new growth strategy that aimed for a "productivity revolution" and a "human capital formation revolution." The government would use tax incentives, government spending, and regulatory reform to promote innovations that would strengthen Japan's position in the race for market leadership in the advanced technologies of the "fourth industrial revolution," including robotics, the Internet of things, big data, and artificial intelligence. It was the clearest answer yet that the Abe administration had given to "fourth industrial revolution" strategies developed by Germany, China, and other governments. To strengthen Japan's workforce, meanwhile, the Abe administration indicated that it would prioritize free and universal early childhood education, cost reductions for higher education, and place a new emphasis on information technology from primary school onwards to help address critical skill shortages in the IT sector. The 2017 growth strategy, however, did not explain how the government would fund these new mandates; "regulatory sandboxes," the project-specific relaxation of regulations, would do much of the work to encourage advances in critical sectors.

But Abenomics was at the mercy of the political calendar. The 2017 election, called largely for politically opportunistic reasons, vacated the autumn Diet session, sparing Abe months of questioning about his scandals but delaying the passage of what it called "working styles" reform legislation, reforms it had begun drafting in 2016 to address equal pay for regular and non-regular workers, teleworking, long working hours, overtime pay, family leave policies, and training.

These issues were intimately connected not only to productivity but also to Japan's demographic crisis. Office cultures that emphasize long workdays and pressure employees not to take vacation days or parental leave force mothers to choose between careers and families, and have prevented fathers from being more involved in childrearing. This package would be delayed until the summer of 2018, which in turn delayed the implementation of the 2017 growth strategy. The shift to universal free preschool, meanwhile, was linked to the next consumption tax hike, from eight percent to ten percent, which would not be implemented until October 2019.

By the time Abe began his bid for a third term, the urgency that had once animated Abenomics seemed to have faded. In his reelection bid, he touted his economic record and promised merely to implement the policies from the party's manifesto the previous year. It was unclear whether Abe still harbored great ambitions for Japan's economy.

Certainly, the economy performed well. In February 2019, the cabinet office certified that Japan's GDP had grown for the seventy-fifth-consecutive month, marking the longest postwar economic boom.[21] Unemployment had reached an all-time low and stayed there. The number of jobs per applicant reached record highs, meaning that new school graduates enjoyed better opportunities than young Japanese had enjoyed in years.[22] More women were working—the share of working-age women in the workforce soared from 63.4 percent in 2012 to 71.3 percent in 2018, surpassing the United States and the G7 average—and Japan's "M curve," the pattern whereby female labor force participation plummets among women in their childbearing years and then recovers as children grow, flattened significantly. Women were increasingly staying in their jobs, at least in part due to the Abe government's efforts to increase the availability and affordability of childcare. And corporate Japan was booming. Corporate profits continued to set records well into Abe's seventh year in office, even as anxiety grew what about the US–China trade war and slowing global growth would mean for Japan. On 1 October 2018, the Nikkei 225 closed at 24,245.76, its highest level in nearly twenty-seven years. Land prices, particularly in Tokyo and major tourist hubs, continued to grow, and Tokyo's skyline was transformed as new towers rose as part of a pre-Olympics construction boom.

But these results, the recitation of which had become a staple of Abe's stump speeches, masked a growing unease about what exactly Abenomics had achieved. Average GDP growth during Abe's tenure was only a little over one percent, better than the previous decade but far below the two-percent real GDP growth and three-percent nominal GDP growth that Abe had hoped for. More Japanese were working, but employers were still replacing too many retiring regular workers with low-paid, lightly regulated temps and part-time workers—and many workers were shifting into lower-paid nursing and eldercare jobs as aging baby boomers needed more assistance. More women were in the workforce, but women were still missing from leadership positions. Japan Inc. was enjoying record profits, but it was also accumulating record cash reserves and using it on large share buybacks, while resisting the Abe government's now-routine pressure for wage increases. Despite critical labor shortages, real wage growth was sluggish and consumer spending remained weak.[23]

The stock market boom, abetted by the Bank of Japan's (BOJ) and Government Pension Investment Fund's (GPIF) equity purchases, also contributed to widening inequality.[24] The underlying constraints on long-term growth—the demographic crisis and low productivity—remained essentially unchanged. In 2019, the total number of births fell below 900,000, the lowest number of births since just after the Meiji Restoration.[25] Population decline appeared to be accelerating rather than stabilizing.

There was, nevertheless, a sense of drift even as these problems became apparent. The BOJ, after introducing its yield curve control policy in 2016, took a back seat, slowing its asset purchases even as inflation remained well below its inflation target. The BOJ ensured that the government's borrowing costs would remain dramatically low—like Germany and other European countries, by 2019 most of Japanese government debt was yielding negative interest rates for bondholders.[26] Kuroda, however, was reluctant to experiment with cutting interest rates deeper into negative territory. Abe effectively endorsed Kuroda's cautious approach when he granted Kuroda a second five-year term in March 2018, instead of opting for a more unconventional choice like his adviser Honda Etsurō. By the time of his third leadership bid, Abe's commitment to macroeconomic experimentation was waning.

Honda and some of Abe's other more heterodoxical advisers had called for more radical experiments. Honda, for example, thought Japan should embrace "helicopter money," the term coined by Milton Friedman to describe the central bank's distributing cash directly to households. As Abe prepared to implement the long-delayed tax hike from eight percent to ten percent in 2019, some tried to draw Japan into a growing debate over the soundness of the heterodoxical Modern Monetary Theory, an increasingly popular approach on the American left which argues that a government that borrows in its own currency and has a floating exchange rate can run larger deficits for longer without risking significant inflation.[27] Abe and his principal advisers were uninterested in Japan's being a laboratory for MMT—they denied that its past experiences had anything to do with the theory—even as some lawmakers, including Nishida Shōji, a new conservative ally of Abe's, called on the prime minister to defy MOF and embrace the theory.[28]

MMT theorists were not the only ones arguing against the tax hike. More conventional economists like former IMF chief economist Olivier Blanchard also argued for scrapping it, stating that persistently weak demand—what Larry Summers calls "secular stagnation"—meant that to grow, Japan must continue to run deficits.[29] But despite a widespread intellectual consensus that to raise the consumption tax would be a mistake, particularly given mounting signs of a global economic slowdown, Abe simply seemed to have less of an appetite for bold or unconventional economic policymaking.

Abe seems to have decided to proceed with the 2019 tax hike partly due to political reasoning—he was afraid that delaying a third time would amount to an admission that he had failed to revitalize Japan's economy—and partly because his government prepared so many offsetting measures that in the immediate term the impact on household spending could be contained. Abe had also decided that the consumption tax hike was an opportunity to shift spending to childcare and early childhood education, a policy that not only would be popular but would help shift towards what he called a "social security system for all generations."[30] Nevertheless, this approach was a far cry from Abe's conducting a radical fiscal policy experiment like MMT.

Abenomics will therefore leave a problematic legacy for Abe's successor. Japan avoided a third "lost decade"—enjoying growth, price increases, and a strong labor market—but also failed to address longer-term demographic challenges, concerns about productivity and innovation, and the future of macroeconomic policy. He will leave future prime ministers with a more pliable BOJ, but one already wedded to "unconventional" easing policies from which there appears to be no exit. Abe's successors may have more fiscal room—under Abe, tax revenues reached the highest levels since the bubble burst and the debt-to-GDP ratio stabilized—but may face a less benign global economic environment than Abe faced for much of his tenure. They will also have to cope with the fiscal impact of baby boomers advancing deeper into old age and placing a heavier burden on the healthcare system—and perhaps also begin bearing more of the costs of climate change and the transition to a zero carbon economy. Japan's future leaders may therefore not have the luxury of rejecting radical (and riskier) ideas about macroeconomic policy or, if orthodoxy prevails, postponing deeper cuts to social security spending as part of the pursuit of a budget surplus.

* * *

Abe's successors will also inherit what has become a "post-populist" democracy. In 2019, less than half of the electorate voted in upper house elections, the second-lowest rate in postwar history and the first time turnout had fallen below fifty percent since 1995. As other democracies fretted about the rise of right-wing populism, "post-truth" politics, and deepening polarization—schisms that would leave them vulnerable to Russian influence operations—Japan was an island of stability.

There were disagreements, but none threatened social solidarity. There were protests, but they never threatened political stability. The Abe government was often on the wrong side of public opinion on key issues, but Abe's political instincts and a sense of complacency on the part of the citizenry prevented disagreements from boiling over. Having risen to power as a conservative iconoclast determined to settle the postwar culture war once and for all, in power Abe was conciliatory, willing to compromise his past hardline ideals when preserving his government and advancing the national interest made it prudent to do so. Abe was able to govern—and to dominate the political system, marginalizing his LDP rivals and breaking the two-party system that had emerged in the first decade of the century—by being a competent, flexible administrator. He had achieved a political virtuous cycle, where stable government translated into strong parliamentary majorities which translated into stronger government, making it progressively harder for the fractured opposition to regain the public trust needed to dent Abe's power. The uncertainties of the post-2016 world would only reinforce this trend. None of Abe's rivals could claim to have a superior ability to deal with Trump, Xi, or Kim.

* * *

While Abe's efforts to preserve a liberal global economic order and expand Japan's strategic independence have been consequential, it is an open question whether, in decades to come, Abe will be remembered for his efforts to defend an open world or whether his legacy will be overwhelmed by a single issue: climate change.

"The eyes of all future generations are upon you," said Swedish climate activist Greta Thunberg at the United Nations in September 2019. "And if you choose to fail us, I say: We will never forgive you." Thunberg's message was intended for all the world's leaders, but may prove especially damning for Abe.

Abe has a decent record of saying the right things about climate change. He has not denied or downplayed the dangers. "The problem is exacerbating more quickly than we expected. We must take more robust actions. And swiftly," he wrote in September 2018.[31] He has recognized that Japan is not immune from the dangers of runaway climate change. During his tenure, Japan has been struck by record-breaking heat waves and battered by super typhoons, which have killed hundreds. Major urban centers—most notably greater Osaka—lie just above sea level, vulnerable to rising oceans in a hotter world.

Post-Paris, Japan's emissions have declined, due to the Abe government's efforts to promote more efficient energy use and its retention of post-3/11 policies to encourage the introduction of renewable energy sources. Abe, meanwhile, has touted corporate Japan's role in developing advanced technologies in the areas of carbon capture, batteries, and advanced clean and renewable energy. His government has also pioneered the use of a joint credit mechanism to help developing countries in Asia adopt cleaner technologies. While Japan's commitment to build new coal-fired power plants at home and abroad tarnishes this record, it is still superior to some of Japan's peers in the developed world.

However, Abe has enjoyed a durable political mandate unmatched in the rich world. While his peers were hobbled by domestic opposition or institutions that limited their ability to lead on climate change, Abe faced few constraints.[32] If any world leader could have rallied his people behind a radical climate mitigation program—a Japanese "Green New Deal"—and led by example and diplomatic initiative, it would have been Abe. But he struggled to convince the Japanese people to support nuclear power—still Japan's best hope for reducing carbon emissions in the immediate term—let alone to embrace a wider-reaching mitigation plan. While Japan ratified the Paris Climate Agreement, the Abe government made voluntary commitments in Paris that were woefully inadequate to meet the challenge of preventing runaway climate change.[33] By 2019, Japan's commitments were viewed as "highly insufficient" relative to what was needed to avoid more devastating levels of warming, beyond the 1.5°C target in Paris or the 2°C viewed as a critical threshold.[34]

If the world fails to avoid catastrophic, runaway climate change, other leaders will bear more responsibility. But Abe is vulnerable to the charge that he did not do all he could with the power he wielded. What difference would constitutional revision make to future generations of Japanese in a world that has blown past two degrees of warming?

Indeed, as nations shift from climate mitigation to climate adaptation, Abe's legacy could look dramatically different. The social and political consequences of a hotter world—food and water shortages, resource wars, climate refugees, and new pandemic diseases—could overwhelm his efforts to protect an open, rules-based world order. How would a liberal rules-based order led by Asian democracies fare in a world of militarized xenophobia as nations struggle to contain transnational security threats? Abe's most enduring legacy could be the national security establishment that he erected, which could become the foundation for Japan's own attempt to build what writer Christian Parenti calls "the politics of the armed lifeboat," a "green authoritarianism" that would erect barriers, police populations, and fight brush wars in order to keep chaos away from Japan's shores.[35]

Abe has been fixated on ensuring national survival in a turbulent century and he has shown an admirable flexibility in the face of the significant challenges he has faced in his own time. But whether he is remembered as the leader who laid the groundwork for a more resilient Japan that could help lead the world away from catastrophe, or as another leader unable to meet the challenge posed by anthropogenic climate change, is out of his hands. The radical transformation Abe sought may lie in Japan's future.

* * *

As Abe heads into his final years, the shape of his legacy is already apparent. He committed Japan to a new vocation as the defender of the global rules-based economic order. He navigated a rapidly changing Asia, preserving ties with a volatile America, stabilizing relations with China, and articulating a new approach for building closer relationships with Australia, India, and ASEAN. He gambled on a macroeconomic policy experiment that boosted growth and inflation. Yet Abe's legacy could be subject to change in his final months in office. A global downturn, a rift with Trump over his approach to North Korea or China, or new scandal allegations would cast his legacy in a less favorable light.

But his place in Japan's history will be ambiguous. In a sense, he has achieved what he had set out to achieve. As a young politician, he wrote of how he envied members of his grandfather's generation, who were brimming with self-confidence and had built a Japan that was "shining" in the world. As prime minister, he showed the world that Japan was a country to admire and convinced the Japanese people to feel proud of their country, its achievements and its place in the world. If the Japanese people could feel confident about their country and its future—even in the face of significant and intractable challenges—the country could achieve anything. By fighting his way back to power, Abe demonstrated the power of this conviction.

In a larger sense, however, Abe demonstrated the limits of strong leadership. As Japan's longest-tenured prime minister, he dominated Japanese democracy as no leader had done, wielding outsized parliamentary majorities and commanding an empowered political executive. He was dominant while the leaders of other advanced industrial democracies were hamstrung by domestic crises. But while he made some significant reforms by patiently deploying the power he had accumulated, he was unable to reverse the underlying causes of national decline.

Japan still faces a challenging future. The next generation of the Abe–Kishi dynasty may face more significant challenges than any of its predecessors.[36] Japan's most momentous decisions still lie ahead, as the planet warms, China's power grows, US leadership fades, and the Japanese population ages. It is unknown whether his successor—whether that is his longtime rival Ishiba Shigeru, former foreign minister Kishida Fumio, current Foreign Minister Motegi Toshimitsu, current Defense Minister Kōno Tarō, Chief Cabinet Secretary Suga Yoshihide, or some dark horse—will convince the Japanese people and the world that Japan is still capable of great things in a turbulent and uncertain future.

It will be up to future generations of Japanese to determine whether they look back at the age of Abe as Japan's last moment in the sun before the inevitable decline, or as the beginning of a new age in which Japan helped lead the world through a volatile twenty-first century.[37]

AFTERWORD

"Together with the Japanese people, I will make this historic year—the year in which we will once again host the Olympic and Paralympic Games—a year for carving out a new era for Japan," Abe Shinzō said in his first press conference of 2020. "I have renewed my determination to do so here as we start the second year of the Reiwa era."[1]

As the new year dawned, 2020 promised to be a good year for Abe. True, he was again battling scandal, after being accused of using the government's annual cherry-blossom viewing party to reward political supporters—potentially in violation of campaign finance laws—and then covering up misconduct when relevant records were found to have been shredded improperly. Most Japanese said they did not trust his explanations and his approval ratings suffered.[2]

Abe's luck continued to hold. The opposition was still divided, and unpopular. Talks about a merger between the two surviving Democratic Party splinters would collapse in January.[3] His would-be successors in the LDP seemed content to wait for his departure. There were even whispers that the LDP could again amend its rules to let him seek a fourth term in September 2021, particularly if Donald Trump were reelected in November. After all, would the Japanese people trust any other leader to parley with him?

And Abe would soon host the Olympics, in Tokyo in July, showcasing his new Japan. Maybe the goodwill generated by the summer games would enable him to call another snap election—which could make it impossible for the LDP to deny him another term, if he wanted it.[4]

Only two weeks into the year his dreams for 2020 were shattered.

* * *

On 11 January, the *Nikkei Shimbun* published a short item on the first death in the Chinese city of Wuhan from pneumonia caused by a "novel coronavirus." By 16 January, the prime minister's office established a crisis management centre and Japan's first case of Covid-19 was reported, a thirty-something man who had recently traveled to Wuhan. A week later, China locked down Wuhan, a manufacturing hub of eleven million people. By the end of January, the World Health Organization (WHO) would declare the disease a Public Health Emergency of International Concern. Governments around the world would begin imposing restrictions on travelers from China and then, as the outbreak spread, travelers from other countries. By late March, the International Olympic Committee (IOC) would postpone the Tokyo Olympics until 2021, after WHO declared the disease a pandemic and national Olympic federations warned that they would not participate in the games. By that time, the Covid-19 pandemic had shut down national economies, overwhelmed healthcare systems, and confined billions of people to their homes.

Japan would weather the pandemic better than nearly all of its peers in the developed world. As of July 2020, Japan has had only 771 deaths from Covid-19, or 6.1 deaths per million people.[5] While slightly worse than some of Japan's Asian neighbors, Japan has performed significantly better than any of its peers in the G7, far ahead of Germany, which has received considerable praise for its response to the pandemic while still suffering nearly ninety deaths per million people. Despite fears and warnings from medical professionals that Japan's healthcare system would be overrun, leading to a surge in deaths, thus far the medical infrastructure has proved resilient, and authorities have introduced some timely reforms—telemedicine, centralized quarantine facilities for mild cases—that have significantly eased the burden on doctors, nurses, and other medical personnel. The country has not only avoided a surge in mortality but has also seen a relatively limited number of cases that have required intensive care. While there are sadly cases of patients unable to receive tests or who were turned away from hospitals and later succumbed to the illness, the fact remains that compared to much of the world, Japan's handling of the pandemic has been exemplary, all the more so considering that no country has a greater share of its population older than sixty-five.[6]

Despite this record, however, Abe appears to be one of only a handful of leaders whose approval ratings have fallen during the Covid-19 crisis. The fall has not been precipitous—and has fluctuated. His approval dipped in February after the *Diamond Princess* episode, when the Japanese government mishandled its decision to quarantine the 2,500 passengers and roughly 1,000 crew members of a cruise ship docked at Yokohama as the virus spread freely among the population. It recovered in March, and then fell again as a growing outbreak in Tokyo forced Abe to declare a state of emergency in April.

From the docking of the *Diamond Princess*, Abe would be repeatedly wrong-footed by the outbreak. He would cycle between indecision and rash action, would struggle to communicate his plans to the public, and would all too often yield the initiative to other actors, whether the populist governors of Tokyo and Osaka or backbenchers in his coalition partner Kōmeitō, who forced Abe to take the virtually unprecedented step of withdrawing an emergency stimulus budget to replace the prime minister's more modest, means-tested program with a plan to distribute cash payments to every individual in the country.[7] His ability to communicate his government's outlook of the pandemic and its intentions were wanting, and he was repeatedly criticized for tone-deaf public messaging, whether his roundly mocked "Dance at Home" Instagram video to promote social distancing or his poorly executed plan to distribute two reusable masks to every household that was michievously dubbed "Abenomasks."[8]

The Covid-19 crisis has dramatically—and most likely irreparably—damaged Abe's reputation as a strong leader determined to protect his country from threats to life and property. He no longer appeared to be a safe pair of hands. As this book has argued, his most fundamental belief as a politician is that, when lives are at stake, a political leader cannot be indecisive or hesitant. The state, meanwhile, must deploy national resources to ward off threats. Having failed to play the role that he himself believed that he must play—a failure for which he had lambasted the leaders of the former Democratic Party of Japan when he plotted his comeback in 2011 and 2012—Abe's standing has been unmistakably diminished. Whether he lingers on past the acute stage of the crisis and survives to host a rescheduled Tokyo Olympics in July 2021—assuming they can take place at all—the idea of a fourth three-year term at the helm of his party and the nation is increasingly unthinkable.[9]

The reasons for Abe's political missteps are mundane. He started the year distracted by political scandals: not only the cherry-blossom viewing one but also an ongoing campaign finance scandal that had forced his lieutenant Kawai Katsuyuki to resign as justice minister the previous fall and a bribery scandal connected to the government's casino legalization scheme that led to the arrest of an LDP lawmaker. The months of battling scandals—Suga was heavily implicated in the cherry-blossom viewing allegations—had frayed the relationship between him and Abe, undermining the administration's key decision-making apparatus just when it needed to function at a higher gear.[10]

The administration was also showing its age. After seven years in power, Abe's government was no longer the well-oiled machine of its early years. Experienced ministers and advisers had given way to more inexperienced officials. Abe's point man for the pandemic, for example, was Nishimura Yasutoshi, a rising star who had served ably in deputy posts earlier in the administration but was serving in his first ministerial post when the crisis struck. Nishimura would be panned for his poor communications in the acute stage of the outbreak. The same slack may have led the prime minister to gamble on passing a controversial reform of prosecutorial personnel practices in the midst of the pandemic, one that sparked fears that the prosecutors' political independence would be compromised. This legislation, and Abe's decision to withdraw it after polls showed that it enjoyed virtually no public support, would cement the impression that his grip was slipping.

However, although the pandemic appears to have finally rendered Abe a lame duck as he approaches his final year in office, the crisis itself has not discredited his vision of a strong state led by a powerful prime minister. If anything, it is conventional wisdom that further reforms—the creation of a Japanese version of the US Centers for Disease Control, an emergency powers amendment to the constitution—are needed. Nevertheless, the pandemic has highlighted the extent to some norms that constrained the exercise of power by the national government have survived despite the efforts of Abe and other reformers. For instance, while Abe successfully gained the power to declare a state of emergency through a legislative change early in the pandemic, a state of emergency, which Abe declared in April, empowered prefectural governors, not the prime minister, to request that individuals limit non-essential activities and non-essential businesses suspend operations—and those requests were not backed by the threat of legal sanction.

Like his grandfather, Abe may be followed by a "low posture" prime minister, the Japanese political term used to describe leaders more willing to defer to critics and tolerate dissent. But his model of leadership—in which an administration's success will depend on its ability to dominate the agenda-setting and decision-making processes—will in all likelihood survive him. The challenges Japan faces in the twenty-first century will continue to militate in favor of centralization.

* * *

Those challenges will become more apparent in the post-Covid-19 world. The pandemic and its consequences will, if not entirely recast Abe's legacy, then cast a shadow over all of his achievements during his historically long tenure as prime minister. The wide-reaching impact of the pandemic on Japan, Asia, and the global order mean that his victories will seem more modest, while his failures will loom larger.

Economically, the crisis revealed the fragility of Abenomics's achievements. Thanks to Abe's decision to raise the consumption tax from eight per cent to ten percent in October 2019, Japan's economy was likely already in recession by the time the pandemic struck. The Covid-19 recession, however, will cut deeper. It has already ended a streak of record-low unemployment, as the demand for workers has plummeted.[11] Inflation, which had been below the Bank of Japan's (BOJ) two-percent inflation target but above zero, may well retreat. Wage increases for 2020 already looked disappointing before Japan's outbreak worsened. A global recession—and, no less significant, global uncertainty about the resilience of economies amidst a pandemic—will make it difficult for Japan's companies to invest. Meanwhile, tourism, a key pillar of Abe's growth strategies, has all but vanished. In April 2019, Japan welcomed 2.7 million international visitors. In April 2020, only 2,900 visitors entered Japan.[12]

At the same time, the combination of a worse-than-expected contraction after the consumption tax hike—despite assurances from the finance ministry that the Japanese economy would be resilient enough to weather it—and the extraordinary demands of the pandemic have effectively undone his efforts to strike a balance between growth and fiscal sustainability. As of July 2020, Abe's government has already passed two supplementary budgets totaling more than more than ¥55 trillion, which will be entirely covered by government bonds, increasing the amount of debt to be issued in the fiscal year to twenty percent of GDP. After stabilizing Japan's debt-to-GDP ratio for much of his tenure, thanks to the largest haul of tax revenues since before the bubble burst, the fiscal stimulus needed to cushion the economy from the twin blows of the consumption tax hike and the global pandemic could lead to a sharp increase in Japan's deficit in 2020 and with it, Japan's debt-to-GDP ratio.[13] Even before the pandemic it was apparent that Abe had merely postponed a reckoning with Japan's public finances. His successors will still have to grapple with the question of whether a can grow and reflate its way to fiscal sustainability or whether tax hikes and spending cuts are unavoidable as the aging population puts a greater burden on the social safety net. The BOJ will continue to dominate the market for Japanese government debt for years to come, perhaps enabling future prime ministers to continue to muddle through, but the debate will continue—and, as other governments contend with the fiscal hangover of the pandemic, heterodox proposals like modern monetary theory will continue to get a hearing in Tokyo. For all of Abe's willingness to entertain unconventional economic policies, there could be more radical experiments in the future.

The economic impact of the Covid-19 pandemic for Abe's legacy and Japan may not be entirely negative. The need for employers to encourage teleworking, accommodate parents faced with school closures with a few days' notice, and reduce gatherings in enclosed, poorly ventilated spaces has encouraged greater changes to Japan's "working styles" in three months in 2020 than the Abe government accomplished after years of a deliberate initiative to make Japan's workplaces more flexible and equal. If Keidanren's guidelines for businesses after the economy reopens are any indication—the business federation has recommended that its members consider telecommuting, flexible hours and leave schedules, staggered commutes, greater use of video conferencing, and even four-day workweeks—life for Japan's white-collar workers could be dramatically different.[14] The impact of the crisis on office culture could be even greater if drinking establishments face heavy regulations to prevent new infections, thereby reducing the role of after-hours socializing.

The geopolitical consequences of the pandemic may be no less important. While the post-pandemic world is still inchoate, it seems increasingly likely that the pandemic could upset the delicate tightrope act that Abe was treading between the United States and China. While in the early phase of the pandemic, it appeared that the crisis might bring Japan and China closer together—Abe, for example, resisted closing Japan's borders to all Chinese travelers until after the outbreak peaked—ultimately the pandemic has revealed just how tenuous their post-2017 rapprochement was. Japan has thus far avoided the heavy-handed "wolf warrior" diplomacy that has spurred backlashes against China in Europe and Australia, although in May, Chinese coast-guard vessels chased a Japanese fishing boat near the Senkakus.[15] The Abe government, for its part, included financial incentives to encourage Japanese corporations to bring manufacturing back to Japan or relocate elsewhere in Asia in its crisis budget in April. It has also endorsed Australia's call for an independent Covid-19 inquiry, the proposal that has led China to impose steep tariffs on Australian agricultural exports, and backed WHO observer status for Taiwan. While neither Abe nor his successors is likely to opt for decoupling from Japan's powerful neighbor, if the Covid-19 crisis leads China to take a more assertive approach to its neighbors and in international institutions—much like after 2008—Abe's modest steps towards rapprochement may well have been for naught.

At the same time, the crisis may also serve as a reminder of the dangers of Abe's decision to invest in Japan's continued dependence on the United States for its security. "The US is renowned for helping others in an emergency," Edward Luce of the *Financial Times* writes. "In hindsight, Trump's claim to global leadership leaps out. History will mark Covid-19 as the first time that ceased to be true. US airlifts have been missing in action. America cannot even supply itself."[16] After the pandemic it will be impossible to deny that America's dysfunctional political system has had ruinous consequences for US global leadership and therefore the reliability of the US as an ally over the long term.[17] Even if a Donald Trump is defeated in November, no US ally can assume that the US will return easily to old patterns or that political polarization will not hinder a future Democratic administration much as it hamstrung the Obama administration.

Abe's successors will have a harder time balancing a confident, assertive China—which has alternated between bullying countries that have criticized its response to the pandemic and deploying its largesse in pursuit of international goodwill—and a United States that is increasingly bent on conducting a new cold war against China, with the support of most Americans and policymakers in both parties, but may also be increasingly incapable of marshaling national resources effectively. It is possible that a future US administration opts for an approach that stresses cooperation with Japan and other allies who may be reluctant to decouple from China entirely. But a harder-edged, multi-dimensional competition between the US and China is here to stay, and the "China question" could become a significantly more salient issue for Abe's successors as the Japanese people debate the risks of dependence on trade, investment, and tourism ties with China versus the risk of participation in what Beijing will inevitably see as a US-led campaign of encirclement. Over the final year of his term, that debate will include a fundamental reconsideration of Japan's national security strategy, as an abrupt decision by Defense Minister Kōno Tarō to suspend the controversial Aegis Ashore missile defense system – foisted upon Abe with little warning, another sign of Abe's waning clout – has prompted the government to update its key strategic documents by the end of 2020.[18]

After Abe, Japan is unlikely to relinquish the leadership role it has assumed as he has sought to articulate a vision of an open Asia in which China also has a leading role but does not dominate its neighbors. Abe's steady investment in bilateral relationships across the region means that future prime ministers will continue to look to Australia, India, and the countries of ASEAN for support and friendship in pursuing this vision, even as Beijing and Washington push for their own alternatives. Despite think pieces about how Covid-19 means the end of globalization, that is unlikely to be the case in Asia, whose governments have not only handled the pandemic better than the Atlantic countries but which have also continued to support regional economic cooperation, whether by expanding TPP or concluding RCEP.[19]

But in foreign policy too Abe's failings stand out. Not only does the pandemic mean that during the remainder of his term it is highly unlikely that Abe will recover any of the Northern Territories from Russia or resolve the abductees issue with North Korea once and for all—part of his desired "settling of accounts" for postwar diplomacy—but his failure to reach a modus vivendi with a South Korea could have increasingly large opportunity costs for a Japan that needs all the friends it can find the region. Repairing the relationship with South Korea, now a global model for public health and a leading champion for democracy after it held a general election (with record turnout!) in the middle of the pandemic, will be imperative for whoever succeeds him.

* * *

There is no doubt now that the age of Abe is drawing to a close. Whether in September 2021, or, if the public abandons him and his party, sometime sooner, Abe will yield the premiership. To some extent, he may be a casualty of the Covid-19 pandemic, in that it revealed Abe's premiership as increasingly exhausted and the public increasingly fatigued by the prime minister—and turned what was supposed to be his valedictory year into a crisis without parallel.

But the pandemic has not fundamentally changed how Abe is likely to be remembered after his political career draws to a close. His efforts to spark a national renaissance—to fill the Japanese people with the belief that their country is capable of anything and to cement Japan's place in the ranks of the great powers—already appeared tenuous and the long-term strength of the Japanese economy was in doubt before a new recession began in 2020. The crisis has perhaps accelerated the competition between China and the US, putting Japan in an uncomfortable position, but it was already apparent that Japan's leaders would struggle to balance between Asia's dominant powers going forward.

Japan's future is already here, and the final task left for Abe will be to ensure a smooth transition to a new leader who can begin building anew with the tools—new central government institutions, international partnerships, and an example of pragmatic, risk-taking statecraft—that Abe will leave behind.

Bethesda, Maryland, July 2020

NOTES

1. THE LAST HEISEI PRIME MINISTER

1. 「首相がダメ出ししてた！？元号の選定で何が」NHK 政治マガジン, 15 May 2019, https://www.nhk.or.jp/politics/articles/feature/17483.html, last accessed 4 May 2020.
2. "Press Conference by the Prime Minister Shinzo Abe," Cabinet Public Relations Office, Cabinet Secretariat, Tokyo, Japan, 1 April 2019, https://japan.kantei.go.jp/98_abe/statement/201904/_00002.html, last accessed 4 May 2020.
3. Jake Adelstein, "Japan Has a New Emperor and a New Era, but a Dark Future," *Daily Beast*, 1 May 2019, https://www.thedailybeast.com/japan-has-a-new-emperor-naruhito-and-a-new-era-but-a-dark-future-under-shinzo-abe, last accessed 4 May 2020.
4. See Ellen Kay Trimberger, *Revolution from Above: Military Bureaucrats and Development in Japan, Turkey, Egypt, and Peru*, New Brunswick, NJ: Transaction Books, 1978.
5. Abe Shinzō, "Policy Speech to the 166th Session of the Diet," Tokyo, 26 Jan. 2007, http://japan.kantei.go.jp/abespeech/2007/01/26speech_e.html, accessed 23 Nov. 2019.
6. Abe Shinzō, "Policy Speech to the 183rd Session of the Diet," Tokyo, 28 Jan. 2013, https://japan.kantei.go.jp/96_abe/statement/201301/28syosin_e.html, accessed 23 Nov. 2019.
7. On the "age of entropy," see Randall Schweller, *Maxwell's Demon and the Golden Apple*, Baltimore: Johns Hopkins University Press, 2014, introduction *passim*. On the decline of US leadership, see Alexander Cooley and Daniel Nexon, *Exit from Hegemony: The Unraveling of the American Global Order*, New York: Oxford University Press, 2020.

8. 「元号案見た首相「うーん」 追加案依頼、看板政策重ねた」, 朝日新聞, https://digital.asahi.com/articles/ASM4Y5D15M4YUTFK00R.html, accessed 23 Nov. 2019.
9. Abe Shinzō, "Japan is Back," speech at the Center for Strategic and International Studies, Washington, DC, 22 Feb. 2013, https://japan.kantei.go.jp/96_abe/statement/201302/22speech_e.html, accessed 23 Nov. 2019.
10. Abe Shinzō, "Defeatism about Japan is now defeated," speech at the World Economic Forum, Davos, Switzerland, 23 Jan. 2019, https://www.weforum.org/agenda/2019/01/abe-speech-transcript, accessed 23 Nov. 2019.
11. *Naiyū gaikan*—"troubles at home and dangers from abroad"—was a slogan coined early in the nineteenth century to capture the problems increasingly besetting the Tokugawa shogunate. See Chushichi Tsuzuki, *Pursuit of Power in Modern Japan, 1825–1995*, New York: Oxford University Press, 2000, 33.

2. THE BIRTH OF A DYNASTY

1. 安倍洋子, 『私の安倍晋太郎』, Tokyo: Nesco, 1992, pp. 109–111.
2. Although his mother-in-law disapproved as a matter of principle, since, she thought, a journalist would work long hours and would be uncouth. Ibid.
3. To this day, Japanese political reporters engage in *asamawari* (morning rounds) and *yomawari* (evening rounds), following powerful politicians around as a standard practice of newsgathering, often in the process developing close relationships with their subjects. The result is that, as the late foreign correspondent Sam Jameson once told me, Japanese journalists know much more than their American colleagues but report significantly less of what they know.
4. 野上忠興, 『安倍晋三 沈黙の画面』, Tokyo: Shōgakukan, 2015, p. 32.
5. "Why are so many adults adopted in Japan?," *The Economist Explains*, 17 April 2013, https://www.economist.com/the-economist-explains/2013/04/16/why-are-so-many-adults-adopted-in-japan, last accessed 23 Nov. 2019.
6. Mark Ravina, *To Stand with the Nations of the World: Japan's Meiji Restoration in World History*, New York: Oxford University Press, 2017, pp. 148–149.
7. On Taishō Democracy, see Peter Duus, *Party Rivalry and Political Change in Taishō Japan*, Cambridge, MA: Harvard University Press, 1968.

8. Margaret Macmillan, *Paris 1919: Six Months That Changed the World*, New York: Random House, 2003, ch. 23 passim. See S.C.M. Paine, *The Wars for Asia, 1911–1949*, New York: Cambridge University Press, 2012 on how geopolitical change in the early decades of the twentieth century laid the roots for the Second World War in Asia.
9. On Kita Ikki's ideas, see Walter A. Skya, *Japan's Holy War: The Ideology of Radical Shintō Ultranationalism*, Durham: Duke University Press, 2009, ch. 4 passim.
10. Dan Kurzman, *Kishi and Japan*, New York: Ivan Obolensky, 1960, p. 92.
11. 原彬久, 『岸信介—権勢の政治家』, Tokyo: Iwanami Shoten, 1995. Chapters 2 and 3 address his student years and early bureaucratic career. While Kishi denied any attraction to Marxism as a student and after the war was outspoken in his anti-communism, his biographer Hara Yoshihisa suggests that between his interest in the first Soviet five-year plan as a young bureaucrat, his close cooperation with Socialist politicians in the early postwar period, and his willingness to borrow ideas from the Japan Socialist Party, he may have been attracted to socialism as a student radical.
12. Michael A. Barnhart, *Japan Prepares for Total War*, Ithaca: Cornell University Press, 1987, p. 18.
13. Janis Mimura, *Planning for Empire*, Ithaca, NY: Cornell University Press, 2011.
14. Haruo Iguchi, *Unfinished Business: Ayukawa Yoshisuke and US–Japan Relations, 1937–1953*, Cambridge, MA: Harvard University Press, 2003, p. 30.
15. Eri Hotta, *Pan-Asianism and Japan's War*, New York: Palgrave Macmillan, 2007, p. 125.
16. Hara, op. cit., p. 76.
17. Files from the International Military Tribunal for the Far East make note of the *ni-ki, san-suke* as the "Manchurian gang" that seized power. Kishi's relationship with Tōjō as part of the "Manchurian gang" was cited as a reason for treating him as a Class A war criminal. "Kishi, Kikuchi, Kihara, Iwamura, Ishihara," General Reports and Memoranda from June 1947, Official Records of the International Military Tribunal for the Far East, University of Virginia Law Library, http://imtfe.law.virginia.edu/collections/tavenner/5/1/kishi-kikuchi-kihara-iwamura-ishihara, last accessed 23 Nov. 2019.
18. 原, op. cit., p. 97. For his role in this plot, Kishi was targeted for assassination by the *Kempeitai*, Japan's wartime secret police.
19. Ibid., p. 98.

20. Dan Kurzman, who in 1960 wrote an English-language biography with extensive input from Kishi himself, suggests that Kishi was sincerely trying to "cultivate the seeds of an antimilitarist popular movement" and therefore had to mask his true intentions behind talk of rallying the people behind the war effort, but Kurzman makes no mention of the brotherhood. Later scholarship strongly suggests that Kishi sincerely supported the prosecution of the war until the end.
21. 東中野多聞, 「岸信介と護国同志会」史学雑誌108 (9), 1999, pp. 1619–1638. As part of his tour of the prefecture, Kishi paid a visit to Abe Kan in the spring of 1945. Virtually the only record of the meeting that survives is a photograph of the two men, which surfaced after Abe Shintarō's death. Kan would die less than a year later and neither had any idea that their children would marry. This meeting is described in 青木理, 『安部三代』, Tokyo: Asahi Shimbun Publications, 2017, p. 75.
22. 原, op. cit., p. 105.
23. Paul J. Heer, *Mr. X and The Pacific: George F. Kennan and American Policy in East Asia*, Ithaca, NY: Cornell University Press, p. 51 and ch. 3 passim.
24. John Dower, *Embracing Defeat*, New York: Norton, 1999, p. 525.
25. 原, op. cit., pp. 127–128.
26. Sandra Wilson, Robert Cribb, Beatrice Trefalt, and Dean Aszkielowicz, *Japanese War Criminals*, New York: Columbia University Press, 2017.
27. In April 1949, less than half a year after Kishi's release, the occupation reestablished the former MCI as the Ministry of International Trade and Industry (MITI) to guide Japan's reindustrialization. Michael Schaller, *Altered States*, New York: Oxford University Press, 1997, p. 18.
28. 原, op. cit., p. 140.
29. 松田賢弥, 『絶頂の一族』, Tokyo: Kōdansha, 2015, pp. 60–61. See Kurzman, op. cit., pp. 254–256 for a colorful description of Kishi's first night out of Sugamo.
30. Richard Samuels, *Machiavelli's Children*, Ithaca, NY: Cornell University Press, 2003, p. 230.
31. Schaller, op. cit., p. 27.
32. See John Dower, *Empire and Aftermath: Yoshida Shigeru and the Japanese Experience 1878–1954*, Cambridge, MA: Harvard University Press, 1988, ch. 11 on conflict between Japanese conservatives over the Yoshida Doctrine.
33. Quoted in Kenneth Pyle, *Japan in the American Century*, Cambridge, MA: Harvard University Press, 2018, p. 167.
34. Kurzman, op. cit., p. 256.

35. 原, op. cit., pp. 150–151.
36. Ibid., p. 152.
37. Dower, *Empire and Aftermath*, p. 372.
38. Liberal Democratic Party, "Party Platform," 15 November 1955, https://www.jimin.jp/aboutus/declaration/100285.html, last accessed 23 Nov. 2019.
39. 原, op. cit., pp. 168–177.
40. 安藤俊裕,「岸信介の娘婿、新聞記者から政界へ 「悲運のプリンス」安倍晋太郎(1)」, 日経新聞 9 June 2013, https://www.nikkei.com/article/DGXNASFK0301I_T00C13A6000000, last accessed 23 Nov. 2019.
41. 松田, op. cit., pp. 127–8; 安藤, ibid.
42. 青木, op. cit., p. 20.
43. 松田, op. cit., p. 113.
44. 野上忠興,『気骨—安倍晋三のDNA』, Tokyo: Kōdansha, 2004, p. 58.
45. 野上,『安倍晋三』, p. 22.
46. 野上,『安倍晋三』, p. 16.
47. 青山和弘,『安倍さんと本音で話した７００時間』, Tokyo: PHP, 2015, p. 67.
48. 青木, op. cit., p. 207.
49. 野上,『気骨』, p. 67.
50. 野上,『安倍晋三』, p. 49.
51. Kurzman, op. cit., 11.
52. Nick Kapur, *Japan at the Crossroads*, Cambridge, MA: Harvard University Press, 2018, p. 11.
53. Pyle, op. cit., p. 205.
54. George Packard, *Protest in Tokyo*, Princeton: Princeton University Press, 1966, p. 53.
55. Schaller, op. cit., p. 136.
56. *Foreign Relations of the United States*, 1958–1960, Volume XVIII, Japan; Korea, Document 18, https://history.state.gov/historicaldocuments/frus1958-60v18/d18, last accessed 23 Nov. 2019. See also Packard, op. cit., pp. 54–80 for an account of intra-LDP debates about treaty revision. On the creation of the Self-Defense Forces, see Sheila A. Smith, *Japan Rearmed: The Politics of Military Power*, Cambridge, MA: Harvard University Press, 2019, pp. 27–32.
57. 石川真澄,『戦後政治史』新版, Tokyo: Iwanami Shoten, 2004, pp. 85–86.
58. Packard, op. cit., pp. 180–181.
59. Ibid., p. 103.
60. Ibid., pp. 186–187.
61. Ibid., p. 237.
62. Kapur, op. cit., pp. 25–27.

63. 長谷川隼人,『岸内閣期の内政・外交路線の歴史的再検討：「福祉国家」、「経済外交」という視点から』, Ph.D. dissertation, Hitotsubashi University, 2015, http://doi.org/10.15057/27304, accessed on 23 Nov. 2019.
64. 北岡伸一,「日本外交の座標軸」,『外交』6, October 2011, https://www.mofa.go.jp/mofaj/press/pr/gaikou/vol6/pdfs/gaikou_vol6_07.pdf, last accessed 23 Nov. 2019.
65. Samuels notes another advantage: Kishi ensured that reparations would be provided in the form of Japanese manufactured goods and services, creating new market opportunities for politically connected trading houses. *Machiavelli's Children*, pp. 238–239.
66. *Congressional Record*, Senate, 103rd Congress, Volume 103, Part 7, 20 June 1957, p. 9777.
67. Japan's economic miracle had many fathers, and, as Minister of International Trade and Industry under Kishi as well as the prime minister who advanced the "income-doubling" plan, Ikeda's claim is stronger than most. See Mark Metzler, *Capital as Will and Imagination*, Ithaca, NY: Cornell University Press, 2013, p. 183.
68. 松田, op. cit., p. 132; 安藤俊裕,「福田派の若手エースに「悲運のプリンス」安倍晋太郎 (2) 」日経新聞, 16 June 2013, https://www.nikkei.com/article/DGXNASFK10028_R10C13A6000000, last accessed 23 Nov. 2019.
69. Ibid., 130.
70. 安倍晋三、『美しい国へ』, Tokyo: Bungei Shunjū, 2006, pp. 22–23.
71. 野上,『安倍晋三』, p. 41.
72. He famously recounts the story of the protests early in『美しい国へ』while in a 2005 essay he recounts visiting his grandfather at Keio University Hospital—which would be an important setting in his own career—after the stabbing. See 安倍晋三,「吉田松蔭の言葉」in『奇跡—安倍晋三語録』, Tokyo: Kairyūsha, 2013, p. 9.
73. 松田, op. cit., p. 70.
74. Ibid., p. 209.
75. On Japan's political dynasties, see Daniel M. Smith, *Dynasties and Democracy: The Inherited Incumbency Advantage in Japan*, Stanford, CA: Stanford University Press, 2018.

3. THE WORLD THAT MADE SHINZŌ

1. Paul Droubie, "Playing the Nation: 1964 Tokyo Summer Olympics and Japanese Identity," Ph.D. Dissertation, University of Illinois, 2009, ch. 3 passim.

2. 安倍晋三、『美しい国へ』, Tokyo: Bungei Shunjū, 2006, p. 76.
3. Christian Tagsold, "The 1964 Tokyo Olympics as Political Games," *The Asia-Pacific Journal*, Vol. 23–3–09, June 8, 2009, https://apjjf.org/-Christian-Tagsold/3165/article.html, last accessed 23 Nov. 2019.
4. 安倍晋三, op. cit., p. 78.
5. Quoted in Jordan Sand, *Tokyo Vernacular*, Berkeley: University of California Press, 2013, p. 128.
6. Aoki Kumiko, a scholar at the Open University of Japan, has discussed the "ideologization" of Shōwa nostalgia, how appreciation or fetishization of the era has reshaped political preferences. She includes Abe's discussion of *ALWAYS: San-chome no yuhi* as an example. 「変わりゆく『昭和30年代ブーム』」『社会科学論考』 32 (2011) pp. 83–107.
7. 安倍晋三, op. cit., p. 219.
8. See Abe's future economic policy adviser Hamada Koichi's reflections on this milestone. Koichi Hamada, "Japan 1968: A Reflection Point During the Era of the Economic Miracle," Economic Growth Center Discussion Paper No. 764, Yale University, August 1996, http://www.econ.yale.edu/growth_pdf/cdp764.pdf, last accessed 23 Nov. 2019.
9. Carol Gluck, "The Past in the Present," in Andrew Gordon, ed., *Postwar Japan as History*, Berkeley: University of California Press, 1993, p. 75. See also 吉川洋, 『高度成長』, Tokyo: Chukō Bunko, 2012, ch. 2 passim on the creation of a mass consumption society.
10. On Tanaka and his politics, see Jacob Schlesinger, *Shadow Shoguns: The Rise and Fall of Japan's Postwar Political Machine*, Stanford, CA: Stanford University Press, 1997.
11. 安藤俊裕, 「無情の中曽根裁定、病に倒れる 「悲運のプリンス」安倍晋太郎 (4)」日経新聞, 30 June 2013, https://www.nikkei.com/article/DGXNASFK24019_U3A620C1000000, last accessed 23 Nov. 2019.
12. 青木理, 『安部三代』, Tokyo: Asahi Shimbun Publishers, 2017, p. 156.
13. 安倍晋三, 「私の保守政治家宣言」 in 栗本慎一郎, 安倍晋三, and 衛藤晟一, 『「保守革命」宣言』, Tokyo: Gendai Shorin, 1996 p. 44. Author's translation.
14. 野上, 『安倍晋三』, p. 35.
15. 青木, op. cit., p. 210.
16. 野上, 『安倍晋三』, p. 27.
17. 青木, op. cit., p. 220.
18. Ibid., p. 238.
19. See Thomas P. Rohlen, "The *Juku* Phenomenon: An Exploratory Essay," *The Journal of Japanese Studies*, 6, 2 (Summer 1980), pp. 207–242.
20. Ibid., pp. 62–63, 72.

21. Oguma Eiji, "Japan's 1968: A Collective Reaction to Rapid Economic Growth in an Age of Turmoil", Nick Kapur with Samuel Malissa and Stephen Poland, trans., *The Asia-Pacific Journal*, Vol. 13, Issue 11, No. 1, March 23, 2015. https://apjjf.org/2015/13/11/Oguma-Eiji/4300.html, last accessed 4 May 2020.
22. 青山, op. cit., p. 28. Author's translation.
23. 青木, op. cit., p. 208.
24. 野上, 『気骨』, p. 98.
25. 安倍, 『美しい国へ』, pp. 20–21.
26. 青木, op. cit., p. 226.
27. See, for example, ibid., p. 230.
28. Japan's academic year starts in April and ends in March.
29. 野上, 『気骨』, pp. 103–104.
30. 野上, 『安倍晋三』, p. 64. See also 青木, op. cit., p. 260.
31. 青山, op. cit., p. 54.
32. 野上, 『安倍晋三』, p. 74.
33. 野上, 『気骨』, pp. 107–108.
34. Abe Shinzō, "Toward an Alliance of Hope," Address to a Joint Meeting of the US Congress, 29 April 2015, https://japan.kantei.go.jp/97_abe/statement/201504/uscongress.html, last accessed 4 May 2020.
35. 野上, 『気骨』, p. 109.
36. Hayashi's son Yoshimasa would go on to a political career of his own, winning a seat in the House of Councillors, serving under Abe in several cabinet posts, and vying for the LDP's leadership in 2012.
37. 野上, 『気骨』, pp. 110–113.
38. 野上, 『安倍晋三』, p. 86.
39. 安倍, 『美しい国へ』, p. 30. Author's translation.
40. 安倍, 『美しい国へ』, p. 31. Author's translation.
41. 野上, 『安倍晋三』, p. 98.
42. 野上, 『気骨』, p. 133.
43. Matthew M. Carlson and Steven R. Reed, *Political Corruption and Scandals in Japan* (Ithaca: Cornell University Press, 2018) pp. 38–42.
44. Samuels, *Machiavelli's Children*, p. 226.
45. 野上, 『安倍晋三』, p. 100.
46. 安倍, 『美しい国へ』, p. 32.
47. Ibid., p. 33.
48. At the time, his 1,333 days as foreign minister were the longest tenure for a postwar Japanese foreign minister and the longest since Kishi's foreign minister, Fujiyama. In the interim, only one foreign minister had even come close to 1,000 days in office. Shintarō's record

would last until it was broken by Kishida Fumio during Shinzō's second administration.

49. Foreign Relations Committee, House of Representatives, National Diet of Japan, 1 August 1984. Available at http://kokkai.ndl.go.jp, last accessed 16 February 2019.
50. 安藤俊裕, 『政客列伝』, Tokyo: Nikkei Shimbun, 2013, p. 402.
51. 菊池正史, 安倍晋三 「保守」の正体』, Tokyo: Bungei Shinsho, 2017, pp. 143–159.
52. 野上, 『気骨』, pp. 152–153. Years later, in a video recorded when receiving an award at the Mt. Fuji Dialogue, an annual gathering of US and Japanese alliance managers, Shultz was misty-eyed recalling his relationship with Shintarō.
53. 野上, 『気骨』, pp. 154–155.
54. 野上, 『安倍晋三』, pp. 112–113.
55. Ibid., pp. 114–116.
56. On the meeting, see 塩田潮 『密談の戦後史』, Tokyo: Kadokawa, 2018, p. 160.
57. 野上,『気骨』, pp. 156–158.
58. 松田, op. cit., p. 142.
59. Carlson and Reed, op. cit., pp. 49–50.
60. Uno also embarrassed the LDP when reports surfaced that he had treated a mistress poorly. See Paul Blustein, "The Feminist Geisha," *The Washington Post*, 19 July 1989, https://www.washingtonpost.com/archive/lifestyle/1989/07/19/the-feminist-geisha/e8348ea5-5042-48a8-96a1-0fffcc521614/?utm_term=.7a78aca2a5bf, last accessed 4 May 2020.
61. 安倍, 『美しい国へ』, pp. 36–37.

4. THE ICONOCLAST

1. This idea was suggested to me by Yamaguchi upper house member Hayashi Yoshimasa.
2. As the Scottish writer Robert Louis Stevenson wrote of Yoshida, "He hoped, perhaps, to get the good of other lands without their evil; to enable Japan to profit by the knowledge of the barbarians, and still keep her inviolate with her own arts and virtues." Robert Louis Stevenson, *Familiar Studies of Men and Books* New York: Charles Scribner's Sons, 1908, p. 150.
3. 安倍晋三, 「吉田松陰の言葉」 in 『軌跡—跡安倍晋三語録』, Tokyo: Kairyusha, 2013, p. 9.

4. Plenary session, House of Councillors, National Diet of Japan, 21 November 2017, http://kokkai.ndl.go.jp/SENTAKU/sangiin/195/0001/19511210001004a.html, last accessed 4 May 2020.
5. In Japanese politics, a candidate's strength has been assessed based on the so-called three "ban": *jiban* (a support base), *kanban* (name recognition), and *kaban* (money). Abe had inherited all three from his late father. On the three "ban," see Daniel M. Smith, *Dynasties and Democracy: The Inherited Incumbency Advantage in Japan* Stanford, CA: Stanford University Press, 2018, p. 120.
6. 安倍洋子, 『私の安倍晋太郎』, p. 179.
7. 野上, 『安倍晋三』, p. 133. Author's translation.
8. On "Japan bashing" in the United States in the 1980s and 1990s, see M.J. Heale, "Anatomy of a Scare: Yellow Peril Politics in America, 1980–1993," *Journal of American Studies* 43 (2009) 1, 19–47.
9. Abe recounts this slight in 『美しい国へ』, p. 136.
10. Jun Hongo, "Tokyo's Stock Bubble: 25 Years on From Nikkei Peak," *Japan Real Time*, 29 December 2014, https://blogs.wsj.com/japanrealtime/2014/12/29/tokyos-stock-bubble-25-years-on-from-the-nikkei-peak, last accessed 4 May 2020.
11. 野上, 『気骨』, pp. 177–179.
12. 青木, op. cit., pp. 262, 266.
13. On Nakasone's legacy, see Kenneth Pyle, *The Japanese Question*, 2nd ed. Washington, DC: AEI Press, 1996, pp. 103–105.
14. 菊池, op. cit., 179. See also Amy Catalinac, *Electoral Reform and National Security in Japan*, New York: Cambridge University Press, 2016, pp. 47–50 especially.
15. J. Patrick Boyd and Richard J. Samuels, *Nine Lives?: The Politics of Constitutional Reform in Japan*, Washington, DC: East-West Center, 2005, p. 26; 菊池, op. cit., pp. 183–185.
16. 安倍, 『美しい国へ』, p. 38. Author's translation. From context, it is clear that Abe is using "conservative mainstream" to refer to the right wing and not the center-right Yoshida wing that had historically been called the LDP's mainstream. In this usage, Abe may be reflecting the views of an informal adviser, Kyoto University international relations professor Nakanishi Terumasa, who believed that Kishi, Hatoyama Ichirō, Nakasone, and Abe actually represented the conservative mainstream. See 大下英治, 『安倍晋三と岸信介』, Tokyo: Kadokawa, 2013, p. 129.
17. 菅野完, 『日本会議の研究』, Tokyo: Fusōsha, 2016, pp. 62–68.
18. 野上, 『気骨』, p. 217.
19. Ibid., p. 188. Nishibe, who committed suicide in 2018, was a prom-

inent right-wing public intellectual who, in his numerous publications and television appearances, was stridently opposed to postwar Japan and its dependence on the United States. For a concise summary of Nishibe's views, see Richard Samuels, *Securing Japan*, Ithaca, NY: Cornell University Press, 2007, pp. 121–122. Samuels identifies Nishibe as a "Gaullist" who wanted Japan to be both heavily armed and independent from the US. Nishibe wanted Japan to introduce conscription, spend more on defense, and even acquire its own nuclear deterrent.

20. Ibid., pp. 44–45.
21. 柿崎 明二, 『検証　安倍イズム』, Tokyo: Iwanami Shoten, 2015, pp. 89–90.
22. 安倍, 美しい国へ』, p. 4; 栗本慎一郎, 安倍晋三, and 衛藤晟一, op. cit., p. 51.
23. Quoted in 菊池, op. cit., p. 61. Author's translation.
24. Kishi's protégé Fukuda, when he became the first and thus far only incumbent LDP prime minister defeated in a party leadership election in 1978, famously said, "Sometimes the voice of heaven has a strange voice."
25. Gerald Curtis, *The Logic of Japanese Politics* New York: Columbia University Press, 2000, 118–120.
26. Looking back to the Meiji Restoration, pragmatism has been a hallmark of otherwise highly idealistic Japanese politicians. It is perhaps not coincidental that Richard Nixon opens an essay about pragmatism with a quote from Nakasone.
27. Sometimes translated as the "ethic of ultimate ends."
28. H.H. Gerth and C. Wright Mills, eds., trans., *From Max Weber: Essays in Sociology* New York: Oxford University Press, 1946, p. 127.
29. 栗本慎一郎, 安倍晋三, and 衛藤晟一, op. cit., p. 45.
30. Another intellectual influence would be Okazaki Hisahiko. A career diplomat, Abe first became acquainted with Okazaki when he served as his father's secretary at MOFA. Okazaki, who had spent time at the Japan Defense Agency in the 1970s and would serve as the first chief of the intelligence bureau in the 1980s, believed that Japan needed a strong state that could defend lives, liberty, and property from external threats. Okazaki and Abe published a book together in 2004 in which they made this argument, and Okazaki was an informal adviser to Abe until his death in 2014. Okazaki, unlike some of the other more "Gaullist" thinkers in Abe's circle, argued emphatically that Japan needed to be a maritime power allied with the United States.

31. 安倍,『美しい国へ』, pp. 60–61.
32. Some Meiji statesmen, including Yamaguchi's Itō Hirobumi, traveled to the United States and Europe in 1871–1873 as part of the Iwakura mission, which included a meeting with German Chancellor Otto von Bismarck. Bismarck, fresh from victory over France, warned the visiting Japanese about the realities of the international order. "Weak countries are always at a disadvantage. This was true for Prussia, but Prussia was able to change it, helped by the patriotism of its people." See Ulrich Wattenberg, "Germany 7–28 March, 15–17 April, 1–8 May 1873," in Ian Nish, ed., *The Iwakura Mission in America and Europe: A New Assessment* London: Japan Library, 1998, p. 76. As a popular song of the Meiji era—"Song of Diplomacy"—went, "In the West there is England / In the North, Russia. / My countrymen, be careful! / Outwardly, they make treaties, / But you cannot tell / What is at the bottom of their hearts. / There is a Law of Nations, it is true, / But when then moment comes, remember, / The Strong eat up the Weak."
33. 安倍,『美しい国へ』, p. 66.
34. Abe lamented that for too long the LDP was simply a party for "anyone who rejects communism." 栗本慎一郎, 安倍晋三, and 衛藤晟一, op. cit., p. 37. See also 安倍,『美しい国へ』, p. 27.
35. See Ozawa's *Blueprint for a New Japan* New York: Kodansha USA, 1994. In the early days of his political career, Abe's mother connected Shinzō with Ozawa, who had of course already left the LDP but felt indebted to Shintarō for kindnesses bestowed as Ozawa rose through the party's ranks. In an October 1993 appearance in deliberations of the House of Representatives Foreign Affairs Committee, one of his first appearances in Diet deliberations, Shinzō also voiced his approval of Ozawa's vision of Japan as a "normal nation." Foreign Affairs Committee, House of Representatives, National Diet of Japan, 22 October 1993, http://kokkai.ndl.go.jp/SENTAKU/syugiin/128/0110/12810220110003a.html, last accessed 8 March 2019.
36. Special Committee regarding Guidelines for US-Japan Defense Cooperation, House of Representatives, National Diet of Japan, 1 April 1999, http://kokkai.ndl.go.jp/SENTAKU/syugiin/145/0072/14504010072005a.html, last accessed 18 March 2019.
37. Thomas U. Berger, *Cultures of Antimilitarism* (Baltimore: Johns Hopkins University Press, 1998). In the 1996 manifesto with Kurimoto and Etō, Abe argues that the prime minister ought to have a uniformed aide from the Self-Defense Forces, mocking the idea that just because the prime minister has uniformed personnel in his vicinity Japan will

suddenly invade China. 栗本慎一郎, 安倍晋三, and 衛藤晟一, op. cit., p. 187.

38. Abe is not alone in scorning the role played by "New Dealers" in drafting the constitution. Notwithstanding the antipathy between Kishi and Yoshida Shigeru, Yoshida also has unkind words for the occupation's "New Dealers" in his memoirs: "Not only in the Government Section, but in all sections outside the General Staff, there seems to have existed a good sprinkling of radical elements—what might be called 'New Dealers'—among the younger members, particularly at the beginning of the Occupation. These belonged to the group that I have classified as the idealists, and traces still remain of their having sought to utilize occupied Japan as an experimental ground for testing out their theories of progress and reform. They included elements that were rather more than radical, and which made friends with Japan's own Left-wingers and, in some cases, worked on them for their own purposes." Shigeru Yoshida, *The Yoshida Memoirs*, Kenichi Yoshida trans. London: Heineman, 1961, p. 54.
39. 栗本慎一郎, 安倍晋三, and 衛藤晟一, op. cit., p. 45.
40. "Press Conference by Prime Minister Abe," Cabinet Public Relations Office, Cabinet Secretariat, 26 September 2006, http://warp.ndl.go.jp/info:ndljp/pid/11236451/www.kantei.go.jp/jp/abespeech/2006/09/26press.html, last accessed 19 March 2019.
41. 安倍, 『美しい国へ』, p. 91.
42. Ibid., p. 96.
43. 栗本慎一郎, 安倍晋三, and 衛藤晟一, op. cit., p. 38.
44. Kenneth Ruoff, *The People's Emperor* Cambridge, MA: Harvard University Press, 2001, pp. 258–259.
45. Nippon Kaigi, 「日本会議が目指すもの」, http://www.nipponkaigi.org/about/mokuteki, last accessed 19 March 2019.
46. Helen Hardacre's *Shinto: A History* New York: Oxford University Press, 2017, pp. 441–447.
47. "Transcript of Emperor Akihito's Speech," *The New York Times*, 8 August 2016. https://www.nytimes.com/2016/08/09/world/asia/transcript-japan-emperor-akihito-speech.html, last accessed 20 March 2019.
48. Hardacre, *Shinto*, 395–397. Hardacre notes that the tradition of war memorial sites began in Choshū in 1864 before spreading to other domains and then becoming "nationalized" at Yasukuni.
49. In *Towards a Beautiful Country*, Abe uses the words of Georgetown University professor Kevin Doak to make this point. 安倍, 『美しい国へ』, p. 74.

50. In the 1960s, the LDP suggested that the shrine should desacralize, which would enable it to receive public funds; Nakasone would later favor a national war memorial because he thought it would be impossible for the shrine ever to become nonreligious. See Hardacre, *Shinto*, pp. 461–463.
51. Kevin Doak, *A History of Nationalism in Modern Japan* Boston: Brill, 2007, p. 39.
52. 安倍, 『美しい国へ』, p. 202. Author's translation.
53. Dower, *Embracing Defeat*, p. 250.
54. Helen Hardacre, *Shintō and the State, 1868–1988* Princeton: Princeton University Press, 1989, pp. 121–122.
55. Michiya Shimbori, "A Historical and Social Note on Moral Education in Japan," *Comparative Education Review* 4, 2 (October 1960) 97–101.
56. Edward Beauchamp, "The Development of Japanese Educational Policy, 1945–85," *History of Education Quarterly* 27, 3 (Autumn 1987) 304.
57. Abe regularly cites the conformist progressivism of his teachers and other intellectual elites during his teenage years as one factor that pushed him to embrace conservatism. See, for example, 栗本慎一郎, 安倍晋三, and 衛藤晟一, op. cit., pp. 43–44.
58. Committee on Foreign Affairs, National Diet of Japan, House of Councillors, 24 October 1996, http://kokkai.ndl.go.jp/SENTAKU/sangiin/134/1110/13410241110002a.html, last accessed 22 March 2019.
59. 「日本歴史教科書問題」, Abe Shinzō homepage, 16 April 1998. https://web.archive.org/web/20000301131156/http://www.s-abe.or.jp/index2.htm. Accessed 23 March 2019.
60. Abe would eulogize Nakagawa as a particularly dogged foe of "masochistic history" in meetings of the junior parliamentarians group. 安倍, 『軌跡』, p. 133.
61. See, for example, Abe's remarks in a Diet debate on history textbooks in 1997. http://kokkai.ndl.go.jp/SENTAKU/syugiin/140/0414/14005270414002a.html.
62. 安倍, 『美しい国へ』, p. 207. Author's translation.

5. CHAMPION OF THE ABDUCTEES

1. The Japan Socialist Party had long enjoyed close relations with Pyongyang, but the Japanese Communist Party was at odds with North Korea and JCP legislators had raised questions about the abductions as early as 1988. See 「拉致問題88年以来、質問を積み重ね解決の道開いた日本

共産党国会議員団」, *Shimbun Akahata*, 18 November 2002, https://www.jcp.or.jp/akahata/aik/2002-11-18/04_0401.html, last accessed 4 April 2019.

2. 安倍,『美しい国へ』, p. 44.
3. Christopher W. Hughes, "The Political Economy of Japanese Sanctions Towards North Korea: Domestic Coalitions and International Systemic Pressures," *Pacific Affairs* 79, 3 (Fall 2006) 470. On Kanemaru's trip, see Victor Cha, *The Impossible State*, updated edition New York: Ecco, 2018, pp. 373–374. North Korea may have been the source of the gold bullion that was found when Kanemaru was arrested in 1993
4. Robert Boynton, *The Invitation-Only Zone* New York: Farrar, Straus and Giroux, 2016, pp. 62–64.
5. 安倍,『美しい国へ』, p. 45.
6. Foreign Relations Committee, House of Representatives, National Diet of Japan, 16 May 1997, http://kokkai.ndl.go.jp/SENTAKU/syugiin/140/0110/14005160110014a.html, last accessed 3 April 2019.
7. As Richard Samuels notes, media organizations were no less responsible for Japan's dilatory response to the abductions than other establishment institutions, since, other than the conservative *Sankei Shimbun*, mainstream news outlets completely ignored the suspected abductions for more than a decade. Richard J. Samuels, "Kidnapping Politics in East Asia," *Journal of East Asian Studies* 10, 3 (2010): 363–395.
8. 野上,『気骨』, pp. 217–218.
9. Nicholas Kristof, "Japan Intercepts Two Boats That May Be North Korean," The *New York Times*, 24 March 1999, https://www.nytimes.com/1999/03/24/world/japan-intercepts-two-boats-that-may-be-north-korean.html, last accessed 4 April 2019.
10. Foreign Relations Committee, House of Representatives, National Diet of Japan, 29 October 1997, http://kokkai.ndl.go.jp/SENTAKU/syugiin/141/0110/14110290110002a.html, last accessed 4 April 2019.
11. On the evolution of abductee activism—and the role of elite allies like Abe in raising the issue to national prominence, see Celeste Arrington, *Accidental Activists: Victim Movements and Government Accountability in Japan and South Korea*, Ithaca, NY: Cornell University Press, 2016, ch. 5 passim.
12. Cabinet Office of Japan, "Public Opinion Survey Concerning Diplomacy—2000," 22 January 2001, https://survey.gov-online.go.jp/h12/gaikou_01/index.html, last accessed 4 April 2019.
13. 野上,『気骨』, p. 223. Hasuike Toru, brother of Hasuike Kaoru, who was one of the abductees who returned to Japan after Koizumi's meet-

ing with Kim Jong Il, was heavily involved in abductee activism even after his brother returned home and supported a hardline approach to pressure North Korea to resolve the issue fully. However, by 2008, he became skeptical of the wisdom of pressuring North Korea via sanctions, and eventually left the activist groups. In December 2015, he published a book that explicitly accused Abe of exploiting the abductees for political gain.

14. Ibid, p. 231.
15. Gerald L. Curtis, *The Logic of Japanese Politics* New York: Columbia University Press, 2000, p. 172. See also Robert M. Uriu, *Clinton and Japan* New York: Oxford University Press, 2009, p. 224.
16. 星浩, 「小選挙区時代の総選選び」『安倍政権の日本』, Tokyo: Asahi Shimbun Publishing, 2006. Digital.
17. Hashimoto Ryutarō, "Policy Speech to the 136th session of the Diet," 22 January 1996, The World and Japan Database, National Graduate Institute for Policy Studies, http://worldjpn.grips.ac.jp/documents/texts/pm/19960122.SWJ.html, last accessed 28 March 2019. He would pursue "six great reforms," transforming social security, public administration, government finances, the financial system, local government, and education. 石川, op cit., p. 193.
18. "Central Government Reform of Japan," Prime Minister of Japan, January 2001, https://japan.kantei.go.jp/central_government/frame.html, last accessed 28 March 2019. See also Brian Woodall, *Growing Democracy in Japan* Lexington, Kentucky: University Press of Kentucky, 2014, pp. 174–179.
19. 清水真人, 『平成デモクラシー史』, Tokyo: Chikuma Shinsho, 2018, pp. 153–155.
20. Edward J. Lincoln and Robert E. Litan, "'The 'Big Bang'? An Ambivalent Japan Deregulates Its Financial Markets," Brookings Institution, 1 December 1998, https://www.brookings.edu/articles/the-big-bang-an-ambivalent-japan-deregulates-its-financial-markets, last accessed 29 March 2019.
21. Edward Lincoln, "Japan's Financial Problems," *Brookings Papers on Economic Activity* 2 (1998) 347.
22. Karube Kensuke, "Lessons of the 1997 Financial Crisis in Japan," *Nippon.com*, 30 October 2017, https://www.nippon.com/en/currents/d00360/lessons-of-the-1997-financial-crisis-in-japan.html, last accessed 28 March 2019.
23. Phillip Y. Lipscy and Hirofumi Takinami, "The Politics of Financial Crisis Response in Japan and the United States," *Japanese Journal of Political Science* 14 (3) 2013, 345.

24. Curtis, op. cit., pp. 208–209.
25. Stephanie Strom, "Cold Pizza Hits the Spot in Japanese Politics," *The New York Times*, 23 July 1998, https://www.nytimes.com/1998/07/23/world/cold-pizza-hits-the-spot-in-japanese-politics.html, last accessed 1 April 2019.
26. 石川, op. cit., p 196.
27. Aurelia George Mulgan, *Ozawa Ichirō and Japanese Politics: Old Versus New* New York: Routledge, 2015, p. 191.
28. On the LDP's antipathy to Kōmeitō and Sōka Gakkai and the 1995 law, see Levi McLaughlin, "Did Aum Change Everything? What Soka Gakkai Before, During, and After the Aum Shinrikyō Affair Tells Us About the Persistent 'Otherness' of New Religions in Japan," *Japanese Journal of Religious Studies* 39/1 (2012): 51–75.
29. Shiozaki was later described by Koizumi adviser Takenaka Heizō as "one of the few true economic policy experts" in Japanese politics. See Heizo Takenaka, *The Structural Reforms of the Koizumi Cabinet: An Insider's Account of the Economic Revival of Japan*, trans. Jillian Yorke Tokyo: Nikkei Books, 2008, p. 37.
30. Shiozaki Yasuhisa, "Changes in the Japanese Policymaking Process," in Thomas E. Mann and Sasaki Takeshi, eds., *Governance for a New Century: Japanese Challenges, American Experience* Tokyo: Japan Center for International Exchange, 2002, p. 53–62.
31. *Yomiuri Shimbun*, 21 December 1999. The website can be viewed at https://web.archive.org/web/20000301162229/http://sousai.cypress.ne.jp, last accessed 5 May 2020.
32. 阿比留瑠比,『総理の誕生』, Tokyo: Bungei Shunjū, 2016, p. 23.
33. This appointment was particularly noteworthy given how seniority-based the LDP had become over its life. Nogami notes that a chairmanship of one of the LDP's policy committees is the kind of post that a veteran with three electoral victories and ten years of service could expect to receive, not a second-termer in his sixth year in office. 野上,『安倍晋三』, p. 159.
34. 野上,『安倍晋三』, pp. 162–164. On the split in Abe's own faction, then headed by Mori Yoshirō, see 大下英治,『清和会秘録』, Tokyo: East Press, 2015, p. 96.
35. 安倍,『軌跡』, p. 111.
36. 阿比留, op. cit., p. 17.
37. Mulgan, op. cit., p. 191.
38. 大下,『清和会秘録』, pp. 105–107; 石川, op. cit., p. 202.
39. 五百籏頭眞, 伊藤元重, and 薬師寺克行, eds.,『森喜朗 自民党と政権交代』, Tokyo: Asahi Shimbun, 2007, p. 25.

40. James Babb, "The Seirankai and the Fate of its Members: The Rise and Fall of the New Right Politicians in Japan," *Japan Forum*, 24, 1 (2012) 75–96.
41. 石原慎太郎 et al, 『青嵐会』, Tokyo: Rōman, 1973, pp. 195–207.
42. Ibid., pp. 121–145.
43. Babb, op. cit., pp. 83–84.
44. 大下, 『清和会秘録』, pp. 84–86.
45. Kamei Shizuka, who at the time was sparring with Abe over long-term care, also attended. Abe Shinzō homepage, 13 April 2000, https://web.archive.org/web/20000829115404/http://www.s-abe.or.jp/index2.htm, last accessed 5 May 2020.
46. 大下, 『清和会秘録』, p. 109.
47. In another sign of his affinities with the new conservatives, his maiden policy speech, delivered on 7 April, used the phrase "beautiful country"—which Abe would later popularize—four times. Mori Yoshirō, "Policy Speech to the 147th session of the Diet," 7 April 2000, The World and Japan Database, National Graduate Institute for Policy Studies, http://worldjpn.grips.ac.jp/documents/texts/pm/20000407.SWJ.html, last accessed 8 April 2019. Author's translation. In this excerpt, Mori uses the word 国家, which is generally translated as "state," but in this context he seems to be referring to the Japanese nation.
48. Mori Yoshirō, 森首相のいわゆる「神の国発言」の全文, Shinto Association of Spiritual Leadership, 15 May 2000, https://web.archive.org/web/20041225080505/http://www.okazaki-inst.jp/material.mor-ishinto.html, last accessed 8 April 2019.
49. "Statement by Prime Minister Yoshiro Mori at the Press Conference," Cabinet Secretariat, 26 May 2000, https://japan.kantei.go.jp/souri/mori/2000/0526press.html, last accessed 8 April 2019.
50. 「首相「無党派層は寝ていてくれれば」・その後、記者団に訂正」, *Nikkei Shimbun*, 20 June 2000, http://www.nikkei.co.jp/topic3/elecnews/archive/20000620diii210020.html, last accessed 10 April 2019.
51. See David Leheny, *Empire of Hope* Ithaca: Cornell University Press, 2018, ch. 2 for an account of the politics of the Ehime Maru sinking.
52. Abe Shinzō homepage, 13 April 2000, https://web.archive.org/web/20000829115404/http://www.s-abe.or.jp/index2.htm, last accessed 5 May 2020.
53. 野上,『気骨』, p. 225.
54. 「人間・安倍晋三の実像」 (2), *Livedoor News*, 21 September 2006, http://news.livedoor.com/article/detail/2473487, last accessed 5 May 2020.

6. THE WEIRDO

1. "The United States and Japan: Advancing Toward a Mature Partnership," Institute for National Strategic Studies, National Defense University, Washington, DC, 11 October 2000, https://apps.dtic.mil/dtic/tr/fulltext/u2/a403599.pdf, last accessed 5 May 2020.
2. "Remarks by the President and Prime Minister Koizumi of Japan in Photo Opportunity," George W. Bush White House Archives, 30 June 2001, https://georgewbush-whitehouse.archives.gov/news/releases/2001/06/20010630–2.html, last accessed 27 April 2001.
3. Itō Masaya, longtime secretary to Ikeda Hayato, used this term as the title to his history of the LDP in the 1970s. 『自民党戦国史』, Tokyo: Chikuma, 2009.
4. Kathryn Tolbert, "For Japanese, a Typical Tale of Divorce," The *Washington Post*, 19 May 2001, https://www.washingtonpost.com/archive/politics/2001/05/19/for-japanese-a-typical-tale-of-divorce/38e28942-cc7d-44b7-b7cd-696cc1782f61/?utm_term=.20e0927a00ce, last accessed 15 April 2019.
5. Phil Arnold, "Junichiro Koizumi Presents My Favorite Elvis Songs," *ElvisBlog*, 2 July 2006, http://www.elvisblog.net/2006/07/02/junichiro-koizumi-presents-my-favorite-elvis-songs, last accessed 15 April 2019.
6. David Pilling provides a colorful eyewitness account of the Koizumi phenomenon. *Bending Adversity* New York: Penguin, 2014, pp. 131–133.
7. On Koizumi's populism, see Yū Uchiyama, *Koizumi and Japanese Politics*, trans. Carl Freire New York: Routledge, 2010, pp. 8–9.
8. Political scientist Margarita Estévez-Abe argues that these programs were "functional equivalents" for the welfare states of Western Europe, providing welfare through employment. Margarita Estévez-Abe, *Welfare and Capitalism in Postwar Japan: Party, Bureaucracy, and Business*, New York: Cambridge University Press, 2008.
9. 大下, 『清和会秘録』, pp. 139–144.
10. One prefecture failed to submit its votes, possibly Hiroshima, which did not embrace open voting and whose favorite-son candidate Kamei Shizuka dropped out during the voting.
11. 清水, 『平成デモクラシー史』, p. 165.
12. Ibid., pp. 166–167.
13. 阿比留, op. cit., p. 47.
14. Ibid., p. 42.

15. "Prime Minister Koizumi Press Conference," Cabinet Secretariat, 27 April 2001, https://web.archive.org/web/20010606185357/http://www.kantei.go.jp/jp/koizumispeech/2001/0427kisyakaiken.html, last accessed 20 April 2019.
16. 小泉内閣メールマガジン, 14 June 2001, https://web.archive.org/web/20011203181621/http://www.kantei.go.jp/jp/m-magazine/backnumber/2001/0614.html, last accessed 28 April 2019.
17. 信田智人、『政治主導vs官僚支配 』, Tokyo: Asahi Shimbun Publishers, 2013, pp. 102–106.
18. Leonard J. Schoppa, *Race for the Exits*, Ithaca: Cornell University Press, 2006, ch. 3 passim.
19. On Koizumi's "one-phrase politics," see 瀬良晴子, 兵庫県立大学「人文論集」第44巻 第1· 2号 2009年 (平成21年) 3月 抜刷.
20. Koizumi Junichirō, "Policy Speech to the 151st session of the Diet," 7 May 2001, The World and Japan Database, National Graduate Institute for Policy Studies, http://worldjpn.grips.ac.jp/documents/texts/pm/20010507.SWJ.html, last accessed 20 April 2019.
21. On the logic of Koizumi's personnel decisions, see Takenaka, op. cit., pp. 19–20.
22. Edward Lincoln, "Japan in 2001: A Depressing Year," *Asian Survey* 42, 1 (January/February 2002) 67–80.
23. 清水真人, 『財務省と政治』, Tokyo: Chukō Shinsho, 2015, p. 116.
24. 藤田勉, 『安倍晋三の経済政策を読む』, Tokyo: Index Communications, 2006, p. 64.
25. See Takenaka, op. cit., ch. 2 passim on his appointment as financial affairs minister and the fight to launch the Takenaka plan.
26. 栗本慎一郎, 安倍晋三, and 衛藤晟一, op. cit., pp. 179–185.
27. 春原剛, 『ジャパン· ハンド』, Tokyo: Bungei Shunjū, 2006, p. 8.
28. 飯島勲, 『小泉官邸秘録』, Tokyo: Nikkei Books, 2006, p. 122.
29. Shinoda Tomohito, *Koizumi Diplomacy* Seattle: University of Washington Press, 2007, pp. 91–93.
30. Ibid., pp. 95–98. See also "Armitage wants bills on SDF role passed soon," *Japan Times*, 7 October 2001, https://www.japantimes.co.jp/news/2001/10/07/national/armitage-wants-bills-on-sdf-role-passed-soon, last accessed 30 April 2019.
31. Gregory W. Noble, "What can Taiwan (and the United States) Expect from Japan," *Journal of East Asian Studies* 5 (2005) 2–3. Japanese conservatives have rallied in support of Taiwan, and Lee Teng-hui has been a strong supporter of Japan in its skirmishes with China over the Yasukuni shrine, the Senkaku Islands, and other issues, reflecting lin-

gering affinities in Taiwan towards the country's former colonial master.

32. Foreign Relations Committee, House of Representatives, National Diet of Japan, 23 May 2001. http://kokkai.ndl.go.jp/SENTAKU/syugiin/151/0005/15105230005009a.html, last accessed 2 May 2019.
33. 野上, 『安倍晋三』, pp. 168–169.

7. ABE'S RISE

1. Yoichi Funabashi provides a richly detailed account of the Pyongyang trip in *The Peninsula Question*, Washington, DC: Brookings Institution Press, 2007.
2. As John Bolton, then the undersecretary of state for arms control, later wrote, the uranium enrichment was "the hammer I had been looking for to shatter the Agreed Framework." John Bolton, *Surrender is Not an Option: Defending America at the United Nations* New York: Simon and Schuster, 2008, p. 106.
3. 田中均, 『外交の力』, Tokyo: Nikkei Books, 2009, p. 118.
4. Ibid., p. 103.
5. Cabinet Affairs Committee, House of Councillors, National Diet of Japan, 30 October 2001, http://kokkai.ndl.go.jp/SENTAKU/sangiin/153/0058/15310300058004a.html, last accessed 5 May 2020.
6. 飯島, op. cit., p. 147. See also Special Committee on Preventing International Terrorism and Japan's Support and Cooperation Activities, House of Representatives, National Diet of Japan. 29 March 2002, http://kokkai.ndl.go.jp/SENTAKU/syugiin/154/0104/15403290104002a.html, last accessed 5 May 2020.
7. Yoichi Funabashi, *The Peninsula Question* Washington, DC: Brookings Institution Press, 2007, pp. 15–18.
8. "Japan–DPRK Pyongyang Declaration," Ministry of Foreign Affairs of Japan, 17 September 2002, https://www.mofa.go.jp/region/asia-paci/n_korea/pmv0209/pyongyang.html, last accessed 9 May 2019.
9. Funabashi, op. cit., pp. 24–25.
10. 清水, 『平成デモクラシー史』, p. 190.
11. 田中, op. cit., pp. 119–120.
12. "Announcement by Chief Cabinet Secretary on Prime Minister Koizumi's Visit to North Korea," Ministry of Foreign Affairs of Japan, 30 August 2002, https://www.mofa.go.jp/region/asia-paci/n_korea/pmv0209/ccs0830.html, last accessed on 9 May 2019.
13. 大下, 『安倍晋三と岸信介』, p. 113; 野上, 『気骨』, p. 242; 阿比留, op. cit., p. 61.

14. Funabashi, op. cit., p. 38.
15. 大下,『清和会秘録』, pp. 160–161.
16. 安倍,『美しい国へ』, p. 50.
17. 田中, op. cit., p. 128.
18. 飯島, op. cit., p. 150.
19. Funabashi, op. cit., 5.
20. From 20 September through the end of 2002, Tanaka would testify before the Diet about North Korea seventeen times. See Funabashi, op. cit., p. 39 on the attacks directed at Tanaka.
21. Ministry of Foreign Affairs,「田中外務審議官自宅への爆発物設置について」, 10 September 2003, https://www.mofa.go.jp/mofaj/press/danwa/15/dga_0910.html, last accessed 12 May 2019.
22. Prime Minister's Office,「拉致問題への対処に関する基本方針」, 26 September 2002, https://www.kantei.go.jp/jp/singi/rati/ugoki/020926housin.pdf, last accessed 12 May 2019.
23. 阿比留, op. cit., p. 69.
24. On Kelly's trip to Pyongyang, see Don Oberdorfer, "My Private Seat at Pyongyang's Table," *Washington Post*, 10 November 2002, https://www.washingtonpost.com/archive/opinions/2002/11/10/my-private-seat-at-pyongyangs-table/824c6e6f-4971-4784-b14c-d771b1cf49ac/?utm_term=.0fefff8d9dcb, last accessed 12 May 2019.
25. 安倍,『美しい国へ』, pp. 48–49.
26. Funabashi, op. cit., p. 40.
27. 田中, op. cit., p. 133.
28. 安倍,『美しい国へ』, p. 49.
29. Funabashi, op. cit., pp. 58–59.
30. 野上,『気骨』, p. 23.
31. Ibid., p. 25.
32. 橋本五郎,『官房長官と幹事長』 Tokyo: Yomiuri Shimbun Publishers, 2018, pp. 43–44.
33. 野上,『安倍晋三』, p. 178.
34. 野上,『気骨』, pp. 26–27.
35. 野上,『安倍晋三』, p. 180.
36. Ibid., pp. 186–188.
37. Asahi Shimbun, 10 November 2003, https://web.archive.org/web/20040215233248/http://www2.asahi.com/senkyo2003/news/TKY200311090171.html, last accessed 16 May 2019.
38. Carlson and Reed, op. cit., pp. 74–75.
39. Smith, *Japan Rearmed*, p. 73.
40. Shinoda, op. cit., pp. 124–126.

41. NHK,「イラク自衛隊派遣と国民意識」, April 2004. https://www.nhk.or.jp/bunken/summary/yoron/social/pdf/040401.pdf.
42. 安倍,『美しい国へ』, pp. 134–135. Ishiba Shigeru, who was head of the Japan Defense Agency at the time of the dispatch and would later challenge Abe for the LDP's leadership, cites similar reasons for the dispatch but says the US–Japan relationship was the fourth reason for going to Iraq, so that the bilateral security treaty would not just be a scrap of paper. 石破茂,『国防』, Tokyo: Shinchōsha, 2005, p. 49.
43. See a 2005 interview with Katō by military affairs journalist Kuroi Buntarō. https://news.yahoo.co.jp/byline/kuroibuntaro/20160911-00062076. Accessed 22 May 2019.
44. In an interview conducted after the vote, Kamei said he challenged Abe to do his worst, arguing that when the government is making a mistake, someone must be willing to speak up. http://www.kamei-shizuka.net/action/2004/040211.html. Accessed 22 May 2019. See 野上,『安倍晋三』, pp. 189–192 on this episode.
45. Shinzo Abe, "An Evolving Relationship: Japan and the United States in 2004," American Enterprise Institute, 29 April 2004. https://www.aei.org/publication/an-evolving-relationship/print. Accessed 22 May 2019.
46. 大下,『安倍晋三と岸信介』, p. 127. In her memoirs, however, Rice would compare Abe unfavorably with Koizumi. Condoleeza Rice, *No Higher Honor* New York: Crown, 2011, pp. 527–528.
47. 春原, op. cit., pp. 9–12.
48. In February 2005, Abe began writing a column for the right-wing evening newspaper, the *Yūkan Fuji* and he used his first column to address the alleged interference in the NHK programming. See https://web.archive.org/web/20050527003558/http://newleader.s-abe.or.jp/modules/news, last accessed 5 May 2020.
49. The DNA incident led to a dispute between the Koizumi government and the journal *Nature*, which questioned the process of testing the remains provided by North Korea and said that the Japanese government was not justified in claiming that the remains were fraudulent when it was possible that the test was either contaminated or inconclusive. Ironically, in its editorial criticizing the Japanese government's interference with a scientific procedure, the journal articulated a position not altogether different from Abe's. "If a totalitarian country had abducted US citizens from a beach and carried them back to teach language to potential spies for 25 years," the journal wrote, "would George Bush or any other US president be standing there with a bag

of ashes haggling over DNA test results?" "Politics versus reality," *Nature* 434, 257, 16 March 2005, https://www.nature.com/articles/434257a, last Accessed 22 May 2019. See also David Cyranoski, "DNA is a burning issue as Japan and Korea clash over kidnaps," *Nature* 433, 445, 2 February 2005, https://www.nature.com/articles/433445a, last accessed 22 May 2019.

50. Funabashi, op. cit., pp. 60–61.
51. Patricia Maclachlan, "Storming the Castle: The Battle for Postal Reform in Japan," *Social Science Japan Journal* 9, 1 (April 2006) 1–18.
52. Takenaka, op. cit., p. 131.
53. Ibid., p. 155.
54. 飯島, op. cit., pp. 269–270.
55. 大下,『清和会秘録』, p. 175.
56. Later, as prime minister, Asō would state that he had actually opposed postal privatization but went along with it and Koizumi's decision to call a snap election over the issue because there did not seem to be much he could do stop it. 清水真人,『首相の蹉跌』, Tokyo: Nikkei Books, 2009, p. 16.
57. "Press Conference by Prime Minister Junichiro Koizumi," Cabinet Secretariat, 8 August 2005, https://japan.kantei.go.jp/koizumispeech/2005/08/08kaiken_e.html, last accessed 23 May 2019.
58. See https://web.archive.org/web/20050811002109/http://newleader.s-abe.or.jp/modules/news, last accessed 5 May 2020.
59. Kamei Shizuka, a leader of the rebels and a onetime member of Abe's faction, said: "The politics of these four years of Mr. Koizumi have sought to create market fundamentalism in the name of structural reform, that is a survival of the fittest society. At the urging of globalization, Japan is being overwhelmed by foreign capital." 29 July 2005, http://www.kamei-shizuka.net/action/2005/050729.html, last accessed 31 May 2019.
60. See https://web.archive.org/web/20051021003110/http://newleader.s-abe.or.jp/modules/news, last accessed 5 May 2020.
61. 青山, op. cit., p. 56.
62. Kenneth Mori McElwain, "How Large Are Koizumi's Coattails? Party Leader Visits in the 2005 Japanese Election," Stanford University, Conference on Electoral and Legislative Politics in Japan, 11–12 June 2007.

8. THE SUCCESSOR

1. Yomiuri Shimbun, 12 August 2006. Evening edition.

2. 吉田貴文, 『世論調査と政治』, Tokyo: Kōdansha, 2008, p. 118.
3. http://www.magazine9.jp/key/018/index.html.
4. 柿崎 明二 and 久江 雅彦, 『空白の宰相, Tokyo: Kōdansha, 2007, pp. 32–33.
5. 「安倍内閣総理大臣記者会見」, Cabinet Secretariat, archived by the National Diet Library, 26 September 2006, http://warp.ndl.go.jp/info:ndljp/pid/244428/www.kantei.go.jp/jp/abespeech/2006/09/26press.html, last accessed 5 May 2020.
6. 吉田, op. cit., p. 119.
7. 野上, 『気骨』, p. 272.
8. 飯島, op. cit., p. 147.
9. 清水, 『平成デモクラシー史』, p. 224.
10. Economist Noah Smith explores the mystery of the Koizumi boom and concludes that Japan's total trade with China—both exports and imports—was probably the most important factor in the recovery. "The Koizumi years: A macroeconomic puzzle," *Noahpinion*, 9 February 2013, https://noahpinionblog.blogspot.com/2013/02/the-koizumi-years-macroeconomic-puzzle.html, last accessed 28 May 2019. Smith was responding to a blog post by Paul Krugman that noted that when looking at Japan's GDP per capita—or, better yet, its GDP per worker—Japan's decline relative to the US was more modest than the narrative about economic stagnation would suggest, since Japan's working-age population had begun shrinking. Paul Krugman, "Japanese Relative Performance," *The Conscience of a Liberal*, 9 February 2013, https://krugman.blogs.nytimes.com/2013/02/09/japanese-relative-performance, last accessed 28 May 2019. See also David Pilling, "Japan's Economy and the Koizumi Myth," *Financial Times*, 17 October 2007, https://www.ft.com/content/4e506f06-7cc3-11dc-aee2-0000779fd2ac, last accessed 29 May 2019.
11. The phrase 格差社会—"gap-widening society"—was recognized as one of the top ten phrases of the year in 2006 in the annual "Words of the Year" list compiled by publisher Jiyū Kokumin Sha and adult education company U-Can. See https://www.jiyu.co.jp/singo/index.php?eid=00023, last accessed 5 May 2020.
12. "NEET": Not in education, employment, or training. "Freeter": portmanteau from "freelance" and "arbeiter," the latter being a common term for a part-time job or side job. See Akio Inui, "Why Freeter and NEET are Misunderstood: Recognizing the New Precarious Conditions of Japanese Youth," *Social Work & Society* 3, 2, 2005, https://www.socwork.net/sws/article/viewFile/200/260, last accessed 29 May 2019.

13. According to Japan's National Police Agency, suicides peaked in 2003 and have plummeted over the past decade. See https://www.npa.go.jp/safetylife/seianki/jisatsu/H30/H30_jisatunojoukyou.pdf, last accessed 25 Nov. 2019.
14. See Yuki Sekine, "The Rise of Poverty in Japan: The Emergence of the Working Poor," *Japan Labor Review* 5, 4 (Autumn 2008), pp. 49–66 for a comprehensive overview of concerns about poverty and inequality during the first decade of the twenty-first century.
15. According to the OECD, Japan's pre-tax Gini coefficient, the most common measure of inequality, increased from 0.403 to 0.462 from 1996 to 2006. Post-tax inequality had worsened too, and by 2006 Japan was in the bottom half of OECD member states, closer to the United Kingdom and the United States than the more egalitarian advanced industrial democracies of northern Europe. Meanwhile, its poverty rate had risen to 15.3 percent, not far behind the United States's 17.1 percent poverty rate.
16. 「好況の日本、高まる格差への不安」, *Asahi Weekly*, 7 May 2006, http://www.asahi.com/english/weekly/column/herald.html, last accessed 4 May 2020.
17. 川北隆雄, 『「失敗」の経済政策史』, Tokyo: Kodansha, 2014, pp. 170–172.
18. Budget Committee, House of Councillors, National Diet of Japan, 2 February 2006, http://kokkai.ndl.go.jp/SENTAKU/sangiin/164/0014/16402020014003a.html, last accessed 30 May 2019.
19. "Re-challenge" was not the last time Abe would use an awkward neologism drawn from English as a slogan.
20. Plenary session, House of Councillors, National Diet of Japan, 10 March 2006, http://kokkai.ndl.go.jp/SENTAKU/sangiin/164/0001/16403100001006a.html, last accessed 4 May 2020.
21. 柿崎 and 久江, op. cit., p. 15.
22. It finished the year at seventeen on Japan's bestseller list. See https://www.tohan.jp/pdf/2006_best.pdf, last accessed 30 May 2019.
23. 安倍, 『美しい国へ』, p. 228. Author's translation.
24. Ibid., p. 170. Author's translation.
25. 藤田, op. cit., p. 117.
26. Carlson and Reed, op. cit., p. 123.
27. Nakagawa's program was in certain respects an ancestor of what would be called Abenomics after 2012. Nakagawa was the first person to use the word "Abenomics." In a parliamentary debate on 2 October 2006, Nakagawa said, "The current lineup of the Abe cabinet acutely feels that the basic philosophy of Abe's economic policies, of Abenomics is

that if business activity is activated, employment will increase and tax revenues will increase, so there is no contradiction between economic growth and fiscal consolidation." Nakagawa's term did not, however, catch on during Abe's first term. Plenary session, House of Representatives, National Diet of Japan, 2 October 2006, http://kokkai.ndl.go.jp/SENTAKU/syugiin/165/0001/16510020001004a.html, last accessed 4 May 2020.

28. 清水,『財務省と政治』, p. 158.
29. Ibid., pp. 162–164.
30. 経済財政運営と構造改革に関する基本方針 2006, 7 July 2006, https://www5.cao.go.jp/keizai-shimon/minutes/2006/0707/item1.pdf, last accessed 5 May 2020.
31. 藤田, op. cit., p. 129.
32. 上川龍之進,『日本銀行と政治』, Tokyo: Chukō Shinsho, 2014, pp. 122–128.
33. Ibid., p. 130.
34. The Bush administration did not only abandon the heavy-handed approach of its predecessors. It concluded, in the words of John Taylor, Under Secretary of the Treasury for International Affairs (2001–2005), that "economic stagnation in Japan was clearly not in the best interests of the United States." Remarkably, in light of widespread US elite and public opposition to "currency manipulation" by US trading partners in the years since, the Bush administration actually gave the green light to the "great intervention," a massive program of exchange rate intervention by the Koizumi government in 2003 and 2004 intended to devalue the yen. John Taylor, *Global Financial Warriors* New York: W.W. Norton, 2007, pp. 285–287.
35. "President Bush Visits Graceland with Japanese Prime Minister Koizumi," George W. Bush White House Archives, 30 June 2006, https://georgewbush-whitehouse.archives.gov/news/releases/2006/06/text/20060630–6.html, last accessed 4 May 2020. See also, Sheryl Gay Stolberg, "Foreign Policy Tries a Little Shake, Rattle and Roll," *New York Times*, 30 June 2006, https://www.nytimes.com/2006/06/30/world/asia/30cnd-elvis.html, last accessed 3 June 2019.
36. Victor Cha, *The Impossible State*, updated edition New York: Ecco, 2018, p. 261.
37. Ibid., p. 266.
38. See Jessica Chen Weiss, *Powerful Patriots: Nationalist Protest in China's Foreign Policy* New York: Oxford University Press, 2014.
39. 上杉隆,『官邸崩壊』, Tokyo: Shinchōsha, 2007, p. 36; 柿崎 明二 and 久江 雅彦, op. cit., pp. 30–31.

40. 大下,『安倍晋三と岸信介』, pp. 139–142.
41. 薬師寺克行,『公明党』, Tokyo: Chukō Shinsho, 2016, pp. 204–205.
42. In Ozawa's first exchange with Abe after he became prime minister, Ozawa offered his heartfelt congratulations to the new leader by first fondly recalling the late Shintarō and lamenting his tragic death. "Now," he said, "his son Abe Shinzō has assumed the office of prime minister. I think Shintarō-sensei would of course be delighted by this, and I myself, having such a relationship with him, am delighted to also offer my congratulations as a personal sentiment." Committees on Fundamental National Policies, National Diet of Japan, 18 October 2006, http://kokkai.ndl.go.jp/SENTAKU/ryoin/165/9001/16510189001001a.html, last accessed on 4 May 2020.
43. On Ozawa's rise as DPJ leader, see 塩田潮,『民主党の研究』, Tokyo: Heibonsha, 2007, ch. 8 passim.
44. 大下,『清和会秘録』, p. 197; 上杉, op. cit., pp. 54–55.

9. INFERNO

1. Referenced in 「安倍首相 第1次政権時代は「KY総理」と呼ばれていた?」, 5 June 2017. http://news.livedoor.com/article/detail/13158174. Accessed 12 June 2019.
2. 安倍晋三「年頭所感」, Cabinet Secretariat, archived by the National Diet Library, 1 January 2007, https://warp.ndl.go.jp/info:ndljp/pid/244428/www.kantei.go.jp/jp/abespeech/2007/01/01syokan.html, last accessed 5 May 2020.
3. 「安倍内閣総理大臣年頭記者会見」Cabinet Secretariat, archived by the National Diet Library, 4 January 2007, http://warp.ndl.go.jp/info:ndljp/pid/244428/www.kantei.go.jp/jp/abespeech/2007/01/01syokan.html, last accessed 5 May 2020.
4. 「欧州訪問における内外記者会見」, Cabinet Secretariat, archived by the National Diet Library, 13 January 2007, http://warp.ndl.go.jp/info:ndljp/pid/244428/www.kantei.go.jp/jp/abespeech/2007/01/13press.html, last accessed 5 May 2020.
5. Speech by Mr. Taro Aso, Minister for Foreign Affairs on the Occasion of the Japan Institute of International Affairs Seminar "Arc of Freedom and Prosperity: Japan's Expanding Diplomatic Horizons," 30 November 2006, https://www.mofa.go.jp/announce/fm/aso/speech0611.html, last accessed 13 June 2019. These themes would be moribund after Abe's resignation but similar concepts would return to Japan's strategic vocabulary after Abe's comeback in 2012.

6. "Policy Speech by Prime Minister Shinzo Abe to the 166th Session of the Diet," Cabinet Secretariat, archived by the National Diet Library, 26 January 2007, http://japan.kantei.go.jp/abespeech/2007/01/26speech_e.html, last accessed 5 May 2020.
7. Plenary session, House of Representatives, National Diet of Japan, http://kokkai.ndl.go.jp/SENTAKU/syugiin/166/0001/16601290001003a.html, 29 January 2007, last accessed 14 June 2019.
8. At the time, the law allowed political groups to declare a total amount for office expenses without itemizing or submitting receipts, a loophole that would be closed later in 2007.
9. Carlson and Reed, op. cit., p. 78. For a biography of Matsuoka and his participation in "structural corruption," see Aurelia George Mulgan, *Power and Pork* Canberra: ANU Press, 2007.
10. As a Japanese-American, Honda was subjected to particularly egregious vitriol from the Japanese right for his advocacy on behalf of the comfort women. See Norimitsu Onishi, "A Congressman Faces Foes in Japan as He Seeks an Apology," *New York Times*, 12 May 2007, https://www.nytimes.com/2007/05/12/world/asia/12honda.html, last accessed 17 June 2019. Japanese conservatives also attributed the resolution to anti-Japanese sentiments on the part of Chinese and Korean Americans, and, behind them, the Chinese and South Korean governments, but while Asian-American activists were part of a broad network of activists fighting to advance the resolution, its passage depended heavily on Henry Hyde, a conservative Republican from Illinois who was a veteran of the Pacific War, and a group of scholars, analysts, and translators organized by Mindy Kotler, director of a small DC-based think tank that monitors the Japanese right wing. Kotler, who would testify in support of Honda's resolution, used her network of experts to push back against Abe and the Japanese government's arguments and line up congressional support. See Kinue Tokudome, "Passage of H.Res. 121 on 'Comfort Women', the US Congress and Historical Memory in Japan," *Japan Focus*, 1 August 2007. https://apjjf.org/-Kinue-TOKUDOME/2510/article.html.
11. Honda built on the work of Lane Evans, a Democratic congressman from Illinois, who had sought to raise awareness of the issue for nearly a decade but retired in 2006. See http://www.donga.com/en/article/all/20141108/409454/1/Lane-Evans-dies-first-US-lawmaker-raised-comfort-women-issue, last accessed 5 May 2020.
12. See "Protecting the Human Rights of the Comfort Women," Hearing, Subcommittee on Asia, the Pacific, and the Global Environment,

Committee on Foreign Affairs, House of Representatives. 110th Congress, 15 February 2007, https://www.govinfo.gov/content/pkg/CHRG-110hhrg33317/pdf/CHRG-110hhrg33317.pdf, last accessed 5 May 2020.

13. 上杉, op. cit., p. 133.
14. *Yomiuri Shimbun*, 1 March 2007, https://web.archive.org/web/20070303105453/http://www.yomiuri.co.jp/politics/news/20070301ia01.htm, last accessed 5 May 2020.
15. Hiroko Tabuchi, "Japan's Abe: No Proof of WWII Sex Slaves," The Associated Press, 1 March 2007, http://www.washingtonpost.com/wp-dyn/content/article/2007/03/01/AR2007030100578.html, last accessed 17 June 2019.
16. In fact, in April, ahead of Abe's visit to Washington, right-wing intellectuals condemned Abe for being insufficiently combative on history issues by continuing to abide by the Kōno statement. 阿比留, op. cit., p. 96.
17. Budget Committee, House of Councillors, National Diet of Japan, 5 March 2007, http://kokkai.ndl.go.jp/SENTAKU/sangiin/166/0014/166030500140003a.html, last accessed 5 May 2020.
18. "Cosponsors," H.Res. 121, House of Representatives, 110th Congress, https://www.congress.gov/bill/110th-congress/house-resolution/121/cosponsors, last accessed 5 May 2020.
19. "Shinzo Abe's Double Talk," *Washington Post*, 24 March 2007, http://www.washingtonpost.com/wp-dyn/content/article/2007/03/23/AR2007032301640.html?noredirect=on, last accessed 17 June 2019.
20. Norimitsu Onishi, "Japan Stands by Declaration on 'Comfort Women,'" *New York Times*, 16 March 2007, https://www.nytimes.com/2007/03/16/world/asia/16cnd-japan.html, last accessed 17 June 2019.
21. While the establishment and management of the imperial military's brothel system was more complicated than the crude vision of Japanese troops wantonly rounding up women—and much historical evidence was destroyed—there is little doubt that the system was "coercive" by any reasonable understanding of the concept of coercion, even if at some times and in some places the Japanese government relied on outside agents and contractors to recruit women (often through deceptive means), who would then be employed as virtual slaves by the imperial military. Of course, as Japan's conservatives are quick to point out, imperial Japan was neither the first nor the last state to establish a system of military prostitution through cruel, coercive means. Abe's foreign policy adviser, the late Okazaki Hisahiko, went a step further,

suggesting that because the comfort women system was a less egregious violation of human rights than mass murder by Stalin and Mao or even the US atomic bombings of Hiroshima and Nagasaki, it was not a particularly serious issue to address. On Okazaki, see Michael Cucek, "Now I have to apologize…," *Shisaku* (blog), 6 June 2007, http://shisaku.blogspot.com/2007/06/now-i-have-to-apologize.html, last accessed 5 May 2020.

22. 上杉, op. cit., p. 145.
23. "President Bush and Prime Minister Abe of Japan Participate in a Joint Press Availability," George W. Bush White House archives, 27 April 2007, https://georgewbush-whitehouse.archives.gov/news/releases/2007/04/20070427-6.html, last accessed 17 June 2019.
24. The right-wing manga artist and provocateur Kobayashi Yoshinori recounted in 2014 that in a 2010 dialogue with Abe, he made clear that although Bush said he accepted his apology, he did not actually apologize. 「ブッシュに慰安婦問題で謝罪した安倍首相」, Yoshinori Kobayashi Blog, 16 March 2014, https://yoshinori-kobayashi.com/4134, last accessed 17 June 2019.
25. "As competent and pragmatic as Kenichiro Sasae was, I found, especially, after Koizumi retired in 2006, that the Japanese had lost their way in dealing with others and, as the Six Party meetings unfolded, were often the delegation least in line with the others." Christopher R. Hill, *Outpost* New York: Simon & Schuster, 2014, p. 226. See also Michael J. Green, *Special Providence* New York: Columbia University Press, 2017, p. 508.
26. "Visit by Premier Wen Jiabao of the People's Republic of China to Japan Establishment of the Japan-China High-Level Economic Dialogue," Ministry of Foreign Affairs of Japan, 12 April 2007, https://www.mofa.go.jp/region/asia-paci/china/pv0704/dialogue.html, last accessed 5 May 2020.
27. Carlson and Reed, op. cit., p. 75.
28. 上杉, op. cit., p. 185.
29. 安倍, 『美しい国へ』, pp. 178–197.
30. Nagatsuma asked a series of questions about the possibility of missing pension records on 16 June 2006. Health and Labor Committee, House of Representatives, National Diet of Japan, 16 June 2006, http://kokkai.ndl.go.jp/SENTAKU/syugiin/164/0097/16406160097032a.html, last accessed 5 May 2020.
31. The *Nikkei Shimbun*'s report on the Social Insurance Agency's internal investigation provides only the slightest hints of the larger scandal that

was to come. See https://web.archive.org/web/20070531144835/http://www.nikkei.co.jp/sp1/nt210/20070527MMSP01000027052007.html, last accessed 5 May 2020.

32. Plenary session, House of Representatives, National Diet of Japan, 8 May 2007, http://kokkai.ndl.go.jp/SENTAKU/syugiin/166/0001/16605080001027a.html, last accessed 5 May 2020.
33. Ali M. El-Agraa, "The Japanese pension scandals," *Pensions* 14, 3: 191–201.
34. Chris Salzberg, "Japan: The Disappearing Pension Accounts," *Global Voices*, 13 June 2007, https://globalvoices.org/2007/06/13/japan-the-disappearing-pension-accounts, last accessed 19 June 2019.
35. Nakagawa Hidenao, facing an increasingly challenging election campaign, described the issue as a "suicide bombing" by the social insurance agency, arguing that it helped raise awareness of the problem precisely to derail the Abe administration's efforts to reform the agency.
36. Suzuki Muneo, a scandal-ridden LDP politician who was convicted of bribery, campaign finance violations, and perjury and served a light prison sentence, had been especially close with Matsuoka and claimed that, when they dined together shortly before his suicide, Matsuoka told him that he wanted to apologize to the public but was prevented from doing so by the administration. See Tobias Harris, "The Matsuoka saga is far from over," *Observing Japan* (blog), 30 May 2007, https://observingjapan.blogspot.com/2007/05/30/the-matsuoka-saga-is-far-from-over, last accessed 5 May 2020. On the Matsuoka-Muneo relationship, see Aurelia George Mulgan, *Power and Pork* Canberra: ANU Press, 2006, ch. 6 passim. Mulgan's book, a biography of Matsuoka published just as he was battling allegations of corruption, is either the best-timed or worst-timed book about Japanese politics ever published.
37. In another example of the way that Japanese politics has become a family business, the grandfather of new minister Akagi Norihiko was Akagi Munenori, who had been director of the Japan defense agency under Kishi in 1960 and famously refused Kishi's suggestion that he might deploy the Self-Defense Forces against the anti-treaty protestors.
38. In *Yomiuri*, his approval plunged from 49.6 percent in a poll conducted on 19–20 May to 32.9 percent only two weeks later, while his disapproval rose from 36.8 percent to 53.7 percent. 吉田, op. cit., p. 226; *Yomiuri Shimbun*, 8 June 2007, https://web.archive.org/web/20070610170748/http://www.yomiuri.co.jp/politics/news/20070608i101.htm, last accessed 5 May 2020.
39. Kyuma got in trouble earlier in 2007 when he bluntly criticized the

US invasion of Iraq as a "mistake," leading the State Department to file a protest with the Japanese embassy in Washington and resulting in Vice President Dick Cheney's avoiding meeting with the defense minister when he visited Tokyo in February 2007. See https://observingjapan.com/tag/kyuma-fumio, last accessed 5 May 2020.

40. The rhetoric from both the Japanese government and the Japanese right grew increasingly heated as the resolution marched to passage. Katō Ryōzō, Japan's ambassador to the United States, warned in a letter to the House leadership that the resolution would have "lasting and harmful effects on the deep friendship, close trust and wide-ranging cooperation our two nations now enjoy." Tobias Harris, "Please explain ambassador," *Observing Japan* (blog), 18 July 2007, https://observingjapan.com/2007/07/18/please-explain-ambassador, last accessed 5 May 2020.
41. 塩田, op. cit., pp. 72–75.
42. 「国民の生活守る「国民重視の政治」打ち立てる　岡山県で小沢代表」, the Democratic Party of Japan, 12 July 2007, https://web.archive.org/web/20080517141638/http://www.dpj.or.jp/news/dpjnews.cgi?indication=dp&num=10343, last accessed 5 May 2020.
43. DPJ Manifesto, http://archive.dpj.or.jp/policy/manifesto/images/Manifesto_2007.pdf, last accessed 5 May 2020.
44. The DPJ would seek limited cooperation with Kamei Shizuka's 国民新党—the People's New Party—in the 2007 election and would form a coalition government with Kamei's party in 2009, giving Kamei the financial affairs and postal reform portfolio, enabling him to oversee the process of rolling back Koizumi's postal privatization scheme.
45. 平野貞夫,『平成政治２０年史』, Tokyo: Gentōsha, 2008, p. 272.
46. Tobias Harris, "What does beautiful country mean anyway?," *Observing Japan* (blog), https://observingjapan.com/2007/07/17/what-does-beautiful-country-mean-anyway, last accessed 5 May 2020.
47. For the state of public opinion before and after the elections, see 河野啓 and 藤岡隆史, 「自民党歴史的大敗と有権者の選択」『放送研究と調査』, November 2007, https://www.nhk.or.jp/bunken/summary/research/report/2007_11/071105.pdf, last accessed 6 May 2020.
48. Tobias Harris, "Desperate to the end," *Observing Japan* (blog), 28 July 2007, https://observingjapan.com/2007/07/28/desperate-to-the-end, last accessed 6 May 2020.
49. Asahi Shimbun, 30 July 2007, https://web.archive.org/web/20130521022130/http://www.asahi.com/senkyo2007/news/TKY200707290301.html, last accessed 6 May 2020.

50. Asahi Shimbun, 「安倍自民が惨敗、続投宣言に党内猛反発」, 30 July 2007, http://www.asahi.com/senkyo2007/nikkan/NIK200707300012.html, last accessed 6 May 2020.
51. Polls suggested that Abe would not have been wrong to believe that the LDP's grassroots supporters—Kishi's "voiceless voices"—were still with him. NHK found that while forty percent of voters overall wanted him to resign compared with twenty-five percent who approved of his staying in office, among ruling-party supporters, fifty-three percent favored his staying on, compared with twenty-one percent who felt he should resign and twenty-six percent who could not say. See 河野啓 and 藤岡隆史, op cit.
52. Months before the upper house elections, Koizumi, at a dinner with Abe and Nakagawa Hidenao, reportedly told his successor that even if he were to lose in the elections, he should not resign since an upper house election, he argued, was not intended to choose the government. 清水, 『首相の蹉跌』, Tokyo: Nikkei, 2009, p. 223.
53. 大下英治, 『安倍官邸「権力」の正体』, Tokyo: Kadokawa, 2017, p. 63.
54. Tobias Harris, "Beautiful no more," *Observing Japan* (blog), 19 August 2007, https://observingjapan.com/2007/08/19/beautiful-no-more, last accessed 6 May 2020.,
55. 柿崎 and 久江, op. cit., p. 232.
56. Shinzo Abe, "Confluence of the Two Seas," Ministry of Foreign Affairs of Japan, 22 August 2007, https://www.mofa.go.jp/region/asia-paci/pmv0708/speech-2.html, last accessed 6 May 2020. Abe's visit to India also included a barely concealed dog whistle for his right-wing supporters, as in his speech to the Indian Parliament he mentioned Judge Radhabinod Pal and visited his elderly son. Judge Pal, who is honored with a statue on the grounds of Yasukuni shrine, served on the International Military Tribunal for the Far East (the Tokyo Tribunal), where he dissented from the other judges and questioned the legitimacy of the entire proceeding on anti-colonialist grounds. His dissent made him a hero to the Japanese right, including Kishi, since it appeared to uphold the arguments made by wartime propagandists that imperial Japan was fighting a holy war of Pan-Asian liberation.
57. "Policy Speech by Prime Minister Shinzo Abe to the 168th Session of the Diet," Cabinet Secretariat, 10 September 2007, https://japan.kantei.go.jp/abespeech/2007/09/10syosin_e.html, last accessed 6 May 2020.
58. Stress is widely recognized as a trigger for episodes of chronic inflammatory bowel diseases like Crohn's disease and ulcerative colitis. See

J.E. Mawdsley and D.S. Rampton, "Psychological stress in IBD: new insights into pathogenic and therapeutic implications," *Gut* 54, 10 (October 2005): 1481–1491, https://www.ncbi.nlm.nih.gov/pmc/articles/PMC1774724, last accessed 6 May 2020.

59. 大下,『清和会秘録』, p. 221.
60. 安倍晋三,「総理の真相」[The Truth Behind the Prime Minister's Resignation], *Bungei Shunjū*, February 2008, reprinted in 安倍,『軌跡』, p. 121. Author's translation.
61. 清水,『平成デモクラシー史』, p. 242.
62. Longtime Japan analyst Michael Cucek provided a witty and succinct account of the dynamics that led Koizumi to throw his weight behind Fukuda. Michael Cucek, "Tarō Francisco Aso's Sudden Fall from Heaven," *Shisaku* (blog), http://shisaku.blogspot.com/2007/09/tar-francisco-asos-sudden-fall-from.html, last accessed 6 May 2020.
63. 阿比留, op. cit., p. 96.

10. ABE IN THE WILDERNESS

1. 「中川昭一先生の葬儀にて　弔辞・麻生太郎　　安倍晋三　　両総理」産経新聞を応援する会 (blog), 15 March 2013, https://ameblo.jp/sankeiouen/entry-11426874612.html, last accessed 6 May 2020.
2. 「中川昭一勉強会　名称は「真・保守政策研究会」」, Sankei Shimbun, 17 December 2007, https://web.archive.org/web/20091119061303/http://sankei.jp.msn.com/politics/situation/071217/stt0712172304005-n1.htm, last accessed 7 May 2020.
3. 青山, op. cit., p. 126. Author's translation.
4. Tomohiko Taniguchi, "Prime Minister Shinzo Abe: Call Him A Born-Again Politician," *Japan Forward*, 20 April 2018, https://japan-forward.com/prime-minister-shinzo-abe-call-him-a-born-again-politician, last accessed on 28 June 2019.
5. 田崎史郎,『安倍官邸の正体』, Tokyo: Kōdansha, 2014, p. 95. He would also, at the recommendation of a former secretary of his father's and Yamamoto Yūji, a member of his cabinet and early backer of his leadership bid, begin practicing Zen meditation in April 2008, taking monthly visits to Tokyo's Zenshōan temple to manage his stress. Nakasone had also been a regular visit to the temple during his premiership. Demachi Yuzuru, "Zen and Politics: The Counsel of Yamamoto Genpō," *Nippon.com*, 9 May 2017, https://www.nippon.com/en/views/b06103, last accessed 2 July 2019.
6. See his discussion with Dr. Hibi Toshifumi, gastroenterologist at Keio

University Hospital, in the autumn 2012 issue of the Japanese Society of Gastroenterology's newsletter, http://jsge.or.jp/citizens/hiroba/pdf/hiroba01.pdf, last accessed on 7 May 2020.
7. 阿比留, op. cit., p. 120.
8. See his December 2007 interview with the *Sankei Shimbun*, https://web.archive.org/web/20071227055006/http://sankei.jp.msn.com/politics/situation/071224/stt0712242102003-n1.htm, last accessed 7 May 2020.
9. 山口敬之, 『総理』, Tokyo: Gentōsha, 2017, p. 112.
10. Ibid., p. 101.
11. By 2012, the former prime minister was deliberately using hikes at Mount Takao as an opportunity to reconnect with voters: on 30 April 2012, with his comeback only months away, he organized a group of nearly 300 to climb the mountain with him, where he was cheered heartily as the group ascended and which Abe marked with a Facebook post featuring a picture in which he is surrounded by his fellow hikers, many of them young. Ibid., 102. See Abe's 30 April 2012 post at https://www.facebook.com/abeshinzo, last accessed 7 May 2020.
12. Terry McCarthy, "Disgraced politicians come back 'cleansed,'" *The Independent*, 20 July 1993, https://www.independent.co.uk/news/world/disgraced-politicans-come-back-cleansed-japans-election-serves-as-a-ritual-purification-for-figures-1485956.html, last accessed 7 May 2020.
13. On Abe's apology tour, see 朝日新聞, 『安倍晋三はなぜ復活できたのか』, Tokyo: Asahi Shimbun Digital Select, Kindle ebook.
14. 田崎, op. cit., pp. 112–113.
15. 安倍昭恵「初めて明かす『安倍辞任』の真相」『週刊新潮』53巻1号、新潮社 2008 年(平成20年)1月3· 10日、29頁。.
16. "Japan PM's wife in rare interview," BBC News, http://news.bbc.co.uk/2/hi/asia-pacific/6044608.stm, last accessed 7 May 2020.
17. Tobias Harris, "The end of Abe politics (for now)," *Observing Japan* (blog), https://observingjapan.com/2007/10/01/the-end-of-abe-politics-for-now, last accessed 7 May 2020.
18. 塩田潮, 『密談の戦後史』, Tokyo: Kadokawa, 2018, pp. 255–262.
19. The Bank of Japan succession battle was fundamentally a question of whether the LDP-led government would genuinely be willing to share power with the DPJ-led House of Councillors or not. The DPJ, which viewed the ministry of finance as the foremost enemy of political leadership of the central government, insisted that the Fukuda government should not nominate an ex-MOF official as governor, despite an infor-

mal convention that dictated that the bank's governors should alternate between career BOJ officials and career MOF officials. Outgoing Governor Fukui Toshihiko was a career BOJ official, so the Fukuda government nominated Deputy Governor Mutō Toshirō, who had had a long career at MOF culminating as administrative vice minister, the top bureaucratic post, before moving over to the BOJ. The DPJ, although initially inclined to support Mutō, decided to reject his appointment. His nomination was nevertheless resubmitted by the Fukuda government and rejected again, resulting in a vacancy that was eventually filled when newly appointed Deputy Governor Shirakawa Masaaki stepped in as the acting and then the permanent governor. Given the worsening global financial outlook, it was perhaps an inopportune moment for a battle over principles, but it was an appropriate battle for the DPJ to press. See 上川, 『日本銀行と政治』, pp. 155–161.

20. On the reaction to the US decision to de-list North Korea, see Tobias Harris, "No surprises," *Observing Japan* (blog), 26 June 2008, https://observingjapan.com/2008/06/26/no-surprises, last accessed 7 May 2020.
21. Tobias Harris, "More stress headed Fukuda's way," 17 June 2008, *Observing Japan* (blog), https://observingjapan.com/2008/06/17/more-stress-headed-fukudas-way, last accessed 7 May 2020.
22. 大下, 『清和会秘録』, p. 249.
23. 塩田潮, 『内閣総理大臣の日本経済』, Tokyo: Nikkei Shimbun, 2015, p. 279.
24. Masahiro Kawai and Shinji Takagi, "Why was Japan Hit So Hard by the Global Financial Crisis?" Asian Development Bank Institute Working Paper No. 153, Tokyo: Asian Development Bank Institute, October 2009, https://www.adb.org/sites/default/files/publication/156008/adbi-wp153.pdf, last accessed 7 May 2020.
25. Justin McCurry, "Japan suffers record fall in GDP," *The Guardian*, 20 May 2009, https://www.theguardian.com/business/2009/may/20/japan-economy-gdp-fall, last accessed 6 July 2019.
26. Richard Koo, *The Escape from the Balance Sheet Recession and the QE Trap* Hoboken, NJ: Wiley, 2014, p. 58.
27. Ibid., pp. 185–186. Koo credits Asō with sacrificing Japan's interests to save the global economy, but it is less obvious to this author that the credit is Asō's versus strong norms regarding the Bank of Japan's independence and a governor (Shirakawa) who was skeptical about the value of the unconventional monetary policies that had originally been pioneered by the BOJ but which had been taken to another level by

the Federal Reserve, Bank of England, and European Central Bank during the crisis.

28. Former Prime Minister Mori did not help matters when he suggested that had Asō consulted him when he formed his cabinet, he would have warned him about naming Nakagawa as finance minister. See: Tobias Harris, "Nakagawa Shoichi is now Aso's problem," *Observing Japan* (blog), 15 February 2009, https://observingjapan.com/2009/02/15/nakagawa-shoichi-is-now-asos-problem, last accessed 7 May 2020.
29. On the "village," see Stephanie Assmann and Sebastian Maslow, "Dispatched and Displaced: Rethinking Employment and Welfare Protection in Japan," *The Asia-Pacific Journal* 8, 15 (April 2010), https://apjjf.org/-Stephanie-Assmann/3342/article.html, last accessed 25 Nov. 2019.
30. 「安倍前首相インタビュー 政界混乱を謝罪 年明け活動再開」, *Sankei Shimbun*, 27 December 2007, https://web.archive.org/web/20071227055007/http://sankei.jp.msn.com/politics/situation/071224/stt0712242102003-n5.htm. last accessed 7 May 2020.
31. 田崎, op. cit., p. 123.
32. 朝日新聞,『安倍晋三はなぜ復活できたのか』Tokyo: Asahi Shimbun Digital Select, ebook.
33. Not unlike how Richard Nixon emerged from his own political purgatory as the "new Nixon" with the help of a savvy media strategy that presented him as the right man for the presidency in 1968. On the "new Nixon," see Joe McGinniss, *The Selling of the President 1968* New York: Trident Press, 1969.
34. 青山, op. cit., 136–139.
35. See: Tobias Harris, "Abe charges in," *Observing Japan* (blog), 18 June 2008, https://observingjapan.com/2008/06/18/abe-charges-in and "Yamasaki's lonely fight," 29 June 2008, https://observingjapan.com/2008/06/29/yamasakis-lonely-fight, last accessed 7 May 2020. Yamasaki lost his seat in 2009 but became, in retirement, a vocal critic of Abe's during his second administration.
36. Ozawa had not helped matters earlier in 2009 when he suggested that the US military presence in Japan ought to be reduced to the naval forces of the Seventh Fleet based in Yokosuka. But no small part of the apprehension in Washington that greeted the DPJ's arrival into power was the result of a critical lack of insight into the new ruling party on the part of the US national security establishment, which had of course long enjoyed close ties with the LDP but had not invested

in relationship building with the Democrats even as it became more likely that they could take power.

37. On the DPJ's plans for administrative reform, see Tobias Harris, "How Will the DPJ Change Japan?" *Naval War College Review* 63, 1 (Winter), https://digital-commons.usnwc.edu/cgi/viewcontent.cgi?article=1618&context=nwc-review, last accessed 25 Nov. 2019.
38. Nagatsuma's memoir of his tenure—『招かれざる大事』, *The Uninvited Minister*—is a revealing look at the DPJ's first year in power. Tokyo: Asahi Shimbun Press, 2011.
39. For Hatoyama's reflection on this episode, see Satoko Oka Norimatsu, "Hatoyama's Confession: The Myth of Deterrence and the Failure to Move a Marine Base Outside Okinawa," *The Asia-Pacific Journal* 9, 9, 28 February 2011, https://apjjf.org/2011/9/9/Satoko-Norimatsu/3495/article.html, last accessed 25 Nov. 2019.
40. Jeffrey Bader, *Obama and China's Rise: An Insider's Account of America's Asia Strategy* Washington, DC: Brookings Institution, 2012, p. 43.
41. 「天皇陛下ご会見の政治利用を糾弾する緊急国民集会」国民運動，日本会議，21 December 2009, https://www.nipponkaigi.org/activity/archives/919, last accessed 7 May 2020.
42. "The Democratic Party of Japan does not have foreign and security policies in the first place," he wrote in the 22 July 2009 edition of his mail magazine. "There cannot be a decent foreign policy that depends the national interest from a political party that will not raise the national flag at its convention." See https://web.archive.org/web/20141218023243/http://www.s-abe.or.jp/topics/mailmagazine/611, last accessed 7 May 2020.
43. In his April 2009 appearance at the Brookings Institution, Abe said that if Maehara Seiji were to become prime minister, "I don't think there would be much change in policy with me." Shinzo Abe, "A New Era Requires New Political Will," The Brookings Institution, Washington, DC, 17 April 2009, https://www.brookings.edu/wp-content/uploads/2012/04/20090417_abe.pdf, last accessed 7 May 2020.
44. See https://web.archive.org/web/20100415205650/http://sosei-nippon.jp/member.html, last accessed 7 May 2020. From the perspective of 2009, the group looks like both a reunion of Abe's first government and a shadow cabinet for his second. In 2010, it included Furuya Keiji, Abe's longtime friend and minister of state for disaster management from 2012–2014; Yamamoto Yūji, minister of state for financial affairs from 2006–2007 and minister of agriculture from 2016–2017; Shimomura Hakubun, deputy chief cabinet secretary from

2006–2007 and minister of education, 2012–2015; Takaichi Sanae, minister of state from 2006–2007 and minister of internal affairs from 2014–2017; Suga, minister of internal affairs from 2006–2007 and chief cabinet secretary from 2012 onwards; Iwaya Takeshi, minister of defense from 2018 onwards; Seko Hiroshige, aide to prime minister from 2006–2007, deputy chief cabinet secretary from 2012–2016, minister of economy, trade, and industry from 2016 onwards; Etō Seiichi, Abe's longtime friend although not a member of his governments; Nishimura Yasutoshi, deputy chief cabinet secretary from 2017 onwards; Katō Katsunobu, head of the group's secretariat and deputy chief cabinet secretary from 2012–2015, minister of state for combating demographic change, gender inequality, and other issues from 2015–2017, and minister of health, labor, and welfare from 2017–2018; Inada Tomomi, minister of state for regulatory reform from 2012–2014 and minister of defense from 2016–2017; Onodera Itsunori, minister of defense from 2012–2014 and again from 2017–2018; Asō, who would be Abe's finance minister from 2012 onwards; Shiozaki, who would return as minister of health, labor, and welfare in 2014; and Ishihara Nobuteru, minister of state from 2012–2014 and again from 2016–2017. It also included his younger brother by birth, Kishi Nobuo, and Hirasawa Katsuei, the LDP lawmaker who had been Abe's childhood tutor and would later work with Abe on the abductee issue.

45. See https://web.archive.org/web/20150803182218/http://www.s-abe.or.jp/wp-content/uploads/220205.pdf, last accessed 7 May 2020.
46. Gideon Rachman, *Easternization* New York: Other Press, 2016, pp. 62–63. On China's fiscal stimulus, see Adam Tooze, *Crashed* New York: Viking, 2018, pp. 242–246. See also Elizabeth Economy, *The Third Revolution* New York: Oxford University Press, 2018, p. 188.
47. 「「菅民主党政権打倒宣言」 中国人船長釈放問題で緊急声明　創生「日本」」, 9 November 2010, https://web.archive.org/web/20141218022019/http://www.s-abe.or.jp/topics/mailmagazine/1997, last accessed 7 May 2020.

11. THE COMEBACK

1. Gregory Smits, "Danger in the Lowground: Historical Context for the March 11, 2011 Tōhoku Earthquake and Tsunami," *Japan Focus*, 9, 20, 9 May 2011, https://apjjf.org/2011/9/20/Gregory-Smits/3531/article.html, last accessed 16 July 2019.

2. Richard Lloyd Parry, *Ghosts of the Tsunami* London: Vintage, 2017, p. 9.
3. 阿比留, op. cit., pp. 131–133.
4. 清水, 『平成デモクラシー史』, p. 305.
5. During the brief campaign for the DPJ's leadership, Noda referred to himself as being like the loach, a bottom-feeding fish often found in rice paddies, suggesting that he would be willing to work unglamorously in the mud on behalf of the Japanese people. See Yuka Hayashi, "Yoshihiko Noda Is Low-Key Politician With Hawkish Bent," *Wall Street Journal*, 30 August 2011, https://www.wsj.com/articles/SB1000142405311190419940457653757125210 7278, last accessed 20 July 2019.
6. Financial Affairs Committee, House of Representatives, National Diet of Japan, 10 November 1993, https://kokkai.ndl.go.jp/#/detail?minId=112804629X00319931110&spkNum=16&single, last accessed 7 May 2020.
7. See Richard Smethurst, *From Foot Soldier to Finance Minister* Cambridge, MA: Harvard University Press, 2009.
8. Paul Krugman, "Japan: Still Trapped," November 1998, http://web.mit.edu/krugman/www/japtrap2.html, last accessed 7 May 2020.
9. Milton Friedman, "Rx for Japan: Back to the Future," Hoover Digest, 17 December 1997, https://www.hoover.org/research/reviving-japan, last accessed 7 May 2020.
10. See, for example, the questions and answers following a 2000 speech to the Bank of Canada. Milton Friedman, "Canada and Flexible Exchange Rates," http://www.bankofcanada.ca/wp-content/uploads/2010/08/keynote.pdf, last accessed 7 May 2020.
11. These decisions, during which Abe was chief cabinet secretary and prime minister respectively, would make him more susceptible to reflationist ideas in 2011 and 2012.
12. Adam Posen, *Restoring Japan's Economic Growth* New York: Columbia University Press, 1998.
13. 小野展克, 『黒田日銀最後の賭け』, Tokyo: Bungei Shunjū, 2015, pp. 38–41. During the 2000s, Hamada Kōichi and Iwata Kikuo moved between academic posts and government advisory jobs; Honda Etsuro served in the final years of his MOF career, before transitioning into academia in 2012; Takahashi Yoichi left MOF and became an academic and public intellectual. Yamamoto pressed the case for monetary policy change in Diet deliberations and opinion pieces, but did so largely by himself.
14. Koichi Hamada and Asahi Noguchi, "The Role of Preconceived Ideas in Macroeconomic Policy: Japan's Experiences in Two Deflationary Periods," Economic Growth Center, Yale University, Discussion Paper No. 908.

15. Paul Krugman, "Japan's Trap," May 1998, http://web.mit.edu/krugman/www/japtrap.html, last accessed 7 May 2020.
16. "Euphoria—that is, a dramatic shift in expectations—was the initial response," wrote Peter Temin and his co-author Barrie Wigmore about the birth of the New Deal.
17. As Bernanke said in 2003, "Addressing the deflation problem would bring substantial real and psychological benefits to the Japanese economy, and ending deflation would make solving the other problems that Japan faces only that much easier." See "Some Thoughts on Monetary Policy in Japan," Tokyo, Japan, 31 May 2003, https://www.federalreserve.gov/boarddocs/speeches/2003/20030531, last accessed 7 May 2020.
18. See Shirakawa Masaaki, "Demographic Changes and Macroeconomic Performance: Japanese Experiences," 2012 BOJ-IMES Conference, 30 May 2012, https://www.boj.or.jp/en/announcements/press/koen_2012/ko120530a.htm, last accessed 23 July 2012.
19. As Ono argues, Yamamoto's perceptive realization that he could use the 3/11 disaster to advance a cause on behalf of which he had been fighting for two decades looks like a textbook example of political scientist John Kingdon's model of policy change. Kingdon argues that policy change happens when circumstances shift to open a "policy window" that enables a "policy entrepreneur" to advance ideas that she had already been pursuing. See 小野, op. cit., p. 39. Also John Kingdon, *Agendas, Alternatives, and Public Policies*, 2nd ed. New York: Pearson, 2003.
20. 「増税反対、超党派211議員が署名」, *Nikkei Shimbun*, 16 June 2011, https://www.nikkei.com/article/DGXNASFS1602T_W1A610C1PE8000, last accessed 7 May 2020.
21. In retrospect, the group looks like the Abe government in waiting. The association included Yamamoto as secretary-general, Tamura as head of the secretariat, Katō Katsunobu, Abe's future foreign minister Kishida Fumio, Abe's future education minister Shimomura Hakubun, Suga, future deputy chief cabinet secretary Nishimura Yasutoshi, future chairman of the National Public Safety Commission Furuya Keiji, and future deputy chief cabinet secretary and METI minister Seko Hiroshige. Other Abe associates included his onetime LDP secretary-general Nakagawa Hidenao (the original coiner of the word Abenomics), his mentor and patron former prime minister Mori Yoshirō, and Kishi Nobuo, Abe's birth brother who was adopted by his uncle and aunt and raised as his cousin. See the statement and list

of members at http://ajer.cocolog-nifty.com/blog/2011/06/post-001f.html, last accessed 23 July 2019.

22. Yamamoto had called on the Kan government to adopt this approach immediately after 3/11, and on 11 May convened a small, multi-party group of parliamentarians interested in monetary policy—including Abe ally Watanabe Yoshimi—to advance this approach. Yamamoto met Abe to inquire about chairing the new association on 19 May, the day after Abe's column ran. This timeline can be found in the *Asahi Shimbun*'s『アベノミクスはどう生まれたか？』, an e-book collecting the newspaper's reporting on the birth of Abenomics. Tokyo: Asahi Shimbun Digital Select, Kindle ebook
23. See for example his 2 November 2011, 4 January 2012, and 15 February 2012 columns, which lambaste Prime Minister Noda Yoshihiko and the BOJ for allowing the yen to strengthen and deflation to remain. He also attacked Noda and the DPJ for considering a consumption tax hike—a position that put him at odds with other members of the LDP—warning that it would be deflationary.
24. The Japan Rebirth manifesto is reproduced in full in 大下,『安倍晋三と岸信介』, pp. 172–183.
25. On the LDP's 2012 draft, see Nakakita, op. cit., pp. 239–241. See also Lawrence Repeta, "Japan's Democracy at Risk—The LDP's Ten Most Dangerous Proposals for Constitutional Change," *Japan Focus* 11, 28, 14 July 2013, https://apjjf.org/2013/11/28/Lawrence-Repeta/3969/article.html; Adam P. Liff, "How Specifically Does Japan's LDP Want to Revise the Constitution?" *The Diplomat*, 14 July 2016, https://thediplomat.com/2016/07/how-specifically-does-japans-ldp-want-to-revise-the-constitution, last accessed 7 May 2020.
26. 読売新聞政治部,『安倍晋三 逆転復活の３００日』, Tokyo: Shinchōsha, 2013, p. 17.
27. Quoted in 塩田潮,『密談の戦後史』, Tokyo: Kadokawa, 2018, pp. 296–297.
28. Ibid., 287–294. See also 朝日新聞,『安倍晋三はなぜ復活できたのか』, Tokyo: Asahi Shimbun Digital Select, Kindle ebook, chs. 6 and 7.
29. 菅義偉,『官僚を動かせ　政治家の覚悟』, Tokyo: Bungei Shunjū, 2013, p. 3.
30. 松田賢弥,『影の権力者　内閣官房長官菅義偉』, Tokyo: Kodansha, 2016, p. 289.
31. 山口,『総理』, pp. 112–113.
32. See an interview with journalist Ohshita Eiji conducted shortly before the LDP election, printed in『安倍晋三と岸信介』, p. 34.
33. 大下,『清和会秘録』, p. 267.

34. 山口, op. cit., pp. 115–116.
35. Ibid., p. 119.
36. Ibid., 112.
37. 石井妙子,『安倍昭恵 「家庭内野党」の真実』, Tokyo: Bungei Shunjū E-Books, 2017.
38. 大下, 『安倍晋三と岸信介』, pp. 218–219.
39. Most of the twenty lawmakers Abe needed to nominate him to run came from the group, and the group's seventy-five members likely made up the bulk of the 108 votes Abe received in the final round. See Christian Winkler, "Right Rising? Ideology and the 2012 House of Representatives Election," in Robert Pekkanen, Steven Reed, and Ethan Scheiner, eds., *Japan Decides 2012: The Japanese General Election* New York: Palgrave Macmillan, 2013, p. 208.
40. 「安倍晋三新総裁　記者会見」, Liberal Democratic Party, 26 September 2012, https://www.jimin.jp/news/press/president/128892.html, last accessed 7 May 2020.
41. 田崎, op. cit., p. 135.
42. Reuters, 4 October 2012, https://jp.reuters.com/article/t9e8kp01j-maehara-boj-idJPTYE89303520121004, last accessed 7 May 2020. On 5 October, Maehara became the first cabinet minister since Takenaka in 2003 to attend a BOJ policy board meeting, where he argued for a one-percent inflation target and greater coordination between the government and central bank on macroeconomic stimulus. Kamikawa, op. cit., p. 234.
43. 上川, op. cit., p. 229.
44. Ibid., p. 235.
45. 清水, 『平成デモクラシー史』, p. 320.

12. "THERE IS NO ALTERNATIVE"

1. It was an unusual reference: whereas Thatcher had used the slogan to argue for the necessity of reforms that would expand the role of markets and roll back the welfare state, Abe was skeptical of free-market capitalism. Instead, in his writings and speeches he would articulate what he called *Mizuho no kuni* capitalism, which referred to an old name for Japan meaning "the land of abundant rice." In an updated version of his 2006 book—now called *Atarashii kuni e* [*Towards a New Country*]—published in early 2013, Abe sketched a picture of a traditional rice-producing society "based on self-reliance and self-help," but in which "if unfortunately someone falls ill, everyone in the village will help."

He wrote: "This kind of ancient Japanese social security is incorporated in a Japanese person's DNA,…I think that in the *Mizuho no kuni*, there is capitalism suitable for the *Mizuho no kuni*. However, while emphasizing free competition and an open economy, it is not the kind of capitalism driven by greed that dominates the world from Wall Street, but rather it is a form of market-based economy suitable for the *Mizuho no kuni* in the *Mizuho no kuni* that respects moral values and knows true wealth." 安部晋三,『新しい国へ』, Tokyo: Bungei Shunjū, 2013, Kindle edition. Author's translation.

2. "Economic Policy Speech by H.E. Mr. Shinzo Abe, Prime Minister of Japan," Cabinet Secretariat, 19 June 2013, https://japan.kantei.go.jp/96_abe/statement/201306/19guildhall_e.html, last accessed 7 May 2020.
3. Shinzo Abe, "Japan is Back," Ministry of Foreign Affairs of Japan, 22 February 2013, https://www.mofa.go.jp/announce/pm/abe/us_20130222en.html, last accessed 7 May 2020.
4. "Policy Speech by Prime Minister Shinzo Abe to the 183rd Session of the Diet," Cabinet Secretariat, 28 January 2013, https://japan.kantei.go.jp/96_abe/statement/201301/28syosin_e.html, last accessed 7 May 2020.
5. Richard McGregor, *Asia's Reckoning* New York: Viking, 2017, p. 300. McGregor notes that two participants in the private session said Russel used this phrase, though Russel himself did not remember saying it.
6. 谷口智彦,『安倍晋三の真実』, Tokyo: Goku Books, 2018, p. 149; 田崎, op. cit., p. 35.
7. Aurelia George Mulgan, *The Abe Administration and the Rise of the Prime Ministerial Executive* New York: Routledge, 2018, p. 39.
8. Ibid., p. 36.
9. Ibid., p. 42.
10. See Giulio Pugliese, "Kantei diplomacy? Japan's hybrid leadership in foreign and security policy," *The Pacific Review* 30, 2 (2017), pp. 152–168 on how Abe's foreign policy leadership depended on his use of trusted, hand-picked officials from MOFA, many of whom he knew from his first government.
11. Quoted in 清水,『財務省と政治』, p. 231.
12. 田崎, op. cit., p. 57.
13. 「佐伯耕三さん 現場主義、難題と向き合う」, Nikkei Shimbun, 9 August 2017, https://www.nikkei.com/article/DGKKZO19813870Z00C17A8EAC000, 7 May 2020.
14. The first reference in the media to "Abenomics" after Abe's return to

the LDP's leadership appears to be an article in the *Nikkei Shimbun*, Japan's leading financial newspaper, by Takita Yoichi on 26 November 2012.

15. A pun in Japanese that used the word for dangerous—*abunai*—in place of Abe's name.
16. Taniguchi uses the phrase "shock and awe."
17. See http://www.kantei.go.jp/jp/96_abe/actions/201301/07keizai.html, last accessed 7 May 2020. The parable of the three arrows, a popular folktale, tells the story of Mōri Motonari, a lord of Chōshu during Japan's Warring States period, who wanted his three sons to work together for the good of the clan. To demonstrate the value of cooperation, he gave each an arrow and instructed them to snap it, which each did easily. He then held three arrows together and instructed them to snap the three arrows, which they were unable to do.
18. 上川, op. cit., p. 243.
19. 「デフレ脱却と持続的な経済成長の実現のための政府・日本銀行の政策連携について（共同声明）」, Council on Economic and Fiscal Policy, Cabinet Secretariat, 22 January 2013, https://www5.cao.go.jp/keizai1/seifu-nichigin/2013/0122_seifu-nichigin.pdf, last accessed 7 May 2020.
20. Makihara Izuru suggests that Suga pressured Shirakawa to resign. "Abe's Enforcer: Suga Yoshihide's Stabilizing Influence on the Cabinet," *Nippon.com*, 25 September 2014, https://www.nippon.com/en/currents/d00135, last accessed 25 Nov. 2019.
21. 読売新聞政治部, op. cit., p. 99.
22. When working at the Japanese consulate in New York in 2000, an economist at the New York Fed asked Honda why on earth the Bank of Japan had decided to lift interest rates with deflation still ongoing. Honda did not have a good answer, which led him to read reflationary economist Iwata Kikuo's books on deflationary economics, turning him into a full-blown reflationist himself. 小野, op. cit., p. 63.
23. 本田悦朗, 『アベノミクスの真実』, Tokyo: Gentōsha, 2013, p. 6. In an interview with the *Wall Street Journal* in 2014, Honda would reveal that he shared Abe's new conservative beliefs about the virtues of Japan's kamikaze pilots, the importance of Abe's worshipping at Yasukuni shrine, and the threat posed by China's rise, among other beliefs. See Andrew Browne, "A More-Muscular Japan, Personified," The *Wall Street Journal*, 18 February 2014, https://www.wsj.com/articles/nationalist-fuel-for-japan8217s-revival-plan-1392717630, last accessed 8 August 2019.
24. 小野, op. cit., p. 80.

25. Ibid., p. 84.
26. 上川, op. cit., p. 248.
27. In a December 2002 op-ed in the *Financial Times*, for example, he argued that the BOJ should "adopt innovative, non-traditional anti-deflationary policies" as part of a coordinated campaign of global reflation by the world's leading central banks. Haruhiko Kuroda and Masahiro Kawai, "Time for a switch to global reflation," *Financial Times*, 2 December 2002.
28. 小野, op. cit., p. 102.
29. Shinzo Abe, "The Bounty of the Open Seas: Five New Principles for Japanese Diplomacy," Ministry of Foreign Affairs of Japan, Jakarta, Indonesia, 18 January 2013, https://www.mofa.go.jp/announce/pm/abe/abe_0118e.html, 7 May 2020.
30. Céline Pajon, "Japan's 'Smart' Strategic Engagement in Southeast Asia," The ASAN Forum, 6 December 2013, http://www.theasanforum.org/japans-smart-strategic-engagement-in-southeast-asia, 7 May 2020.
31. While Hillary Clinton would try to claim ownership of the "pivot to Asia," Obama himself—the Hawaii native who on his first trip to Tokyo as president in November 2009 called himself America's "first Pacific president"—believed in the importance of focusing his administration's attention and resources on Asia. See Jeffrey Goldberg, "The Obama Doctrine," *The Atlantic*, April 2016, https://www.theatlantic.com/magazine/archive/2016/04/the-obama-doctrine/471525, last accessed 7 May 2020.
32. Bader, op. cit., p. 6.
33. Michael Green, *By More Than Providence* New York: Columbia University Press, 2017, pp. 520–521.
34. Ibid., p. 16.
35. Carrie Budoff-Brown, "Obama's no-schmooze diplomacy," *Politico*, 7 June 2011, https://www.politico.com/story/2011/06/obamas-no-schmooze-diplomacy-056470, last accessed 7 May 2020. Unlike his predecessor, who hosted both Koizumi and Abe at Camp David, Obama barely used Camp David for meetings with foreign leaders during his eight years in office. See Juliet Eilperin, "For President Obama, Camp David often ranks as the venue of last resort," *Washington Post*, 20 March 2015, https://www.washingtonpost.com/politics/camp-david-just-isnt-president-obamas-kind-of-retreat/2015/03/20/253de0fc-ce51-11e4-a2a7-9517a3a70506_story.html, last accessed 7 May 2020.
36. As Robert Dujarric notes, this belief seems to have little bearing in

reality. It was, after all, a Republican (Nixon) who had carried out the twin shocks that had so rattled Japan in 1971. Republicans Ronald Reagan and George H.W. Bush were unflinching in their opposition to Japan's trade practices. Abe did not even have to look to the Cold War for evidence of Republican "perfidy": George W. Bush's administration had chided him on the comfort women issue, and then slighted Japan in negotiations with North Korea, to the fury of the abductee movement. "Why does the LDP prefer the GOP?" The *Japan Times*, 3 March 2014, https://www.japantimes.co.jp/opinion/2014/03/03/commentary/japan-commentary/why-does-the-ldp-prefer-the-gop/#.XVbv-ZNKjdc, last accessed 7 May 2020.

37. To this day, well into the Trump administration, Japanese diplomats still accuse Obama of being a weak foreign policy president on these terms.
38. Andrew Erickson and Adam Liff, "Full Steam Ahead: China's Ever-Increasing Military Budget," *China Real Time (Wall Street Journal)*, 5 March 2014, http://blogs.wsj.com/chinarealtime/2014/03/05/full-steam-ahead-chinas-ever-increasing-military-budget/tab/print, last accessed 7 May 2020
39. See, for example, commentator Komori Yoshihisa in the right-wing *Sankei Shimbun*. 「米中２極Ｇ２論の適否」, 9 May 2009.
40. "Transcript of interview with Japanese Prime Minister Shinzo Abe," *Washington Post*, 20 February 2013, https://www.washingtonpost.com/world/transcript-of-interview-with-japanese-prime-minister-shinzo-abe/2013/02/20/e7518d54-7b1c-11e2-82e8-61a46c2cde3d_story.html, last accessed 7 May 2020.
41. Budget Committee, House of Representatives, National Diet of Japan, 12 March 2013, http://kokkai.ndl.go.jp/SENTAKU/syugiin/183/0018/18303120018012a.html, last accessed 7 May 2020. Julian Ryall, "Japan PM dismisses WWII war crimes trials as 'victors' justice," The *Telegraph*, 14 March 2013, https://www.telegraph.co.uk/news/worldnews/asia/japan/9930041/Japan-PM-dismisses-WWII-war-crimes-trials-as-victors-justice.html, last accessed 7 May 2020.
42. "One Man's Invasion Is…" *Wall Street Journal*, 27 April 2013, https://www.wsj.com/articles/SB10001424127887324474004578447213428743382, last accessed 7 May 2020.
43. It almost goes without saying that this was not the first time Abe made comments like these about the Tokyo tribunals or the definition of an "invasion," including in Diet deliberations. 柿崎, op. cit., ch. 2.2 passim.

44. 読売新聞政治部, op. cit., p. 110.
45. Yachi Shōtarō, 「TPP参加は「強い安保」「強い経済」への分水嶺」 WEDGE, 20 December 2010.
46. Aurelia George Mulgan, "Farmers, Agricultural Policies, and the Election," in Robert Pekkanen, Steven R. Reed, and Ethan Scheiner, eds., *Japan Decides 2012: The Japanese General Election* New York: Palgrave Macmillan, 2013.
47. Liberal Democratic Parry manifesto 2012, https://jimin.jp-east-2.storage.api.nifcloud.com/pdf/seisaku_ichiban24.pdf?_ga=2.81474135.1511928292.1565498608–128191866.1562870219, last accessed 7 May 2020. The LDP under Tanigaki had taken a similar stance and had also stressed other preconditions for Japan's participation, including resisting numerical quotas for automobiles, protecting Japan's national health insurance system, ensuring the safety of Japan's food supply, opposing investor-state dispute settlement, and securing carve-outs for government procurement rules.
48. "Joint Statement by the United States and Japan," Ministry of Foreign Affairs of Japan, 22 February 2013, https://www.mofa.go.jp/mofaj/kaidan/s_abe2/vti_1302/pdfs/1302_us_02.pdf, last accessed 7 May 2020.
49. "Press Conference by Prime Minister Shinzo Abe," Cabinet Secretariat, 15 March 2013, https://japan.kantei.go.jp/96_abe/statement/201303/15kaiken_e.html, last accessed 7 May 2020.
50. 清水,『平成デモクラシー史』, p. 334.
51. 『日本再興戦略 JAPAN IS BACK』, Council on Economic and Fiscal Policy, Cabinet Secretariat, 14 June 2013, https://www.kantei.go.jp/jp/singi/keizaisaisei/pdf/saikou_jpn.pdf, last accessed 7 May 2020.
52. Jeff Kingston, "Richard Katz on the failures of 'Voodoo Abenomics,'" The *Japan Times*, 30 August 2014, https://www.japantimes.co.jp/opinion/2014/08/30/commentary/japan-commentary/richard-katz-failures-voodoo-abenomics/#.XVFqXZNKjdc, last accessed 7 May 2020.
53. "Speech on Growth Strategy by Prime Minister Shinzo Abe at the Japan National Press Club," Cabinet Secretariat, 19 April 2013, https://japan.kantei.go.jp/96_abe/statement/201304/19speech_e.html, last accessed 7 May 2020.

13. BUILDING A NEW JAPAN

1. 塩田潮, 『復活！自民党の謎』, Tokyo: Asahi Shimbun Publishers, 2014, p. 219.

2. "Presentation by Prime Minister Shinzo Abe at the 125th Session of the International Olympic Committee," Buenos Aires, Cabinet Secretariat, 7 September 2013, https://japan.kantei.go.jp/96_abe/statement/201309/07ioc_presentation_e.html, last accessed on 25 Nov. 2019.
3. David Leheny, "Shinzo Abe's appeal to nostalgia and nationalism," *Los Angeles Times*, 2 August 2019, https://www.latimes.com/opinion/story/2019-08-01/shinzo-abe-japan-nationalism-parliament-elections-postwar-history, last accessed 7 May 2020.
4. "Press Conference by Prime Minister Shinzo Abe Following His Attendance at the G20 Summit Meeting in Saint Petersburg and the 125th International Olympic Committee Session," Buenos Aires, Cabinet Secretariat, 7 September 2013, http://japan.kantei.go.jp/96_abe/statement/201309/07argentine_naigai_e.html, last accessed 7 May 2020.
5. 「消費税引き上げ「なだらかでも」 首相ブレーンの浜田氏」 Asahi Shimbun, 12 July 2013.
6. 山口, op. cit., p. 133.
7. Prime Minister Ohira campaigned on introducing a five-percent tax in 1979 and the LDP lost its majority for the first time, sparking a crisis that eventually led to a massive heart attack that felled Ohira. In 1988, Takeshita introduced a three-percent consumption tax. In 1989, the LDP lost control of the upper house. In 1997, Hashimoto raised the tax to five percent. The following year, the LDP suffered another big upper house defeat and Hashimoto resigned. The DPJ suffered the tax's curse too. Kan's promise to introduce a tax hike crippled the DPJ's chances in 2010, and Noda's dauntless pursuit of a compromise shattered his party and ensured the LDP's victory in 2012.
8. This is the kind of reasoning—the idea that contractionary fiscal policy can contribute to growth—that economist Paul Krugman has mocked as "figments of the policy elite's imagination." He has regularly referred to them as the "confidence fairy" and the "invisible bond vigilante." See Paul Krugman, "Myths of Austerity," *New York Times*, 1 July 2010, https://www.nytimes.com/2010/07/02/opinion/02krugman.html, last accessed 7 May 2020.
9. The IMF, for example, recommended in its 2013 Article IV report on Japan that "Raising the consumption tax rate is an essential first step to contain fiscal vulnerabilities." See https://www.imf.org/external/pubs/ft/scr/2013/cr13253.pdf, last accessed 7 May 2020.
10. David Pilling and Jonathan Soble, "Shinzo Abe interview: 'I am

convinced that our road is the only way,'" *Financial Times*, 7 October 2013.

11. It was precisely this talent that led to his being dubbed Yokohama's shadow mayor in the early 1990s; his mentor Okonogi had advised the city's mayor, "If there's something you don't know about personnel issues, please talk with Suga."
12. 松田賢弥,『影の権力者 内閣官房長官菅義偉』, p. 150.
13. Aurelia George Mulgan, *The Abe Administration*, p. 45 and pp. 44–47 for the Abe government's approach to administrative personnel decision-making more broadly.
14. "Cabinet Personnel Bureau Sign Hanging and Instructions," Cabinet Secretariat, 30 May 2014, http://www.kantei.go.jp/jp/96_abe/actions/201405/30jinjikyoku.html, last accessed 7 May 2020.
15. 「省庁幹部人事、女性２倍の15人　政権方針を反映」Nikkei Shimbun, 5 July 2014.
16. Richard J. Samuels, *Special Duty: A History of the Japanese Intelligence Community*, Ithaca, NY: Cornell University Press, 2019, pp. 205–207; "Act on the Protection of Specially Designated Secrets," 22 April 2014, http://www.japaneselawtranslation.go.jp/law/detail/?ft=1&re=01&dn=1&x=28&y=10&co=01&ia=03&ja=04&ky=%E7%89%B9%E5%AE%9A%E7%A7%98%E5%AF%86&page=2, last accessed 25 Nov. 2019.
17. "Statement Concerning the Approval of the Cabinet Meeting Regarding the Bill on the Protection of Specially Designated Secrets," Japan Federation of Bar Associations, 25 October 2013, https://www.nichibenren.or.jp/en/document/statements/131025.html, last accessed 7 May 2020.
18. 「特定秘密保護法案「治安維持法」復活の危険性も？」, *Shūkan Asahi*, 20 November 2013, https://dot.asahi.com/wa/2013112000003.html?page=1, last accessed 7 May 2020.
19. 「首相、秘密保全体制の強化へ検討指示　尖閣映像流出受け」, *Nikkei Shimbun*, https://www.nikkei.com/article/DGXNASFS1000D_Q0A111C1NN0000, last accessed 7 May 2020.
20. Catherine A. Traywick, "In Japan's State Secrets Law, Shades of Red, White and Blue," *Foreign Policy*, 5 December 2013, https://foreignpolicy.com/2013/12/05/in-japans-state-secrets-law-shades-of-red-white-and-blue, last accessed 7 May 2020.
21. The DPJ, while in power, revealed the existence of secret agreements between the US and Japan that would, despite Japan's three non-nuclear principles and official denials, allow the US to bring nuclear

weapons into Japan, https://www.npr.org/templates/story/story.php?storyId=124567404, last accessed 7 May 2020. Meanwhile, as the *New York Times* reported in 1994 and the US government officially confirmed a decade later, the CIA funneled money to Kishi and other LDP politicians to strengthen Japan as a bulwark against communism. See Tim Weiner, "C.I.A. Spent Millions to Support Japanese Right in 50's and 60's," *New York Times*, 9 October 1994, https://www.nytimes.com/1994/10/09/world/cia-spent-millions-to-support-japanese-right-in-50-s-and-60-s.html, last accessed 7 May 2020.

22. Smith, *Japan Rearmed*, p. 34.
23. Sabine Frühstück, *Uneasy Warriors* Berkeley: University of California Press, 2007.
24. Adam P. Liff, "Japan's Defense Policy: Abe the Evolutionary," *The Washington Quarterly* (Summer 2015) 82–83.
25. 二階堂勇, 「自衛隊制服組、じわり政治の表に　統幕長しばしば官邸へ」, *Asahi Shimbun*, 25 April 2016, https://digital.asahi.com/articles/ASJ4N3SY5J4NUTFK005.html, last accessed 7 May 2020.
26. Samuels, *Special Duty*, pp. 210–213.
27. Adam P. Liff, "Japan's National Security Council: Policy Coordination and Political Power," *Japanese Studies* 38, 2 (2018) 253–254.
28. Katsuhiko Meshino, "Princelings are ruling not just China," *Nikkei Asian Review*, 31 December 2013. https://asia.nikkei.com/Politics/Princelings-are-ruling-not-just-China, last ccessed 14 August 2019.
29. Rush Doshi, "Hu's to blame for China's foreign assertiveness?" Brookings Institution, 22 January 2019. https://www.brookings.edu/articles/hus-to-blame-for-chinas-foreign-assertiveness.
30. Adam P. Liff, "China and the US Alliance System," *The China Quarterly* 233 (March 2018) 137–165.
31. Xi Jinping, "New Asian Security Concept For New Progress in Security Cooperation," Remarks at the Fourth Summit of the Conference on Interaction and Confidence Building Measures in Asia, Shanghai, 21 May 2014, https://www.fmprc.gov.cn/mfa_eng/zxxx_662805/t1159951.shtml, last accessed 7 May 2020.
32. "China officially labels Senkakus a 'core interest'," *Japan Times*, 27 April 2013, https://www.japantimes.co.jp/news/2013/04/27/national/china-officially-labels-senkakus-a-core-interest/#.XVWfu5NKjdc, last accessed 7 May 2020.
33. According to Japan's Joint Staff Office, the ASDF scrambled fighters 810 times in 2013, the most since the end of the Cold War. 415 of those scrambles were in response to PLAAF planes, an increase from

306 in 2012. As recently as 2009, the ASDF scrambled fighters only thirty-eight times in response to Chinese aircraft.

34. "China And Japan Are Calling Each Other 'Voldemort' As Propaganda War Escalates," *Business Insider*, 7 January 2014, https://www.businessinsider.com/china-and-japan-are-calling-each-other-voldemort-2014-1, last accessed 7 May 2020.
35. Andrew Browne, "Shinzo Abe's History Lesson Haunts Davos," *Wall Street Journal*, 28 January 2014, https://www.wsj.com/articles/no-headline-available-1390900995, last accessed 7 May 2020.
36. Jane Perlez, "Abe's Version of History Doesn't Sit Well With Chinese," *New York Times*, 24 January 2014, https://cn.nytimes.com/asia-pacific/20140124/c24abe/en-us, last accessed 7 May 2020.
37. Jeffrey W. Hornung, "Japan's Growing Hard Hedge Against China," *Asian Strategy* 10, 2 (June 2014): 97–122.
38. On multiple occasions, Abe has recounted how, at the start of his grandfather's premiership, his father, then Kishi's secretary, recommended that he focus on economic prosperity. However, Kishi answered, "Certainly economic policy is important. However, at the same time, security is fundamental for the nation, and we have to accomplish it, because no one other than politicians can strive to do it." Abe Shinzō, Speech at the *Naigai Jyōsei Chōsakai*, 19 September 2014, http://www.kantei.go.jp/jp/96_abe/statement/2014/0919naigai.html, last accessed 7 May 2020. Author's translation.
39. Jane Perlez and Joe Cochrane, "Obama's Absence Leaves China as Dominant Force at Asia-Pacific Meeting," *New York Times*, 7 October 2013, https://www.nytimes.com/2013/10/08/world/asia/asia-pacific-economic-cooperation-summit.html, last accessed 7 May 2020.
40. *Mainichi Shimbun*, 1 November 2013.
41. 山口, op. cit., pp. 210–211.
42. "Statement by PM Abe on visit to war-linked Yasukuni Shrine," Kyodo News, 26 December 2013.
43. http://www.wiesenthal.com/about/news/simon-wiesenthal-center-pm.html
44. US Mission Japan, "Statement on Prime Minister Abe's December 26 Visit to Yasukuni Shrine," 26 December 2013. https://jp.usembassy.gov/statement-prime-minister-abes-december-26-visit-yasukuni-shrine.
45. CCS book.
46. 山口, op. cit., pp. 214–217.
47. Quoted in McGregor, op. cit., p. 321.
48. Warwick's Christopher Hughes also used the term "Abe Doctrine" in

a 2015 monograph but was highly skeptical about whether it actually constituted a break from the past. Christopher W. Hughes, *Japan's Foreign and Security Policy Under the "Abe Doctrine": New Dynamism or New Dead End?* New York: Palgrave Macmillan, 2015.

14. THE SLOW BORING OF HARD BOARDS

1. 「第47回衆議院選挙の結果をうけて 安倍総裁記者会見」Liberal Democratic Party, 15 December 2012, https://www.jimin.jp/news/press/president/126713.html, last accessed 8 May 2020.
2. Gregory Jackson and Hideaki Miyajima, "Introduction: The Diversity and Change of Corporate Governance in Japan," in Masahiko Aoki, Gregory Jackson, and Hideaki Miyajima, eds., *Corporate Governance in Japan: Institutional Change and Organizational Diversity* New York: Oxford University Press, 2007, pp. 1–50.
3. See Ulrike Schaede, *Choose and Focus: Japanese Business Strategies for the 21st Century* Ithaca, NY: Cornell University Press, 2008, on how Japan's more global manufacturers adapted.
4. See Steven K. Vogel, "Japan's Ambivalent Pursuit of Shareholder Capitalism," *Politics & Society* 47, 1 (2019) 117–144.
5. 柿崎, op. cit., 21–22.
6. 「経営者の行動が賃金を増やす (社説) 」, *Nikkei Shimbun*, 23 December 2013.
7. 「2014年賃金交渉・協議の最終集計」Business Labor Trend, October 2014, the Japan Institute for Labor Policy and Training, https://www.jil.go.jp/kokunai/blt/backnumber/2014/10/026–034.pdf, last accessed 8 May 2020.
8. 加藤裕則、滝沢卓、土屋亮 「賃上げ続くか正念場 薄まる「官製春闘」、割れる労組」, *Asahi Shimbun*, 6 February 2019, https://digital.asahi.com/articles/ASM25014YM24ULFA039.html, last accessed 8 May 2020.
9. 「連合メーデーに4万人 首相出席「景気回復実感を」, *Nikkei Shimbun*, 26 April 2014, https://www.nikkei.com/article/DGXNASDG2601J_W4A420C1CC0000, last accessed 8 May 2020.
10. As Ken Hokugo and Alicia Ogawa note, however, there was a critical difference with the British model: unlike in the UK, Japan's stewardship code did not include provisions regarding collective action with other investors to press managers for better returns. "The Unfinished Business of Japan's Stewardship Code," Center on Japanese Economy and Business, Columbia University, Corporate Governance and Stewardship Program Working Paper Series, No. 1, July 2017, https://

academiccommons.columbia.edu/doi/10.7916/D88G8Z39/download, last accessed 8 May 2020.

11. On Suga's role in agricultural reform, see Mulgan, *The Abe Administration*, p. 48.
12. "Speech on the Second Round of Policies under the Growth Strategy by Prime Minister Shinzo Abe at Japan Akademeia," Cabinet Secretariat, 17 May 2013, https://japan.kantei.go.jp/96_abe/statement/201305/17speech_e.html, last accessed 8 May 2020.
13. On the history of Japan's agricultural cooperatives, see Aurelia George Mulgan, *The Politics of Agriculture in Japan*, New York: Routledge, 2000, ch. 4 passim especially. See also Adam D. Sheingate, *The Rise of the Agricultural Welfare State*, Princeton: Princeton University Press, 2001, pp. 150–161 on the politics and policy of agriculture in postwar Japan.
14. Chikako Mogi and Masaaki Iwamoto, "Abe Breaks Micro-Farms to End Japan Agriculture Slide," Bloomberg, 12 December 2013, https://www.bloomberg.com/news/articles/2013-12-12/abe-pushes-biggest-farm-revamp-since-macarthur-broke-landlords, last accessed 8 May 2020.
15. "'Second Gathering with Prime Minister Shinzo Abe' hosted by Japan Akademeia, Speech by Prime Minister," Cabinet Secretariat, 19 December 2013, https://japan.kantei.go.jp/96_abe/statement/201312/19speech_e.html, last accessed 8 May 2020.
16. Kazuhito Yamashita, "Issues concerning the review of the rice paddy set-aside program," The Canon Institute for Global Studies. 27 December 2013, https://www.canon-igs.org/en/column/macroeconomics/20131227_2264.html, last accessed 8 May 2020. In 2018, Yamashita was still fighting back against reports that the system had been demolished, describing them in a piece as "fake news." *WebRonza*, 18 May 2018, https://webronza.asahi.com/business/articles/2018051500007.html, last accessed 8 May 2020.
17. See, for example,「「攻めの農業」の実現に向けて」Ministry of Agriculture, Forestry, and Fisheries, https://www.kantei.go.jp/jp/singi/keizaisaisei/bunka/dai6/siryou1.pdf, last accessed 8 May 2020. On Suga's involvement, see 岸博幸,「農業改革はどこまで実現するか」Diamond Online, 23 May 2014, https://diamond.jp/articles/-/53453, last accessed 8 May 2020.
18. Mireya Solís, *Dilemmas of a Trading Nation* Washington: Brookings Institution, 2017, p. 155.
19. At a press conference in November 2013, Koizumi's first major appearance since he left the Diet in 2009, he challenged Abe to have

the political courage to eliminate nuclear power. "The public has set the stage for you to use your authority to move us in the right direction [of zero nuclear power]. Ultimately, it's a question of the prime minister's judgment and insight," Koizumi said. On Koizumi's anti-nuclear activism, see Harano Jōji, "The Impact of Koizumi's Call for Zero Nuclear Power," *Nippon.com*, 5 Dec. 2013, https://www.nippon.com/en/column/g00140/the-impact-of-koizumi%E2%80%99s-call-for-zero-nuclear-power.html, last accessed 26 Nov. 2019.

20. Andrew Oros, *Japan's Security Renaissance* New York: Columbia University Press, 2017, pp. 137–138.
21. The 2014 budget also marked the introduction of multi-year procurement contracts, enabling the Japanese government to place larger orders and lower unit costs.
22. "The Three Principles on Transfer of Defense Equipment and Technology," Ministry of Foreign Affairs of Japan, https://www.mofa.go.jp/fp/nsp/page1we_000083.html, last accessed 8 May 2020.
23. Masaya Kato, "Japan's defense industry still lacks bang overseas," *Nikkei Asian Review*, 23 May 2019, https://asia.nikkei.com/Politics/International-relations/Japan-s-defense-industry-still-lacks-bang-overseas2, last accessed 8 May 2020.
24. Sheila Smith, "The President as Facilitator in Chief," *Asia Unbound*, Council on Foreign Relations, 26 March 2014, https://www.cfr.org/blog/president-facilitator-chief, last accessed 8 May 2020.
25. McGregor, op. cit., pp. 312–314.
26. Shinzo Abe, "Asia's Democratic Security Diamond," *Project Syndicate*, 27 Dec. 2012, https://www.project-syndicate.org/onpoint/a-strategic-alliance-for-japan-and-india-by-shinzo-abe, last accessed 26 Nov. 2019.
27. 安倍,『美しい国へ』, p. 159.
28. On Pal's dissent, see Kei Ushimura, "Pal's 'Dissentient Judgment' Reconsidered: Some Notes on Postwar Japan's Responses to the Opinion," *Japan Review* 19 (207): 215–224. A monument to Pal stands on the grounds of Yasukuni shrine, and when Abe visited India in 2007, he met with Pal's son Prasanta. George Nishiyama, "Abe risks ire by meeting son of Indian judge," *Reuters*, 23 Aug. 2007, https://www.reuters.com/article/idINIndia-29108320070823, last accessed 26 Nov. 2019.
29. See C. Raja Mohan, "India and the Balance of Power," *Foreign Affairs* (July/August 2006), https://www.foreignaffairs.com/articles/asia/2006-07-01/india-and-balance-power, last accessed 26 Nov. 2019 on Koizumi's approach to India, which Abe had a hand in as part of Koizumi's government.

30. "Japan-India Joint Statement: Intensifying the Strategic and Global Partnership," Ministry of Foreign Affairs of Japan, January 2014, https://www.mofa.go.jp/files/000025064.pdf, last accessed 8 May 2020.
31. Brahma Chellaney, "Narendra Modi: India's Shinzo Abe," *Japan Times*, 20 May 2014, https://www.japantimes.co.jp/opinion/2014/05/20/commentary/world-commentary/narendra-modi-indias-shinzo-abe/#.XXaHiZNKjdc, last accessed 8 May 2020.
32. *Nikkei Shimbun*, 2 September 2014.
33. Gideon Rachman, *Easternization* New York: Other Press, 2016, pp. 133–134.
34. "Remarks by Prime Minister Abe to the Australian Parliament," Cabinet Secretariat, 8 July 2014, https://japan.kantei.go.jp/96_abe/statement/201407/0708article1.html, last accessed 8 May 2020.
35. Hugh White, "Should we become Japan's ally against China?" *The Age*, 8 July 2014.
36. Although Turnbull rattled the relationship in 2016 when he decided to award a submarine contract to a French bidder rather than a Japanese bid, despite assurances from Abbott that Japan would be favored. Franz-Stefan Gady, "Why Japan Lost the Bid to Build Australia's New Subs," *The Diplomat*, 27 April 2016, https://thediplomat.com/2016/04/why-japan-lost-the-bid-to-build-australias-new-subs, last accessed 26 Nov. 2019.
37. "Joint Press Conference with President Obama and Prime Minister Abe of Japan," Barack Obama White House Archives, 24 April 2014, https://obamawhitehouse.archives.gov/photos-and-video/video/2014/04/24/president-obama-holds-press-conference-prime-minister-abe-japan#transcript, last accessed 8 May 2020.
38. Adam P. Liff, "Policy by Other Means: Collective Self-Defense and the Politics of Japan's Postwar Constitutional Reinterpretations," *Asia Policy* 24 (July 2017): 146.
39. "Judgment upon case of the so-called 'SUNAKAWA CASE'," 159 (A) 710, Supreme Court of Japan, 16 December 1959, http://www.courts.go.jp/app/hanrei_en/detail?id=13, last accessed 8 May 2020.
40. Christopher W. Hughes, "Japan's Strategic Trajectory and Collective Self-Defense: Essential Continuity or Radical Shift?" *Journal of Japanese Studies* 43, 1 (Winter 2017): 101–102.
41. 安倍、『美しい国へ』, pp. 130–134.
42. 「安全保障の法的基盤の再構築に関する懇談会の開催について」Cabinet Secretariat, 7 February 2013, https://www.kantei.go.jp/jp/singi/

anzenhosyou2/pdf/member.pdf, last accessed 8 May 2020. Its ranks included, in addition to a number of prominent security and legal experts, Kasai Yoshiyuki, Abe's leading business ally.

43. "Report of the Advisory Panel on Reconstruction of the Legal Basis for Security," The Advisory Panel on the Reconstruction of the Legal Basis for Security, 15 May 2014, https://www.kantei.go.jp/jp/singi/anzenhosyou2/dai7/houkoku_en.pdf, last accessed 8 May 2020.
44. His choice to lead the bureau, Komatsu Ichirō, was the first diplomat named to the post and shared Abe's views on the need for constitutional change. However, Komatsu, suffering from cancer, resigned from the post in May 2014 and died soon thereafter. See "Former Cabinet Legislation Bureau chief Komatsu dies at 63," *Japan Times*, 23 June 2014, https://www.japantimes.co.jp/news/2014/06/23/national/politics-diplomacy/former-cabinet-legislation-bureau-chief-komatsu-dies-63, last accessed 8 May 2020.
45. 清水,『平成デモクラシー史』, p. 341.
46. In the final weeks of negotiations with Kōmeitō, Iijima Isao, Koizumi's former secretary who Abe had brought on as an adviser, suggested in a speech in Washington, DC that the Abe government could revisit a ruling that determined that the relationship between Kōmeitō and the lay Buddhist organization Sōka Gakkai—the source of Kōmeitō's political clout—was not a violation of the constitution's separation of church and state clause. This threat was disavowed by Suga, but the message was clearly received.
47. Liff, "Policy by Other Means," p. 161.
48. 「国の存立を全うし、国民を守るための切れ目のない安全保障法 制の整備について」Cabinet Secretariat, 1 July 2014, https://www.cas.go.jp/jp/gaiyou/jimu/pdf/anpohosei.pdf, last accessed 8 May 2020
49. "Press Conference by Prime Minister Abe," Cabinet Secretariat, 1 July 2014, https://japan.kantei.go.jp/96_abe/statement/201407/0701kaiken.html, last accessed 8 May 2020.
50. "Pacifist principles preserved," Komeito, 2 July 2014, https://www.komei.or.jp/en/policy/stands/20140702.html, last accessed 8 May 2020.
51. Brad W. Setser, "Japan's First Consumption Tax Hike Was a Demand Disaster," *Follow the Money blog*, 2 June 2016, https://www.cfr.org/blog/japans-first-consumption-tax-hike-was-demand-disaster, last accessed 8 May 2020.
52. 「"聖域"自民党税調の敗北　税制牛耳ってきた歴史も首相には通じず」*Yūkan Fuji*, 13 October 2013, https://www.zakzak.co.jp/society/politics/

news/20131013/plt1310130800000-n1.htm, last accessed 8 May 2020.

53. 山口, op. cit., pp. 140–145.
54. Ibid., 146–150. See 岩田規久男,『日銀日記』, Tokyo: Chikuma Shobō, 2018, pp. 143–146 on the BOJ's deliberations ahead of the second bazooka.
55. Gideon Rachman and James Politi, "Abe balances tax rise against economic damage," *Financial Times*, 19 October 2014, https://www.ft.com/content/25431cfc-57af-11e4-8493-00144feab7de, last accessed 8 May 2020.
56. Eleanor Warnock and Mitsuru Obe, "Japan falls into recession," *Wall Street Journal*, 17 November 2014, https://www.wsj.com/articles/japan-falls-into-recession-1416182404, last accessed 8 May 2020.
57. 「安倍内閣総理大臣記者会見」Cabinet Secretariat, 18 November 2014, https://www.kantei.go.jp/jp/96_abe/statement/2014/1118kaiken.html, last accessed 8 May 2020.
58. Mulgan, *The Abe Administration*, pp. 49–50.
59. 「自民税調会長に宮沢氏起用へ　野田氏、事実上更迭の見方」*Asahi Shimbun*, 10 October 2015, https://digital.asahi.com/articles/ASHBB2V5WHBBUTFK001.html, last accessed 8 May 2020. While Noda was a leading fiscal hawk, his dismissal by Abe may have been a bit of revenge by the prime minister, since Noda had been part of a group pushing for Abe's resignation after the 2007 upper house elections. After his ouster from the tax commission, he would remain a leading critic of Abe's, joining forces with Ishiba Shigeru to create an anti-Abenomics study group in 2017. See 藤原慎一、古賀大己、「自民４０人が「脱アベノミクス」勉強会　経済政策を懸念」*Asahi Shimbun*, 15 June 2017, https://digital.asahi.com/articles/ASK6H4HBNK6HUTFK00P.html, last accessed 8 May 2020.
60. See, in particular, Jeff Kingston, "Nationalism and the 2014 Snap Election: The Abe Conundrum," in Robert Pekkanen, Ethan Scheiner, and Steven R. Reed, eds., *Japan Decides 2014: The Japanese General Election*, pp. 211–225. The volume uses the "bait-and-switch" argument as a motif.

15. ALLIANCE OF HOPE

1. His grandfather, Kishi Nobusuke, and his grandfather's successor, Ikeda Hayato, had addressed meetings of the House of Representatives in 1957 and 1961 respectively, but no Japanese prime minister had ever addressed the entire Congress.

2. Robert D. Blackwill and Kurt M. Campbell, "Xi Jinping on the Global Stage," Council Special Report No. 74, Council on Foreign Relations, February 2016, https://backend-live.cfr.org/sites/default/files/pdf/2016/02/CSR74_Blackwill_Campbell_Xi_Jinping.pdf, last accessed 8 May 2020.
3. "On average two very large crude carriers, each carrying 2 million barrels of oil, and two large liquefied natural gas carriers, each carrying 200,000 cubic metres, must arrive in Japan every day, just to keep the lights on," writes journalist Bill Hayton. *The South China Sea* New Haven: Yale University Press, 2014, p. 150.
4. See Howard W. French, *Everything Under the Heavens: How the Past Helps Shape China's Push for Global Power* New York: Vintage Books, 2018, ch. 6 passim.
5. Admiral Harry B. Harris Jr., "Speech at Australian Strategic Policy Institute," Canberra, Australia, 31 March 2015, https://www.cpf.navy.mil/leaders/harry-harris/speeches/2015/03/ASPI-Australia.pdf, last accessed 8 May 2020. Other claimants had sought to defend their claims with their coast guards and built artificial islands—if not at the same pace as China—and China's island building alone did not pose a threat to commercial shipping through the South China Sea, much of which, after all, was destined for China.
6. Stephen Biddle and Ivan Oelrich, "Future Warfare in the Western Pacific: Chinese Antiaccess/Area Denial, US AirSea Battle, and Command of the Commons in East Asia," *International Security*, 41, 1, Summer 2016, pp. 7–48.
7. Yoji Koda, "The US-Japan Alliance: Responding to China's A2/AD Threat," Alliance Requirements Roadmap Series, Center for a New American Security, May 2016, https://s3.amazonaws.com/files.cnas.org/documents/CNAS_US-Japan-Alliance-Responding-to-Chinas-A2-AD-Threat_FINAL.pdf?mtime=20161005211732, last accessed 8 May 2020.
8. Ministry of Defense, Japan, *Defense of Japan 2015*, pp. 34–35. Russia's conflict with Ukraine, in which Moscow used all of these tools to pressure Kiev, heightened fears of China's using the same approach with Japan or another neighbor in East Asia.
9. Valentina Romei and John Reed, "The Asian century is set to begin," *Financial Times*, 25 March 2019, https://www.ft.com/content/520cb6f6-2958-11e9-a5ab-ff8ef2b976c7, last accessed 8 May 2020.
10. The Democratic staff of the Senate Committee on Foreign Relations issued a report in 2014 that called for strengthening the non-military

components of the rebalance strategy. See https://www.foreign.senate.gov/imo/media/doc/872692.pdf, last accessed 8 May 2020.

11. French, op. cit., p. 258; Bruno Maçães, *Belt and Road: A Chinese World Order* London: Hurst, 2019.
12. In fact, when the AIIB was launched in June 2015, its charter members included major US allies including Australia, South Korea, the United Kingdom, France, Germany, and other NATO members. The Obama administration responded petulantly to British participation in particular, with an anonymous official telling the *Financial Times* that the administration was "wary" about Britain's "constant accommodation of China." George Parker, Anne-Sylvaine Chassany, and Geoff Dyer, "Europeans defy US to join China-led development bank," *Financial Times*, 16 March 2015, https://www.ft.com/content/0655b342-cc29-11e4-beca-00144feab7de, last accessed 8 May 2020. On the diplomacy surrounding the founding of the AIIB, see Daniel Bob, ed., *Asian Infrastructure Investment Bank: China as Responsible Stakeholder?* Washington: Sasakawa Peace Foundation USA, 2015.
13. *Nikkei Shimbun*, 12 May 2015.
14. "Press Conference by Prime Minister Shinzo Abe Following the Cabinet Decision on the 'Legislation for Peace and Security'," Cabinet Secretariat, 14 May 2015, https://japan.kantei.go.jp/97_abe/statement/201505/0514kaiken.html, last accessed 8 May 2020.
15. 徳山喜雄,『安倍晋三「迷言」録』, Tokyo: Heibonsha, 2016, pp. 27–34.
16. "Japan PM Shinzo Abe under fire for short fuse," The *Straits Times*, 31 December 2014, https://www.straitstimes.com/asia/japan-pm-shinzo-abe-under-fire-for-short-fuse, last accessed 8 May 2020; Moeko Fujii, "Japan PM Abe Defends Use of Facebook," *Japan Real Time* (blog), *Wall Street Journal*, 3 July 2013, https://blogs.wsj.com/japanrealtime/2013/07/03/japan-pm-abe-defends-use-of-facebook, last accessed 8 May 2020.
17. Although *Asahi* was not alone in publishing the account, in 2014 the paper was virtually alone in retracting reporting.
18. Mulgan, *The Abe Administration*, p. 64.
19. See Michael Cucek, "Abe and Press Oppression: Guilty, not guilty, or not proven?" in Jeff Kingston, ed., *Press Freedom in Contemporary Japan* New York: Routledge, 2017, pp. 84–86.
20. Martin Fackler,『安倍政権にひれ伏す日本のメディア』(Tokyo: Futabasha, 2016) 46–47.
21. Glen S. Fukushima, "Golf and Gold," *The New York Review of Books*, 8 March 2018, https://www.nybooks.com/articles/2018/03/08/japan-shinzo-abe-golf-gold, last accessed 8 May 2020.

22. 徳山, op. cit, ch. 1 on Abe's frustrations with the heated parliamentary debates.
23. *Yomiuri Shimbun*, 27 July 2015.
24. The emergence of SEALDs would be hailed by foreign observers as evidence of the birth of a new political consciousness among young Japanese, but by 2019, the prevailing narrative regarding young Japanese in politics would be not their opposition to "Abe politics" but their puzzling support for the prime minister. Abe's strongest support in opinion polls and at the ballot box came from Japanese under forty years old, while baby boomers—his own generation—were generally the most consistent source of opposition to the prime minister. See, for example: 「若年層を重視する安倍政権」, *Nikkei Shimbun*, 30 January 2019, https://www.nikkei.com/article/DGXMZO40658860Q9A130C1EN2000, last accessed 8 May 2020.
25. 山口, op. cit., pp. 222–226.
26. Motoko Rich, "Japanese Warship Escorts U.S. Supply Ship on Its Way to Join Strike Force," *New York Times*, 1 May 2017, https://www.nytimes.com/2017/05/01/world/asia/japanese-warship-us-navy-ship.html, last accessed 8 May 2020.
27. "The Guidelines for U.S.-Japan Defense Cooperation," 27 April 2015, https://archive.defense.gov/pubs/20150427_—_GUIDELINES_FOR_US-JAPAN_DEFENSE_COOPERATION.pdf, last accessed 8 May 2020.
28. The Koizumi government had decided to buy land- and sea-based missile defense systems from the US in 2003, and over time missile defense had become one of the most important components of bilateral defense cooperation. See Emma Chanlett-Avery, Caitlin Campbell, and Joshua Williams, *The US–Japan Alliance*, CRS Report RL33740, Congressional Research Service, 13 June 2019: 34–35.
29. Ashton Carter, "Remarks on the Next Phase of the US Rebalance to the Asia-Pacific," US Department of Defense, 6 April 2015, https://www.defense.gov/Newsroom/Speeches/Speech/Article/606660/remarks-on-the-next-phase-of-the-us-rebalance-to-the-asia-pacific-mccain-instit, last accessed 8 May 2020.
30. "As we speak, China wants to write the rules for the world's fastest-growing region. That would put our workers and our businesses at a disadvantage. Why would we let that happen? We should write those rules. We should level the playing field." Barack Obama, "Remarks by the President in State of the Union Address," Barack Obama White House Archives, 20 January 2015, https://obamawhitehouse.archives.

gov/the-press-office/2015/01/20/remarks-president-state-union-address-January–20–2015, last accessed 8 May 2020.

31. Although Orrin Hatch, the new Senate Finance Committee chairman, who had oversight authority for trade negotiations, would press US Trade Representative Michael Froman to take a harder line on intellectual property rights protection, particularly for biologic drugs, a demand that would be the last major hurdle in negotiations.
32. "Transcript of the Trans-Pacific Partnership Atlanta Ministerial Closing Press Conference," Office of the US Trade Representative, 5 October 2015, https://ustr.gov/about-us/policy-offices/press-office/speeches-transcripts/2015/october/transcript-trans-pacific#, last accessed 8 May 2020.
33. For more on how the Abe government made the case for the agreement, see Solís, op. cit., pp. 168–172.
34. "Policy Speech by Prime Minister Shinzo Abe to the 190th Session of the Diet," Cabinet Secretariat, 22 January 2016, http://japan.kantei.go.jp/97_abe/statement/201601/1215627_10999.html, last accessed 8 May 2020.
35. Anne Gearan and David Nakamura, "Hillary Clinton comes out against Obama's Pacific trade deal," *Washington Post*, 7 October 2015, https://www.washingtonpost.com/news/post-politics/wp/2015/10/07/hillary-clinton-comes-out-against-obamas-pacific-trade-deal, last accessed 8 May 2020.
36. Trump's first tweet on TPP mentioned that it did not "stop Japan's currency manipulation." See also Adam Taylor, "A timeline of Trump's complicated relationship with the TPP," *Washington Post*, 13 April 2018, https://www.washingtonpost.com/news/worldviews/wp/2018/04/13/a-timeline-of-trumps-complicated-relationship-with-the-tpp, last accessed 8 May 2020.
37. Cristiano Lima, "Trump calls trade deal a 'rape of our country'," *Politico*, 28 June 2016, https://www.politico.com/story/2016/06/donald-trump-trans-pacific-partnership-224916, last accessed 8 May 2020.
38. See Judith Stein, *Pivotal Decade: How the United States Traded Factories for Finance in the Seventies*, New Haven: Yale University Press, 2011, on the internal debates that saw strategic arguments repeatedly trump economic arguments, particularly in the Democratic Party.
39. Kazuhito Yamashita, "A First Step Toward Reform of Japan's Agricultural Cooperative System," *Nippon.com*, 20 April 2015, https://www.canon-igs.org/en/column/macroeconomics/20150427_3086.html, last accessed 8 May 2020.

40. Later in the year, Abe would pressure the MHLW's minimum wage-setting council to recommend a substantial minimum wage increase. The council delivered a 2.3 percent increase in the average national minimum wage, the largest annual increase since the council began setting an hourly minimum wage rate in 2002.
41. Nicholas Benes, "How Japan's Corporate Governance Code Was Born," Board Director Training Institute of Japan, https://bdti.or.jp/en/blog/en/cgcodejapanbirth, last accessed 8 May 2020.
42. Mike Bird, "Shinzo Abe's Record and the Continuing Revolution in Japanese Stocks," *Wall Street Journal*, 20 Nov. 2019, https://www.wsj.com/articles/shinzo-abes-record-and-the-continuing-revolution-in-japanese-stocks-11574248293, last accessed 26 Nov. 2019.
43. Despite high-profile efforts by the Abe government to attract FDI, as of 2018, Japan's inbound FDI stocks were only four percent of GDP, a marginal increase from 2013 and still at the bottom of the OECD, well behind its G7 peers and even South Korea, which was also near the bottom. OECD (2019), FDI stocks (indicator). doi: 10.1787/80eca1f9-en, last accessed on 21 September 2019. See also Takeo Hoshi, "Has Abenomics Succeeded in Raising Japan's Inward Foreign Direct Investment?" *Asian Economic Policy Review* 13 (January 2018). On corporate cash hoards, see Ishika Mookerjee, Fox Hu, Min Jeong Lee, "Japan Inc. sitting on ¥506.4 trillion mountain of cash," *Bloomberg*, 3 September 2019, https://www.japantimes.co.jp/news/2019/09/03/business/corporate-business/japanese-firms-record-4-8-trillion/#.XYZg9fxKjdd, last accessed 8 May 2020.
44. Curtis J. Milhaupt, "Evaluating Abe's Third Arrow: How Significant are Japan's Recent Corporate Governance Reforms?" October 2017, https://papers.ssrn.com/sol3/papers.cfm?abstract_id=2925497, last accessed 26 Nov. 2019.
45. In his first press conference as prime minister in December 2012, of Japan's demographic outlook he said only, "Growth is difficult with the size of our population in decline. But while this is certainly a difficult condition, I believe that a country that abandons the pursuit of growth or a country that loses the desire to grow has no future." Cabinet Secretariat, 26 December 2012, https://japan.kantei.go.jp/96_abe/statement/201212/26kaiken_e.html, last accessed 8 May 2020.
46. 安倍, 『美しい国』, ch. 6 passim.
47. Of course, a major problem was that the BOJ was not actually flooding the economy with cash: "Friedman's 'helicopter drop' came not to

mean putting money in people's pockets, but rather casting money blindly onto international financial markets without regard to where it would end up." See Frances Coppola, *The Case for People's Quantitative Easing* (Cambridge: Polity, 2019) 24. The BOJ expanded the quantity of money, but relied on banks as an intermediary—and banks mostly sat on it.

48. Quoted in David Pilling, "This will be a crunch year for the Japanese economy," *Financial Times*, 15 January 2014, https://www.ft.com/content/b94e6c00-7dd3-11e3-95dd-00144feabdc0, last accessed 8 May 2020. See Edward Hugh, *The A-B-E of Abenomics* (e-book, 2014) for an articulation of the demographics-based critique of Abenomics.
49. National Institute of Population and Social Security Research, "Population Projections for Japan (2016–2065): Summary," http://www.ipss.go.jp/pp-zenkoku/e/zenkoku_e2017/pp_zenkoku2017e_gaiyou.html, last accessed 8 May 2020.
50. "Press conference by Prime Minister Shinzo Abe," Cabinet Secretariat, 7 October 2015, https://japan.kantei.go.jp/97_abe/statement/201510/1213721_9930.html, last accessed 8 May 2020.
51. "Speech on Growth Strategy by Prime Minister Shinzo Abe at the Japan National Press Club," Cabinet Secretariat, 19 April 2013, https://japan.kantei.go.jp/96_abe/statement/201304/19speech_e.html, last accessed 8 May 2020.
52. Kakizaki notes that there were some uncomfortable antecedents to the wartime militarist government, which did in fact try to mandate population increases. . 柿崎, op. cit., pp. 52–61.
53. 「ニッポン一億総活躍プラン」Cabinet Secretariat, 2 June 2016, http://www.kantei.go.jp/jp/singi/ichiokusoukatsuyaku/pdf/plan1.pdf, last accessed 8 May 2020.
54. See Joshua Hausman and Johannes Wieland, "Overcoming the Lost Decades? Abenomics after Three Years," *Brookings Papers on Economic Activity*, Fall 2015, https://www.brookings.edu/wp-content/uploads/2015/09/HausmanTextFall15BPEA.pdf, last accessed 8 May 2020.
55. The records for these meetings—the "International Finance and Economic Assessment Council"—can be viewed at https://www.kantei.go.jp/jp/singi/kokusaikinyu, last accessed 26 Nov. 2019.
56. Robin Harding, "Abe's grim warning about global economy highlights G7 divisions," *Financial Times*, 26 May 2016, https://www.ft.com/content/6c804178-231c-11e6-9d4d-c11776a5124d, last accessed 8 May 2020.
57. A sizable chunk of this stimulus package would go to building a mag-

lev rail line between Tokyo and Osaka, a pet project of Abe ally Kasai Yoshiyuki and his Central Japan Railways.

58. See Sayuri Shirai, *Mission Incomplete: Reflating Japan's Economy*, 2nd ed. Tokyo: Asian Development Bank Institute, 2018, ch. 5 passim.
59. Mio Tomita, "Bank of Japan to be top shareholder of Japan stocks," *Nikkei Asian Review*, 17 April 2019, https://asia.nikkei.com/Business/Markets/Bank-of-Japan-to-be-top-shareholder-of-Japan-stocks, last accessed 8 May 2020.
60. "Remarks by President Obama and Prime Minister Abe of Japan at Hiroshima Peace Memorial," Barack Obama White House Archives, 27 May 2016, https://obamawhitehouse.archives.gov/the-press-office/2016/05/27/remarks-president-obama-and-prime-minister-abe-japan-hiroshima-peace, last accessed 8 May 2020.
61. Ben Rhodes, *The World As It Is* New York: Random House, 2018, p. 377.
62. That said, the statement flirted with the new conservatism's core beliefs about imperial Japan's actions as legitimate resistance to western colonialism, referring to "waves of colonial rule [that] surged toward Asia in the 19th century" and Japan's "sense of isolation" during the Great Depression. See "Statement by Prime Minister Shinzo Abe," Cabinet Secretariat, 14 August 2015, https://japan.kantei.go.jp/97_abe/statement/201508/0814statement.html, last accessed 8 May 2020.
63. WSJ staff, "Full Text: Japan-South Korea Statement on 'Comfort Women'," *Japan Real Time* (blog), *Wall Street Journal*, 28 December 2015, https://blogs.wsj.com/japanrealtime/2015/12/28/full-text-japan-south-korea-statement-on-comfort-women, last accessed 8 May 2020. It was a problematic agreement, more of an understanding than a treaty, as neither country's legislature ratified it, and it was therefore vulnerable to a change in political circumstances—precisely what happened when Park was impeached and replaced by the left-wing Moon Jae-in.

16. THE GAMBLE

1. "The Power of Reconciliation: Address by Prime Minister Shinzo Abe," Cabinet Secretariat, 27 December 2016, http://japan.kantei.go.jp/97_abe/statement/201612/1220678_11021.html, last accessed 8 May 2020.
2. "Remarks by President Obama and Prime Minister Abe of Japan at Pearl Harbor," Barack Obama White House Archives, 27 December 2016,

https://obamawhitehouse.archives.gov/the-press-office/2016/12/28/remarks-president-obama-and-prime-minister-abe-japan-pearl-harbor, last accessed 8 May 2020.

3. 「ドナルド・トランプ次期米国大統領の選出について」Cabinet Secretariat, 9 November 2016, https://www.kantei.go.jp/jp/97_abe/actions/201611/09kaiken.html, last accessed 8 May 2020.
4. Michael Crowley, "Exclusive: Armitage to back Clinton over Trump," *Politico*, 16 June 2016, https://www.politico.com/story/2016/06/richard-armitage-endorses-clinton-224431, last accessed 8 May 2020.
5. 山口敬之,『暗闘』, Tokyo: Gentōsha, 2017, pp. 40–48, 51.
6. "Full Rush Transcript: Donald Trump, CNN Milwaukee Republican Presidential Town Hall," CNN, 29 March 2016, http://cnnpressroom.blogs.cnn.com/2016/03/29/full-rush-transcript-donald-trump-cnn-milwaukee-republican-presidential-town-hall, last accessed 8 May 2020; see also Michael Flynn interviewed in 『暗闘』(2016米大統領選) トランプ節に日本困惑　米軍駐留費の負担増要求、撤退も示唆」*Asahi Shimbun*, 18 October 2016.
7. For a thorough look at Japan's place in Trump's worldview, see Jennifer Miller, "Let's Not be Laughed at Anymore: Donald Trump and Japan from the 1980s to the Present," *Journal of American-East Asian Relations* 25 (2018): 138–168.
8. Ivo Daalder and James Lindsay, *The Empty Throne* New York: Public Affairs, 2018, p. 29.
9. John Hudson and Josh Dawsey, "'I remember Pearl Harbor': Inside Trump's hot-and-cold relationship with Japan's prime minister," *Washington Post*, 28 August 2018, https://www.washingtonpost.com/world/national-security/i-remember-pearl-harbor-inside-trumps-hot-and-cold-relationship-with-japans-prime-minister/2018/08/28/d6117021-e310-40a4-b688-68fdf5ed2f38_story.html, last accessed 8 May 2020.
10. "The unspoken rule of global trade policy was that the United States would look the other way when American goods were discriminated against," writes Judith Stein. Stein in *Pivotal Decade*. The great fight in US Japan policy in the 1980s was between "revisionists" in the Office of the US Trade Representative and Commerce Department, who believed that Japan played by different economic rules and therefore needed to be treated differently by the United States, and traditional alliance managers in the State and Defense departments, who wanted to preserve the strategic partnership with Japan at the climax of the Cold War. Naturally the end of the Cold War shifted the debate in

favor of the revisionists, whose beliefs about Japan—"the Cold War is over; Japan won," Massachusetts Senator and 1992 presidential candidate Paul Tsongas reportedly said—became mainstream. Trump's beliefs were part of this mainstreaming, but unlike others, he never moved on from the belief that Japan was taking advantage of the US. He just added new countries to the rogues gallery, especially China after its accession to the World Trade Organization in 2001. On the fight between revisionists and traditionalists on Japan, see Robert Uriu, *Clinton and Japan: The Impact of Revisionism on US Trade Policy* New York: Oxford University Press, 2009.

11. Jane Mayer, "Donald Trump's Ghostwriter Tells All," *The New Yorker*, 25 July 2016, https://www.newyorker.com/magazine/2016/07/25/donald-trumps-ghostwriter-tells-all, last accessed 8 May 2020.
12. @realDonaldTrump (Donald Trump), "When someone attacks me, I always attack back...except 100x more. This has nothing to do with a tirade but rather, a way of life!," *Twitter*, 11 November 2012, https://twitter.com/realDonaldTrump/status/267626951097868289?ref_src=twsrc%5Etfw%7Ctwcamp%5Etweetembed%7Ctwterm%5E2676269510978682898&ref_url=http%3A%2F%2Fwww.trumptwitter-archive.com%2Fhighlights%2Fretaliation, last accessed 8 May 2020.
13. "Transcript: Donald Trump's Foreign Policy Speech," *New York Times*, 27 April 2016, https://www.nytimes.com/2016/04/28/us/politics/transcript-trump-foreign-policy.html, last accessed 8 May 2020.
14. "Reforming the U.S.-China Trade Relationship to Make America Great Again," Trump-Pence campaign, 2016, https://web.archive.org/web/20160920080848/https://www.donaldjtrump.com/positions/us-china-trade-reform, last accessed 8 May 2020.
15. Nolan McCaskill, "Obama reminds Trump: 'There's only one president at a time," *Politico*, 14 November 2016, https://www.politico.com/story/2016/11/obama-presser-trump-one-president-at-a-time-231355, last accessed 8 May 2020.
16. Abe would apologize to Obama after the fact for the breach of protocol. Rhodes, op. cit., xiv.
17. 「首相とトランプ氏、会談へ合意　17日で調整」*Nikkei Shimbun*, 10 November 2016, https://www.nikkei.com/article/DGXLASFK10H0Q_Q6A111C1000000, last accessed 8 May 2020; Anna Fifield, "Japan's prime minister hopes to start building 'trusting relationship' with Trump," *Washington Post*, 15 November 2016, https://www.washingtonpost.com/world/asia_pacific/japans-pm-hopes-to-start-building-a-trusting-relationship-with-trump/2016/11/14/e710f6f9-1b60-41cd-

9c89-f247ec97bfd7_story.html, last accessed 8 May 2020. The phone call and subsequent meeting are shrouded in rumor, but it seems it went as smoothly as it did in part because of Ambassador Sasae's outreach to Jared and Ivanka. Another rumor suggests that Sheldon Adelson, who was a major financial backer of Trump's campaign and was also seeking to build a casino in Japan, if and when the country legalized casino gambling, facilitated the meeting. See Justin Elliott, "Trump's Patron-in-Chief," *ProPublica*, 10 October 2018, https://features.propublica.org/trump-inc-podcast/sheldon-adelson-casino-magnate-trump-macau-and-japan, last accessed 8 May 2020.

18. Special Committee on the Trans-Pacific Partnership Agreement, House of Councillors, National Diet of Japan, 14 November 2016, http://kokkai.ndl.go.jp/SENTAKU/sangiin/192/0194/19211140194003a.html, last accessed 8 May 2020.
19. "Remarks by President Trump and Prime Minister Abe of Japan at State Dinner," Tokyo, White House, 6 November 2017, https://www.whitehouse.gov/briefings-statements/remarks-president-trump-prime-minister-abe-japan-state-dinner-tokyo-japan, last accessed 8 May 2020.
20. The Pew Research Center would find that confidence in the US president among Japanese people fell from seventy-eight percent in 2016 to twenty-four percent in 2017. See https://www.pewresearch.org/global/2018/10/01/trumps-international-ratings-remain-low-especially-among-key-allies, last accessed 8 May 2020.
21. It was one of the first indications that his family would play an unusual role in his administration; Ivanka and Jared joined the meeting, which also included Flynn, prompting concerns about conflicts of interest since Ivanka was at the time negotiating a licensing deal with a Japanese company whose largest shareholder was a Japanese government-owned bank. Matt Flegenheimer, Rachel Abrams, Barry Meier, and Hiroko Tabuchi, "Business Since Birth: Trump's Children and the Tangle That Awaits," *New York Times*, 4 December 2016, https://www.nytimes.com/2016/12/04/us/politics/trump-family-ivanka-donald-jr.html, last accessed 8 May 2020; Vicky Ward, *Kushner Inc.* New York: St. Martin's Press, 2019.
22. Simon Denyer and Akiko Kashiwagi, "Japan's Abe won't confirm Trump Nobel Prize nomination, but media reports say he made it," *Washington Post*, 18 February 2019, https://www.washingtonpost.com/world/japans-abe-wont-confirm-trump-nobel-prize-nomination-but-media-reports-say-he-did/2019/02/18/26f62310-3337-11e9-946a-115a5932c45b_story.html, last accessed 8 May 2020.

23. "Donald Trump receives $3,755 driver from Japan's Prime Minister," *Golf Digest*, 20 November 2016, https://www.golfdigest.com/story/donald-trump-receives-dollar3755-driver-from-japans-prime-minister, last accessed 8 May 2020.
24. 「トランプ次期米国大統領との会談」Cabinet Secretariat, 17 November 2016, https://www.kantei.go.jp/jp/97_abe/actions/201611/17usa.html, last accessed 8 May 2020.
25. Special Committee on the Trans-Pacific Partnership Agreement, House of Councillors, National Diet of Japan, 24 November 2016, http://kokkai.ndl.go.jp/SENTAKU/sangiin/192/0194/19211240194009a.html, last accessed 8 May 2020.
26. "Policy Speech by Prime Minister Shinzo Abe to the 193rd Session of the Diet," Cabinet Secretariat, 20 January 2017, https://www.kantei.go.jp/jp/97_abe/statement2/20170120siseihousin.html, last accessed 8 May 2020.
27. While there is some controversy over just how good a golfer Trump is, Abe, despite being an enthusiastic and regular golfer—he had golfed around fifty times during his first four years in office—was not regarded as a particularly talented player, with scores estimated in the nineties.,「日米首脳、似た者同士？ ゴルフ· 肉好き· 世襲· 再起」, *Asahi Shimbun*, 11 February 2017. Golf journalists amused themselves with lengthy analyses of their comparative games before the "golf summit." Josh Sens, "Donald Trump vs. Shinzo Abe: Previewing their weekend golf outing," *Golf*, 10 February 2017, https://www.golf.com/extra-spin/2017/02/10/donald-trump-vs-shinzo-abe-heads-state-golf-course, last accessed 8 May 2020.
28. https://web.archive.org/web/20170213155949/https://www.whitehouse.gov/the-press-office/2017/02/10/remarks-president-trump-and-prime-minister-abe-japan-joint-press; https://www.politico.com/story/2017/02/shinzo-abe-trump-presser-golf-234905
29. Asahi Shimbun,「親密アピール、ゴルフ２７ホール　異例の厚遇、夕食会も連夜　安倍首相· トランプ氏」, 13 February 2017.
30. David A. Fahrenthold and Karen DeYoung, "Trump turns Mar-a-Lago Club terrace into open-air situation room," *Washington Post*, 13 February 2017, https://www.washingtonpost.com/politics/trump-turns-mar-a-lago-club-terrace-into-open-air-situation-room/2017/02/13/c5525096-f20d-11e6-a9b0-ecee7ce475fc_story.html, last accessed 9 May 2020.
31. "Joint Press Conference with President Donald J. Trump of the United States of America on the Missile Launch by North Korea," Cabinet

Secretariat, 11 February 2017, https://japan.kantei.go.jp/97_abe/decisions/2017/pconference.html, last accessed 9 May 2020.

32. John Wagner, "A hastily called news conference caps a surreal day for Trump in South Florida," *Washington Post*, 12 February 2017, https://www.washingtonpost.com/news/post-politics/wp/2017/02/12/a-hastily-called-news-conference-caps-a-surreal-day-for-trump-in-south-florida, last accessed 9 May 2020. Obama's April 2009 statement on a failed North Korea satellite launch—the first major launch of Obama's presidency and a violation of a truce—clearly identified the violation of UN Security Council resolutions, stressed that he would consult with allies (both Japan and South Korea), articulated US goals in the region, and expressed a commitment to pursuing North Korea's denuclearization through the then-still-extant six-party talks. It was not necessarily an especially memorable statement, but it provides a useful reminder of what the US response to a North Korean test, even by a relatively inexperienced president, looked like. See Barack Obama White House Archives, 5 April 2009, https://obamawhitehouse.archives.gov/the-press-office/statement-president-north-korea-launch, last accessed 9 May 2020.
33. Van Jackson, *On the Brink: Trump, Kim, and the Threat of Nuclear War* New York: Cambridge University Press, 2019, p. 100.
34. On Navarro's entry into Trump's circle, see Sarah Ellison, "The Inside Story of the Kushner-Bannon Civil War," *Vanity Fair*, May 2017, https://www.vanityfair.com/news/2017/04/jared-kushner-steve-bannon-white-house-civil-war, last accessed 9 May 2020. On the "globalists" in the administration, Jonathan Swan, "How the globalists fought—and failed," *Axios*, 9 June 2018, https://www.axios.com/how-the-globalists-fought—and-failed-6e26001d-06f5-4d29-b6da-34085d2b2b74.html, last accessed 9 May 2020. This division also runs through Bob Woodward's account *Fear*.
35. See Jeffrey Lewis, *The 2020 Commission Report on the North Korean Nuclear Attacks Against the United States*, New York: Houghton Mifflin, 2018, for a creative exercise in thinking through how a war between the US and North Korea would unfold.
36. Peter Landers, "Trump's Loyal Sidekick on North Korea: Japan's Shinzo Abe," The *Wall Street Journal*, 16 August 2017, https://www.wsj.com/articles/trumps-loyal-sidekick-on-north-korea-japans-shinzo-abe-1502875805, last accessed 9 May 2020.
37. Mira Rapp-Hooper, "Decoupling is back in Asia: a 1960s playbook won't solve these problems," *War On The Rocks*, 7 September 2017,

https://warontherocks.com/2017/09/decoupling-is-back-in-asia-a-1960s-playbook-wont-solve-these-problems, last accessed 9 May 2020.

38. "Policy Speech by Prime Minister Shinzo Abe to the 193rd Session of the Diet," Cabinet Secretariat, 20 January 2017, https://japan.kantei.go.jp/97_abe/statement/201701/1221105_11567.html, last accessed 9 May 2020.
39. "Remarks by President Trump to the 72nd Session of the United Nations General Assembly," White House, 19 September 2017, https://www.whitehouse.gov/briefings-statements/remarks-president-trump-72nd-session-united-nations-general-assembly, last accessed 9 May 2020. Trump rhetorically linked the Japanese abductees with the case of Otto Warmbier, an American college student who had been detained while visiting North Korea and died soon after being released in June. Trump would use Warmbier's death to lambaste North Korea. "The United States once again condemns the brutality of the North Korean regime as we mourn its latest victim," he said. He would invite his parents to attend the State of the Union address the following January, when he would again pay tribute to their son. Fred and Cindy Warmbier would later turn on Trump, when after his second meeting with Kim Jong Un, he said that he believed Kim's denial of responsibility for their son's death. See Christine Hauser, "Responding to Trump, Otto Warmbier's Parents Blame Kim Jong-un and 'Evil Regime' for Son's Death," *New York Times*, 28 February 2019, https://www.nytimes.com/2019/02/28/world/asia/trump-otto-warmbier.html, last accessed 9 May 2020.
40. "Remarks by President Trump in a Meeting with Families of North Korean Abductees," White House, 6 November 2017, https://www.whitehouse.gov/briefings-statements/remarks-president-trump-meeting-families-north-korean-abductees, last accessed 9 May 2020.
41. "President Donald J. Trump's Summit Meeting with Prime Minister Shinzo Abe of Japan," White House, 6 November 2017, https://www.whitehouse.gov/briefings-statements/president-donald-j-trumps-summit-meeting-prime-minister-shinzo-abe-japan, last accessed 9 May 2020.
42. "National Security Strategy of the United States," December 2017, https://www.whitehouse.gov/wp-content/uploads/2017/12/NSS-Final-12-18-2017-0905.pdf, last accessed 9 May 2020.
43. "Remarks by President Trump to U.S. and Japanese Business Leaders," White House, 6 November 2017, https://www.whitehouse.gov/briefings-statements/5769, last accessed 9 May 2020.

44. Ivo Daalder and James Lindsay, "RIP, Axis of Adults," *Politico Magazine*, 21 December 2018, https://www.politico.com/magazine/story/2018/12/21/james-mattis-resigns-rip-axis-of-adults-223553, last accessed 9 May 2020.
45. "Policy Speech to the 193rd Session of the Diet," op. cit., https://japan.kantei.go.jp/97_abe/statement/201701/1221105_11567.html, last accessed 9 May 2020.
46. As Abe argued in his 2015 statement, "With the Great Depression setting in and the Western countries launching economic blocs by involving colonial economies, Japan's economy suffered a major blow. In such circumstances, Japan's sense of isolation deepened and it attempted to overcome its diplomatic and economic deadlock through the use of force." As historian Louise Young writes, Manchuria would be an "economic lifeline" that would be "necessary for Japan's economic security, or even its economic survival." Louise Young, *Japan's Total Empire* Los Angeles: University of California Press, 1998, p. 94.
47. Tomohiro Osaki, "Ex-adviser Steve Bannon says Abe was 'Trump before Trump,' urges him to play hardball with China," *Japan Times*, 8 March 2019, https://www.japantimes.co.jp/news/2019/03/08/national/politics-diplomacy/ex-adviser-steve-bannon-confident-donald-trump-win-2020-despite-probes/#.XZdoD-dKjOQ, last accessed 9 May 2020.
48. "Full Text of Xi Jinping keynote at the World Economic Forum," CGTN America, 17 January 2017, https://america.cgtn.com/2017/01/17/full-text-of-xi-jinping-keynote-at-the-world-economic-forum, last accessed 10 May 2020.
49. See Edward Luce, *The Retreat of Western Liberalism*, New York: Atlantic Monthly Press 2017.
50. Solís, op. cit., ch. 8 passism.
51. "Press Conference by Prime Minister Shinzo Abe Following His Visit to Argentina and His Attendance at the APEC Economic Leaders' Meeting in Lima, Peru and Related Meetings," Cabinet Secretariat, 21 November 2016, https://japan.kantei.go.jp/97_abe/statement/201611/1220102_11019.html, last accessed 10 May 2020.
52. Terada Takashi, "How and Why Japan Has Saved The TPP: From Trump Tower to Davos," *The Asan Forum* Open Forum, 19 February 2018, last accessed http://www.theasanforum.org/how-and-why-japan-has-saved-the-tpp-from-trump-tower-to-davos, 10 May 2020.
53. "Asia's Dream: Linking the Pacific and Eurasia"—Speech by Prime Minister Shinzo Abe at the Banquet of the 23rd International Conference on The Future of Asia," Cabinet Secretariat, 5 June 2017,

https://japan.kantei.go.jp/97_abe/statement/201706/1222768_11579.html, 10 May 2020.

54. *Yomiuri Shimbun*, 22 March 2017.
55. The two sides agreed to split off investor-state dispute settlement and data flows into separate agreements in order to smooth the agreement's ratification by the EU. Separating these issues sidestepped having to secure national or sub-national parliamentary approval, avoiding issues that dogged the EU's trade agreement with Canada.
56. Michael Peel, "EU envoy urges bloc to engage more with Russia over 5G data," *Financial Times*, 13 September 2019, https://www.ft.com/content/725aa5b6-d5f7-11e9-8367-807ebd53ab77, last accessed 10 May 2020.
57. Polls conducted during the Trump administration suggest that Americans largely want the US to play a global leadership role, including on trade. See Dina Smeltz, Ivo Daalder, Karl Friedhoff, Craig Kafura, and Brendan Helm, *Rejecting Retreat*, Chicago Council on Global Affairs, 6 September 2019, https://www.thechicagocouncil.org/publication/rejecting-retreat, last accessed 10 May 2020.
58. Tobias Harris, "The meaning of Abe's polling slump," Sasakawa Peace Foundation USA, 22 June 2017, https://spfusa.org/japan-political-pulse/meaning-abes-polling-slump, last accessed 10 May 2020.
59. 「安倍内閣総理大臣記者会見」, Cabinet Secretariat, 19 June 2017, http://www.kantei.go.jp/jp/97_abe/statement/2017/0619kaiken.html, last accessed 10 May 2020.
60. In 2017, only 53.68 percent of voters showed up, slightly higher than in 2014 but still the second lowest in postwar history.

17. IN SEARCH OF A LEGACY

1. 「3選をうけて安倍総裁記者会見」, Liberal Democratic Party, 20 September 2018, https://www.jimin.jp/news/press/president/138148.html, last accessed 10 May 2020.
2. Tobias Harris, "June poll watcher: despite fluctuations, Prime Minister Abe recovers in the polls," Sasakawa Peace Foundation USA, 29 June 2018, https://spfusa.org/japan-political-pulse/june-poll-watcher-despite-fluctuations-prime-minister-abe-recovers-in-the-polls, last accessed 10 May 2020.
3. On Nikai's role and Abe's taming of the LDP, see Mulgan, *The Abe Administration*, pp. 54–58.
4. Bae Hyun-jung, "Full text of Moon's speech at the Korber Foundation,"

The *Korea Herald*, 7 July 2017, http://www.koreaherald.com/view.php?ud=20170707000032, last accessed 10 May 2020.

5. 「トランプ米国大統領との電話会談についての会見」Cabinet Secretariat, 9 March 2018, https://www.kantei.go.jp/jp/98_abe/actions/201803/09kaiken.html, last accessed 10 May 2020.
6. "Remarks by President Trump and Prime Minister Abe of Japan Before Bilateral Meeting," White House, 7 June 2018, https://www.whitehouse.gov/briefings-statements/remarks-president-trump-prime-minister-abe-japan-bilateral-meeting-3, last accessed 10 May 2020.
7. "US rejects 'freeze-for-freeze' proposal from China, Russia to break North Korea impasse," The *Straits Times*, 7 July 2017, https://www.straitstimes.com/asia/east-asia/us-rejects-freeze-for-freeze-proposal-from-china-russia-to-break-north-korea-impasse, last accessed 10 May 2020.
8. Roberta Rampton, "'We fell in love:' Trump swoons over letters from North Korea's Kim," Reuters, 30 September 2018, https://www.reuters.com/article/us-northkorea-usa-trump/we-fell-in-love-trump-swoons-over-letters-from-north-koreas-kim-idUSKCN1MA03Q, last accessed 10 May 2020.
9. Daalder and Lindsay, op. cit., p. 146.
10. Robin Harding, "Japan plays it cool on response to US steel tariffs," *Financial Times*, https://www.ft.com/content/c7fc9ae0-37e4-11e8-8b98-2f31af407cc8, last accessed 10 May 2020.
11. "Remarks by President Trump at Signing of a Presidential Memorandum Targeting China's Economic Aggression," White House, 22 March 2018, https://www.whitehouse.gov/briefings-statements/remarks-president-trump-signing-presidential-memorandum-targeting-chinas-economic-aggression, last accessed 10 May 2020.
12. Although there was some reason to believe that Trump would not be able to follow through on the threat. No one—not even US automakers and autoworkers—supported imposing automobile tariffs.
13. US Ambassador William Hagerty would accuse Japan of stalling. "Hagerty: U.S. frustrated at pace of trade talks with Japan," *Asahi Shimbun*, 5 February 2019, http://www.asahi.com/ajw/articles/AJ201902050044.html, last accessed 10 May 2020.
14. Lighthizer mentioned Japan as a priority in his confirmation hearing to become USTR. "Nomination of Robert E. Lighthizer," Committee on Finance, United States Senate, 115th Congress, 14 March 2017, https://www.congress.gov/115/chrg/shrg28798/CHRG-115shrg28798.pdf, p. 19, last accessed 10 May 2020.

15. "Remarks by Vice President Pence on the Administration's Policy Toward China," White House, 4 October 2018, https://www.whitehouse.gov/briefings-statements/remarks-vice-president-pence-administrations-policy-toward-china, last accessed 10 May 2020.
16. The administration would even change the name of Pacific Command, which manages all US military activities from the west coast of the United States to the east coast of Africa, into Indo-Pacific Command. Tara Copp, "INDOPACOM, it is: US Pacific Command gets renamed," *Military Times*, 30 May 2018, https://www.militarytimes.com/news/your-military/2018/05/30/indo-pacom-it-is-pacific-command-gets-renamed, last accessed 10 May 2020.
17. Scott W. Harold, Derek Grossman, Brian Harding, Jeffrey W. Hornung, Gregory Poling, Jeffrey Smith, and Meagan L. Smith, *The Thickening Web of Asian Security Cooperation: Deepening Defense Ties Among US Allies and Partners in the Indo-Pacific*, Santa Monica, CA: RAND Corporation, 2019.
18. Peter Navarro and Greg Autry, *Death by China*. Robert Lighthizer issued a comprehensive statement about China's trade practices in testimony before the US–China Economic and Security Review Commission in 2010. Robert E. Lighthizer, "Testimony before the U.S.-China Economic and Security Review Commission: Evaluating China's Role in the World Trade Organization Over the Past Decade," U.S.-China Economic and Security Review Commission, 9 June 2010, https://www.uscc.gov/sites/default/files/6.9.10Lighthizer.pdf, last accessed 10 May 2020.
19. "Full transcript: Donald Trump's jobs plan speech," *Politico*, https://www.politico.com/story/2016/06/full-transcript-trump-job-plan-speech-224891, last accessed 10 May 2020.
20. Alan Rappeport, "In New Slap at China, U.S. Expands Power to Block Foreign Investments," *New York Times*, 10 October 2018, https://www.nytimes.com/2018/10/10/business/us-china-investment-cfius.html, last accessed 10 May 2020.
21. Gerry Shih, "Trump's new North American trade deal also aimed at bigger target: China," *Washington Post*, 3 October 2018, https://www.washingtonpost.com/world/asia_pacific/trumps-new-north-american-trade-deal-is-also-aimed-at-a-bigger-target-china/2018/10/03/5290686c-c705-11e8-9c0f-2ffaf6d422aa_story.html, last accessed 10 May 2020.
22. See, for example, "Joint Statement of the Trilateral Meeting of the Trade Ministers of the United States, European Union, and Japan,"

Office of the US Trade Representative, 23 May 2019, https://ustr.gov/about-us/policy-offices/press-office/press-releases/2019/may/joint-statement-trilateral-meeting#, last accessed 10 May 2020.

23. Tokyo has monitored the growth of Chinese state support for firms in advanced sectors in the years since the Made in China plan was announced. "White Paper on International Economy and Trade," Ministry of Economy, Trade, and Industry, July 2019, https://www.meti.go.jp/english/press/2019/pdf/0718_001b.pdf, last accessed 10 May 2020.
24. Japanese firms suffered from unilateral US trade remedies aimed at China's state-led capitalism even as they shared US concerns about those policies. See Chang Sun, Zhigang Tao, Hongjie Yuan, Hongyong Zhang, "The Impact of the US-China Trade War on Japanese Multinational Corporations," RIETI Discussion Paper Series 19-E-050, the Research Institute of Economy, Trade, and Industry, https://www.rieti.go.jp/jp/publications/dp/19e050.pdf, last accessed 10 May 2020
25. Shortly after becoming secretary-general, Nikai traveled to Beijing and met with Foreign Minister Wang Yi to discuss how to revive the bilateral relationship. 「自民· 二階幹事長、中国外相と会談　尖閣問題などを議論」*Asahi Shimbun*, 24 August 2016, https://digital.asahi.com/articles/ASJ8S2RKHJ8SUTFK002.html, last accessed 10 May 2020.
26. 「トランプ"密使"が官邸にあらかじめ貢ぎ物をレクチャーしていた」*Asahi Shimbun*, 24 February 2017.
27. 「保護主義へ懸念、「日中共通」認識　経済官庁次官級協議」*Asahi Shimbun*, 29 March 2017, https://digital.asahi.com/articles/DA3S12865170.html?iref=pc_ss_date, last accessed 10 May 2020.
28. Interview with Imai Takaya, 『文芸春秋』, June 2018.
29. Ministry of Foreign Affairs of Japan, "Japan-China Summit Meeting," 8 July 2017. http://www.mofa.go.jp/a_o/c_m1/cn/page4e_000636.html, last accessed 14 January 2018.
30. Ministry of Foreign Affairs of Japan, "Japan-China Summit Meeting," 11 November 2017, https://www.mofa.go.jp/a_o/c_m1/cn/page4e_000711.html, last accessed 10 May 2020. The joint statement from Abe's meeting with Li two days later included the same language. Ministry of Foreign Affairs of Japan, "Japan-China Summit Meeting," 13 November 2017, http://www.mofa.go.jp/a_o/c_m1/cn/press3e_000119.html, last accessed 10 May 2020.
31. Shinzo Abe, "Remarks at the Welcome Reception for the 3rd Japan-China CEO Summit," 4 December 2017. https://www.kantei.go.jp/jp/98_abe/actions/201712/04taiwa_kangei.html, last accessed 10 May

2020. Keidanren, "3rd Japan-China CEO Summit Joint Statement," 5 December 2017, http://www.keidanren.or.jp/policy/2017/098.html?v=s, last accessed 10 May 2020.

32. In the Pew Research Center's 2019 Global Attitudes Survey, Japanese respondents were by far the most negative about China. More Japanese—eighty-five percent—said they have an unfavorable opinion of China than any other nationality surveyed, while only fourteen percent said that they have a favorable opinion, the lowest share by far. China's net unfavorability—seventy-one percent—was naturally the worst among Japanese. Laura Silver, Kat Devlin, Christine Huang, "People are around the globe are divided in their opinions of China," *Facttank* (blog), Pew Research Center, 5 December 2019, https://www.pewresearch.org/fact-tank/2019/12/05/people-around-the-globe-are-divided-in-their-opinions-of-china, last accessed 10 May 2020.
33. "Tourism Statistics," JTB Tourism Research & Consulting Co., https://www.tourism.jp/en/tourism-database/stats, last accessed 10 May 2020.
34. "International Students in Japan 2017," Japan Student Services Organization, December 2017, https://www.jasso.go.jp/en/about/statistics/intl_student/data2017.html, last accessed 10 May 2020; 『第六十八回日本統計年鑑　平成31年』 Statistics Bureau, Ministry of Internal Affairs and Communications, 2018, https://www.stat.go.jp/data/nenkan/68nenkan/zuhyou/y680210000.xls, last accessed 10 May 2020.
35. Plenary session, House of Representatives, National Diet of Japan, 24 October 2018, http://kokkai.ndl.go.jp/SENTAKU/syugiin/197/0001/19710240001001a.html, last accessed 10 May 2020.
36. The Soviet Union had actually been prepared to cede Habomai and Shikotan, the smallest of the four, in 1956, but the US, afraid it would lead Japan to demand the return of Okinawa and other islands that the US forces had occupied after the war and perhaps also lead to a broader rapprochement with the communist bloc that would draw Japan out of the US orbit, pressured Japan to stiffen its demands in the negotiations. James D.J. Brown, "Abe's 2016 Plan to Break the Deadlock in the Territorial Dispute with Russia," *The Asia Pacific Journal: Japan Focus*, 15 February 2016, https://apjjf.org/2016/04/Brown.html, last accessed 10 May 2020.
37. James D.J. Brown, "Shinzo Abe's Russia policy risks embarrassment for Japan," *Nikkei Asian Review*, 10 September 2019, https://asia.nik-

kei.com/Opinion/Shinzo-Abe-s-Russia-policy-risks-embarrassment-for-Japan, last accessed 10 May 2020.

38. "Russia's military base worries may put Japan in bind over Northern Territories talks," *Mainichi Shimbun*, 27 November 2018, https://mainichi.jp/english/articles/20181127/p2a/00m/0na/014000c, last accessed 10 May 2020. Putin and other officials have also repeatedly cited the controversies surrounding US bases in Okinawa as evidence that Japan was not truly independent of the US and might not be able to resist US pressure to install troops on returned islands.
39. See Alina Polyakova and Chris Meserole, "Exporting digital authoritarianism: The Russian and Chinese models," Policy Brief, Brookings Institution, August 2019, https://www.brookings.edu/wp-content/uploads/2019/08/FP_20190827_digital_authoritarianism_polyakova_meserole.pdf, last accessed 10 May 2020.
40. Choe Sang-Hun, "Ex-Chief Justice of South Korea Is Arrested on Case-Rigging Charges," *New York Times*, 23 January 2019, https://www.nytimes.com/2019/01/23/world/asia/south-korea-chief-justice-japan.html, last accessed 10 May 2020.
41. B.J. Lee, "Forget Putin and Kim. Trump's real soulmate lives in Tokyo," *Washington Post*, 26 August 2019, https://www.washingtonpost.com/opinions/2019/08/26/forget-putin-kim-donald-trumps-real-soulmate-lives-tokyo, last accessed 10 May 2020.
42. Meanwhile, as South Korea knows well, Trump did not pioneer the use of economic weapons to apply political pressure on trading partners. China, after its rare earth metals embargo of Japan in 2010, would go on to organize a tourism and consumer boycott of South Korea in 2017 in response to South Korea's deployment of the US THAAD missile defense system, a boycott that ultimately forced Korean retailer Lotte to abandon China entirely.

18. A NEW JAPAN

1. "Abe vows all-out effort to beat deflation, eyes Constitutional reform," Kyodo News, 20 November 2019, https://english.kyodonews.net/news/2019/11/c349f4fdfff2-abe-vows-all-out-effort-to-beat-deflation-eyes-constitutional-reform.html, last accessed 10 May 2020.
2. 「憲法改正に関する首相メッセージ全文」*Nikkei Shimbun*, 3 May 2017, https://www.nikkei.com/article/DGXLASFK03H16_T00C17A5000000, last accessed 10 May 2020.
3. Kenneth Mori McElwain, "Constitutional Revision in the 2017 Election,"

in Robert J. Pekkanen, Steven R. Reed, Ethan Scheiner, and Daniel M. Smith, eds., *Japan Decides 2017: The Japanese General Election* New York: Palgrave Macmillan, 2018, 297–312.

4. 「第48回衆議院総選挙の結果をうけて安倍総裁記者会見」Liberal Democratic Party, 23 October 2017, https://www.jimin.jp/news/press/president/135972.html, last accessed 10 May 2020.
5. 清水真人,「仕切り直しの憲法改正　カギ握る「中山ルール」」*Nikkei Shimbun*, 8 October 2019, https://www.nikkei.com/article/DGXMZO50684090X01C19A0I00000, last accessed 10 May 2020.
6. No less an authority on the political dangers of referenda than David Cameron warned a delegation from the lower house's constitutional commission, "Those who want to change the status quo should not be relieved by the support of a majority—it's necessary to be in a position where supporters are at least sixty percent." 「衆議院欧州各国憲法及び国民投票制度調査議員団報告書」Constitution Commission, House of Representatives, National Diet of Japan, 8 November 2017, http://www.shugiin.go.jp/internet/itdb_kenpou.nsf/html/kenpou/report2017.pdf/$File/report2017.pdf, last accessed 11 May 2020.
7. 安倍、『美しい国へ』, pp. 90–92.
8. 「経済財政諮問会議及び経済財政諮問会議・産業競争力会議合同会議」Cabinet Secretariat, 4 April 2014, https://www.kantei.go.jp/jp/96_abe/actions/201404/4kaigi.html, last accessed 11 May 2020.
9. Eri Sugiura, "Japan gets more than it bargained for with tourist boom," *Nikkei Asian Review*, 17 April 2019, https://asia.nikkei.com/Spotlight/Cover-Story/Japan-gets-more-than-it-bargained-for-with-tourist-boom, last accessed 11 May 2020.
10. "Tourism Statistics," JTB Tourism Research & Consulting Co., https://www.tourism.jp/en/tourism-database/stats/inbound/#annual, last accessed 11 May 2020; Brian Ashcraft, "Tourists Are Causing Headaches In Japan," *Kotaku* (blog), 27 May 2019, https://kotaku.com/tourists-are-causing-headaches-for-japan-1835043188, last accessed 11 May 2020.
11. 「【福田政権考】「１０００万移民」日本改造の権利あるのか」Ronna, 26 July 2008, https://ironna.jp/article/155, last accessed 11 May 2020.
12. See, for example, right-wing pundit Sakurai Yoshiko's response to Nakagawa's proposal. 「粗にして雑、移民国家の自民党案」, Yoshiko Sakurai (website) [originally 『週刊新潮』], 4 September 2008, https://yoshiko-sakurai.jp/2008/09/04/752, last accessed 11 May 2020.
13. "69 foreign technical interns die in Japan between 2015 and 2017," Kyodo News, 6 December 2018, https://english.kyodonews.net/

news/2018/12/fefaaa516a27–69-foreign-technical-interns-die-in-japan-between-2015-and-2017.html, last accessed 11 May 2020.

14. 「菅官房長官単独インタビュー詳報 「外国人労働者なしに日本経済は回らない」」*Nishi Nippon Shimbun*, https://www.nishinippon.co.jp/item/n/443663, last accessed 11 May 2020.
15. *Yomiuri Shimbun*, "Behind-the-scenes moves led to Japan's new foreign worker law," *The Japan News*, 11 December 2018.
16. 「外国人受け入れ、スピード重視 迫る選挙「最後の機会」」*Nikkei Shimbun*, 18 December 2018, https://www.nikkei.com/article/DGXMZO39037400X11C18A2PP8000, last accessed 11 May 2020.
17. 「メルケル氏引退ショック...外国人労働者受け入れ問題、日本は大丈夫か? 「独の失敗に学べ」」*Zakzak*, https://www.zakzak.co.jp/soc/news/181030/soc1810300012-n1.html, last accessed 11 May 2020.
18. See, for example, "Number of foreigners in Japan with new working visa totals 1,621," Kyodo News, 7 February 2020, https://english.kyodonews.net/news/2020/02/ecb1475abeb0-number-of-foreigners-in-japan-with-new-working-visa-totals-1621.html, last accessed 11 May 2020.
19. "Foreign population in Japan breaks record with 2.82 million," *Japan Times*, 26 October 2019, https://www.japantimes.co.jp/news/2019/10/26/national/foreign-population-japan-breaks-record-2–82-million/#.XdhNATJKjdc, last accessed 11 May 2020.
20. The conservative public intellectual Nishibe Susumu, whom Abe had read earlier and with whom he had spoken periodically during his wilderness years, accused Abe of not being a conservative but rather a practitioner of an "empty practicalism" in a political testament published after his apparent suicide in January 2018. 西部邁、『保守の遺言』, Tokyo: Heibonsha, 2018.
21. This record was partly due to a decision by the cabinet office in 2016 to recalibrate how Japan calculates its GDP, which turned a 0.9 percent decline in 2014 into 2.4 percent growth.
22. An annual cabinet quality-of-life survey found that Japanese aged 18–39 were the most satisfied age groups, with 85.8 percent of Japanese under twenty-nine and 77.9 percent of Japanese between thirty and thirty-nine expressing satisfaction with their ways of living. (In 2012, the comparable figures were 75.4 percent and 69.4 percent respectively.) For the 2019 version, see 「国民生活に関する世論調査」 Cabinet Office, August 2019, https://survey.gov-online.go.jp/r01/r01-life/gairyaku.pdf, last accessed 11 May 2020. For the 2012 version, see https://survey.gov-online.go.jp/h24/h24-life/index.html, last accessed May 11 2020.

23. Sayuri Shirai, "Japan's labor shortage and low-wage puzzle," *Japan Times*, 26 May 2019, https://www.japantimes.co.jp/opinion/2019/05/26/commentary/japan-commentary/japans-labor-shortage-low-wage-puzzle/#.Xafe8ZNKjdc, last accessed 11 May 2020. See also Yasuo Takeuchi, "Japan's record expansion produces no consumption boom," *Nikkei Asian Review*, 30 January 2019, https://asia.nikkei.com/Economy/Japan-s-record-expansion-produces-no-consumption-boom, last accessed 11 May 2020.
24. James Mayger and Hannah Dormido, "The Rich Are Getting Richer in Abe's Japan," Bloomberg, 13 December 2017, https://www.bloomberg.com/graphics/2017-japan-inequality, last accessed 11 May 2020.
25. Ben Dooley, Japan Shrinks by 500,000 People as Births Fall to Lowest Number Since 1874," *New York Times*, 24 December 2019, https://www.nytimes.com/2019/12/24/world/asia/japan-birthrate-shrink.html, last accessed 11 May 2020.
26. Stephen Spratt, "Japan Lines Up to Join Germany in All-Negative Yield Curve Club," 26 August 2019, https://www.bloombergquint.com/global-economics/japan-lines-up-to-join-germany-in-all-negative-yield-curve-club, last accessed 3 May 2020.
27. On MMT, see Zach Helfand, "The Economist Who Believes the Government Should Just Print More Money," The *New Yorker*, 20 August 2019, https://www.newyorker.com/news/news-desk/the-economist-who-believes-the-government-should-just-print-more-money, last accessed 3 May 2020.
28. See Ben Dooley, "Modern Monetary Theory's Reluctant Poster Child: Japan," *New York Times*, 5 June 2019, https://www.nytimes.com/2019/06/05/business/modern-monetary-theorys-reluctant-poster-child-japan.html, last accessed 3 May 2020; Koichi Hamada, "Does Japan Vindicate Modern Monetary Theory?" *Project Syndicate*, 1 July 2019, https://www.project-syndicate.org/commentary/modern-monetary-theory-japan-inflation-by-koichi-hamada-2019-07?barrier=accesspaylog, last accessed 3 May 2020. Nishida would meet with MMT proponent and Bernie Sanders adviser Stephanie Kelton when the latter visited Japan in summer 2019. Abe would explicitly reject the theory when prompted by an opposition lawmaker in October 2019. http://www.shugiin.go.jp/internet/itdb_shitsumon_pdf_t.nsf/html/shitsumon/pdfT/b200014.pdf/$File/b200014.pdf.
29. Olivier Blanchard and Takeshi Tashiro, "Fiscal Policy Options for Japan," PIIE Policy Brief 19–7, May 2019, https://www.piie.com/system/files/documents/pb19-7.pdf, last accessed 10 May 2020. Blanchard

and Tashiro explicitly differentiate themselves from MMT, arguing, "[deficits] are needed not because they are desirable in and of themselves; they are not, and the high levels of debt come with some risks."

30. This policy was one of Abe's more brazen borrowings from the political opposition: as leader of the Democratic Party Maehara Seiji had worked with economist Ide Eisaku to advocate what he called an "All for All" social security system. See https://www.businessinsider.jp/post-106191.
31. Shinzo Abe, "Join Japan and act now to save our planet," *Financial Times*, 23 September 2018. https://www.ft.com/content/c97b1458-ba5e-11e8–8dfd-2f1cbc7ee27c. Accessed 3 May 2020.
32. See Daniel Aldrich, Phillip Y. Lipscy, and Mary M. McCarthy, "Japan's opportunity to lead," *Nature Climate Change* 9 (July 2019) p. 492 for a similar critique.
33. Japan would reduce its greenhouse gas emissions by twenty-six percent relative to 2013—a problematic benchmark due to Japan's increased post-3/11 dependence on fossil fuels—by 2030.
34. See https://climateactiontracker.org/countries/japan.
35. Christian Parenti, *Tropic of Chaos: Climate Change and the New Geography of Violence* New York: Nation Books, 2011, p. 11.
36. As Shinzō's career wanes, tabloids have speculated that Nobuo's son, Nobuchiyo, currently a reporter at Fuji Television, could be tapped as Shinzō's successor—although his mother is said to prefer that Abe Hiroto, the son of Shinzō's older brother Hironobu, inherit Shinzō's constituency. "Prime Minister Abe Shinzō's nephew Kishi Nobuchiyo is at Fuji TV. A Keio boy from the Keio baseball team," *Sōri no bansan*, 2 March 2017. https://sori-no-bansan.com/256. Accessed 24 March 2019.
37. For an argument that Abe is a last flourish before Japan declines, see Brad Glosserman, *Peak Japan* Washington, DC: Georgetown University Press, 2019.

AFTERWORD

1. "New Year's Press Conference by the Prime Minister (Opening Statement)," Cabinet Secretariat, 6 January 2020, https://japan.kantei.go.jp/98_abe/statement/202001/_nypressconference.html, last accessed 20 May 2020.
2. For an explanation of the scandal, see Eric Johnston, "Cherry blossom-viewing party: Breaking down Abe's latest cronyism scandal," *Japan*

Times, 27 November 2019, https://www.japantimes.co.jp/news/2019/11/27/reference/cherry-blossom-viewing-party-shinzo-abe-cronyism-scandal/#.XsVyRhNKjBU, last accessed 20 May 2020.

3. 「「選択肢ない」「疑心暗鬼募る」不信感深まり、立憲・国民合流見送り」, *Mainichi Shimbun*, 21 January 2020, https://mainichi.jp/articles/20200121/k00/00m/010/295000c, last accessed 20 May 2020.
4. 「首相「9年目に大きな花を」 21年秋の任期意識 解散・4選巡り臆測」, *Nikkei Shimbun*, 8 January 2020, https://www.nikkei.com/article/DGXMZO54117570X00C20A1PP8000, last accessed 20 May 2020.
5. Data drawn from Max Roser, Hannah Ritchie, Esteban Ortiz-Ospina, and Joe Hasell, "Coronavirus pandemic (COVID-19)—Country by country, Japan," *Our World in Data*, https://ourworldindata.org/coronavirus-country-by-country?country=JPN, last accessed 20 May 2020.
6. See Andy Crump, "Japan's coronavirus response is flawed—but it works," *Nikkei Asian Review*, 14 May 2020, https://asia.nikkei.com/Opinion/Japan-s-coronavirus-response-is-flawed-but-it-works, last accessed 20 May 2020.
7. On this episode, see 「補正予算案を午後決定 1人10万円に首相「1日も早く手元に」 異例の組み替え」 *Nikkei Shimbun*, 20 April 2020, https://www.nikkei.com/article/DGXMZO58248080Q0A420C2MM0000, last accessed 20 May 2020; 清宮涼、安倍龍太郎, 「1人10万円、土壇場の修正「首相のメンツ丸つぶれ」」 *Asahi Shimbun*, 16 April 2020, https://digital.asahi.com/articles/ASN4J76W1N4JUTFK00M.html, last accessed 20 May 2020.
8. Gearoid Reidy, "Japan Defends Abe After His 'Dance at Home' Video Sparks Backlash," *Bloomberg*, 13 April 2020, https://www.bloomberg.com/news/articles/2020-04-13/japan-defends-abe-after-his-dance-at-home-virus-foray-stumbles, last accessed 20 May 2020; Alastair Gale and Miho Inada, "Japan's Abe Taken to Task Over Itsy-Bitsy Masks," *Wall Street Journal*, 21 April 2020, https://www.wsj.com/articles/japans-abe-taken-to-task-over-itsy-bitsy-masks-11587469588?redirect=amp, last accessed 20 May 2020.
9. The *Asahi Shimbun* conducted a nationwide survey of political attitudes in March and April 2020 in which sixty-six per cent of respondents opposed a fourth term for Abe. Among self-identified LDP supporters, forty-eight per cent favored a fourth term—but forty-six per cent opposed it. Independents were strongly opposed: seventy-three per cent, with only sixteen percent in favor. 「安倍首相の総裁4選、「反対」66% 朝日新聞世論調査」, *Asahi Shimbun*, 28 April 2020, https://digital.asahi.com/articles/ASN4X7QCPN4SUZPS00B.html?iref=pc_ss_date, last accessed 2020 May 2020.

10. Numerous reports surfaced during the pandemic that showed Abe and Suga to be at odds at critical decision points during the pandemic. See 「永田町大混乱!「新型コロナvs安倍vs菅」最後に勝つのは誰だ!」 PRESIDENT, 6 March 2020, https://president.jp/articles/-/32964, last accessed 20 May 2020; 「新型コロナ対応で浮かんだ亀裂　菅氏「失権」　重み増す今井補佐官」 Jiji Press, 21 March 2020, https://www.jiji.com/jc/article?k=2020031901371&g=pol, last accessed 20 May 2020.
11. "Over 3 mil. jobs could be lost in Japan due to coronavirus," Kyodo News, 20 May 2020, https://english.kyodonews.net/news/2020/05/7c9bafef2333-over-3-mil-jobs-could-be-lost-in-japan-due-to-coronavirus.html?utm_source=dlvr.it&utm_medium=twitter, last accessed 20 May 2020.
12. Gearoid Reidy, "Visitors to Japan Slumped 99.9% Last Month," Bloomberg, 20 May 2020, https://www.bloomberg.com/news/articles/2020-05-20/visitors-to-japan-slump-99-9-as-3-million-tourists-become-3-000, last accessed 20 May 2020.
13. "Japan's Coronavirus Response Increases Public Debt Challenge," FitchRatings, 15 April 2020, https://www.fitchratings.com/research/sovereigns/japan-coronavirus-response-increases-public-debt-challenge-15-04-2020, last accessed 20 May 2020.
14. 「「新型コロナウイルス感染予防対策ガイドライン」について」 Keidanren, 14 May 2020, http://www.keidanren.or.jp/policy/2020/040.html, last accessed 20 May 2020.
15. On "wolf warriors," see Kathrin Hille, "'Wolf warrior' diplomats reveal China's ambitions," *Financial Times*, 11 May 2020, https://www.ft.com/content/7d500105-4349-4721-b4f5-179de6a58f08, last accessed 20 May 2020.
16. Edward Luce, "Inside Trump's coronavirus meltdown," *Financial Times*, 14 May 2020, https://www.ft.com/content/97dc7de6-940b-11ea-abcd-371e24b679ed, last accessed 20 May 2020.
17. The pandemic may be strongly influencing European views of the competition between the US and China. See Noah Barkin, "In the Post-Pandemic Cold War, America Is Losing Europe," *Foreign Policy*, 19 May 2020, https://foreignpolicy.com/2020/05/19/coronavirus-pandemic-europe-opinion-polls-united-states-china-losing, last accessed 20 May 2020.
18. 「「河野さん、分かってるよね?」撤回直訴に驚いた首相」 Asahi Shimbun, 24 June 2020, https://digital.asahi.com/articles/ASN6S6QNGN6SUTFK00D.html, last accessed 9 July 2020.
19. Japan has continued exploring opportunities for TPP's expansion even

as the pandemic has spread. See 「TPP参加「全力で応援」　茂木氏がタイ外相と協議」 *Nikkei Shimbun*, 13 May 2020, https://www.nikkei.com/article/DGXMZO59041780T10C20A5PP8000, last accessed 20 May 2020.

INDEX